पुरातत्त्व

PURĀTATTVA

Bulletin of the Indian Archaeological Society

No. 30 1999-2000

Editors

K. N. Dikshit & K.S. Ramachandran

D.K. Printworld (P) Ltd.
New Delhi

Cataloging in Publication Data — DK
[Courtesy : D.K. Agencies (P) Ltd. <docinfo@dkagencies.com>]

Purātattva : bulletin of the Indian Archaeological
Society, no. 30, 1999-2000 / editor, K.N. Dikshit &
K.S. Ramachandran.
p. cm.
Includes bibliographical references.
ISBN 8124603057

1. Archaeology — India — Periodicals. 2. India
— Antiquities — Periodicals. 3. India — Civilization
— Periodicals. I. Dikshit, K.N. II. Ramachandran,
K.S. (Kattalai Sivasubramanium), 1939- III. Indian
Archaeological Society.

First Published in 2000
First Reprinted in 2005
ISBN 81-246-0305-7
Price for volume 30 (1999-2000): Rs. 800 US $ 40

Reprint authorised by
Indian Archaeological Society
New Delhi - 110 016

Purātattva is published annually.

Manuscripts (whether in the form of articles or notes or book reviews) offered for publication should be sent to the Editor, Purātattva, Indian Archaeological Society, B-17, Qutab Institutional Area, New Delhi - 110 016.

Published and printed by:
D.K. Printworld (P) Ltd.
'Srikunj,' F-52, Bali Nagar
New Delhi – 110015
Phone : (011) 2545 3975, 2546 6019 Fax : (011) 2546 5926
E-mail : dkprintworld@vsnl.net
www. dkprintworld.com

PURĀTATTVA

CONTENTS

Obituary

Dr. B.B. Lal
(1913-2000)

Dr. Bijan Bihari Lal, Chief Archaeological Chemist, (retd), Dehradun, was born at Biswan in U.P. on 14th August, 1913. He studied at Christian College, Lucknow and later at Lucknow University from where he obtained a Doctorate degree n Chemistry. Dr. B.B. Lal got married to Smt. Shakuntala Lal on 18th May, 1943. They had a very happy married life until the cruel hand of death on 2nd June, 2000 separated them.

Dr. Lal was appointed Archaeological Chemist to head the Chemistry Branch of the Archaeological Survey of the India at Dehradun, a position which he held until he retired. He had a deep knowledge of problems of mural paintings, stone monuments, excavated objects etc. and had solved them with scientific approaches and with the best of his ability. He had trained a team of Conservators who are carrying on work on the same principles. He was deputed to the Institute of Archaeology, London for study of Geo-chronology, a subject he introduced later in the Chemistry Branch.

In spite of his scholarship, Dr. Lal was very humble, He was simple, soft spoken and unassuming person. Author of several publications, he was instrumental in introducing many modern scientific methods, hitherto unknown, for the conservation of stone monuments in India.

Dr. Lal had been a member of several important advisory committees like Ajanta Expert Committee, Konark Expert Committee, Puri Expert Committee and Air Pollution committee on Taj Mahal. He was appointed Consultant to undertake studies on impact of pollution on Taj Mahal from Mathura Refinery at the instance of Varadrajan Committee. He was the First president of the Indian Association for the Study of Conservation of Cultural Property.

The present generation of conservators pay their homage to this great soul for his dedication to the cause of conservation and preservation of built in heritage in India.

I.K. Bhatnagar

PURĀTATTVA

Number 30 **1999–2000**

Editorial

We are happy to inform our members that as anticipated in the editorial of the last number of our Bulletin, the construction of the building is complete. We have shifted our office to the new building. Our library consisting of more than two thousand books has also been shifted and is ready for our members and scholars to utilize it.

As promised we have also commenced our academic activities also: two projects viz., An Atlas of the Indus-Sarasvati Civilization and Methodology in Archaeological Research are underway. Research Associates and other technical personnel are busy in collating and collecting data for the succesful completion of these projects.

A third project Growth of Cities in Ancient India is also in the offing and work on this will commence very soon. We are thankful to ICHR for supporting these projects.

The Society also invites projects from interested members of the Society.

The Society also underlook excavations of the ancient city of Kampilya in collaboration with 'Ca' Foscari University, Venice.

The present issue, as usual, carries articles of varied interest—from prehistory to Early historic times. The major contribution in this issue is about the different aspects of the excavation of chalcolithic site at Chichali. Other reports on excavations include Sirpur, Mansar, Dhalewan and also Mandi from where a hoard of jewellary consisting of gold spacer, terminal beads, bracelets, silver anklets besides beads of gold, banded agate, onyx and other semi-precious stones were found. Articles on ethnoarchaeology and archaeotechnical studies have also been included which will be of special interest to scholars.

In spite of our repeated request, our contributors have been following different types of referencing. We will be grateful if they would follow American style henceforth.

At the out set we, the editors are thankful for all the help and encouragement we received from Dr. S.P. Gupta, Chairman of the Society.

Dr. Y.D. Sharma, Shri M.N. Deshpande and Shri K.M. Srivastava deserve our thanks for their monetary donation.

It would not have been possible to publish this Bulletin without the generous financial aid received from the Archaeological Survey of India and Indian Council of Historical Research. We are grateful for this.

Thanks are also due to Smt. Anita Mehta and her staff for their cooperation in bringing out the issue in time.

KND
KSR

The Significance of the Acheulian Site of Isampur, Karnataka, in the Lower Palaeolithic of India

K. PADDAYYA, RICHA JHALDIYAL AND MICHAEL D. PETRAGLIA*

I. INTRODUCTION

Isampur is one among the 200 Acheulian sites of the Lower Palaeolithic stage discovered by the first author in the Hunsgi and Baichbal valleys located in the Shorapur Taluk of Gulbarga District, Karnataka. The two valleys constitute an amphitheatre shaped erosional basin of Tertiary age (the total basin area including uplands and valleys floor measuring about 1000 km^2) and contain one of the densest concentrations of Acheulian sites known so far in the Old World (fig. 1). Detailed investigations in the area during the last two decades and a half, comprising both intensive foot-surveys and excavations, have provided a wealth of data pertaining to the depositional and cultural contexts of the Acheulian sites and their spatial distribution. Radiometric dates and relative dating by fluorine analysis suggests that the sites belong to the Middle Pleistocene and range from 200,000 to beyond 350,000 years B.P. (Kshirsagar and Paddayya 1989; Szabo *et al.* 1990). The field data and observations arising from experimental and ethnoarchaeological studies, have helped in reconstructing the Acheulian culture from a settlement system perspective (Paddayya 1982; 1991). More recently, following a formation processes approach, the site contexts have been reinvestigated (Paddayya 1987a; Paddayya and Petraglia 1993, 1995; Jhaldiyal 1997). This approach has provided fresh data about the sedimentary and cultural contexts of the sites as well as about the functioning of the Acheulian settlement system. The ongoing investigations at the site of Isampur are an aspect of these more recent studies.

At Isampur two Acheulian localities were discovered by the first author in 1983 when a large portion of the brown and black silts overlying the limestone floor of the valley was quarried for preparing the embankment of a major irrigation canal (the Narayanapur Left Bank Canal forming part of the Upper Krishna Project), which is located about a kilometre to the west of the site. In 1994 a more extensive scatter of artefacts, exposed to the surface due to subsequent erosion of silt cover, was noticed at locality II. The surface features gave good indications of the existence of an extensive Acheulian workshop (Paddayya and Petraglia 1997, 1998). Subsequently field studies comprising detailed explorations of both the basin floor and plateau surfaces, contour survey and mapping work, and regular excavation were undertaken for four seasons (1997-2000) at this site. More than 30 trial pits (1 m^2) were dug to ascertain the presence of undisturbed cultural level at the locality. The results were encouraging and subsequently five regular trenches were excavated at the site, covering a total area of 159 m^2. These studies have shown that this site is not merely another addition to the list of known Acheulian sites of the region. The

*Department of Archaeology, Deccan College, Pune 411006, India
Department of Anthropology, National Museum of Natural History, Smithsonian Institution, Washington DC, 20560, USA

uniqueness of the site lies in the fact that it has provided fresh insight into the Acheulian culture of the area by exposing a workshop for stone tool manufacture, including evidence pertaining to the exploitation of limestone blocks for tool manufacture at the raw material source itself.

II. ENVIRONMENTAL SETTING

Geomorphic Context

The village of Isampur (16° 30'N; 76° 29'E) is situated in the northwestern part of the Hunsgi valley. The Acheulian site occurs about 2 km to the northwest of the village (fig. 2). Both the modern village and the Acheulian site are located in a narrow sub-valley, which measures about 12 km in length (east-west) and 1 to 3 km in width (north-south). The head of the Isampur valley is towards the west and is formed by badlands carved into the Deccan Trap plateau. The shale-limestone plateaus (occasionally capped by remnant Deccan Trap patches) flank the valley on the southern and northern sides and while its eastern edge is formed by a southward extending spur of the northern plateau. Following the contours of this spur, the Isampur valley takes a southerly bend near the village of Isampur and merges with the Hunsgi valley after a distance of 5 km. The Isampur valley has been sculpted by a continuous backwearing of the surrounding uplands and like the Hunsgi and Baichbal valleys it is erosional in origin. The valley floor is covered by limestone formation and gradually slopes down from an elevation of 500-520 m AMSL in the west to 450 m AMSL where it opens out into the Hunsgi valley.

The Isampur valley is drained by a seasonal, fourth order stream which is locally known as the Kamta Halla. This stream originates in the Trap-covered badlands in the west and following the valley floor contours flows in an easterly and then southeasterly direction for a distance of 19.5 km before it joins the Hunsgi nullah on its left bank. The total catchment area of this stream is about 80 km^2.

The Acheulian site lies 150 m from the left bank of the Kamta Halla where it takes a southerly bend and at a distance of about 750 m from the foot of the plateau which defines the eastern side of the valley. The site occurs on the limestone-covered valley floor (460m AMSL) and is located at the confluence of two shallow water courses which drain the pediment surface and valley floor. One of these originates on the northern plateau near the village of Gundalgera and the second originates on the eastern upland. However, extensive soil quarrying by the Irrigation Department in 1983 (for making the embankment o the irrigation canal mentioned earlier) has caused some changes in the courses of these streams.

The site is spread over an area of about 7200m^2 (fig. 3). A major portion of the site occurs in farmland while the rest lies in the shallow bed of the watercourse that descends from the northern plateau. A large part of this area is now covered with 10 to 20 cm thick blackish sticky clay of more recent times and supports scrub jungle vegetaion (mostly thick grasses and plants belonging to *Cassia* and *Acacia* species) in the uncultivated parts. The Stone Age cultural material and the underlying limestone valley floor are exposed due to stripping of the silt cover by quarrying and subsequent erosion. The watercourse, which has exposed part of the Acheulian occupation level, is narrow on the northern side as it is flanked on either side by field bunds while the southern portion of the watercourse is ill-defined and shallow and occupies a broader area. It is also lower in elevation by about a metre as compared to the upper part of the water course. As a result some patches of the lower portion of the site have witnessed scouring by water action. The site modification has taken place in more recent times after soil quarrying by the Irrigation Department.

Palaeotopography

Geoarchaeological investigations comprising examination of the rain gullies, field bunds and cuttings resulting from soil quarrying have brought to light the existence of a shallow eroded tract on the limestone valley floor (Paddayya et al. 1999). This tract lies between the Stone Age site and the limestone plateau strip that defines the eastern margin of Isampur valley. It is 1.5 km long (north-south) and 200 to 300 m wide (east-west) and has been carved out due to the erosional activity of the drainage ancestral to present-day watercourses that descend from the plateaus on the northern and eastern sides. In fact, this palaeodrainage tract forms part of a network of shallow fluves and low interfluves that make up the floors of Hunsgi and Baichbal basins. These fluves and interfluves are the products of backwearing of plateaus and have given a gently undulating topography to the basin floor.

The Acheulian site lies on the western edge of the plaeodrainage tract. This setting of the site by the side of a waterbody is confirmed by the discovery of a few fossilized shell fragments of pond turtle belonging to the genus *Clemmys* in Trench 1. In Late Pleistocene times the drainage tract was filled up with a 3 to 4 m thick body of black/brown sediment.

Sedimentary and Stratigraphical Context

Five cuttings dug in the palaeodrainage tract, inspection of the sections preserved in rain gullies and cuttings of the quarried area and the study of sediments found in test pits and excavated trenches have made it possible to understand the thickness and character of the sediments filling up this ancient drainage tract as well as the stratigraphical position of the Stone Age cultural material (figs. 4 and 5).

In four of the cutting a small number of Acheulian artefacts were found on the eroded surface of the limestone, thereby establishing the pre-Acheulian age of the drainage tract. At a few places in the quarried area covering the palaeodrainage tract a 25 cm thick conglomerate horizon consisting of angular limestone blocks within calcrete encrustation was found resting on the limestone bedrock. This encrustation represents a precipitate formed in a pool-like environment containing carbonate-rich waters. The conglomerate horizon is overlain by a 3 to 4 m thick silt deposit. The upper half of this sediment is dark brown/black, while the lower half is light brown in colour. The particle size analysis has revealed that the sediments are clayey silts, which are essentially the weathered products of the Traps and were deposited on the valley floor by the interplay of colluvial and fluvial processes. They also contain angular to subangular pieces of basalt and chert derived from the Deccan Trap formations and quartzite pebbles and cobbles washed down from the pre-Trappean conglomerate beds that occur on the northern plateau. Further, each deposit showed evidence of internal stratification, which implies that several depositional episodes were involved in their formation. In one of the cuttings (Cutting I) the two sediments were separated from each other by a disconformity, which clearly shows that these deposits are distinct sedimentary bodies. In two of the cuttings Middle Palaeolithic artefacts were found in the upper part of the brown silt. It is possible that under conditions of landscape stability soil formation took place on these silts though no true soil profiles could be identified due to disturbances caused by intensive cultivation and quarrying.

The sediment cover in the area occupied by the Stone Age site is lesser in comparison. This is in conformity with the elevated nature of the valley floor. The *kankar* conglomerate horizon found in the palaeodrainage tract is absent here. The Acheulian cultural level lies on the limestone bedrock and occurs in a matrix of clacareous brown silt and measures about 15 to 30 cm in thickness. It is overlain by brown and black silt cover which measures from 15 cm to 1 m in thickness. In Trenches 1 and 3 Middle Palaeolithic artefacts were found in colluvial gravel lenses occurring in the bottom portion of the silt cover.

Preservational Context

The excavations have rvealed significant intrasite differences in the preservational contex of the Acheulian level. In Trench 2 (5 x 3 m) a loose rubble horizon (10 to 15 cm thick) was found overlying the original level; this rubble consists of limestone blocks and artefacts eroded from the upper elevated parts of the site and was deposited here in more recent years (fig. 6). In Trench 3 (6 x 7 m) an in sity Acheulian horizon was exposed under the silt cover varying from 15 cm to 60 cm in thickness. However, some portions of the Acheulian level were either partially scooped out or their contexts suffered some degree of spatial rearrangement due to soil quarrying and digging of field channels. The disturbed patches were subsequently filled up with loose black/brown silt; these present a sharp contrast to the undisturbed portions of the Acheulian level with its well-cemented, carbonate rich matrix (fig. 6).

Trenches 1 (7 x 10 m), 4 (4 x 3 m) and 5 (4 x 5 m) exposed the cultural horizon in a condition unaffected by post-depositional processes (fig. 7). Artificial clustering and spatial jumbling of pieces noticed in Trenches 2 and 3 were absent here. Trench 1 was of particular importance because many of the stone blocks and artefacts even seemed to fulfil the criterion of point provenance (i.e.pieces still lying in their original contexts). The flat positions and fresh and unrounded surfaces of artefacts and other clasts, their being embedded in a matrix of hard carbonate rich brown silt, and the occurrence of debitage pieces even smaller than a centimetre in size all bear testimony to the high level of integrity in the preservation of the site. It would seem that the cultural material did not remain exposed to the surface for a long time, before it was buried under silt cover. It is inferred that the flat nature of the surface and presence of ground vegetation protected the assemblage from processes like surface runoff, though minor spatial displacement of debitage belonging to the small size category would have occurred in some cases.

Fossil Fauna

The Acheulian level in Trenches 1, 4 and 5 yielded a small amount of fossil fauna comprising dental and bone pieces of wild cattle (*Bos* sp.), limb bone fragments of some unidentified medium-sized mammals and shell fragments of pond turtle (genus *Clemmys*). This evidence, slender though it is, is helpful in reconstrucing both past environments and hominid food habits (Pls. 1–3).

II. HOMINID BEHAVIOUR

Site Selection

Surface studies as well as digging of trial pits brought to light that the selection of this locality by th hominids was determined mainly by the occurrence of suitable raw material in the form of hard and highly siliceous limestone blocks resulting from the weathering of the valley floor. These blocks have a tabular form and are rectangular, squarish or triangular in shape. In size, they measure from 30 to 40 cm in length and 10 to 15 cm in thickness. Other favourable factors which would have influenced the selection of this site by the hominids included, the sheltered topography of the valley, the possibility of obtaining a clear view of the uplands from this spot, low heights (30 to 40 m above the valley floor) and flat surfaces of the uplands wich facilitated free movement of the hominids in their hunting-gathering activities, the availability of water in the drainage tract, and the ocurrence of a vaiety of wild plant and animal foods, as suggested by ethnobotanical evidence (Paddayya 1982: 71) and the discovery of small quantitites of fossil fauna in the Isampur excavation and at other sites in the Hunsgi and Baichbal valleys (Paddayya 1985, 1989).

Technological Organization

The assemblages from the five trenches, taken together with the surface collection from the site, provide excellent evidence both for understanding the overall character of the Isampur site and for reconstructing the organization of hominid technology.

Middle Palaeolithic

The Middle Palaeolithic assemblage from the Isampur excavation compares well with the assemblages found from other sites in the two valleys (Paddayya 1974, 1987b), both with respect to raw material preference and typo-technological features. The cultural material consists of flake tool assemblages, based on the working of chert nodules derived from Inter-Trappean chert beds and limestone formations. A limited number of artefacts are also made on quartzite derived from pre-Trappean conglomerate beds exposed on the plateau separating the Hunsgi and Baichbal valleys. The assemblage consists of finished tools, cores, hammerstones, flakes and debitage. Other than chert and quartzite limestone has also been utilized though in a limited way. Essentially two flaking techniques were adopted for the removal of flake blanks. One is the simple flaking technique aimed at the production of flakes which retain full or partial cortex on their dorsal surfaces. The second technique consists of detaching flakes from prepared cores. Such flakes tend to have regular shapes and fully worked dorsal surfaces. Flakes obtained by these techhniques were transformed into regular tools by the application of edge retouch or, in some cases, steep flaking. The most common tool type is the scraper, with the side, end, straight-edged, concave-edged, round, notched and core scrapers forming the major subtypes. In comparison to the scraper group other tool types like points and borers are fewer in number (fig. 8).

Acheulian

The Acheulian level, exposed in Trenches 1, 3, 4 and 5, measured 15 to 30 cm in thickness. The trenches were divided into 1m^2 grids to facilitate recording and plotting of the cultural material and limestone blocks. As a matter of convenience, the total deposit was exposed as successive, 5 to 10 cm thick units during the actual process of excavation. The following table presents the artefactual data recorded from various plotted levels (in which all exposed artefacts and stone blocks were plotted and a full record was kept of their spatial contexts) and also the material obtained from actual digging preceding exposing of each one of the plotted surfaces. The counts of artefacts for all the levels are not yet available. Nevertheless even a brief glance at the figures given in the following table will reveal the rich nature of the cultural assemblage from the site of Isampur.

Levels	Culture	Artefact No.	Description
Trench 1			
1997 Season (1.5x1.5m)			
0-15 cm (digging level)	MP	47	Black clayed silt with colluvial gravel
25-35 (digging level)	A	51	Brown kankary clayey silt
15/20-30 cm (plotted level)	A	182	Brown kankary clayey silt
30-40 cm (plotted level)	A	63	Brown kankary clayey silt
1998 Season (4x6 m)			
5-10 cm (digging level)		450	Loose black clayey silt mixed with light brown clayey silt
10-15 cm (digging level)	MP	864	Hard brown kankary clayey silt with colluvial gravel
15 cm (plotted level)	MP	204	Hard brown kankary clayey silt with colluvial gravel
15-20 cm (digging level)	MP	NA	Hard brown kankary clayey silt with colluvial gravel
20 cm (plotted level)	MP	158	Bottom portion of colluvial gravel lens
20-25 cm (digging level)	A	NA	Hard brown kankary clayey silt
25-30 cm (digging level)	A	NA	Hard brown kankary clayey silt
30 cm (plotted level)	A	463	Hard brown kankary clayey silt
1999 Season (6x10 m)			
0-5 cm (digging level)			Loose sediment with no antiquities
5-10 cm (digging level)			Compact blackish/brown clayey silt
10-15 cm (digging level)			Compact blackish/brown clayey silt
5-15 cm (digging level)			Compact blackish/brown clayey silt
15 cm (plotted level)	MP	69	Hard brown kankary clayey silt with colluvial gravel
15-20 cm (digging level)	MP	NA	Hard brown kankary clayey silt with colluvial gravel
20 cm (plotted level)	MP	110	Hard brown kankary clayey silt with colluvial gravel
20-25 cm (digging level)	MP	NA	Hard brown kankary clayey silt with colluvial gravel
25 cm (plotted level)	MP	164	Hard brown kankary clayey silt with colluvial gravel
25-30/35 cm (digging level)	MP	NA	Hard brown kankary clayey silt with colluvial gravel
30/35 cm (plotted level)	MP & A	210	Hard brown kankary clayey silt with colluvial gravel
35-40 (digging level)	A	NA	Hard brown kankary clayey silt
40 cm (plotted level)	A	473	Hard brown kankary clayey silt
40-45 cm (digging level)	A	3027	Hard brown kankary clayey silt
45 cm (plotted level	A	1023	Hard brown kankary clayey silt
2000 Season (7x10 m)			
0-10 cm (digging level)	A	NA	Blackish/brown clayey silt
10-15 cm (digging level)	A	NA	Blackish/brown clayey silt
15 cm (plotted leel)	A	18	Blackish/brown clayey silt
15-25 (digging level)	A	NA	Blackish/brown clayey silt
25 cm (plotted level)	A	115	Brown clayey silt
45-50 cm (digging level)	A	5233	Hard brown kankary clayey silt
50 cm (plotted level)	A	1233	Hard brown kankary clayey silt
Bedrock			

Trench 2 1997 Seaon (5x3 m)			
10-15 cm (digging level)	A	NA	Compack black/brown clayey silt
15 cm (plotted level)	A	329	Brown kankary clayey silt
15-25/30 cm (only E1-3)	A	NA	Hard white/brown kankary clayey silt
30 cm (plotted level) (only E1-3)	A	92	Hard white/brown kankary clayey silt
Trench 3 1998 Season (6x7m)			
Surface			Black clayey silk
0-5 cm (digging level)	Disturbed	NA	Black clayey silk
20-25 cm (digging level)	Disturbed	NA	Black clayey silk
25 cm (plotted level)	Disturbed	NA	Black clayey silt with loose colluvial gravel
25-30 cm (digging level)	Disturbed	NA	Black clayey silt with loose colluvial gravel
30 cm (plotted level)	MP & A	NA	Black clayey silt with loose colluvial gravel
30-35 cm (digging level)	MP & A	NA	Brown clayey silt with loose colluvial gravel
35 cm (plotted level)	A	162	Brown clayey silt with loose colluvial gravel
35-45 cm (plotted level)	A	NA	Hard brown kankary clayey silt
45 cm (plotted level)	A	415	Hard brown kankary clayey silt
45-55 cm (digging level)	A	NA	Hard brown kankary clayey silt
55 cm (plotted level)	A	628	Hard brown kankary clayey silt
Bedrock			
Trench 4 (4x3 m) 1999 Season			
0-5 cm (digging level)		NA	Loose black clayey silt
5-10 cm (digging level)		NA	Loose black clayey silt
1cm (plotted level)		59	Black clayey silt with colluvial gravel
10-15 cm (digging level)		NA	Compact brown clayey silt mixed with black clayey silt
15 cm (plotted level	A	106	Compact brown clayey silt mixed with black clayey silt
15-20 cm (digging level)	A	NA	Brown kankary clayey silt though not very hard to dig
20 cm (plotted level)	A	281	Hard brown kankary clayey silt with limestone rubble
20-25/30cm (digging level)	A	NA	Hard brown kankary clayey silt with limestone rubble
30 cm (plotted level)	A	250	Hard brown kankary clayey silt with limestone rubble
Bedrock			
Trench 5 1999 Season (3x3m)			
Surface			Loose black clayey silt rich in Acheulian debitage
0-5 cm (digging level)	A	NA	Black clayey silt
5 cm (plotted level)	A	133	Black clayey silt
5-10 (digging level)	A	NA	Black clayey silt
10 cm (plotted level)	A	321	Hard brown kankary clayey silt
2000 Season (4x5 m)			
0-5 cm (digging level)	A	Na	Black clayey silt
5-10 cm (digging level)	A	NA	Black clayey silt
10 cm (plotted level)	A	333	Hard brown kankary clayey silt
10-15 cm (digging level)	A	NA	Hard brown kankary clayey silt
15 cm (plotted level)	A	362	Hard brown kankary clayey silt
15-20 cm (digging level)	A	NA	Hard brown kankary clayey silt
Bedrock			

A-Acheulian, MP-Middle Palaeolithic, NA-Not Available

Though a detailed techno-typological analysis of the assemblage is still underway, a few comments about the striking features of the Isampur Acheulian assemblage are made here. First, the composition of the assemblage is characterized by the predominance of cores of various types of shapes, large flakes and debitage and relatively fewer finished tools (bifacial and unifacial). Secondly, the debitage belonging to different classes (fig. 9) and sizes and shaped tools in various stages of manufacture also occur at the site. Thirdly, a large number of hammerstones of varying sizes and made of harder rocks like quartzite, chert and basalt hav been found on the surface and also in the excavations (fig. 10). These features have enabled us to reconstruct the complete sequence of tool manufacture.

The principal reduction stages identified at the site are as follows. First there is the selection of raw material which was easily available on the surface of the site in the form of siliceous limestone blocks and slabs. These blocks and slabs on account of the angularities formed at the intersection of flat surfaces and steep sides, served as ideal cores for flaking (for further details see, Petraglia et al.1999). The site also preserves evidence of quarrying in the form of prying disjointed blocks from bedrock. Several cores in various stages of working have been recorded in the assemblage. A large number of cores show that they were trimmed/dressed (to obtain a suitable platform) prior to the removal of large flakes (fig. 11). Several such core-trimming flakes were recorded during excavation. Then these is the removal of flake blanks from selected limestone blocks by using one of the steep sides (i.e.along the thickness of blocks) as the platform. These flakes generally preserve the cortical surface of parent blocks, possess very prominent bulbs of percussion and are massive in size, measuring 15 to 20 cm along the major axis (fig. 12). Once flaking was initiated on the blocks, it was continued, sometimes in alternate direction, in order to obtain flake blanks. The dorsal surfaces of these blanks are either partially cortical or non-cortical. In some cases massive flakes also served as cores for detaching flakes. The next level involves transforming these large flakes into chopping tools and knives with a minimum of secondary chipping or shaping them into bifacial tools especially handaxes and cleavers by elaborate trimming (fig. 13). Smaller hammerstones (8 to 9 cm across) were used for this purpose. A large quantity of thin and small debitage flakes having small striking platforms and heavily flaked dorsal surfaces confirm that this stage of secondary reduction also took place at the site. Flaking of thinner limestone slabs (2 to 8 cm thick) for fashioning them into bifaces and chopping tools (fig. 14) and manufacture of expedient tools which occur in the form of modified flakes and chunks or utilised flakes are the other manufacturing processes noticed in the Isampur assemblage.

Chopping tools, knives, handaxes, cleavers and scrapers are the main tool-types of the Isampur assemblage. Given the massive sizes of artefacts and their thick cross-sections and pointed shapes of bifaces, it is easy to infer that both in terms of technology and typological composition, this assemblage presents a primitive appearance as compared to the assemblages from other sites in the Hunsgi and Baichbal valleys. A few fossile tooth samples from Trenches 1 and 5 have been submitted to Dr. B.Blackwell, U.S.A., for ESR dating. It is presumed that the age of the new site could easily be of the order of 500,000 to 600,000 years.

In Trench 1 it was possible to identify activity areas in the form of four chipping clusters or circles, each measuring 88 to 10 m^2 in extent. These clusters consisted of dense concentrations of thick limestone blocks, cores of various sizes, chips and flakes forming debitage, and finished artefacts (Pl. 4).

Hominid Landuse Pattern

Excavations and surface mapping revealed several features which have brought about a new understanding of the role of function of the site was have thrown fresh light on the landuse patterns of the hominids. First, it is clear that this site was an important location which witnessed not one but a series of occupations by the hominids spread over a long period of time during which a tremendous amount of chipping took place. This observation is attested by the unstratified and palimpsest nature of the 30 cm thick Acheulian horizon, the high density of artefacts, and the large area over which the site is spread. Secondly, the surface distribution of artefactual material and limestone blocks and the evidence provided by trial pits and regular trenches excavated at the site show that the site consisted of four sub-localities, each measuring 300 to 400 m^2 in size and containing numerous limestone blocks and slabs suitable for tool manufacture (see fig. 3). These rocky patches would have been the foci of activity of individual groups or families, all making up a band. Thirdly, from the large spatial extent of the site and the tremendously rich nature of the lithic assemblage, one could say that the Isampur site was a localised hub of tool manufacturing activities. From here the hominids radiated onto the valley floor and uplands for their daily foraging activities. Many of the finished tools were also being removed from the site to form a part of the tool-kit of the hominids on their daily foraging rounds. In this connection it is encouraging to note that surveys of the valley floor and uplands around Isampur since 1994 have brought to light about a dozen occurrences of he non-site type and also a large site at Kolihal (Paddayya and Jhaldiyal 1998-99), all lying within a radius of 2 to 3 km. This new data has greatly elevated our understanding of the Acheulian settlement system of the region. One would infer that several other hubs of manufacturig and occupation activities existed in the two basins, e.g. Hunsgi V, Yediyapur VI, Mudnur X and Fatehpur V. Fourthly, the presence of weahered artefacts, use-marks on several tools and identification of a large number of modified and utilised pieces confirm that this spot was also an occupation site which witnessed other subsistence related activities like food processing.

IV. CONCLUSION

In the foregoing pages a fairly detailed account has been presented of the new Acheulian site of Isampur — its geomorphic and sedimentary contexts, variability in the preservational context of the Acheulian cultural level and hominid behavioural aspects such as site selection criteria and various lithic manufacturing strategies adopted by the hominids. Against this background one may try to evaluate the significance of the Isampur first in the context of existing knowledge of the Acheulian culture phase of the Hunsgi and Baichbal valleys and then the place of the site *vis-a-vis* other excavated Lower Palaeolithic site (for a recent review see, Pappu- In press) in other parts of the country.

Contrary to the general notion which gives scant regard to surface sites of the Lower Palaeolithic phase, the work at Isampur clearly shows how detailed studies comprising both surface survey and excavations can reveal totally new dimensions or aspects of an archaeological site which could be easilyy missed by cursory work. An important aspect brought into focus by the work at Isampur concerns the so-called surface character of many of the Acheulian sites. It is worth emphasizing here that the present-day surface character of sites is a post-depositional feature caused by various natural and anthropogenic processes. The real fact as highlighted by the work at Isampur is that these sites were originally covered by sediments of variable thickness; it is this sedimentary cover which has preserved the site in their *in situ* context for a long period of time.

Another noteworthy feature highlighted by th work at Isampur concerns the recognition of tremendous variability in the preservational context of the Acheulian cultural level — fluvially altered in more recent times; partially disturbed due to construction of field channels and quarrying; and *in situ* contexts. The Isampur excavatons unexpectedly also gave for the first time valuable stratigraphic data for ascertaining the chronological position of the Middle Palaeolihic culture in the Stone Age sequence of the Hunsgi and Baichbal valleys.

The various details provided in the paper about the locational setting of the Isampur site enable one for the first time to reconstruct the kind of cognitive mapping of the landscape done by the hominids — particularly the recognition of the siiliceous character of the limestone blocks at this patch of the valley floor and their suitable sizes and shapes, location of the spot close to an assured source of water and a complete view of the surrounding uplands.

As mentioned in detail in the paper, the unusually rich character of the assemblage consisting of both finished products and byproducts has made it possible to reconstruct for the first time the *chaine operatoire* or the principal manufacturing stages and strategies adopted by the hominids. Very little of this understanding of the Acheulian culture of the two valleys has been afforded by the sites studied so far. No less insightful are the data pertaining to the typological repertoire, especially the occurence in good numbers of nearly finished flake blanks which could serve as chopping tools, knives and other heavy duty tool forms.

Last but by no means the least important, this work at Isampur has led to a more refined understanding of the functioning of the Acheulian settlement system — a series of medium and small sites and non-sites located on the valley floor and plateau surrfaces forming units of a sub-regional system with a major site like Isampur serving as the hub of manufacturing and occupation activities.

Seen in a pan-Indian context, many of the observations made above are equally valid. But perhaps attention needs to be focussed on two or three specific aspects. First, the work at Isampur serves to emphasise that Stone Age studies, far from being considered a cursory hit-and-run job, could shed light on the lifeways of even the remotest phases of human past. Secondly, it is now abundantly clear that the Indian Lower Palaeolithic record is no longer a matter of only secondary sites or surface sites; intensive field studies will undoubtedly bring to light sites like Isampur or even better ones in different regions, affording a greater chronological control and yielding crucial data for reconstructing palaeoenvironments and early human adaptation strategies.

Thanks to the pioneering discoveries of Robert Bruce Foote, Lower Palaeolithic research commenced in India almost on the heels of he epoch-making discoveries of Boucher de Perthes in northern France. Since then hundreds of sites have been explored in the southern, eastern, central, western, and northwestern parts of the subcontinent. Over the last forty years about 20 sites comprising both open-air and cave/rock-shelter localities have been excavated leading to a more elaborate understanding of the regional cultural settings. All the same fresh work at sites like Isampur described in the present article prompts one to look for new sites in different regions which can place at our disposal more comprehensive data about the palaeoenvironmental, chronological and cultural aspects of early human adaptations and even provide hominid skeletal material which has been the tour de force of East African prehistory.

Acknowledgements

We would like to express our deep appreciation to the people of Isampur and Hunsgi villages particularly Dr. S.R.Biradar, Shri Naganna Dandi, Shri Nagappa Hadkyal, Shri Bhimanna Udidamani and the late Shri Aminappa Harnal (owner of the farmland on which the Stone Age site is located) for their cooperation and help. Drs. Bilal R. Khrisat and S.K.Aruni provided tremendous support by their participation in the excavations. We also thank the technical staff of the Institute —Dr. P.S.Joshi, Shri D.D. Phule, S.D.Rokade, D.V.Karanjkar, B.S.Waghmode, S.A.Pradhan and V.G.Vishwasrao — who participated in the fieldwork and have prepared the site maps, plottings of the excavated cultural levels and the lithic illustrations and Shri Sunil Jadhav and Ravi Dhamapurkar who carried out the photo-documentation. Our thanks are also extended to Shri Ashok Omble, Chandrakant Shendge and H.S.Balakrishna for the management of the excavation camp. A large number of M.A., M.Phil and Ph.D. students of the Institute participated in the Isampur excavation as a part of their field training in field archaeology. We are grateful to Dr. G.L.Badam for the identification of fossil fauna.

REFERENCES

Jhaldiyal, R.1998. Formation Processes of the Prehistoric Sites in the Hunsgi and Baichbal Basins, Gulbarga District, Karnataka. Unpublished Ph.D. Thesis, University of Pune.

Kshirsagar A. and Paddayya K. 1989. Relative Chronology of Stone Age Cultures of Hunsgi-Baichbal valleys, North Karnataka, by Fluorine Analysis. *Bulletin of Deccan College Post Graduate and Research Institute,* 47-48:143-146.

Paddayya, K.1974. The Middle Palaeolithic Culture of the Shorapur Doab, Karnataka. *Journal of Indian History*, 52: 1-19.

Paddayyya, K. 1982. *The Acheulian Culture of Hunsgi Valley, Peninsular India: A Settlement System Perspective.* Pune : Deccan College.

Paddayya K. 1985. Acheulian Occupation Sites and Associated Fossil Fauna from the Hunsgi-Baichbal Valleys, Peninsular India. *Anthropos* 80:653-658.

Paddayya, K. 1987a. The Place of the Study of Site Formation Processes in Prehistoric Research in India, in *Natural Formation Processes and the Archaeological Record* (D.T.Nash and M.D.Petraglia Eds.), pp.74-85. Oxford: BAR International Series 352.

Paddayya, K. 1987b. The Stone Age Cultural Systems of the Baichbal Valley, Gulbarga District, Karnataka: a Preliminary Report. *Bulletin of the Deccan College Post-Graduate and Research Institute* 46: 77-100.

Paddayya, K. 1989. The Acheulian Culture Localities along the Fatehpur Nullah, Baichbal Valley, Karnataka (Peninsular India), in Old Problems and New Perspectives in the *Archaeology of South Asia*(J.M.Kenoyer Ed.) pp. 21-28. Madison: University of Wisconsin Press.

Paddayya, K. 1991. The Acheulian Culture of the Hunsgi-Baichbal Valleys, Peninsular India: a Processual Study, *Quartar* 41/42: 111-138.

Paddayya, K. and M.D.Petraglia. 1993. Formation Processes of Acheulian Localities in the Hunsgi and Baichbal Valleys, Peninsular India. In *Formation Processes in Archaeological Context.*(P.Goldberg, D.T. Nash and M.D.Petraglia Eds.), pp. 61-82 Madison: Prehistory Press.

Paddayya, K. and M.D. Petraglia. 1995. Natural and Cultural Formation Processes of the Acheullian Sites of the Hunsgi and Baichbal Valleys, Karnataka. In *Quaternary Environments and Geoarchaeology of India* (S. Wadia, R.Korisettar and V.S.Kale Eds.) pp. 333-351. Bangalore:Geological Society of India.

Paddayya, K. and M.D. Petraglia 1997. Isampur: an Acheulian Workshop Site in the Hunsgi Valley, Gulbarga District, Karnataka. *Man and Environment* 22(2): 95-100.

Paddayya, K. and M.D. Petraglia 1998. Acheulian Workshop at Isampur, Hunsgi Valley, Karnataka: a Preliminary Report. *Bulletin of the Deccan College Post-Graduate and Research Institute* 56-57 (1996-97):3-26.

Paddayya, K.R.Jhaldiyal, and M.D.Petraglia. 1999. Geoarchaeology of the Acheulian Workshop at Isampur, Hunsgi Valley, Karnataka, *Man and Environment* 24(1): 167-184.

Paddayya, K. and R. Jhaldiya. 1998-99. A new Acheulian Site at Kolihal in the Hunsgi Valley, Karnataka. *Puratattva* 29:1-7.

Petraglia, M.D., P.LaPorta and K. Paddayya. 1999. Isampur, The First Acheulian Quarry in India: Stone Tool Manufacture, Biface Morphology and Behviours, *Journal of Anthropological Research* 55: 39-70.

Pappu, R.S. In Press. The Lower Paleolithic Cullture of India. In Recent Advances in *Indian Archaeology* (K.Paddayya, Ed.). New Delhi: Munshiram Manoharlal Publishers.

Szabo, B.J., Curtis Mckinney, T.S.Dalbey and K.Paddayya. 1990. On the Age of the Acheulian Culture of the Hunsgi-Baichbal Valleys, Peninsular India. *Bulletin of the Deccan College Post-Graduate and Research Institute* 50: 317-21.

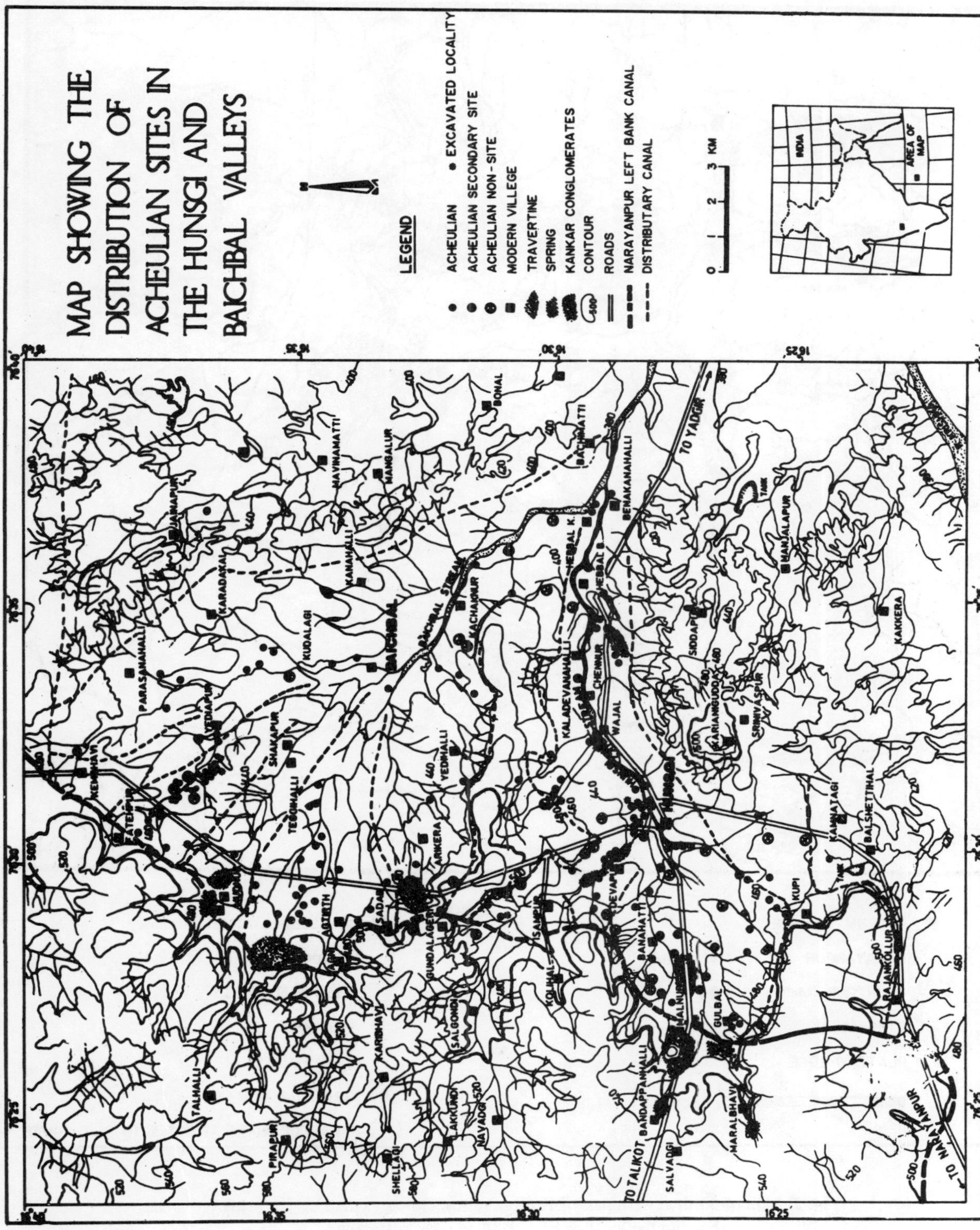

Fig. 1. Map showing the distribution of Acheulian Sites in the Hunsgi and Baichbal valleys, Gulbarga district, Karnataka.

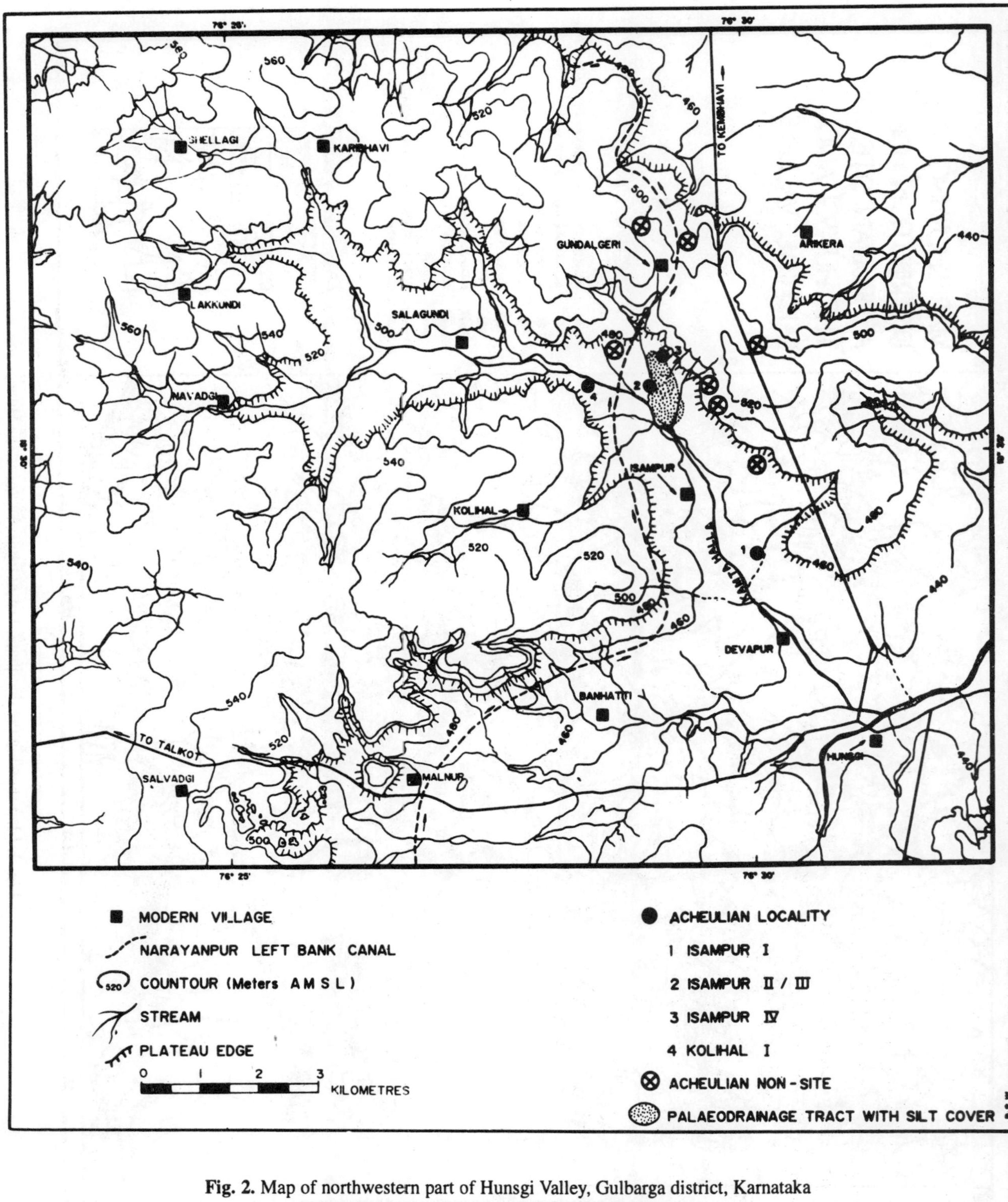

Fig. 2. Map of northwestern part of Hunsgi Valley, Gulbarga district, Karnataka showing the location of Acheulian sites at Isampur.

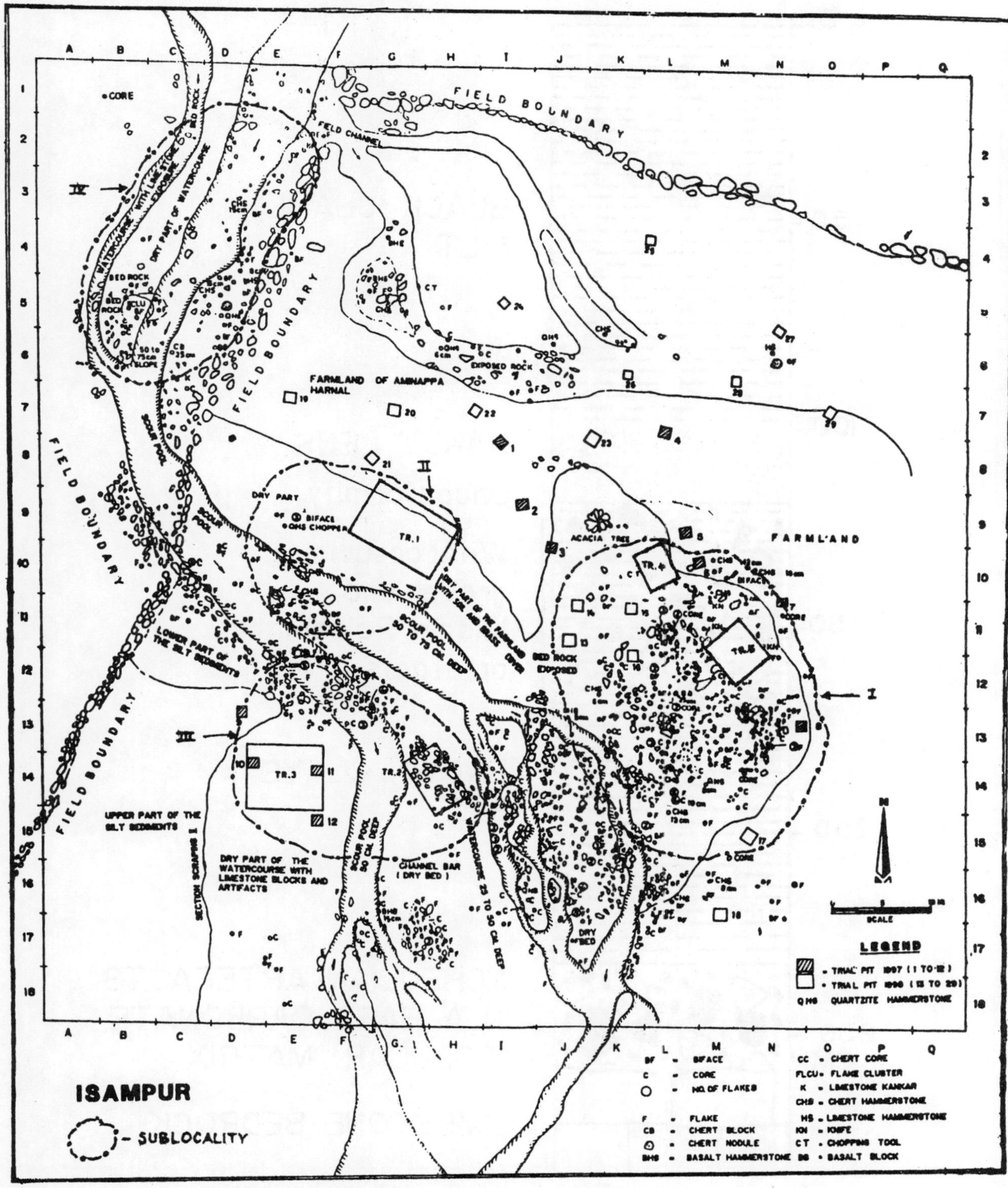

Fig. 3. Map of Isampur Acheulian site showing the surface distribution of artefacts and location of excavated trenches and trial pits.

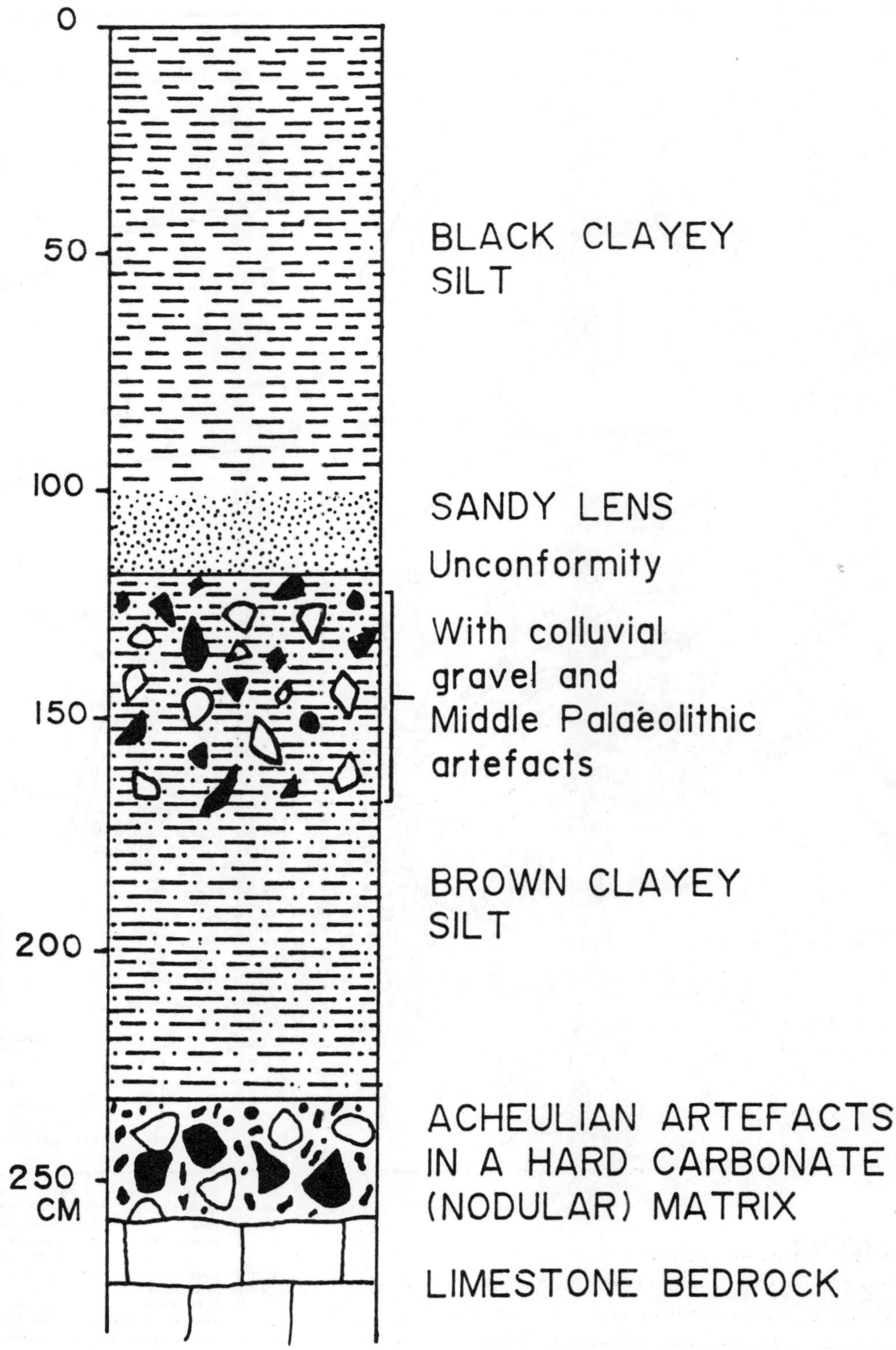

Fig. 4. Stratigraphy exposed in Cutting 1 dug in the palaeodrainage tract near Isampur Acheulian site.

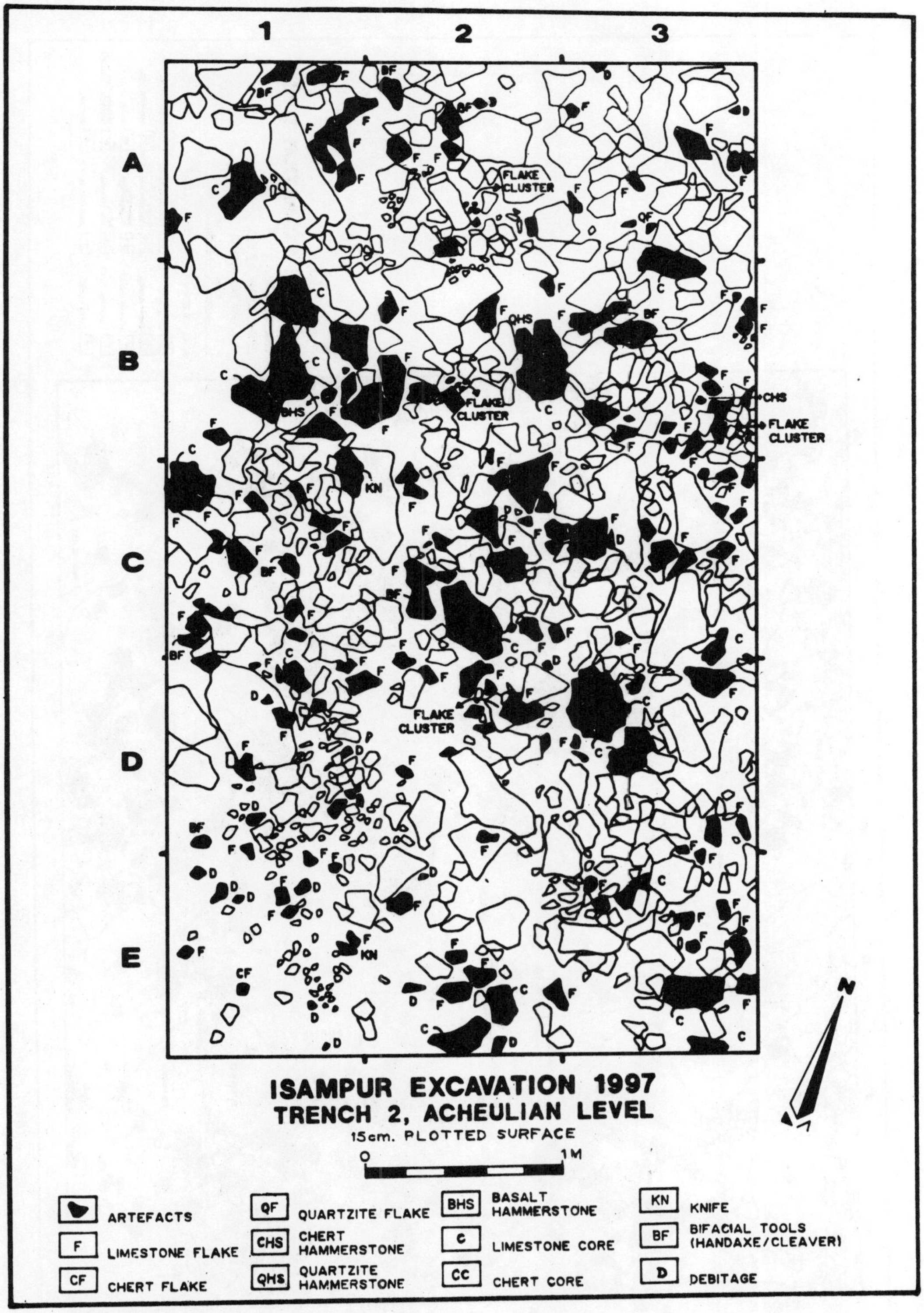

Fig. 5. Rubble horizon containing redeposited limestone blocks and Acheulian artefacts exposed at a depth of 15 cm below surface in Trench 2, Isampur.

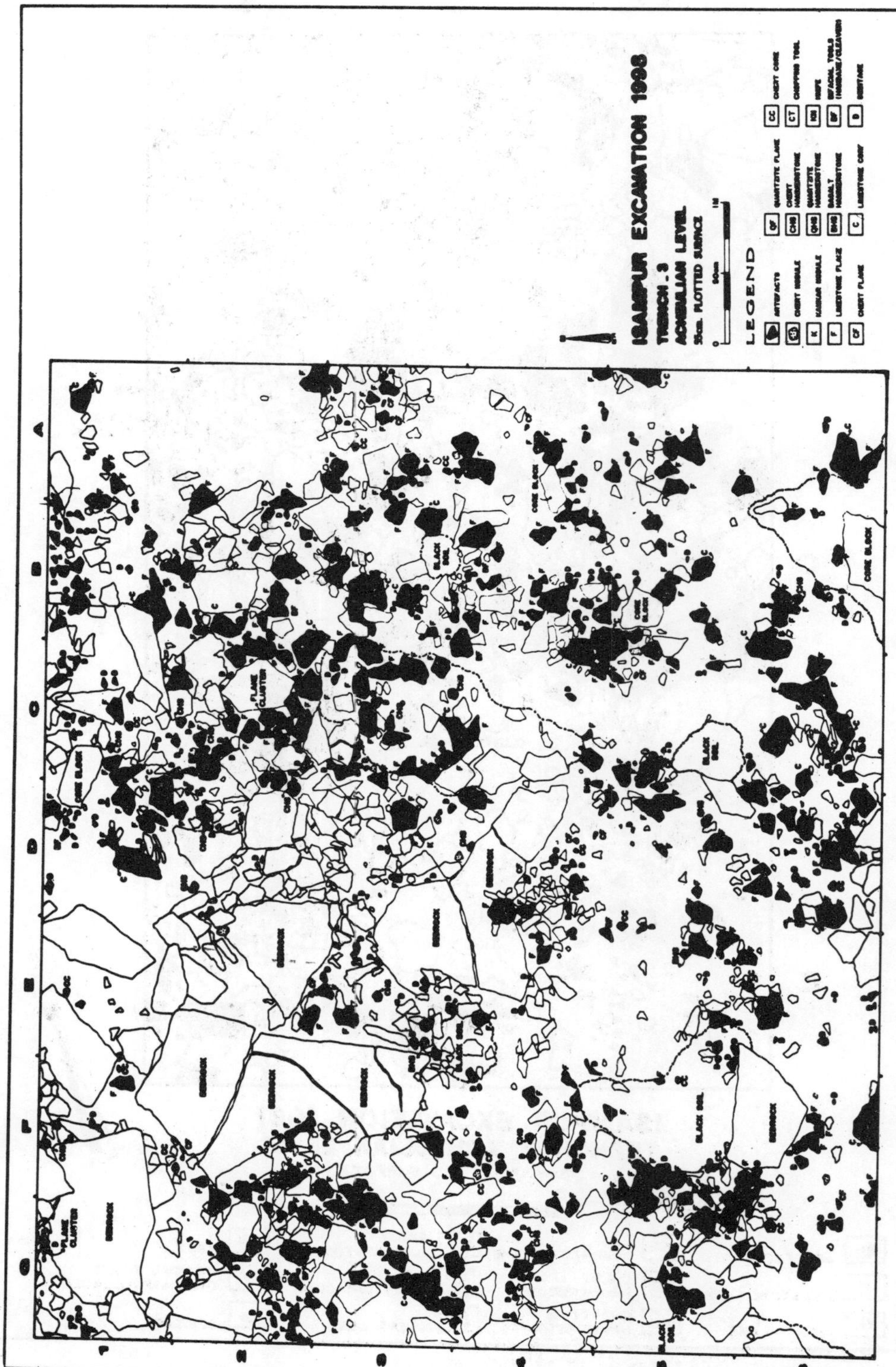

Fig. 6. Acheulian level exposed at a depth of 55 cm below surface in Trench 3, Isampur showing in situcultural material interspersed with localised patches of black soil indicating disturbance of more recent times (denoted by dotted lines).

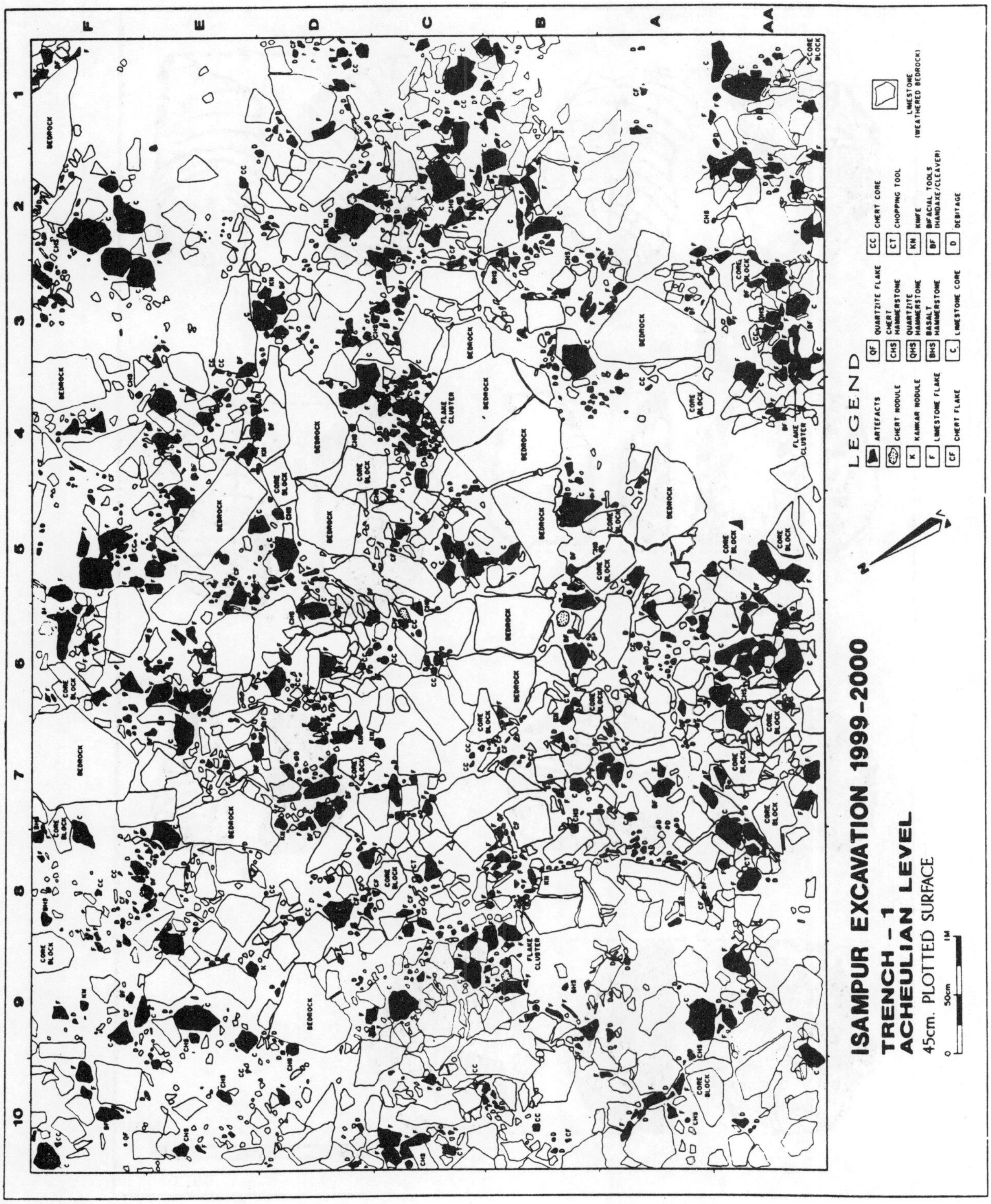

Fig. 7. Acheulian level exposed at 45 cm below surface in Trench 1 at Isampur, showing the distribution of limestone blocks and artefacts. Note the flat positions of the limestone blocks and artefacts.

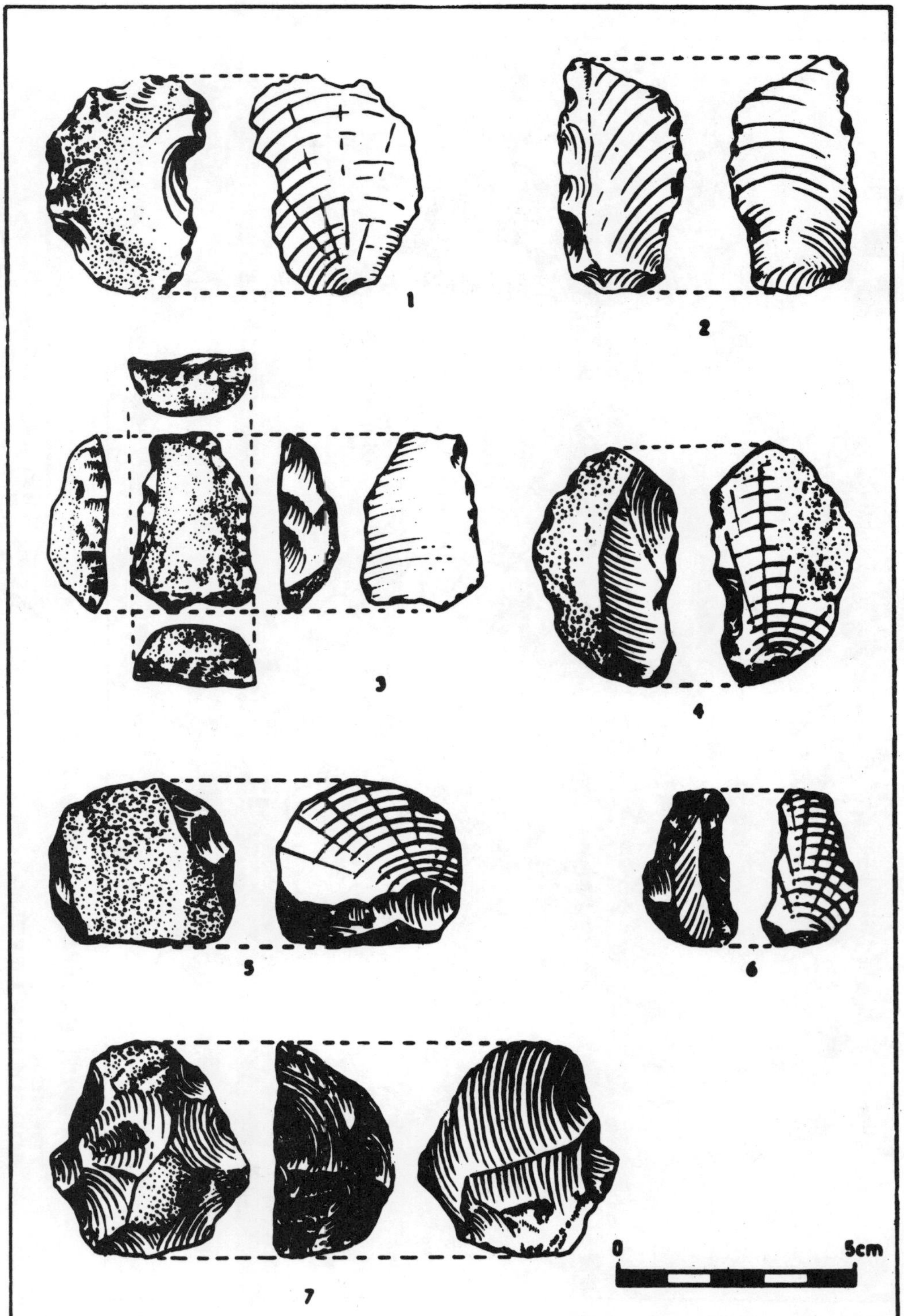

Fig. 8. Limestone Debitage from Acheulian level exposed in Trench 1, Isampur.

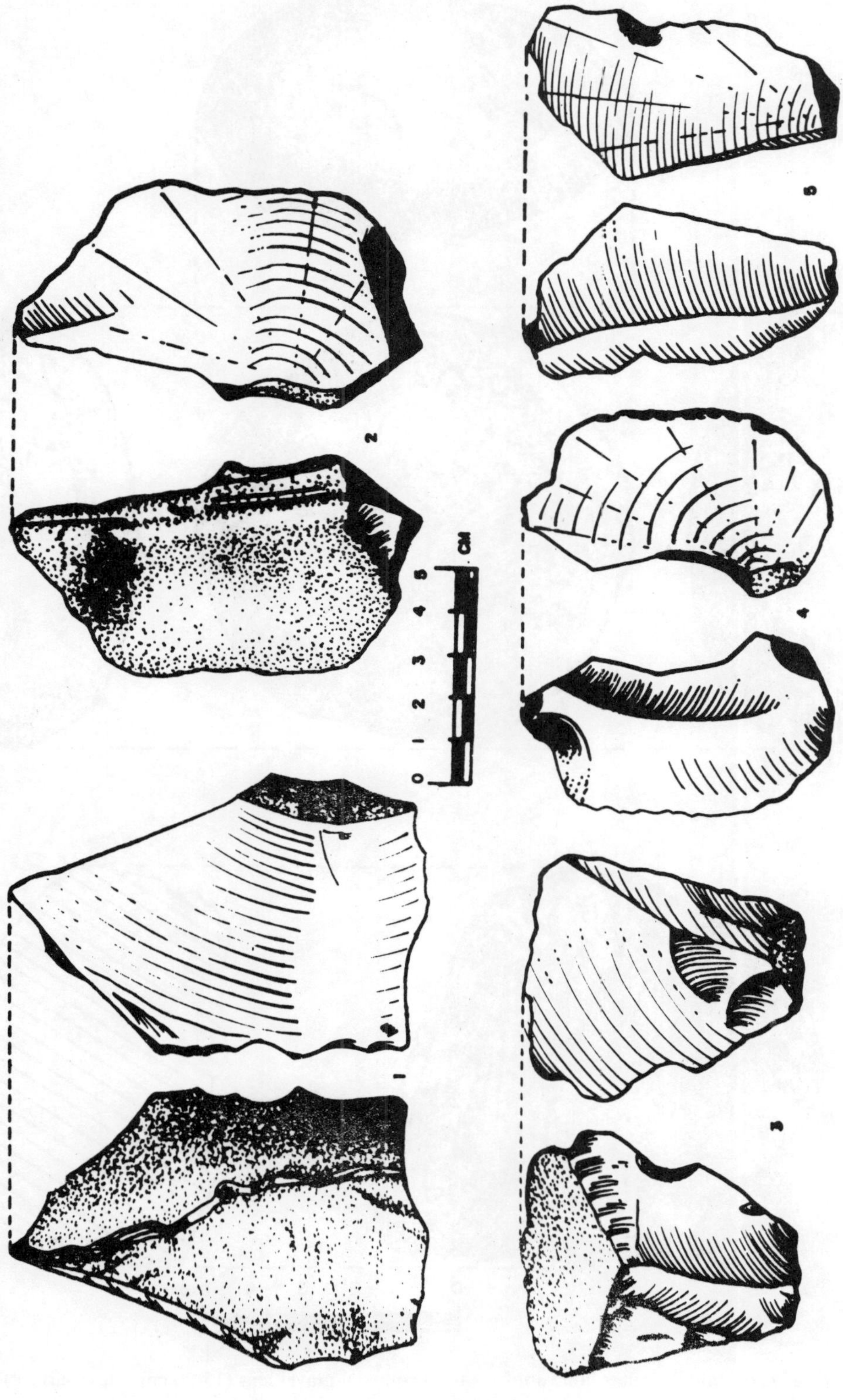

Fig. 9. Hammerstones with use-marks from surface of Acheulian site of Isampur : 1) made of dolerite; 2) made of quartz crystal.

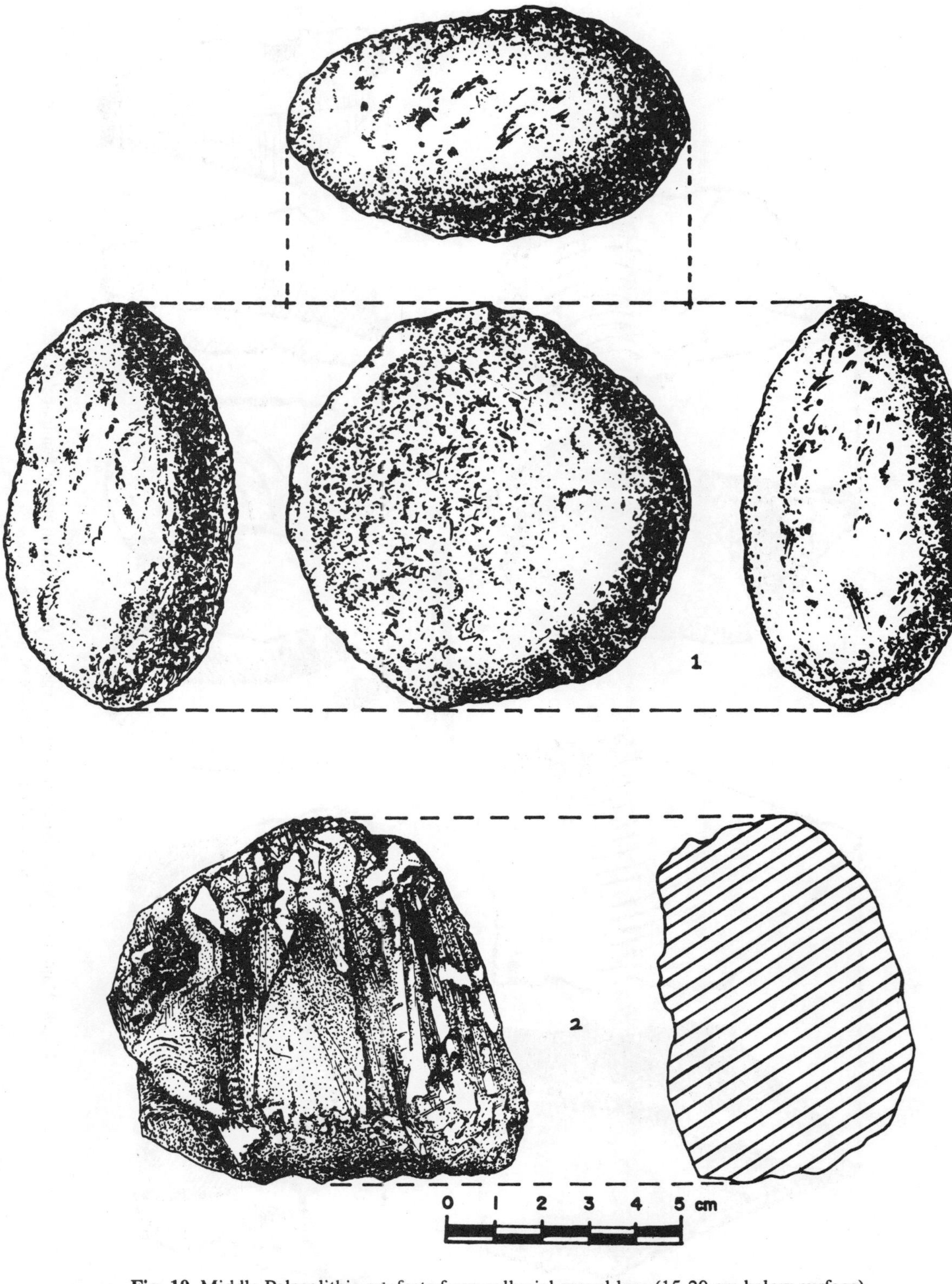

Fig. 10. Middle Palaeolithic artefacts from colluvial gravel lens (15-20 cm below surface) overlying the Acheulian horizon in Trench 1, Isampur.

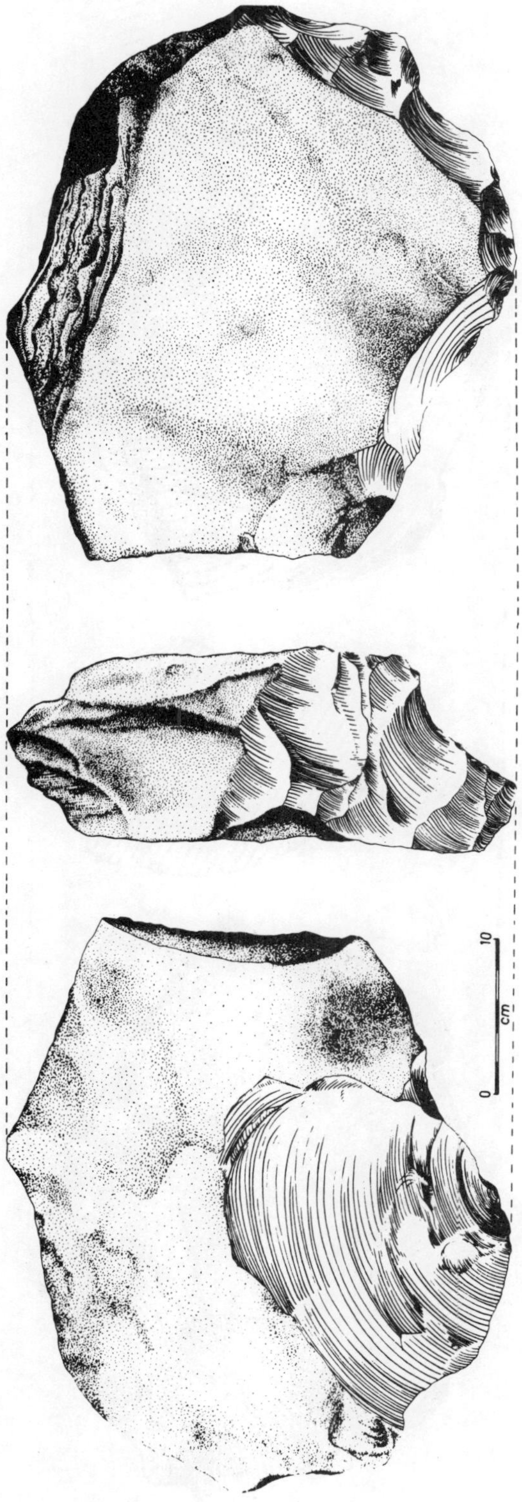

Fig. 11. Large limestone core showing dressing along a portion of the periphery and removal of a lage flake detached from one of the surfaces.

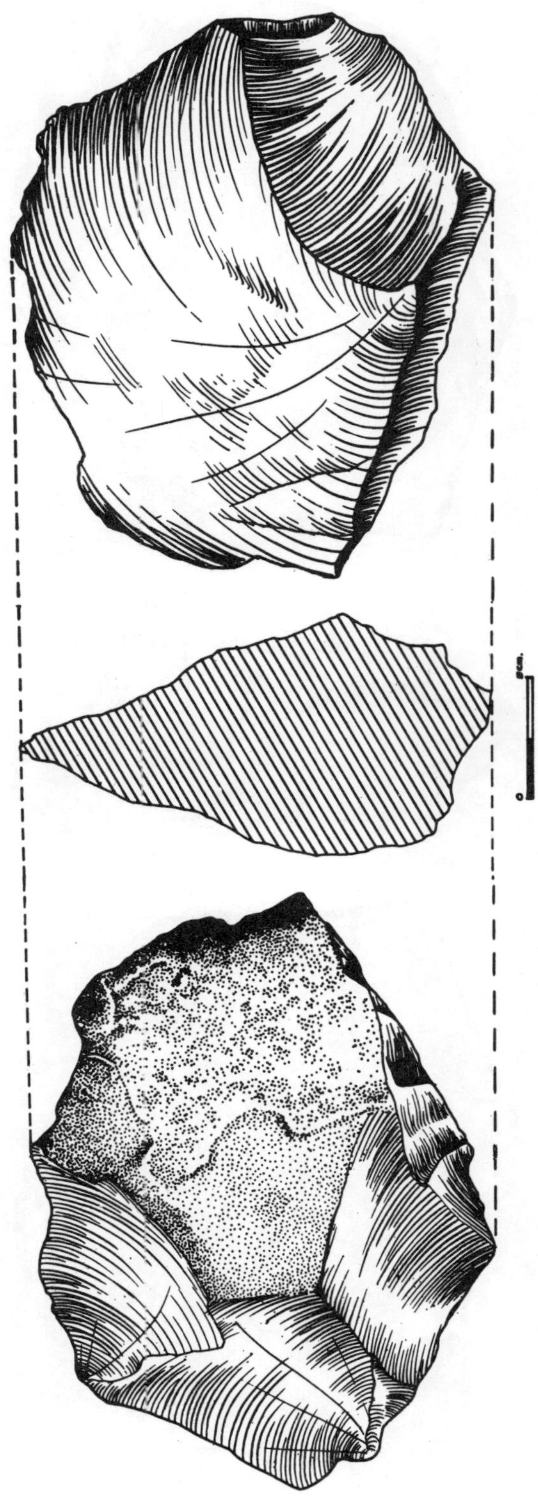

Fig. 12. A large limestone flake showing partial working on the dorsal surface.

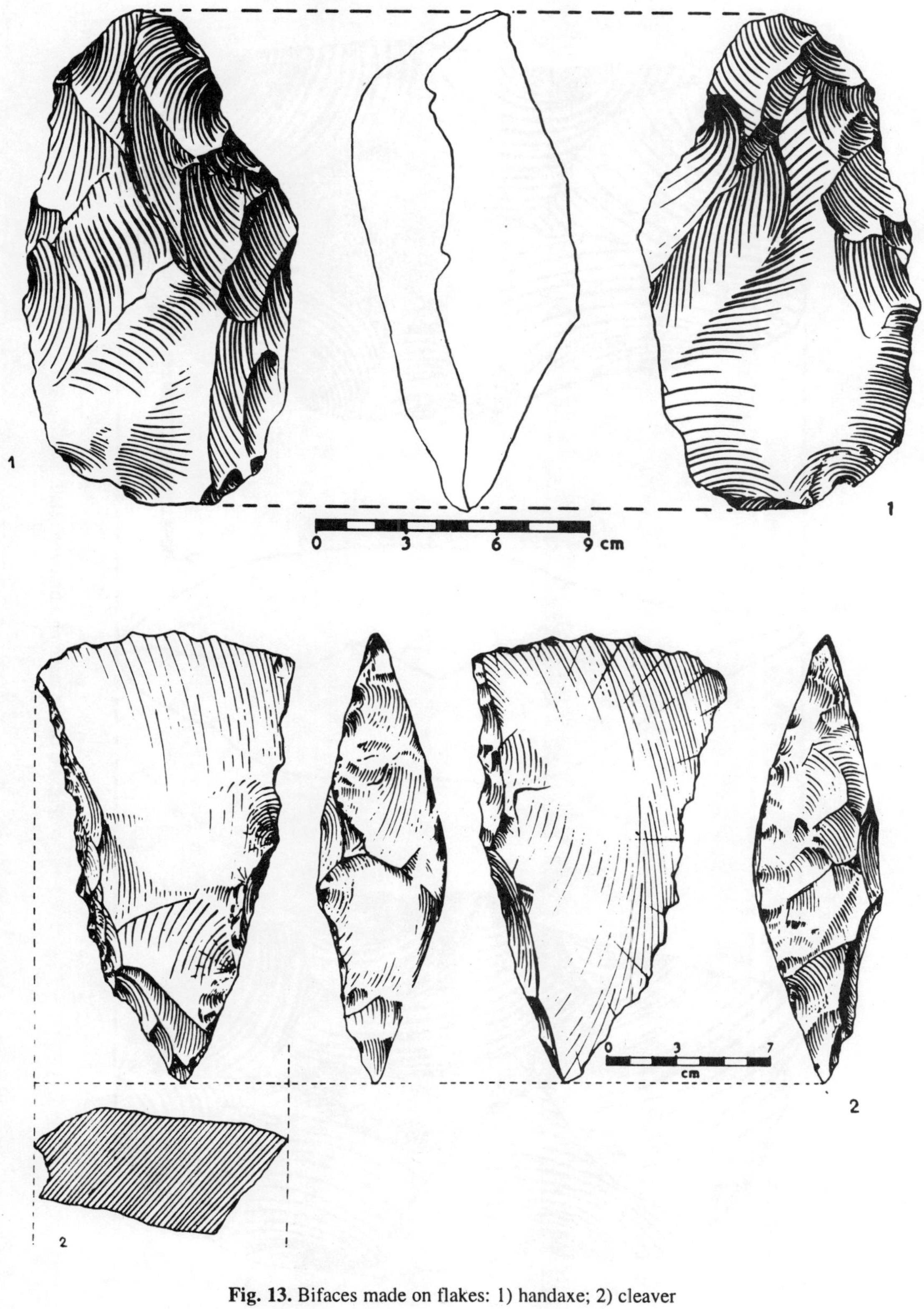

Fig. 13. Bifaces made on flakes: 1) handaxe; 2) cleaver

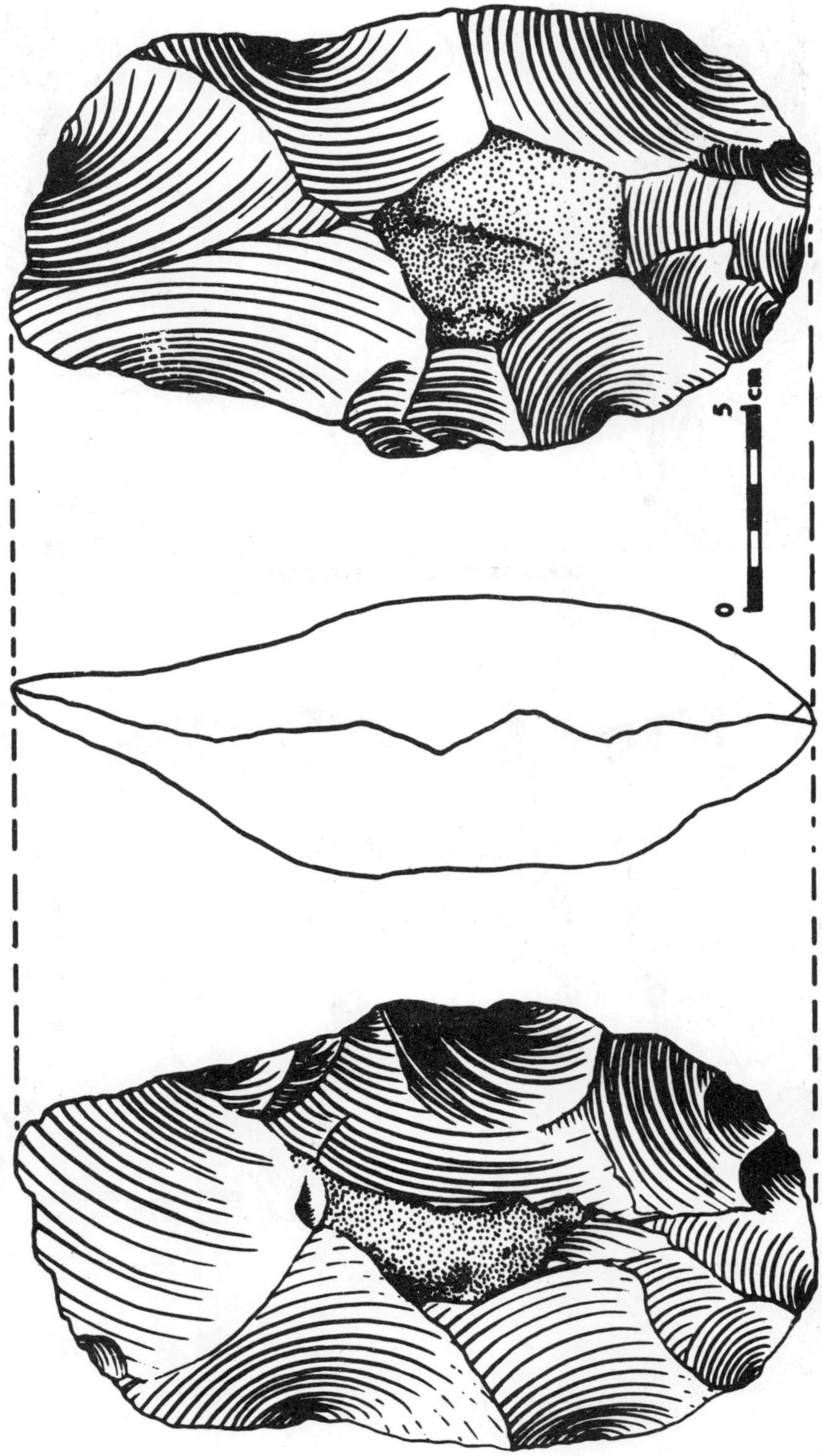

Fig. 14. Biface made on a limestone slab.

Economy of the Neolithic Cultures of Southern Uttar Pradesh and Western Bihar

DR. ANIL KUMAR AND PROF. P.C. PANT*

Although the evidence of the Neolithic settlement and culture patterns of neolithic settlers is still scanty, an objective and critical persual of the available details indicates that it will not be justifiable to treat the cultures of all the excavated sites as belonging to one period and of the same stage of development. The evidences available from the excavations at Mahagara and to a certain extent those from Koldihwa and Panchoh of Southern Uttar Pradesh as well as from Chirand, Chechar-Kutubpur, Taradih, Maner and Senuwar of western Bihar indicate a mixed economy characterised by incipient farming, pastoralism, hunting-fishing and gathering. On the basis of the evidence of pottery as well as that of carbonised grains unearthed from some of the sites, it may be inferred that it is possible to discern three developmental stages in the Neolithic economy of the above regions. While reconstructing the economy, the ethnographic data of the four tribes of Chhotanagpur plateau of Bihar - the Santals, the Mundas, the Oraons and the Hos, practicing primitive agriculture, domestication of animals, gathering of forest products, fishing and hunting for subsistence, may also be considered.

Stage I

This stage (*ca.* 2300 B.C. - 1950 B.C.) was represented by the Sub-Period IA of Senuwar and the entire Neolithic complex of Mahagara-Koldihwa. This stage was based on the economy of the cultivation of only one cereal, i.e.. rice and domestication of various animals, partly supplemented by, gathering hunting and fishing.

The totality of evidence gathered from these sites suggests tribal economy, to a certain extent comparable with that of the present day tribes of the Chhotanagpur plateau, viz, the Santal, the Munda, the Oraon and the Ho. This is best exemplified by the study of faunal remains from Senuwar by G. L. Badam (Courtesy B. P. Singh), who observed that bones of different parts of the body of animals are not found at one place, but were found scattered in different trenches of the site. This applies to both wild and domesticated animals. This may imply that the hunted as well as butchered domesticated animals were considered the property of the entire community, and the flesh was distributed among all the members. It may be noted that even today among the above mentioned tribes and also several others, hunting is a community affair in which all the eligible male members participate. Irrespective of the fact that the animal was killed by the weapons of whichever individual, the flesh of the hunted animal is shared by all the families. The practice of equal sharing of the hunted animal was also perhaps prevalent among the neolithic settlers of the area of our study. Although at present each tribal family owns some domes-

*A.Kumar, Ratan Sen Degree College, Bansi, Siddharth Nagar 273153
P.C. Pant, 10, Amaravati Colony, Indira Nagar, Lucknow, 226017.

ticated animals, it may be surmised that the concept of joint ownership of the community was applicable for the domesticated animals as well during the Neolithic period. G.L. Badam's findings appear to support this hypothesis. Moreover, attention may also be drawn in this connection to the discovery of cattle pen located almost in the middle of the settlement at Mahagara (Sharma, *et. al.* 1980: 146). It may be noted that as many as eighteen huts have been unearthed at this site, but none of them were found associated with any cattle shed (Sharma, *et. al.* 1980: 189). On the contrary, each family of the present day tribes makes provision for the domesticated animals within the house complex. The evidence of cattle pen at Mahagara may indicate community ownership over the domesticated animals. It is difficult to determine whether the cultivation of rice was practised separately by each family, or this too was a community affair in which the agricultural produce was shared by all the members. Since only rice was cultivated during this stage agriculture might have contributed marginally to the economy of the people; who, it appears, might have sustained by mainly intensive gathering of wild rice, grasses, such as job's tear and fox tail, and wild fruits like *ber*, hunting of big games, particularly big ungulates, and exploitation of aquatic fauna such as turtle and fish (Sharma, *et.al.* 1980: 182; Singh, 1995–96: 90). It may be observed that not only in hunting but also in gathering forest products most of the members of the present day tribal communities jointly participate. It is only logical to believe that in the Neolithic culture also, all means of subsistence involving hunting, gathering, fishing and perhaps cultivation was a community affair. If the proposed hypothesis is accepted, the Neolithic culture was an egalitarian society in which perhaps no socioe-conomic hierarcy existed.

The excavations at Mahagara and Senuwar reveal that cattle and sheep were domesticated at both the sites (Sharma, *et.al.* 1980: 184). While buffaloes and pigs were domesticated at Senuwar; they were absent at Mahagara (Badam, in press). The evidence of wild goat is present at the former site, but it was domesticated at the latter site, where remains of domesticated horse have also occured (Sharma, *et. al.* 1980: 184). The domestication of pig at Senuwar and that of horse at Mahagara is indeed significant. It may be recalled that pigs were also domesticated in the Southern Neolithic complex. (Ghosh, 1989: 47). It is note worthy that the Santhal, the Munda and the Oraon not only domesticate pigs, but the pig-sty is also set up within the compound of the house, beside the cattle pen (Datta, *et al.*, Nabendu 1956; Bodding 1931: 103-4; Roy 1912; Roy 1915). Moreover, pig also has sacrificial significance among the Santals and the Mundas. They are sacrificed to god along with goat and/or fowl on special occasions. There is no way to determine whether the pig also occupied sacrificial position in the Neolithic set up of Senuwar.

It is also note worthy that some of the Burnished Grey Ware pots bear post firing ochre painting on the rim from the very beginning at Senuwar (Singh 1997:9). Thus, two culture patterns, viz., domestication of pig and post-firing ochre painting are common both in the Southern Noelithic complex and Senuwar. The domestication of pig may be explained by the evolutionists' theory of the psychic unity of mankind (Majumdar and Madan 1985: 17). But, the other pattern may be the result of diffusion. However, it is difficult to determine whether this feature first developed in the Southern Neolithic complex or at Senuwar, since it occurs at both the places more or less simultaneously.

The above account clearly demonstrates that there was a mixed economy, perhaps dominated by pastoralism, during this stage. The cultivation of rice must have been in an incipient stage and must have contributed marginally to the subsistence. On the contrary, hunting and gathering would have been two other major sources of the economy along with pastoralism.

Stage II

The Stage II (*ca.* 1950 B.C. - 1650 B.C.) is marked by the introduction of the cultivation of some new cereals and pulses, *viz.*, barley (*Hardeum vulgare*), dwarf-wheat (*Triticum spaeorococcum*), jowar-millet (*Sorghum bicolor*), finger-millet/Ragi (*Eleusine corcane*), Lentil (*Lens culinaris*), field pea (*Pisum arvense*) and *Khasari* (*Lathyrus sativus*) (Singh, 1995–96 : 91). This stage was reached at Senuwar more or less in the middle level of the Sub Period A, which has been dated by us around *ca.* 1950 B.C. and continued up to the end of the Sub-Period in *ca.* 1650 B.C. Carbonised grains of somewhat similar agricultural products have been reported from Chirand and Taradih*. Nothing is known about the agricultural

* I express my gratitude to Prof Basudev Narayan of the Patna University for giving some details of the botanical remains of Taradih through a personal communication.

products from Chechar, Kutubpur and Maner. The excavation at Senuwar reveals that in spite of the introduction of two crop system in agriculture, surprisingly no marked change has been observed in other cultural patterns, e.g., mode of habitation, pottery, stone objects, bone objects, etc. The study of palaeobotanical remains from Senuwar by K. S. Saraswat denotes that the species of wheat, barley and pulses found at Senuwar are similar to those of the Indus Valley Civilization**.

This observation is indeed very revealing and may indicate diffusion of agricultural traits from the Harappan Civilization in the Neolithic complex of Bihar. Presumably, this occurred with the decline of the Harappan cities around ca. 2000 B.C., when the population probably started migrating eastwards.

It is very surprising to note that these new cereals and pulses were never introduced in the Mahagara-Koldihwa complex in spite of the fact that the people continued to pursue the neolithic, life-style for a period of at least 700 years up to *ca.* 1600 B.C. or a little later. As observed earlier, the twin sites of Koldiwa and Mahagara were never examined by any palaeo-botanist during the excavation and no particular effort was made by an expert to retrieve tiny botanical remains from the excavated floors. And hence, it is not unlikely that the valuable evidence of the introduction of new cereals was altogether missed at these sites. However, an alternative explanation for the absence of the cultivation of new species at the two sites may also be offered. It may be held that probably the diffusionary patterns from the Indus Valley Civilization bypassed the Belan valley and reached the southern part of Bihar directly. Since, after the beginning of sedentary life in the Belan valley, the nucleus of the culture shifted from there to the Kaimur foot-hills of Bihar, the Belan valley remained an area of isolation where the neolithic way of life continued uninterruptedly for about seven centuries without any observable chances. The explanation appears plausible, though not supported by any archaeological evidence.

After the introduction of cereals like wheat and barley besides a few pulses, and the knowledge of two crop system, it is only reasonable to believe that the people must have realised the significance of agriculture and fertile land. It appears that a few groups of people now started migrating towards east and north, presumably in search of fertile land and better facilities for cultivation. As a result, new settlements were established, such as Taradih in the east, and Chirand, Chechar-Kutubpur and Maner in the Gangetic valley in north. Thus, this stage of cultural evolution witnessed the expansion of the culture into new areas.

Side by side along with agriculture, domestication of animals hunting and gathering continued to be significant part of the economic structure. Although there is hardly any archaeological evidence to support, it is reasonable to surmise that in this new economic setup, the share of agriculture must have increased substantially.

Stage III

The most significant feature of the Stage III (*ca.* 1650 B.C. – 1300 B.C.) is the introduction of copper in the Neolithic economy (Singh 1990: 6–7). Since all the major culture patterns of the earlier stages remained more or less unaltered during this stage, the economy remained basically Neolithic. The excavator of Senuwar thus rightly recognises this stage as a Sub-Period B of the Neolithic Period. Besides Senuwar, where this stage is well defined, it was perhaps also represented at Chirand, Chechar-Kutubpur, Taradih and Maner where many of the traits of Senuwar IB occur. However, no evidence of copper has so far been found at these sites except Senuwar.

Agriculture based on two crop system, domestication of various animals, gathering of forest products, practice of big game hunting and increased fishing activities may be mentioned as significant features of the economic structure of this stage. Some new species of wheat, millets and pulses were introduced at Senuwar; the earlier species also continued (Singh 1995-96: 91). Besides, the evidence for the seeds of *bhang* and *dhatur* and an uncarbonised piece of iron wood, which grow in Assam and north Bengal, also occur at this site (Singh 1995 – 96: 91). Obviously, the use of new plant species was the result of diffusion, although it is difficult to identify the source. It appears that the people have now started using comparatively bigger antler implements for primitive cultivation. Such implements as were presumably used as agricultur-

** Personal communication from Dr. K.S.Saraswat

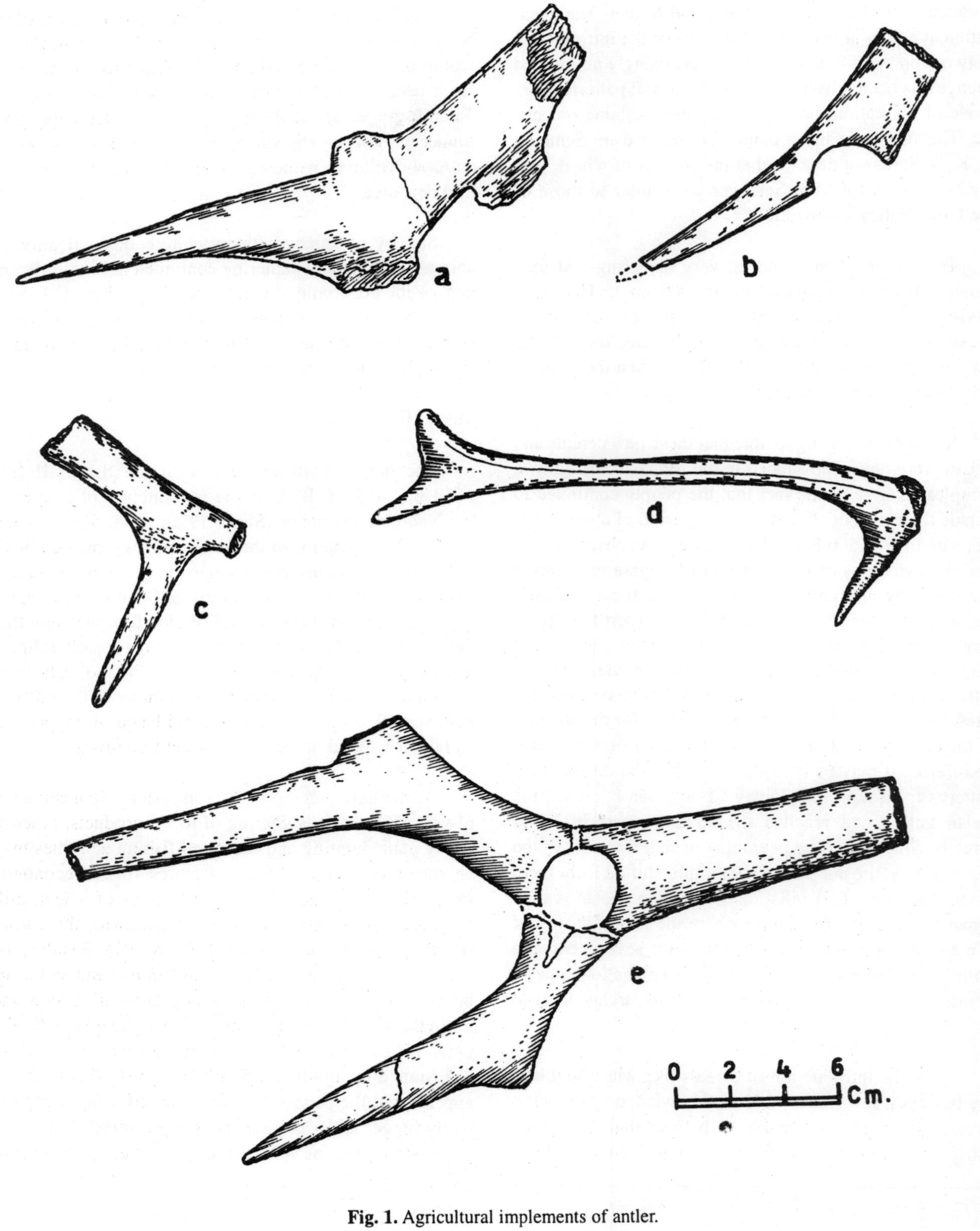

Fig. 1. Agricultural implements of antler.

al implements have been found at Chirand as well as Chechar at Kutubpur (fig.1).

As many as nineteen copper objects have been found in this stage at Senuwar, which include a fish-hook, a broken needle, a borer, a couple of rings, a wire and many fragmented objects (Singh 1990: 13). The introduction of copper, it appears, did not bring about a revolutionary change in life patterns of the people, since almost all the earlier traits continued uninterruptedly, though some refinement and modifications are observed in certain objects. However attention may be drawn to the fact that there is a marginal increase in the number and also perhaps types of almost all the antiquities during this stage. For example, not only the number of stone beads increases substantially, but also new types such as barrel, tubular collared, truncated bicone, tiny: globular and micro-beads, were introduced during this stage (Singh 1995-96 :84). Similarly, the number of shell objects exibit marked increase from 6 in the Sub-Period IA at Senuwar to as many as 73 in the Sub-Period lB (Singh 1995-96: 88). It is difficult to determine whether the significant increase in antiquities was the result of the introduction of copper technology. However, the change may denote increase in population at Senuwar and also probably higher standard of living. It may also be surmised that the use of copper might have resulted in the introduction of new crafts activities.

REFERENCES

Badam, G.L. (In Press) 'Faunal remains from Senuwar'. Typed copy of the report made available by courtesy Dr. B.P. Singh.

Bodding, P.O. (1931). 'Notes on the Santals', *Census of India* Vol. l, Part III.

Datta -Majumdar, N. 1956. *The Santal:A study in cultural change*, Memoir. No. 2 (1955), Department of Anthropology, Government of India.

Ghosh, A. (ed.). 1989. *An encyclopaedia of Indian Archaeology,* Vol.1.

Majumdar, D.N. and T.N. Madan l985. *An Introduction to Social Anthropology*, Mayoors Paperbacks, Noida.

Ray, S.C. 1912. *The Mundas and their country*, Calcutta.

Ray, S.C. 1915. *The Oraon*, Ranchi.

Sharma, G.R., V.D. Mishra, D. Mandal, B.B. Mishra and J.N. Pal. 1980. *From Hunting and Food Gathering to Demestication of Plants and Animals: Beginning of Agriculture. Allahabad.*

Singh, B.P. 1990. Early Farming Communities of Kaimur Foot Hills, *Puratattva*, No. 19.

——1995-96. Transformation of Culture in the Middle Ganga Plain: A case study of Senuwar, *Pragdhara*, No.6

——1997. Neolithic and Chalcolithic Pottery of the Middle Ganga Plains: A Case study of Senuwar', *Ancient ceramics: Historical Enquiries & Scientific Approaches.*

Verma, B.S. 1970-71. Excavation at Chirand: New light on the Indian Neolithic culture complex, *Puratattva,* No. 4.

Neolithic Ceramics and their Decorative Patterns in Kashmir Valley

P.C.CHAUDHARI*

Various Archaeological investigations have revealed that the Kashmir Valley had a well developed neolithic culture spread through out the valley. Based on excavations at Burzahom and Gufkral the entire neolithic culture can be divided into two main stages of development, viz Aceramic and ceramic neolithic. This is also supported by recent excavation at Kanispur in Dist. Baramulla. Besides a new developed neolithic stage could be identified within the Ceramic Neolithic (Mature Ceramic) at the site. The Neolithic culture, therefore, can be divided into three different phases—Phase IA (Aceramic), Phase IB (Ceramic) and Phase IC (Mature Ceramic). The later two divisions are largely based on the nature of ceramic assemblages and structural remains recovered from the excavations. Hand-made neolithic pottery, decorated with various incisions and impressions made its appearance in phase IB. They not only continued in phase IC but also became more prolific with addition of new fabric, shapes, decoration and a few wheel-made pots of Harappan signatory.

This paper presents the study of ceramics and the type of decorations of the neolithic pottery of Kashmir valley. Due to limited published literature on Burzahom and Gufkral, my major concentration of the study is based on recently excavated site at Kanispur in which I was also a member of the excavation team. However the material published on Burzahom, Gufkral and other explored sites have also been studied.

*C/o ASI, Chhni Himmat, Jammu-180015

The Ceramic Assemblage

One of the characteristic features of the neolithic culture of Kashmir valley is the ceramic industry. Clay, raw material of the ceramic, is formed by the decomposition of rock forming minerals. The larger part of volcanic rock, quartz, quartzite, limestone, sandstone and mudstone deposited proximal to the source area in Kashmir valley is the primary clay, whereas lighter parts of same minerals, besides mud, rich in plant debris, silt and loess deposited distant from source by various natural agencies is known as 'secondary clay'. The sources of both the clays are readily available throughout the valley.

The basic technique of forming the pots is hand-made, however, wheel-turned pots are also available in the last phase (IC). Both "Strip" and "Coil" techniques were widely used in their production. Thick rods of paste are made by rolling between hands and then added in successive layers to a disc or base made on mat or other materials. The ropes are firmly joined at the point of overlap by pressing between figures and thumb and further smoothed together by downward strokes of thumb. In majority of cases the ring of paste ropes are not set directly on top of each other, but rather always overlap slightly on the inside or outside. However, considerable variation existed in the manner in which these ropes wire applied in forming vessels. For example, some pots have internal overlap of ropes while other have external overlap. Internal and external overlap alternating each other are also found. Finally, neck/rims are made in various forms by using strips joined together; while doing this grass straws or reeds have been used for support and to stabilized circular forms as the marks of grasses and reed are frequently met on neck portion. Similar marks are also observed on body portion, specifically on pots made of coarse clay. Besides the above mentioned techniques, hollow ball of clay by pressing in the thumbs and then thinning the walls between thumb and finger is also used, specifically in shaping the simple and small size vessel. When vessel is completely formed, it is ready for finishing and decorating. Varying sections of the body may be lightly wetted with the hand and one or more type of rouletts, besides straw of grass or reed are applied for further smoothening on surface of pot.

The ceramics of this culture belongs to two technological classes i.e. coarse and fine fabrics.

(i) *Coarse Fabric:* This ware is characterised by crude and handsome pottery. The clay used for manufacturing the pottery is not well levigated and contains large particles of quartz, quarzite, and limestone. The uncontrolled firing resulted sometimes into a variety of colours — grey, black, dull and buff. Some sherds have black inner and red and buff outer surface. The core is generally dark ashy, black and very rarely completely oxidised which perhaps indicates fast rise in temperature in the initial stage and a short duration of high temperature. In other words, almost no control could be exercised over the amount of heat produced. The shapes in this fabric are mainly big jars with everted rim, smal' pot with rounded and triangular rim, bowls with slightly everted and perpendicular rim, short neck *lota* and *handi.*

(ii) *Fine Fabric:* The clay used for this fabric is well levigated and refined by elutriation. Hence, content of mineral particles are small and fine. The burnished grey ware and the red ware are the dominent wares in this fabric. The different shades of these wares such as grey, black, ashy, buff and occasionally red are achieved through controlled firing. Finally, burnishing on the surface of pots is achieved through frequently rubbing with smooh pebble. Characteristic shapes in this fabric are long neck jars with everted externally projecting and flarring rims, bowls of everted and perpendicular rims, small lota, basin, lid and dishes-on-stand.

Decorations : The neolithic pots of Kashmir valley is generally not painted, but the surface of a large percentage of the pots is decorated by various forms of incisions, impressions and applied strips. These are executed by using different tools when clay is still soft, and during shaping and smoothing processes depending on the type of vessel and the spot at which the decoration is done. As many as thirteen different decorative patterns from various sites are reported so far. Of these, some are decorative while a few others are functional in nature.

Mat impression: Mat impression is a common decoration found at the base of pots. These must have been made by straw, grass, twigs and wiker as the lakes, swamps and forests of Kashmir are rich in these vegetational growths. Even today the use of these natural vegetation to form mats and baskets is closely integrated with daily life of people. Three main variations in mat making are distinguished in the mat-impression on pot-bases.

Type I: In this two elements —the coilor ore and the wrapping of sewing strip—are employed. The coil or core may have consisted of bundle of grass or rushes coiled spirally in shape required or single read used as core. These have been gathered by sewing strip made of similar material or differnt. The strip passes round the latest coil piercing the edge of the one below already in place (fig. 1) A large number of bone points and needles are reported from excavations which may bave been used as peircing tools.

Type II: This type is called 'twined plaint' or 'twined weave'. A single rush or bundle of rushes were laid side by side and inter-placed by two threads which twine between each bundle or single rush.

Type III: In this type the grasses, reed or twigs being twisted together as in a two-played thread. It has two variants.

Variant 1: Rushes interlaced over and under forming diagonal lines.

Variant 2: Rushes interlaced at right angles

Incised lines: These are simple decorations consisting of verticals, obliques, zig-zag lines. Of these vertical and oblique incisions, at regular inervals, are found on the everted, externally projected rim of pots of coarse fabric, while groups of four oblique lines in reverse directions are found on the body. The short and deep incised lines at regular intervals in rows and the long zig-zag lines joining at 45° angle at proportionate intervals from bottom to the tapering top are the characteristic decorations on the dish-on-stand. The precise nature and perfection of these decorations suggest the use of precise tools and instruments.

Ridging: The ridging is a common decoration found on short necked and triangular rim, made of coarse and fine fabric. These are created by down and upward pressing of clay by thumb and fingers.

Comb and boss: The ridges are created, as mentioned above, on external surface of the rim, then the comb-like tool was pressed at regular intervals on these ridges to produce comb-like designs, while doing the remaining part became raised boss. Thus the 'comb-and-boss impression' was produced. This decoration is found only in very coarse grey ware.

Punching : Punching is a rare decorative technique used by neolithic men with the help of pointed and blunted tools. Two main varieties of punched decorations are found so far in the Neolithic Context. There are : (a) two rows of punched dots on the rims of bowls, and (b) haphazardly punctured dots bordered by a triangle on the body of bowls. The equal size triangular shape punching in a row spread uniformly on the stem of dish-on-stand is also found. These are punched in such a way that the upper part became slightly deeper than the lower one.

Notches: This decoration is found as incision on lower portion of long neck jar and on the stem of dish-on-stand. The oblique shallow notches, even space in one row, executed on long neck jar are a rare decoration found on pots from phase IC at Burzahom, whereas the shallow but triangular in shape is spread uniformly in row, from top to bottom, is one of the characteristic decorations on dish-on-stand.

Reed impressions: This is the most common impression found on the neck and sometimes on the body portion of some of the pots of coarse as well as fine fabric. This may have been purely functional in nature as the reed avoided saging of vessele while paste was still soft and also helped in smoothening and removing the impurities from the surface of pot.

Applied strips: A narrow strip of clay was applied, generally horizontally, forming ridges where two ropes of paste are luted together. However, a few potsherds show vertical and circular strips too.

Concentric circles: This is a rare decoration found in the interior of bowls. In this pattern of decoration inner concentric circle is encircled by another concentriic circle and the space between two concentric circles is filled with groups of oblique lines.

Thumb and finger impression: Thumb and finger impressions are generally found where two ropes are luted together. The original purpose is to spread extra clay but the impression so formed are in a row that eventually it became a decorative pattern.

Triangles: The triangular shape but hollow incised decoration is one of the characteristic decorations on stem of dish-on-stand. It is executed from top to bottom on stem with perfection. It is so precise and executed at regular intervals in a row in a precise manner from top to bottom that it gives artistic look. Other triangles are decorated in the form of double triangles in horizontal row as found on the body of bowls. These are cordened and divided up with incised dots whereas the lower one has single dots.

Criss-cross: Only a single sherd of this decorative pattern is found so far. Nearly horizontal and vertical lines are incised on surface of pot at regular intervals. Thus, the rows of small squares in relief became prominent.

Nail impression: This is simple, yet effective, decoration used on the body of vessel. It is in horizontal vertical rows.

Conclusion

The pre-historic man of Kashmir valley must have

started the new way of life before the production of pottery is evident from polished tools and cultivation of grains from aceramic phase. In course of cultural development pottery manufacturing became a regular practice. As with other neolithic cultures initial pottery was handmade and very coarse in fabric. For the production of this pottery mats made of grass and rushes and grass may have been used, as most of pot sherds yielded impressions of these. Besides these, boss and pinch decorations are commonly found on the surface of the pots. In the mature phase, coarse ware along with a few wheel-made pots with new decorative patterns were introduced. The patterns included triangular shape but hallow, triangular punch, long incised lines on the stem of dish-on-stand, oblique strokes, ridging, applied strips, concentric circles, nail impressions and notches on the body of vase. However, hand-made pots and decorative patterns which were started earlier continued with the same percentage.

Acknowledgement: My most sincere thanks are due to Dr. B.R. Mani, Superintending Archaeologist, Srinagar Circle, ASI, who allowed me to work on pottery collected from the excavation at Kanispora and to study the neolithic potery available in the collection of circle. I am thankful to Shri B.S.Jamwal, Sr. Photographer, Shri R.K.Koul, Draftsman, Shri Gulzar Singh, Sr. Surveyor, Shri Raghuvir Singh, Virander Koul and Arun Sidha for helping at various stages of the study.

REFERENCES

Agarwal D.P.1992: *Man and environment in India through Ages*, Books and Books New Delhi.

Agarwal D.P. and Rekha Dodia, 1985: *Late Quaternary environment and archaeological changes in Kashmir, South Asian Archaeology.*

Dikshit K.N. 1982: The neolithic cultural frontiers of Kashmir, *Man and Environment*, Vol. VI.

Gupta S.P.1979: *Archaeology of Soviet Central Asia and Indian Borderlands*, New Delhi

Indian Archaeology - a Review, 1961-62; 1966-67; 1971-72, 1981-82.

Joshi J.P.and Madhu Bala 1982.: Manda. A Harappan site in Jammu and Kashmir, *Harappan Civilization*, (ed. G.L.Possehl) Oxford an IBH Publishing co.

Khazanchi T.N.1977: North-western neolithic Culture and India, *News letter 7 and 8*, Indian Institute of Advance Study, Simla.

Mani B.R. 1998–99: *Preliminary Report on excavation at Kanispur.*

Mahapatra, G.C. 1978-79. Neolithic of western Sub-Himalaya, *Puratattva,* 13–14.

Ranov V.A. 1982. The Hissar neolithic culture of Soviet Central Asia, *Man and Environment.*

Sali S.L.1993. *Kashmir: History and Archaeology through the Ages.* Indus Publishing Company, New Delhi.

Saar S.S. 1992. *Ancestors of Kashmir*, Lalit Art Publishers, New Delhi.

Sharma A.K. 1979-80. Excavations at Gufkral, *Puratattva*, 15.

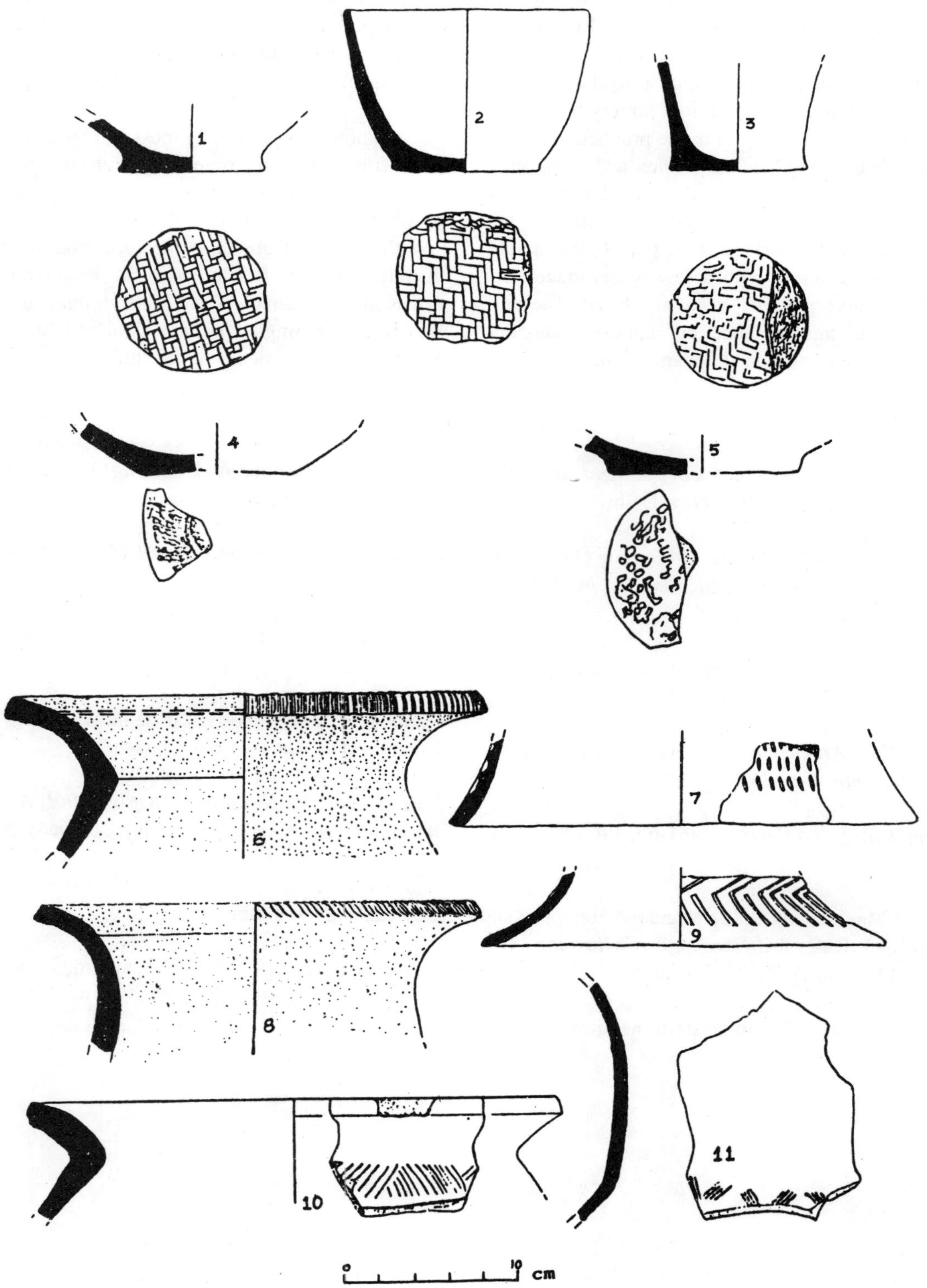

Fig. 1. Decorative Pottery, Neolithic Period (Kashmir)

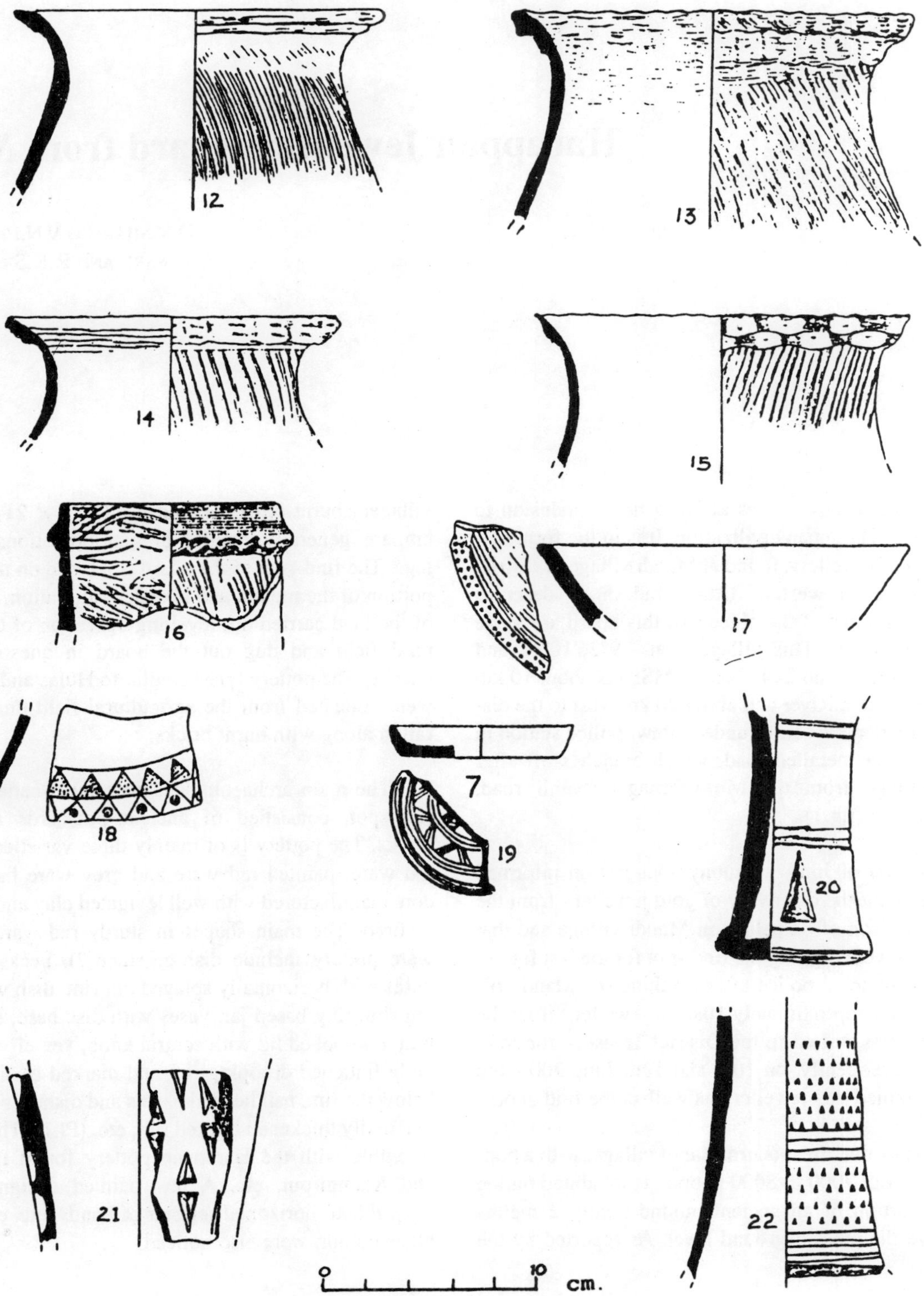

Fig. 2. Decorative Pottery, Neolithic Period (Kashmir)

Harappan Jewellery Hoard from Mandi

D.V.SHARMA, V.N.PRABHAKAR*
R.TEWARI AND R.K.SRIVASTAVA**

A chance discovery has added a new dimension to the studies of Harappan civilization. It is in the form of a huge hoard of jewellery, found at Mandi village of district Muzaffarnagar in western Uttar Pradesh. It deserves emphasis that most of the objects of this hoard are made of gold and silver. This village (Lat. 29°26'10"N. and Long. 77°34'35"E and 244m above MSL) is about 10 km east to the Hindon River and about 20 km west to the district headquarters. It comes under Titawi police station in Tehsil Sadar. A metalled road, which branches off after Baghra village from the Muzaffarnagar-Shamli road, leads to Mandi (fig.1).

On the 1st of June, an anonymous person informed the police about the discovery of gold jewellery from the field of Anil, son of Satpal Jat in Mandi village and that the villagers were digging the find spot for the last four to five days. The local police after reaching the Mandi village recovered approximately 10kg of jewellery from the site, which was shifted to the District Treasury for safe-custody. Subsequently, on 10th and 13th June 2000, the author examined this jewellery as well as the find-spot.

It appears that the modern Mandi village, with a population of about 7000 to 8000 people, is inhabited on the southern portion of an ancient mound nearly 2 metres high above the present ground level. As reported by the villagers burnt-brick, measuring 31-33 × 21-23 × 9-11 cm, are generally found in digging operations in the village. The find-spot of the hoard is located on the northern portion of the mound and is under cultivation. The owner of the land carried out levelling operation of the agricultural field and dug out the hoard in question by the chance. The pottery types similar to Hulas and Alamgirpr were collected from the agricultural field during exploration along with burnt bricks.

The main archaeological material, scattered on the find-spot, consistied of ancient potsherds and burnt-bricks. The pottery is of mainly three varieties i.e., plain red ware, painted red ware and grey ware having thick core manufactured with well levigated clay and adequately fired. The main shapes in sturdy red ware and grey ware pottery include dish-on-stand(?), neck portion of vases with horizontally splayed out rim, dish with drooping rim, ring based jar, vases with disc base, storage jar, button knobbed lid with central knob, vessels with externally flattened drooping rim and marked by a carination below the rim, nail headed basins and dishes, vessels with externally thickened beaked rim, etc. (Pl.1). These shapes resemble with the Harappan pottery found from Hulas and Alamgirpur, etc. A few painted designs such as *Peepal* leaf, horizontal register of bands, etc. executed in black colour, were also noticed.

*ASI, Agra; **Deptt. of State Archaeology, U.P.

A few shapes in red ware of medium to fine fabric such as bowls with in-turned carinated rim and flat base, bowls with flared rim, bowls with straight or vertical featureless rim, thick storage jar, etc. were also present in the assemblage. These shapes represent Kushan-Gupta and later periods at most of the sites in U.P., such as Mathura.

On the basis of the above observations it may be surmised that the ancient pottery of Mandi represents broadly two cultural phases:

(i) contemporary to that of Hulas and Alamgirpur-placed around 2000 BC onwards, and

(ii) Kushan period of A.D. 100 onwards.

It may be noted that this observation is tentative and subject to the results of further investigations.

The measurements of bricks are 8×22×31 cm, 9×23×33 cm, 9×20×30 cm. A few of them bear frog marks (finger marks depicted obliquely). The proportion of measurements of these bricks is unusual. Though these bricks appear to be related to the earlier phase, it is difficult to ascertain their precise cultural association at this stage.

The hoard found from Mandi and kept in the district treasury is said to have been recovered from the lower levels of the field in association with the pottery assemblage considered to be related with the above mentioned first period. It comprises of beads made of gold, banded agate, onyx, and copper. There are a large number of etched cornelian beads also with trefoil and eye designs. Two copper containers are also kept along with the beads, and were found at the same find-spot (Pl. 2). The whole of the material under consideration weighs about 10kg.

The gold beads may further be divided into following types,

(i) spacer beads
(ii) circular beads
(iii) hollow terminal heads
(iv) single and double bell shaped beads
(v) disc beads

The *spacers* 37 in number, are of different sizes. Out of them, seventeen have two holes each, four with three holes, fifteen with four holes, while one bears six holes to accommodate two, three, four and six strings of beads (Pl. 3). These spacers are of two types, i.e. plain and segmented (sides). Disc beads, in very large number were found by ASI and are on display in the National Museum. The *circular beads* form the most sizeable proportion of the entire lot. Apparently their number appears to be in thousands. Their sizes vary from water thin micro to medium (Pl. 4). A few examples show these beads were stuck together to make a long string of necklace.

Hollow *terminal beads* are also known as half moon shaped or 'D' shaped terminals. Seventeen beads of this type have been found in the Mandi hoard. These beads are of different sizes (Pl.5). On the consideration that two terminals would have been used in one necklace, it appears that they belong to at least eight necklaces.

Bell-shaped beads are 42 in number, 39 with single hole and three with double holes (Pl. 6)

Beads of semi-precious stones include about half a dozen beads of onyx and over 200 of banded agate (Pl.7).

Copper beads are only six in number. Besides, one thin gold foil is also included in this assemblage(Pl.7).

Copper containers found along with the jewellery are of two shapes,

(i) large deep bowl with convex sides and flat base, and

(ii) rectangular.

Both of them are in a bad state of preservation. The earlier one is partly broken from the upper side. The radius of the bowl is 21 cm. Its internal and outer depths are about 14.8 and 15.3 cm respectively. The length, width and inner depth of the rectangular container measures 47.5, 9.5, 4.5 cm. It appears that these containers had some sort of cover too, which have not been found with the hoard.

Apart from the above mentioned components of jewellery kept in government Treasury, a few broken silver ornaments and bits and pieces of silver pots were also observed in the possession of Titavi Police Station. This

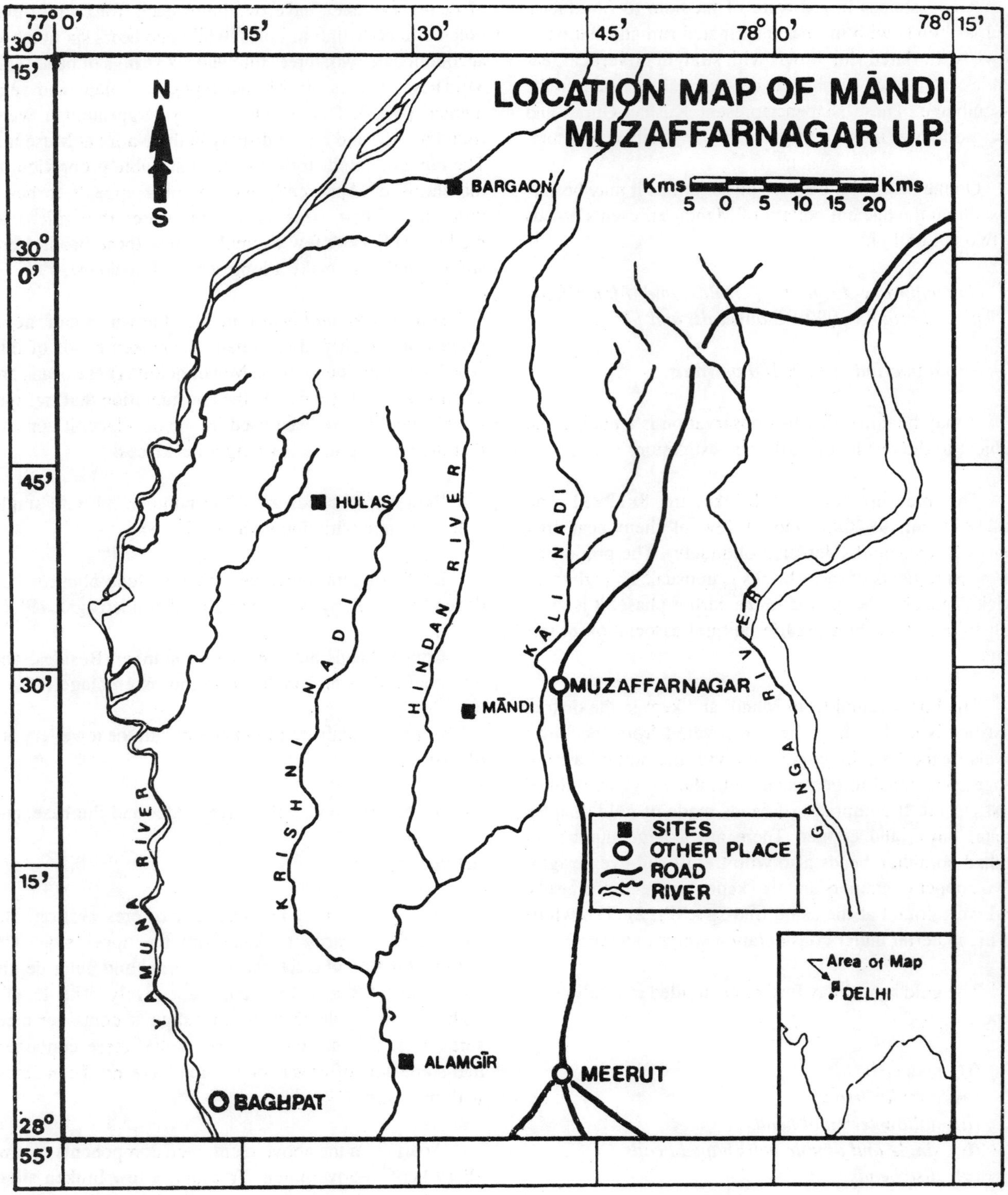

Fig. 1. Location map of Mandi.

includes three broken parts of anklets or bangles *(padkatak or kangans)*. Two of them put together appear to be of one *padkatak or kangan* while the third is the broken half of another. More of them were recovered by ASI and are on display in the National Museum.

Spacer beads of gold have also been found at Mohenjodaro (Marshall 1931:517-18, Pl. CXLVII, No. 20) and Lothal (Rao 1985: 633-34, Pl.CCXCV A). Bronze spacer beads are found in Allahdino hoard (Kenoyer 1998: 138, Fig. 7.30; 199, Cat. no. 48). Examples of spacer beads of copper are known from Mohenjodaro (Marshall 1931: op. cit Nos. 18, 19; CXLIII, Nos. 15, 17) and Harappa (Vats 1940: 439, Pl. CXXXVII, No. 46). Besides, copper and terracotta spacer beads are also known from Lothal and other Harappan sites (Rao 1985: 584, 605, 607, 608). These beads are comparable to those represented in the Mandi hoard.

Circular gold beads of Mandi resemble the steatite and gold micro or wafer beads of Mohenjodaro (Mackay 1937, Pls. CXI, 1; CXXXVI, 1, 2; CXXXVII, 68-71, CXXXiX, 29-32; 1938: 517-18) and Lothal (Rao 1985: 583, 595, 633-35, Pl. CCLXVII) and steatite beads of Harappa (Vats 1940: 395-96, 436, Pls. CXXXIII, Fig. 1).

Hollow terminal beads are also known as half moon-shaped terminals, hemispherical terminals and 'D' shaped beads. Such gold beads are reported from Lothal (Rao 1985: 633-35, Pl. CCXVI A) and Mohenjodaro (Marshall 1931: 520, 22, Pls. CLI, CXLI, 3). Examples of bronze terminal beads are represented in Allahdino hoard (Kenoyer 1998: 199, Cat. no. 48). This type of terracotta terminal beads resembling those of gold and copper are also occasionally noticed at Lothal (Rao 1985:584) and other Harappan sites.

Beads of banded agate have been found in considerable numbers from different sites, such as, Mohenjodaro (Marshall 1931: 536-37, Pl. CL; Mackay 1938: 497, 501-3, 513, 516, 527), Lothal (Rao 1985: 585, 597-9, Pl. CCLXIX B Allahdino (Kenoyer 1998: 138, fig. 7.30), Kunal (Khatri & Acharya 1995: 86), etc.

Some onyx beads have been found at Indus Valley sites (Marshall 1931: 536-37; Mackay 1938:500; Mackay 1943: 204, 209), however, at Lothal they were more popular (Rao 1985: 565, 586-7, 603-5). The same is true of etched cornelian beads.

Though the copper containers have not been found containing the jewellery of Mandi hoard, on the basis of circumstantial evidence it may be surmised that most of it was kept in the large bowl. The shape of this container broadly resembles to that of earthen vessel containing the Allahdino hoard (Kenoyer 1998: 138, fig.7.29). Not a single jewellery of the size and shape accomodable in the rectangular container is represented in the material kept in the recovered hoard of Mandi. The gold fillets or ribbons found from Mohenjo-daro and other Harappan sites are notable in this regard. Such fillets are shown on the forehead of a few Harappan sculptures (Lal and Gupta: Pls. 204 B and C). The length and width of a fillet, from Mohenjo-daro, i.e. 42 cm and 1.4 cm respectively (Kenoyer 1998: 200, Cat. no. 52), indicate that the rectangular container of Mandi might have contained a number of such fillets, which have been most probably taken away by the villagers.

The above description shows that several potsherds, found from the lowest levels of the find-spot of the Mandi hoard, have Harappan affinity and are comparable to the pottery found at the Harappan sites of Hulas and Alamgirpur. As the jewellery discovered at Mandi is clearly comparable with those found at different Harappan sites mentioned above, both on circumstantial and comparative considerations the jewellery of the Mandi hoard appears to be of Harappan workmanship.

Major hoards of Harappan jewellery have been found so far from Mohenjo-daro, Harappa and Allahdino in Pakistan and Lothal and Kunal (Early Harappan) in India. Mandi is the next addition to this list. However, considering the quantity of gold beads and bracelets* it is the most important and largest amongst all. It may be noted in this regard that the circular wafer gold beads are found in comparatively lesser proportion at the Harappan sites, while the Mandi hoard contains mainly such beads, thou-

* Gold bracelets were not included in the material kept in the Treasury these were subsequently handed over to ASI by the villagers. They are thick hollow type, heart-shaped forms as well as solid and thin ones, both on display in the National Museum.

sands in number and roughly over 7 kg in weight. It should be noted in this regard that this quantity is only of the gold beads included in the hoard kept in treasury. It does not include the material taken away by the villagers. On a rough estimate it may be surmised that the Mandi hoard might have contained objects at least three to four times of this quantity.

Earlier a number of Harappan sites were brought to light during the extensive explorations carried out in Saharanpur, Mujaffarnagar, Bulandshahar and Meerut districts. Besides, a few such sites are also known from the neighbouring districts of Etah and Bijnor (Joshi, 1984: 521-23). A few of them, i.e., Alamgirpur and Hulas, etc. have also been excavated. The discovery of Mandi hoard, however, has drawn renewed attention towards this area of western Uttar Pradesh. In view of this discovery, it seems that a lot many hitherto unknown aspects of the culture, represented by the habitation deposits of these sites, may be revealed in future investigations.

Since the aforementioned finds of Mandi have not been found from their stratified cultural context, scientific archaeological excavation* is necessary to corroborate the above surmises and to understand different aspects related to the hoard as well as ancient cultures represented at this site. We will have to wait for that till the conclusion of such operations, but from the very on set Mandi has already earned a place of distinction in the context of Harappan civilization for its incomparable hoard.

Above description is based on the observation of the first author of this paper.

Acknowledgement

The author are grateful to Sri Manmohan Dimri, Surveyor, U.P.State Archaeological Dept. for preparation of the map illustrated in this paper.

REFERENCES

Joshi, J.P., Madhubala and Jassu Ram 1984. "The Indus Civilization: A Reconsideration on the Basis of Distribution Maps", *Frontiers of Indus Civilization* (Eds. B.B.Lal and S.P. Gupta), pp. 511-530, Books and Books, C4A/20A, Janakpuri, New Delhi-110058.

Kenoyer, Jonathan Mark 1998. *Ancient Cities of the Indus Valley Civilization* Oxford University Press, American Institute of Pakistan Studies.

Khatri, J.S. and M. Acharya 1995. 'Kunal: A New Indus—Saraswati Site', *Puratattva*, No. 25, Indian Archaeological Society, New Delhi, pp. 84-6

Khatri 2000. 'Excavation at Kunal District Hissar', *Indian Archaeology 1993-94: A Review*, Archaeological Survey of India, pp 47-50.

Mackay, Earnest J.H. 1937. *Further Excavations at Mohenjo-daro*, Vol. II, Govt. of India Press, New Delhi.

Mackay, 1938 *Further Excavations at Mohenjo-daro* Vol. I, Govt. of India Press, New Delhi.

Mackay, 1943 *Chanhu-daro Excavations 1935-36*, Reprinted in 1976, Bhartiya Publishing House B9/45, Pilkhana Sonpur, Varanasi.

* It is worthwhile to mention herein that the Archaeological survey of India has recently carried out a limited excavation under the direction of Sri R.S. Bisht at the find-spot of the above hoard to recover the remaining part of it and to ascertain its cultural context. The excavated area is, however, found highly disturbed partly due to the aforesaid levelling operations and treasure hunt. The excavation yielded approximately 500 gm. of jewellery consisting of circular wafer beads, spacers, conical beads, and beads of banded agate, microsteatite, faience beads, a few terracotta sling balls, terracotta animal figurines, broken silver pieces and arecanut shaped terracotta beads. A kiln was also exposed. Its upper portion is damaged. It measures 127 cm x 84cm x 80 cm and was found filled with ash, broken potsherds, burnt bricks (38x28x10cm) with finger impressions and other burnt materials. A burnt brick structure measuring 97 x 90 cm was also revealed to the south-east of the kiln at a distance of about 25 m. The structure has three courses and runs in northeast-southwest direction. The bricks used therein measure 36 x 22 x 10 cm. The total habitation deposit revealed in the excavation is 65-80 cm. The pottery types such as plain and painted red ware, thick grey ware, and red polished ware with stamped designs represent two cultural deposits namely, Harappan and Kushan.

Marshall, Sir John 1931 *Mohenjo-daro and the Indus Civilization*, Arthur Probsthain, London.

Rao, S.R. 1985 *Lothal: A Harappan Port Town* (1952-62), Vol. II, Archaeological Survey of India, New Delhi.

Vats, M.S.1940 *Excavations at Harappa*, reprinted 1974, Bhartiya Publishing house, B9/45, Pilkhana Sonpur, Varanasi.

Dhalewan — An Early Harappan site in Pubjab

MADHU BALA AND VISHNU KANT*

The ancient site at Dhalewan, (Lat. 300 1' 20" N; long 75° 35' 45" E.) in Mansa District Punjab is situated about 30 km northeast of district headquarters and about 7 km from the township of Bhikhi. The approach to Dhalewan from Bhikhi is by a road which is negotiable by any mode of surface transport. The mound suddenly emerges out from the adjoining low sand dunes and lush green fields. Presently the mound is situated on the eastern side of the canal locally called drain which has been dug on the dried up bed of the ancient Sirhind Nallah. As one could see from far away the mound is very impressive, having a height of about 8m. and measuring 81,000 sqm. The mound is capped by a *Marhi*, surrounded by *Neem, Babul* and a huge banyan tree around which a circular depression has been dug. The mound had more area of ancient occupation which has been now brought under cultivation which is attested to by the find of pottery in the adjoining fields. The site was explored during an extensive exploration of Mansa district in 1984 by a team headed by Shri J.P. Joshi and assisted by Ms. Madhu Bala.

The availability of twenty five sites of Early Harappan, Harappan and Late Harappan periods in an area of approximately 1250 sq. Km in Mansa District shows that this area was a very important zone in the Harappan culture-area (fig. 1). The Early Harappan and Harappans preferred the Ghaggar and its tributaries, as this was a more static river-system than the Beas, Satluj and Ravi which were erratic in their behaviour and changing their courses very often. The Sirhind, a tributary of the Ghaggar, was one of the most important lines of communication between Punjab and Rajasthan for getting raw materials like timber, especially *Deodar* used in house-building activities, as noted earlier. This channel appears to be buzzing with activity in the third and second millennia. Studies of the settlement pattern of the area suggests that it had three types of settlements. This area, therefore, gives the best evidence of all the three types of settlements placed near each other, creating an ideal situation of an urban complex. Their commercial interaction was the pre-requisite for a developed civilization. It seems that Sirhind was an important 'economic pocket' which mobilized the resources of the northern region of the lower Himalayas and transported them to Bahawalpur area via Kalibangan, and also to Harappan sites in Haryana and Punjab.

Excavation have been carried out at this site between January to May 2000 by a team of the Excavation Branch-II of Archaeological Survey of India under the direction of Ms. Madhu Bala, Superintending Archaeologist.

The Excavation at Dhalewan has yielded a sequence

*Archaeological Survey of Inda, Excavation Branch II, Purana Quila, New Delhi.

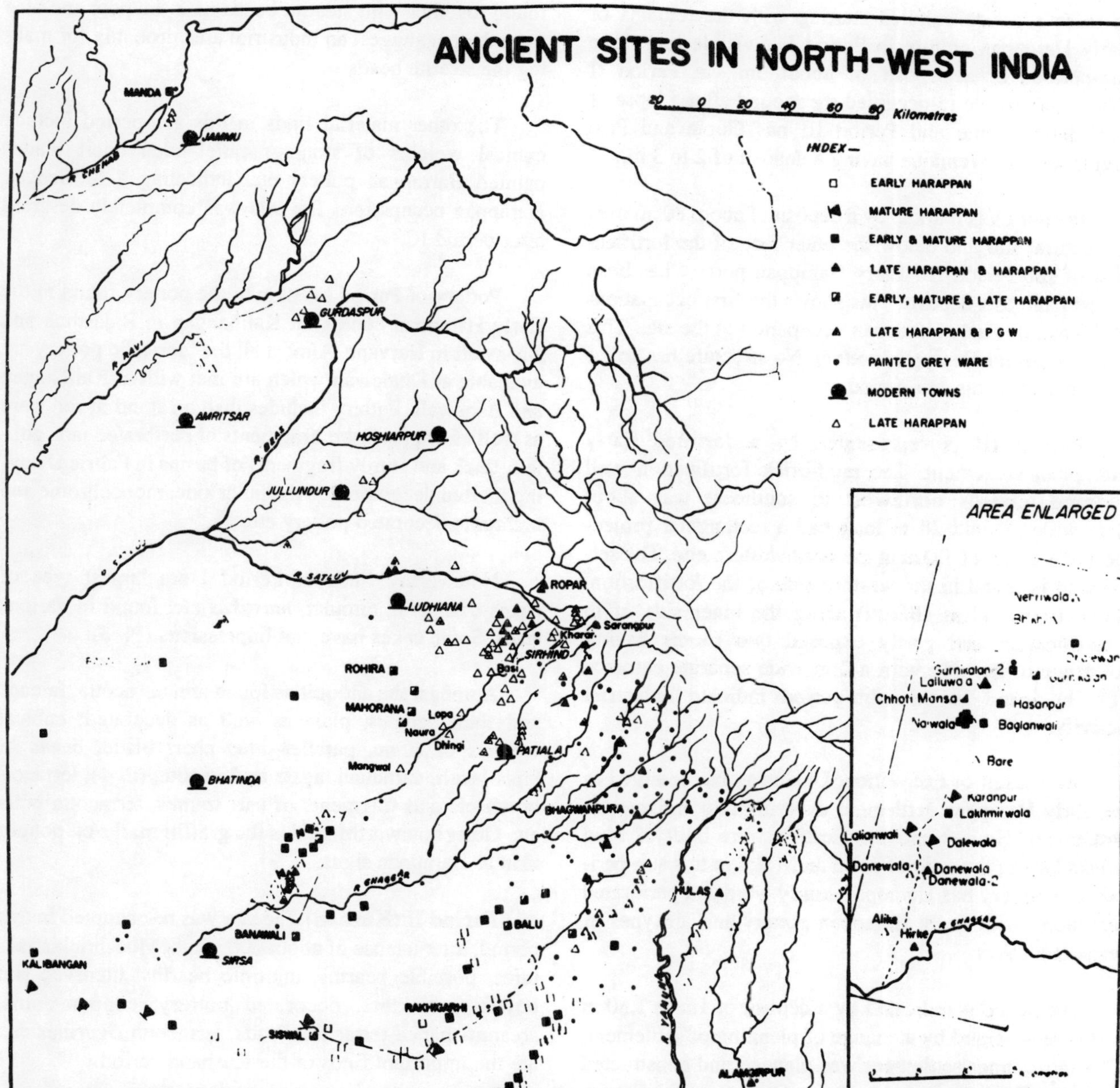

Fig. 1. Ancient sites in Northwest India.

of three separate cultures starting with the remains of Early Harappan culture in Period I, divisible into three sub-periods in a deposit of about 3m., in Period II (Kushana) people re-occupied the mound after a lapse of considerable time and Period III has Gupta and Post Gupta and later remains having a deposit of 2 to 3 m.

Period IA is marked by a deposit of about 80cm over the natural soil and below the outer face of the fortification of sub-Period IB. Early Harappan pottery has been found from this deposit. This shows the first occupational deposit of Early Harappan occupation at the site. This horizon has no Harappan pottery. No structure has so far been found in this sub-period.

Period IB is represented by a fortified Early Harappan settlement. The mud-brick fortification wall running towards northwest to southeast was about 2 m wide (?) and 28 m long had a rectangular projection of 8.00 m x 6.00 m at the northwestern end. The settlement is found in the western side of the fortification. Two circular kilns (*Bhatti*) along the inner side of th fortification and partly exposed two rooms having evidence of burning with a 2 m wide separate entrance (Pl. 1) found in this sub-period indicate industrial activity.

As a result of excavation, Dhalewan has emerged as an Early Harappan settlement evolving into a Harappan settlement. Houses and fortification were built of Mud bricks having the ratio of 1:2:3 and 1:2:4 in this sub-period. The pottery has Harappan sturdy ware and perforated jars along with Early Harappan pottery and all types of terracotta cakes.

Period IC is indicated by a deposit of 1m to 1.50 m and is represented by a change of planning of settlement. The entire inner settlement was planned and constructed *de novo.* This sub-period contains two structural phases. The fortification of the previous sub-period was also used in this sub-period. A room of size 3.45 x 2.20 m having narrow galleries with a huge platform was found in the first phase of this sub-period. The circular kiln, two pots and multiple hearths and partly exposed room with small circular ovens (Pl. 2) represent the phase II of this sub-period. A circular kiln, two pots and the multiple hearths found together with steatite beads near the pots and also from the pot suggest an industrial area probably for making the steatite beads.

The other material finds in this sub-period include cubical weights of stone, parallel-sided chert blades painted Harrappan pottery etc. indicating a fullfledged Harappan occupation. The site was completely deserted after period IC.

Pottery of Period I is akin to the pottery found in the Early Harappan context at Kalibangan in Rajasthan and Banawali in Haryana. Almost all the fabrics in pottery are available at Dhalewan which are met with at Kalibangan and Banawali. Pottery includes dish on stand of red ware as well as of grey ware, fragments of perforated jars, goblets, thick and sturdy fragments of basins in Fabric D having incised decoration on the inner side, monochrome and bichrome decorated pottery etc.

Noteworthy finds of Period I are largest type of cakes-triangular, circular, *mustikas* etc. found in various sizes. Some cakes have mat impressions (Pl. 3).

Amongst the antiquities found are, terracotta, faience and shell bangles, plain as well as decorated; cubical weights of stone, parallel-sided chert blade, beads of lapis-lazuli, carnelian, agate and steatite, (Pl 4); terracotta wheels and fragments of cart frames, terracotta bulls etc. Other noteworthy find is the graffiti marks on pottery akin to Harappan signs.

Period II (Kushan) The site was re-occupied in this period, after a lapse of about 200 years. Mud-brick structures, portable hearths, multiple hearths, incurved rim bowls, sprinklers, decorated pottery, copper coins, arcanut-shaped terracotta beads, terracotta figurines etc. are the important finds of the Kushana period.

Period III (Gupta and later) Over the open parts of fortification of Early Harappans, circular and deep pits were dug for clayey soil and for dumping refuse. The structures are made of mud-lump walls. Hearths, have also been found. Sharp-edged bowls, handled-incense burners (lamps), tiles, lids etc. are the other characteristic finds of this period.

Chalcolithic Settlements at Chichali

DRS. S.K. MITTRA AND SHIVANANDA, V*

The lifeline of Madhya Pradesh (Madhya Desa), Narmada catered to the needs of many a cultural society of protohistoric India since third millennium B.C. It was a natural barrier for many, because of its turbulent ferocious and gigantic look. Others embraced it because of its parennial water and fertile land. The Prehistoric man right from his early stages has lived in this region, i.e. 'Early Stone Age'. In fact the only specimen of Prehistoric man has come from Narmada with the discovery of fossilized skull from Hatnora, near Hoshangabad. Chichali 22°08'N; 75°22'E) in Khasrawad taluk of Khargaon district of Madhya Pradesh (fig. 1) also has yielded large number of prehistoric artefacts belonging to all the stages of Prehistoric period.

In the present paper we shall emphasise upon the Chalcolithic finds and the settlement patterns unearthed during the excavations between 1998 to 2000. Chichali is located on the left bank of river Narmada, 7 km west of village Nimrani on the Mumbai-Agra National Highway. The site was discovered in 1996-97 by the Prehistory Branch of Archaeological Survey of India, during the course of exploration headed by Shri S.B.Ota[1]. The ancient Chalcolithic mound of Chichali is locally known as 'Ghosai Tawda' meaning the habitat of the Gosais or present day Goswamis. A single family of Goswamis are among the Chichali habitants even today. The site is situated about 1 km east of the village overlooking the river on its north. The main mound raises to a height of 33 metres from the present water level of river and measures 100 m N-S x 90 m E-W. in a horse-shoe shape. A smaller mound is found 60 m west of the bigger mound also overlooking the river measures 40 m E-W x 30 m N-S. The surface collection during explorations provided vary important and number of ceramic repertoire which includes white painted black-and-red ware, thick incised red ware, black on red ware, red slipped ware, dull red ware, grey ware, black and red ware and black burnished ware. The other finds include a chalice, beads of lapis lazuli, carnelian, terracotta, steatite, T.C. ear studs, broken quern, mullers, shell bangles, microlithic cores and blades.

The finds immediately remind us the famous sites of Navadatoli[2] and Maheswar.[3] Not much work was carried out in the East Nimar region since the completion of the work at Navadatoli. In the recent past the Prehistory Branch of the Survey conducted small scale excavations in this region at Pipri[4] Utawad[5] and Navrakheri.[6] All the three sites turned out to be Chalcolithic in character with sporadic influence of early historical finds in the later stage. Like Chichali all these sites are located to the south of Narmada though not exactly on the river bank unlike Chichali, except Navrakheri. As crow flies Chichali is

*Archaeological Survey of India, Prehistory Branch, Nagpur.

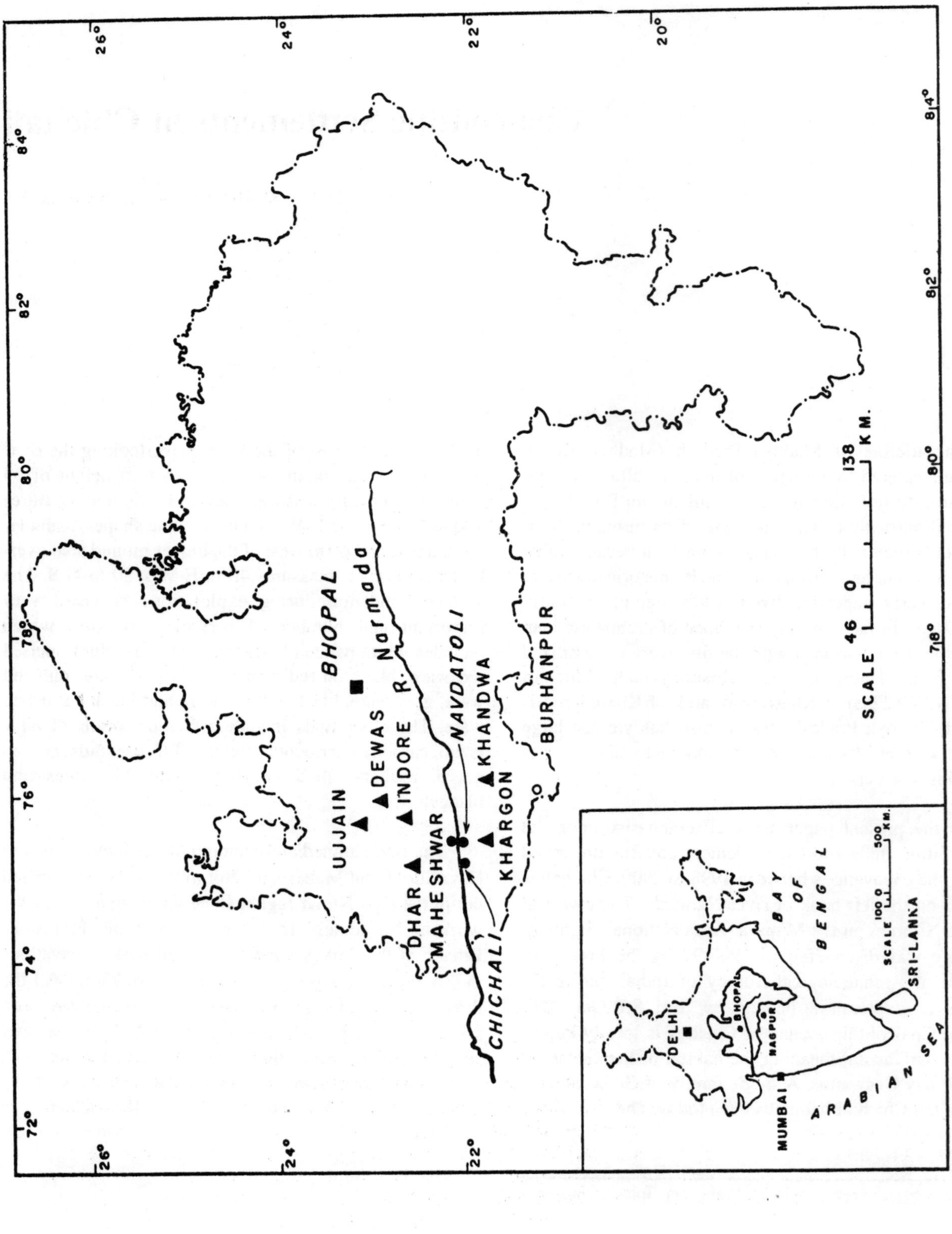

Fig. 1. Location Map of Chichali.

located about 10 km downstream of Narmada. Thus the recent works carried out in this region has thrown more light on the chalcolithic culture of Nimar province and their possible interaction among themselves. Rich exploration finds and over four metres of cultural deposit ascertained from the exposed cliff of the mound overlooking the river deserved large scale excavation to record various aspects of chalcolithic culture. The site is located on an ancient river-crossing zone very close to the Khalghat bridge linking the north to south on the National Highway. In fact the Khalghat bridge can be seen clearly from the mound itself.

Chichali mound was subject to major excavations in two consecutive field seasons of 1998-2000 under the direction of Dr. S.K.Mittra. The excavations have established the maximum deposit of approximately 4.5 m mainly confined to the north of the bigger mound and 3.25 m towards south (fig. 2). While the smaller mound had yielded a maximum deposit of 2.60 m, there is hardly any cultural differences in their deposits between the two mounds except that the smaller mound was not preferred much for the habitation during the early historical times. Similarly, from the centre of the larger mound towards the south the early historical deposit was much less than the northern half of the mound. This shows that right from the Chalcolithic levels to the culmination of early historical period at Chichali people preferred to stay towards river side for better view of the river and fresh air. The excavation has confirmed in all four periods of cultural assemblage at Chichali; the relative dates cultures an as below:

<u>Relative Dates</u>

Period I — Ahar — c. 2000 to 1800 B.C.

Period II — Malwa — *c.* 1800 to 1100 B.C.

Period III — Jorwe — *c.*1100 to 700 B.C.

Period IV — early historical — *c.* 700 to Pre-2nd cent. B.C.

Period I: Aharians inhabited both the mounds simultaneously and accounted for nearly 40 cm of cultural deposit. In fact they are the first settlers at Chichali over the natural black cotton soil. They constructed houses with mud walls having single opening for a room with average thickness of the walls ranging between 20 to 28 cm with well-rammed mud floors. (Pl.1). New evidences have come to light for the first time from the larger mound, associated with the Aharians, where they have constructed a huge wall to serve as a boundary made of thick mud wall with an (average thickness of 55-60 cm) supported by vertically placed reinforced posts at regular intervals of 20-25 cm distance. The wall was provided with a maximum 1.10 m foundation cut through the natural black cotton soil. Considering the depth of the foundation it is likely that the boundary wall must have been raised to an height of over 2 m. Thus it is new evidence that has come to light in context to chalcolithic settlement pattern. Within this enclosure wall the Aharians built their small huts or circular and oval shape and later constructed single, double and multi-roomed houses of mud walls.

The typical white painted black-and-red ware of the Aharians constituted the bulk of ceramic finds besides red ware and thick incised red ware. The white painting chiefly comprises dots, slashes, lines, criss-cross, parallel lines and vertical wavy lines. In most of the occasions the painting is executed in groups. Sporadic presence of black painted buff wash ware during this period is noteworthy. White painted black and red ware mainly accounted for the shapes of bowls and dishes. So also the black on buff ware while the red ware consisted of vases, dough plates, storage jars and basins.

The ȃntiquarian finds account for small terracotta bull (Pl. 2) and decorated beads, steatite and shell beads. Most of the houses have single hearth and saddle querns *in situ*. Besides a couple of houses yielded *in situ* mace-heads, dull red ware vase and querns. Microlithic blade industry accounted for a large number among the antiquities mainly fashioned out of chalcedony and occasionally on chert and carnelian. The raw material abundantly available locally, has helped in fashioning of these tools in large number which comprises parallel-sided, pen-knife, and serrated blades, lunates and points.

The quantity of animal bones accounts for the food habits of Aharians besides large amount of charred wheat grains widely found in all the trenches and couple of lintels like *moong* and *tuwar* accounts for their food habits.

Period II: Malwans succeeded the Aharians at

Chichali with no time gap and accounted for the maximum deposit of 1.5 m amongst the chalcolithic levels. Like their predecessors Malwans also built the is houses with mud-walls in square, rectangular shapes, circular (Pl. 3) and ovalish huts with provisions of tatched bamboo roof. Number of houses have yielded *in situ* single, double and occasionally triple hearths with quern and large quantity of ceramic evidence. The ceramic industry of this period mainly accounted for thick paste/black on red ware, black on buff ware, red slipped ware, red ware, dull red ware. Special mention is made of very bright slipped red ware only associated with Malwans at Chichali. Besides lesser quantity of chacolate slipped ware and grey ware is also found. The lower levels of Malwa has produced survivals of white painted black-and-red ware of the preceeding period. Dish-on- stand, pottery stand, chalice jar, vase, channelled bowl, dish, dough plates, basins, elongated necked vase, accounted for shapes in black on red ware, red slipped ware and red ware. A special mention is made here of a conical based elongated barrel shaped narrow necked jar resembling Harappan pot found *in situ* on a Malwan floor. Most of the slip is made of red , orangish and buff mixed colours. A large variety of painted motifs which includes flora, fauna and geometric designs are executed with black, purple, red and occasionally with white pigments. The painted designs include simple lines wavy pattern, strokes, hollow and solid triangles, loops and curves diagonally placed mesh design, chequer board and sporadic human representations. Mostly the upper belly and neck part was preferred for the execution of paintings. A red slipped ware sherd containing gunny bag impression is among the noteworthy finds. Malwa level at Chichali has produced a number of *in situ* full storage jars in red ware and red slipped ware. Interestingly enough, several stone floor polishers were arranged round the pot covered with an inverted dish on stand, may bespeak of a kind of religious activity. (Pl. 4).

Antiquarian finds of the Malwans at Chichali include copper objects representing chisel (Pl. 5), a *parsú* (Pl. 6), fish-hooks, antimony rods and needles. terracotta animal figurines and beads of steatite, agate, shell, bone, chert, chalcedony, jasper and carnelian; bangles of shell besides huge quantity of microliths fashioned out of chalcedony, chert and carnelian. Among the cereals and lintels charred grains of wheat, black gram, green gram, barley are some of the finds besides huge quantity of slaughtered animal bones. Some of them are charred and represent their foood habits.

Period III: Malwa is closely succeeded by Jorwe culture at Chichali with an average deposit of a metre. During this period they constructed houses of mud wall of an inferior character as compared to their preceeding periods and plastered from either sides. Occasionally the plaster was decorated with stucco finish. The house floor was well-rammed and burnt hard for a longer life and was subsequently repaired on several times. Besides the Jorweyans constructed huts in circular and ovalish shapes over a rammed rubble floor and the superstructure supported by posts arranged in circular fashion. The ceramic is represented by typical of the Jorwe black on red ware finished with high bright red colour from the exterior and bright orangish to buff finish carrying painting. Besides, red ware, red slipped ware, dull red ware, chocolate slipped ware, grey ware and black burnished ware formed the other ceramics of this period. Pottery shapes include small high necked, pear, lota shaped out flaring featureless rimmed flask with and without painting and with the without graffiti marks are noteworthy Channelled bowls externally decorated, deep bowls, basin, miniature pots, chalice, small to medium sized vases often painted and storage jars are also found. Painted motifs which occurs inside the rim and exterior of the pots upto shoulder level often depicts parallel strokes placed diagonally, suspending curves, sun motifs, dots arranged in wavy fashion, other geometrical designs and occasionally depicting faunal representations. A unique find in red ware is large sized storage jar extensively decorated with applique finger pressed concentric circle pattern from this level (Pl. 7) has its parallels from Jorwe levels of Navdotoli.

The antiquarian finds include copper fish hooks, antimony rods, needles, rings, terracotta human and animal figures, net sinkers, beads of steatite, shell, chalcedony, agate and jasper; bangles of shell, querns, mullers and polishers.

From the cutting a stratigraphical observation made reveals a significant evidence of faulting of strata, perhaps caused due to earthquake at Chichali may have brought an end to Jorwe period as seen from the uniform collapsed houses noticed in several trenches in the same level and further corroborated by uniformly burnt horizon throughout the site occurring at a time. In such case it can be presumed that anatural disaster has taken place at a time when most of the Jorweyans were busy in cooking their food.

Period IV: This period accounts for the early historical deposit which followed the Jorweyans without a gap. It has produced a large quantity of antiquities typical of the period comprising of carnelian beads, semi-precious stone beads of different silicious materials; terracotta objects, beads, net sinkers; ivory combs; bone points; large quantity of iron objects comprising axe, hoe, points, arrow-heads, nails and clamps. A unique find amongst the ceramics of this period is a three-handled *gajamukha* red ware, globular bodies wide mouthed jar (Pl. 8). During this period they lived in huts measuring 2 to 3 m in dia. and have extensively used lime for their houses and surroundings. Surprisingly one of the post-holes has yielded a portion of post in tact *in situ*.

Thus we find Chichali enjoyed the status of an important centre for more than 1500 years in the Narmada basin. This excavation has further thrown light on the chalcolithic settlement with enough evidences of their living in semi-urban conditions.

REFERENCES

1. *IAR 1996-97* (unpublished).

2. Sankalia.,H.D., Subarao, B. Deo, S.B. 1958 *Excavations at Maheshwar and Navdatoli (1952-53)*, Poona, Baroda.

3. *Ibid.*

4. *IAR-1994-95*, pp. 46-48

5. *Ibid.*, pp. 48-50

6. *IAR 1996-97* (Unpublished).

Chalcolithic Painted Human Representations from Chichali

CH. BABJIRAO*

The genesis of paintings in general and depiction of human motifs in particular dates back to the prehistoric times when the early man began experimenting to freeze his ideas and observations over the rocky canvas of caves and rock-shelters.Though incipient in nature, the earliest painted human motifs were impressions of hand-prints noticed variously from Europe[1] to Central Indian rock-shelters[2]. Subsequently he had envisaged a method of recording events of day-to-day life pertaining to the subsistance, game and socio-religious aspects. These basic elements of theme of magico-religious nature rules the canvas down to early historical times parallel to emergence of other modes of organic and inorganic material, amongst which ceramics played a significant role resulting in expansion and greater mobility of paintings, its form, theme, concept, execution and techniques during the protohistoric period. The river valleys of Narmada, Chambal and Tapti witnessed the emergence of many a chalcolithic settlement in Central India. Most of these sites exhibit initial inroads of Kayatha-Ahar cultural traits and the rise of Malwa chalcolithic culture. The characteristic features and core elements of Malwa chalcolithic entity were adequately known from the evidences from a number of sites like Navadatoli, Nagda, Awra, Manoti, Kayatha, Beasnagar, Atudkhas, Dangawada, Pipliya-Lorka and Runiji[3] and recent evidences reported from lower Narmada at Pipri-utawad,[4] Navlakheri[5] and Chichali.[6]

The ceramic data available from these sites were indeed abundant to help us in estimating and to reconstruct the demography and social life patterns of Central Indian Chalcolithic settlements. The paintings over the ceramics generate finer inputs of the social life, environment and the artistic talents of their authors. However, occurrence of painted human motifs were confined to few sites viz. Navadatoli[7], Nagda[8], Awra[9] and Dangawada[10] in the Malwa region of Madhya Pradesh and Inamgaon[11] and Diamabad[12] from adjacent Maharashtra. While the Malwa group was essentially identified as of Malwan entity the latter represents Jorwe and Savalda cultures. Navadatoli had produced fairly good number of ceramics bearing painted human figures than the rest; thus providing substantial evidence about the chalcolihic Narmada population. Within the proximity of Navadatoli, the recent excavations conducted by Dr. S.K. Mittra between 1998–2000, at Chichali 22°08'N, 75°22'E, right on he southern bank of Narmada in Kasarawad taluk of Khargaon district have brought to light four fold cultural sequence of Ahar, Malwa, Jorwe and Early historical periods.[13] The ceramic industry of Malwa period has produced some of the finest examples of hitherto unknown painted motifs, reflecting fauna and flora besides geometric designs. Occurrence of animal depictions out number

*Archaeological Survey of India, Excavations Branch-I Nagpur.

human motifs yet they throw adequate light on the chalcolithic life at Chichali.

In all seven specimens, bearing human depictions were noticed at the site and all belong to different levels of Malwa period (fig. 1). A close scrutiny of these specimens suggest that the artists adhered to naturalistic and stylistic themes. The paintings were invariably executed in black pigment obtained from organic and inorganic substances. The treatment of body-form was attained through adopting geometric symbols, angular and curved strokes besides constant use of fine brush.

The specimens retrieved were storage jar, vase and bowls of medium to coarse fabric treated with bright red, red, dull-red and buff-slip. Based on thematic and stylistic grounds the painted human figures of Chichali are broadly classified into three different catagories viz. dancing human figures; portraits or individual figures and human figures in association with animals.

Dancing Human Figures: Two specimens accounts for this category and both are on bowls and bear identical paintings. The artist had depicted a theme representing dance scene of a social or community festive moment in a simple way with the help of lines and strokes. The human figures exhibit total uniformity with regard to their size, thus indicating the precision involved in the execution of these motifs.

But for surface treatment and breakage of painted portion both the specimens bear dancing scene of identical nature (nos. 1 & 2). The former executed in black over red surface depicts the scene of a community/group dancing by four individuals in a joyful mood. The figures are slender and each measures 3 cm in height. The body is represented by relatively thicker vertical lines and the heads are marked by hollow circle connected to the torso with stretched neck and the legs are depicted by small horizontal and slender vertical strokes as if half crouched. The hands are delineated by oblique strokes connected to each other showing that the group holding their hands to each other while dancing. Further, each human figure is shown with two pairs of hands to denote the effect of body motion involved in the act of dancing and to animate the movements of hands while dancing, thus denoting the all important rythm. The second specimen shows the vestiges of below the waist portion of three human figures similar to the specimen above, which is bordered by horizontal lines above head and below the feet respectively. The dancing human motifs of Chichali can very well be identified with those reported from Navadatoli[14] and to some extent with Nagda[15] dancing figures.

Portrait or individual motifs: Four examples of this kind are reported from the site. As these figures exhibit different style and mode of depiction each specimen is dealt separately. The first specimen of portrait (no. 3) is very interesting and totally differs from others in regard to their form of depiction as the figure is shown standing to its right. The 2.2 cm motif shows the vestiges of human body below bust level. The denoted body resembles that of a dumb-bell shape showing waist and pelvic portions. The legs are depicted by two parallel lines, terminating towards left at the end thus forming the feet. The stylistically drawn curved features could be its headgear. This human motif is the only evidence at the site shown with feet. Navdatoli produces a variant of the illustrated example, also from Malwa level.[16] The second figure of this series (no.4) is painted in black on a storage jar of red ware. The painted human motif of, 6/5 x 4 cm depicts bust and above waist portions in a stylistic way. The head is denoted by a solid circle connected to solid triangular body with a long neck. The gently raised and curvelinear suspended hands are probably holding suspending flower bunch. The available portion of the figure may resemble boat at a glance owing to its missing portions below bust line. However, similar figures with raised hands were reported from the chalcolithic rock-paintings at Kanjadei[17] of Chambal valley, Malwa levels of Nagda[18], a variant from Jorwe levels of Inamgaon[19] and from the Malwa level of Dangawada[20]. The only example in full (no.5) on a vase is also of black on red variety of typical Malwan character. Here he human figure is executed with two solid triangles opposite to each other like a mirror image, with short slender neck supporting a roundish small head flanked by a dot each on either side perhaps denoting a bunch of hair knot. If so, it is a finest example to depict a small girl. The hands are depicted little muscular and fine enough to indicate a healthy character. the right hand holds an indeterminate object near to the constricted waist line. The slightly curved legs shown adds to the momentum of the finished art representation. No.6 is depicted on a red ware hopescotch with the human bust waist portion intact (1.5 x 1.5 cm), with both the hands placed on the waist resembling like a *katibhanga* posture.

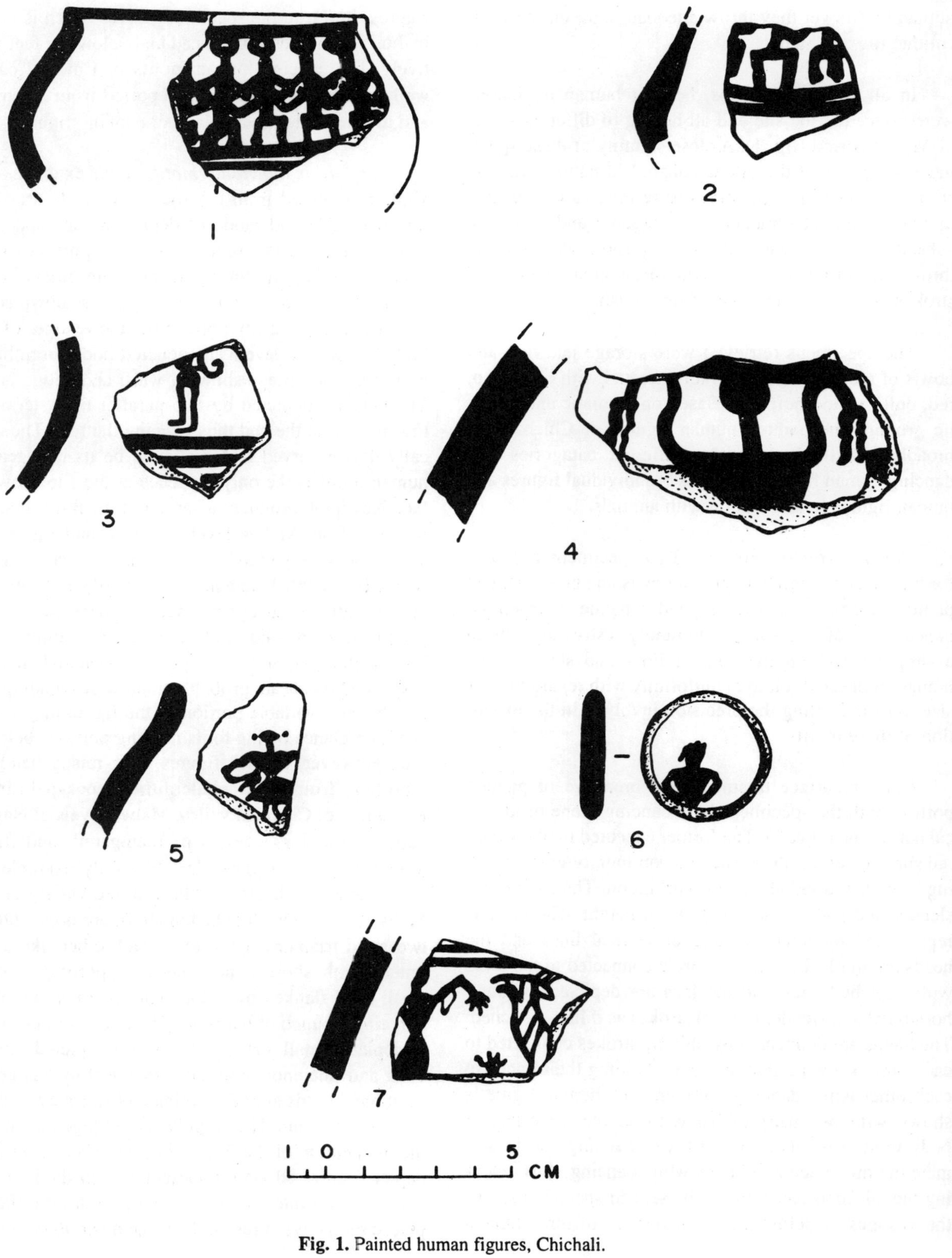

Fig. 1. Painted human figures, Chichali.

The head is denoted by a thickened sub-triangle connected to a solid triangular body. The comparables of nos. 5 and 6 are not available from other chalcolithic sites.

Human figure in association with animals: A solitary example in this category (no. 8) is reported from the site comes from upper Malwa level. Here a man and animal is shown together, a practice in vogue since long. Some of the domisticated and pet animals together with human figures variously reported are from Navadatoli[21] and Dangawada.[22] Besides domisticated ones, wild animals too occasionally figure together with man as in the case of Diamabad[23] from Savalda level.

The specimen under scrutiny is of a vase fragment bearing a human motif of 2.8 cm high with its right portion partially missing and neck portion of an animal to its left side. The human figure is depicted with chest in solid diamond shape and curvelinear lower portion and a solid circular head connected to a short neck. The left hand is shown raised above the shoulder and bent downward at elbow with fingers stretched to the extent that it can be counted clearly. Hear the middle finger is shown little longer to match the anotomical feature more effectively. The human figure has a hollow circular object to its left arm suspended and wearing an ornament around its neck(?). The long necked animal shown to the left of the human figure, is marked by series of oblique bands over its neck. The ears of the animal are well depicted with a pair of horns(?). The animal is looking at the human figure which is interesting for the posture in which it is shown. An unidentified object is delineated below. The figure in totality suggests of its being engaged in the act of dancing(?).

A close examination of these painted motifs of Chichali and similar human figures reported elsewhere in Malwa and extra Malwa region from Maharashtra suggests that the artists at Chichali adopted common art style and theme that prevailed in chalcolithic Malwa region and locally experimented to evolve new concepts of human depictions and further accelerated the mode and execution methods of the paintings.

REFERENCES

1. Paul G Bahn, 1998, *Prehistoric Art*, Cambridge, U.K., p.111–115.
2. Wakankar, V.A.S. *et al.*, 1976 *Stone Age Painting In India*, Bombay.
3. Sharma, R.A., 1991 *Technology and Material Life of Central India*, Delhi, pp.41–102.
4. *Indian Archaeology 1995–96–A Review* (under print).
5. *IAR, 1997–98* (under print).
6. *IAR, 1998–99* (under print).
7. Sankalia, H.D., *et al.*, 1971, *Chalcolithic Navadatoli,* Pune, Baroda, pp. 110–112; 120, 167 & 217.
8. Banerjee, N.R., 1986, *Nagda Excavations,* Delhi, p.182, PL.XXI,B11.
9. Trivedi, H.V., 'Excavations at Awra', *Journal of Madhya Pradesh Itihas Parishad*, vol.4, Bhopal, 1962, p.27, Fig.4.
10. *IAR, 1978–79,* p.70, PL.XLIIB.
11. Sankalia, H.D., *et al.* 1988, *Excavations at Inamgaon*, Pune, figs. 11–43, D71 and 11–12, D21.
12. Sali, S.A., 1986, *Diamabad Excavations,* Delhi, pp. Fig. 25-11, 12, 16; 69–38 and Fig. 71–20.
13. For details of the Cultural sequence refer to introductory article.
14. Sankalia, H.D., *et al., op. cit.,* pp. 110–112, 120 and 168; 217; Fig.37-D-24, 25, 27; 38D–46; 41–D110; 63D 322–23 and 590.
15. Banerjee, N.R., 'A dancing figure on the pottery from Nagda', *Bulletin of Deccan College Postrgraduate Research Institute,*, Vol.20, 1960, pp.

1 & 11.

16. Sankalia, H.D., *op.cit,* p.168, Fig, 63 D 322.

17. Newumayer, Erwin 1983, *Prehistoric Indian Rock Paintings,* Delhi, Fig. 180.

18. Banerjee, *op.cit.,* p.182, PL.XXI B1.

19. Datta, Veena, 2000, *Chalcolithic pottery paintings,* Delhi, p.46, Pl2.11.

20. *op.cit.*

21. Sankalia, H.D., *op.cit.* Fig. 70.D.455.

22. *op.cit.*

23. Datta, Veena, *op.cit.* p.52, pl.4.11.

Anthropomorphic Figurines from Chichali: Some Observations

NANDINI BHATTACHARYA SAHU*

Among the cultural finds anthropomorphic figures always attracted archaeologists and art historians alike and have called for specific attention. Besides the anthropomorphic figures from the copper hoards examples of which can be categorised as same, have also been found from the Early Historical levels from sites like Taxila, Nagda, Ujjain, Prabhas Patan, Kaundinyapur, Sonkh etc., the latest being the ones from Chichali. In the present paper an attempt is being made to elucidate the finds from Chichali which has produced anthropomorphic figures in ivory, bone, terracotta and stone (figs. 1&2).

These figurines were worshipped and sometimes adorned as fertility charms, as a measure to check a sudden breakout of epidemics such as smallpox,[1] as a treatment to some chronic ailment, sometimes for good crop or to end a drought or famine.[2]

The figurines under discussion were found from the Early Historical deposits only. These are conspicuous by their absence in the Chalcolithic levels - Ahar, Malwa and Jorwe, the proceeding horizons at Chichali.

Chichali in all has produced twenty examples of anthropomorhic figurines, variously on pottery (12), in stone (3), ivory (4) and bone (1) from different levels of Early Historical period.

Each category of these anthropomorphic figurines can be subdivided on the basis of material and typology. The site yielded twelve (12) figurines executed on pottery pieces (fig. 1), these can be classified as:

a) Two examples were found, having well marked head, torso and legs. These have parallels from comparable levels at Kaundinyapur,[4] Amravati district, in Maharashtra.

b) Two more have only the head and the torso, without legs.

c) A unique example from Chichali consists of a figurine, made out of a red ware sherd, which does not carry well-marked parts. However, the group of five perforations are arranged so as to mark the head and the body. Four perforations are arranged in two rows of two each, on the sides and fifth marking the head. It is interesting to note that this particular type of anthropomorphic figurine made out of potsherds is still worshipped by the locals during the Navaratri festival as Goddess Durga.

d) The remaining seven figurines are fiddle-shaped and have their parallels from Navdotoli[5], Kakrehta,[6] both in Madhya Pradesh. However, the perfect '8' shaped

*Archaeological Survey of India, Preistory Branch, Nagpur.

figurines are found only from Chichali. One of these seven, carries a circular dent mark in the centre, apparently made with an intention of drilling a hole. The '8' shaped figurines were made by grinding the sides of an ovalish sherd. It was meticulously done so as to produce the required roundness on both ends and give it a perfect '8' shape. Chichali is perhaps the first site to yield anthropomorphic figurines, made out of locally available sandstone, (nos. 13–15). Three such figurines reported, have been made by punching portions from flat pebbles to indicate head and legs. However, one of the three figurines is not very finely finished and has only the legs marked on an undressed rectangular stone nodule. Of the finely finished specimens, one is roundish and the other is a slender, rectangular one.

Apart from the pottery and stone, the site has yielded fragmentary figurines in ivory, (fig.2, nos. 1–4) and in tact specimen in bone, (no. 5.) Such figurines have been found in varying shapes and with different styles of execution from the Early Historical levels even at Taxila,[7] Nagda[8], Prabhas Patan[9], Ujjain[10], Navdatoli[11], Sonkh[12], Kakrehta[13], Atranjikhera[14]. At these sites were found in the time bracket of *c* 5th C BC to 2nd C BC and occur either prior to or along with NBPW. However, fragmentary figurines of this type were found from the earliest levels at Ujjain dating to *c* 800–500 BC and from the Painted Grey ware levels at Alamgirpur[15] dating approximately between *c* 1100–800 BC. These figurines have been found to be decorated all over with 'dot-in-circle' and linear patterns. the 'do-in-circle' motif is found to have been executed in a particular manner and by their style one can easily make out the obverse and reverse of the figurines. Noteworthy are the different patterns of execution on the obverse and reverse.

The first pair of 'dot-in-circle' motif represents the types and just below them a circle denoting the nose. The two others on the two arms (in case of the figurines from Chichali), though do not appear to be so but represent the breasts the other circles on the lower half of the body are probably only decorative. The 'dot-in-circle' motif is known as the 'eye-motif' by scholars.[16] It is believed that the beads, amulets, pendants, etc. with the eye motif were worn because of the magical charm the motif was thought to carry. These figurines resembling the finds from Chichali have been found within a large time bracket and were extremely common particularly in West Asia and Egypt in the 2nd-3rd millennium BC. These were termed as 'eye-goddesses'; so the ones found in the Indian context have also been termed as 'eye-goddesses'.[17]

The figurines from Chichali are found to have a triangular head and a sub-triangular lower half, with a split at the lower end to show the parted legs. None of the ivory figurine is in tact. The largest of all is represented only by the head, without the lower portion and is charred. (fig. 2, 1). The remaining three have only the lower portion in tact of which one is charred, (fig. 2).

In none of the figurines be it of any material, are the feminine physical features emphasised, yet the bulbous curve of the hip portion and the narrow waist in case of the '8'-shaped figurines and the positioning of the 'eye-motif' on the bust prove that these are female figurines. It needs to be clearly mentioned here that there were significant differences in the roles of the terrocotta female figurines in round[18] and these anthropomorphic plaquettes. That these anthropomorphic figurines are cult objects is more emphasised by the fact that these were found in a lesser number compared to other antiquities of the period.

Illuminating still more on the socio-religious lives of the inhabitants of Chichali in the early historical times we find ivory comb fragments from Chichali depicting the 'eye-motif'. It is still believed by the tribals in many parts of India that a comb is a symbol of happiness and prosperity. Even now the brides and the grooms offer combs to each other at the time of marriage.[19] To ward off evils from their prosperity, the 'eye-motifs' could have been used by the Early Historical people at Chichali as it combs are used by many tribes including the present day Santhals.[20]

Apart from throwing significant light on the socio-religious set up of the people in the Early Historical times at Chichali these finds may also be helpful in fixing the chronology on a comparative basis for the Early Historical horizon at Chichali. The total absence of any numismatic and palaeographic evidences and in the light of only stray finds of two sherds of NBP ware and PGW (without painting) the Early Historical dating here becomes a puzzle. On comparing the levels with those from the known dated earlier sites which produced such figurines, mostly in ivory and bone, viz. the 'eye-god-

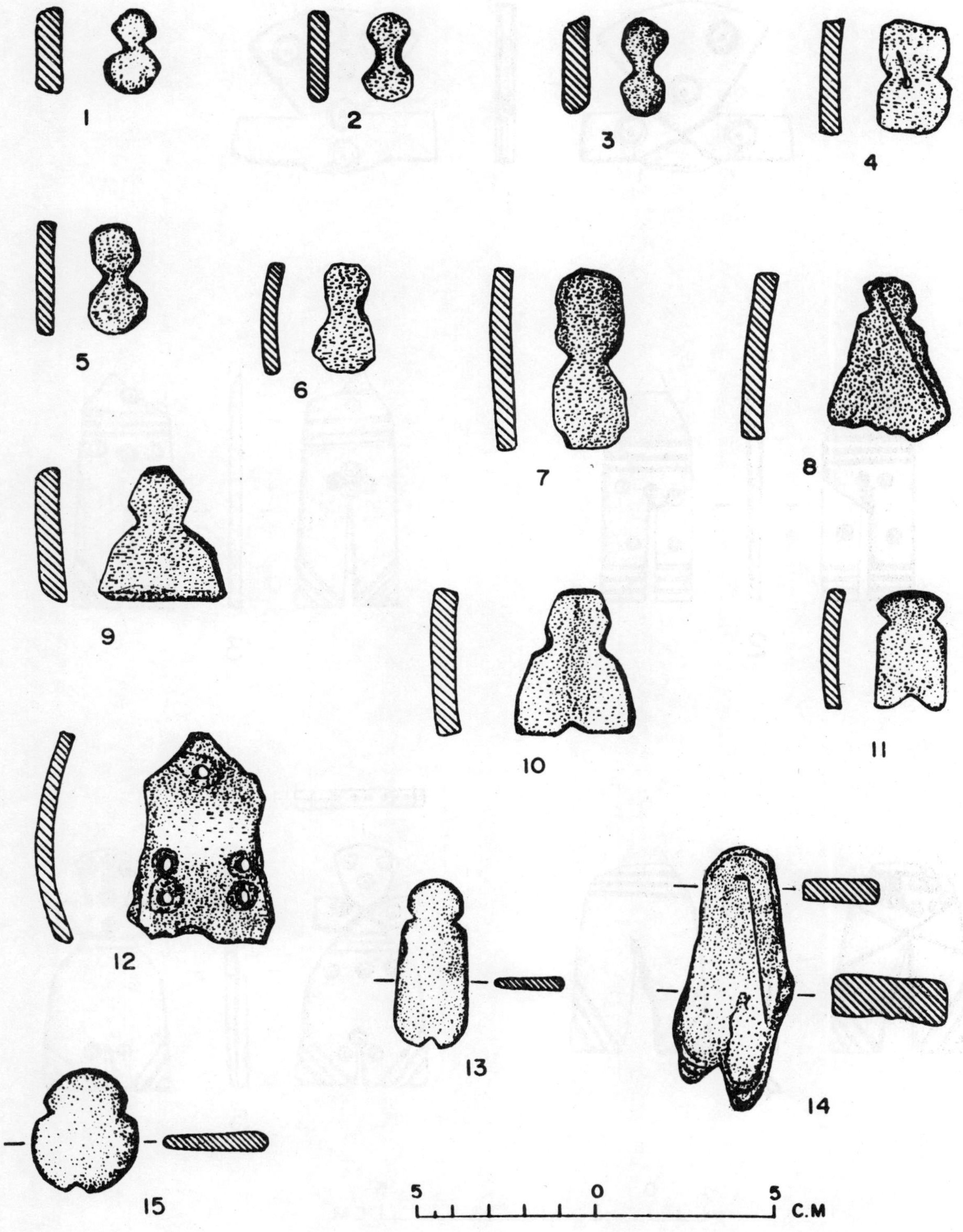

Fig. 1: Anthropomorphic figurines in pottery (1–12) and in stone (13–15), from Chichali.

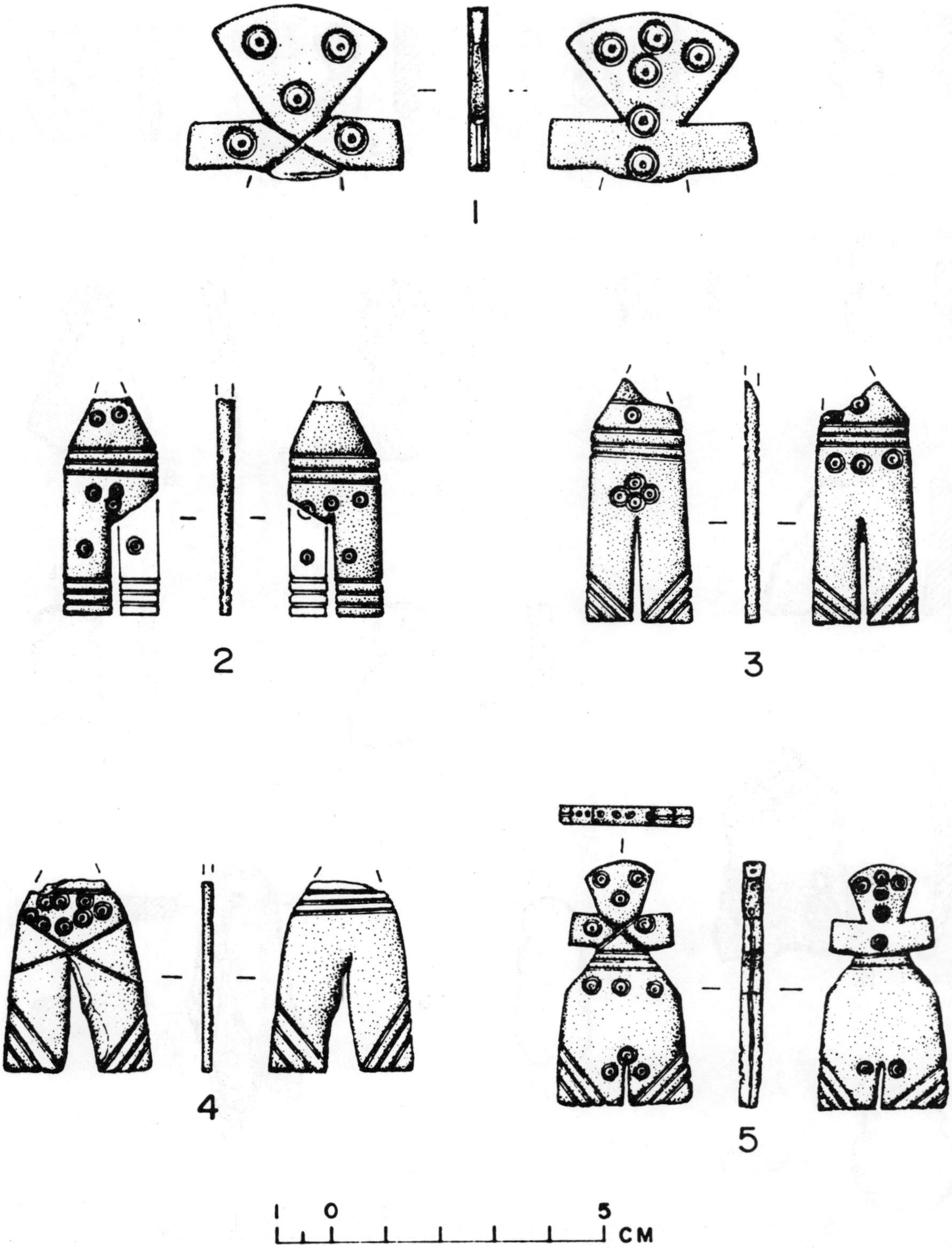

Fig 2: anthropomorphic figurines in ivory (1–4) and in bone (5) from Chichali.

desses', we may infer about the tentative date of the Early Historical levels at Chichali. As at other sites, the dating is confirmed between 4th 5th C B.C. to 2nd C B.C., we may in light of, still earlier fragmentary finds from Ujjain[21] and even prior to that from Alamgirpur[22] date the Chichali finds and consequently the Early Historical levels between *c* 7th C B.C. to *c* 4th C B.C.

Apart from the Early Historical levels discussed above examples are not wanting in preceding cultural horizons as from Harappa and Mohenjodaro[23] though somewhat stylized. However, our dates regarding the Chichali specimens seem to be in proper light in context of the preceeding Chalcolithic horizon and the associated antiquarian remains like the iron objects, pieces of saddle quern bearing Mauryan polish recovered from the uppermost levels of Early Historical period.

Lastly we may discuss in brief about the provenance of these anthropomorphs. It is interesting to note that except two anthropomorphic figurines from Kaundinyapur[24], these were found only in sites north of Narmada. It is also to be marked that most of the occult practices associated with diseases, deaths, etc. are prevalent more in this region. There is every possibility of the figurines being used for a different purpose altogether. The pronounced curve of hips is indicative of its being used as a fertility deity. In case of the bone and ivory figurines of 'eye-goddesses' one is tempted to compare them with the representation of the goddess Sitala in the northern and eastern India. Almost all over these regions particularly in the rural areas, she is worshipped as a deity of smallpox and her representations are most interesting from the point of view of this paper. In Punjab, the deity represented by ring of spots round the neck and is referred to as *Kandi Mata*[25] or the mother of swellings. The Sitala cult appears to be considerably important in eastern India. There she is represented by a block of stone, roughly resembling a face, covered with vermilion and brass points fixed in it.[26] In certain areas of Madhya Pradesh, she is worshipped in the form of a rough stone, indented like a honey comb, to represent the pitting of the malady and is placed under a neem tree.[27]

The discovery of such figurines north of Narmada and the fact that rites and rituals are more popular in these regions, does not seem to be merely coincidental. Dhavalikar opines, these may 'betoken the survival of an age-old Harappan cult through millennia, the traces of which can be even found today among the fatalistic Indian populace.'

Last but not the least I am thankful to Dr. S.K. Mittra for allowing me to utilise the excavated materials from Chichali in the present article.

REFERENCES

1. Dhavalikar, M.K., 'Eye-Goddesses in India and their West Asian Parallels', *Anthropos* 60, 1965, p.540.

2. The site was exacaveted by Dr. S.K. Mittra, Superintending Archaeologist, Excavations Branch-I for two consecutive seasons between 1998–2000.

3. Gaur R.C., *Excavations at Atranjikhera: Early Civilization of the Upper Ganga Basin*, Delhi, p.362–63, Pl.LXXV.

4. Dikshit, M.G., *Excavations at Kaundinyapur,* Bombay.

5. Sankalia, H.D., *et. al. Chalcolithic Navdatoli: The Excavations at Navdatoli 1957–59*, Poona, 1971, Baroda, p.386.

6. Sharma, R.K. and Mishra, S.N., *Excavations at Kakrehta,* Agam Kala Prakashan, Delhi, p.126.

7. Marshall, Sir John, *Taxila* (Cambridge, 1951), Vol.II, p.654, Vol. III, Pl.199, no.12.

8. Banerjee, N.R. *Nagda (1955–57)*, *MASI* 85, Archaeological Survey of India, New Delhi, pp.241–44, Pl.XXXI.

9. *IAR, 1956–57,* p.17, Pl.XVIII B.

10. *IAR, 1956–57,* p.27, PLXXXIII A.

11. Sankalia, H.D., *et. al. op.cit.*, p.404, fig.124, no.3.

12. Hartel, Herbert, *Excavations at Sonkh,* Dietrich Reimer Verlag, Berlin, 1993, p.277, & 280, no.12.

13. Sharma, R.K., *op.cit.*, p.135, Pl.XXXVI.

14. Gaur R.C., *op.cit.*, p.420, Pl. CXXIII, A (1).

15. *IAR, 1958–59,* p.52, Pl.LXII.

16. Dhavalikar, M.K., *op.cit.*, p.534.

17. *Ibid.*

18. Terracotta human figurines in round were found from Early Historical levels yielding the anthropomorphic figurines as also from the preceeding levels.

19. Elwin, Verrier, *The Tribal Art of Middle India,* Oxford University Press, 1951, pp.46–54.

20. *The world of Man,* vol. *6, Asia,* Creative world publications, Inc. Chicago, 1959, p.44.

21. *IAR, 1956–57, op.cit.*

22. *IAR, 1958–59, op.cit.*

23. Dhavalikar, M.K., *op.cit.*, pp.536–7.

24. Dikshit, M.G., *op.cit.*

25. Dhavalikar, M.K., *op.cit.*, p.539.

26. *Ibid.*

27. *Ibid.*

Painted Faunal Depictions from Chalcolthic Chichali

PRABASH SAHU*

The present paper delves into the realm of animal motifs as depicted on the Chalcolithic pottery from Chichali and their significance in the given time frame and probable ecological set up. The archaeological site of chichali (Lat.22°8'N, Long. 75°22'E) located in the Kasravad tehsil, Khargone District, Madhya Pradesh was subjected to scientific excavations by Dr. S.K. Mittra, Superintending Archaeologist, Archeological Survey of India, Excavations Branch-I, Nagpur from 1998 to 2000. The mound here rises to a height of 33 m from the present day water-level and contains cultural deposit of approximately 4.5 m ascribable to four periods viz. Period I, Ahar; Period II- Malwa; Period III-Jorwe and period IV - Early Historical.

The Ahar period, a short-lived one, at Chichali has not produced any painted animal motifs whereas the Malwa and the Jorwe levels which were prosperous produced animal motifs painted over pottery in fairly good number and are the matter of study in the present paper. These paintings are executed invariably in black over red buff or pinkish red wares and the animals motifs include animals like antelope, camel, horse, rabbit; peacock, the lone specimen from the avian family and insects, like centipede and butterfly besides an array of geometrical, Sun and few human representations.

I. ANIMALS (FIGS. 1 AND 2)

A. Antelope:

Antelopes, the earliest known ruminants, having solid, long, cylindrical and often lyre shaped horns, are essentially creatures of open plains and grassland. The relationship of man with antelope is deep-rooted though the former has always acted as an exterminator of the latter. At the same time the aesthetic appeal and agility of this animal has evoked veneration in ancient religious texts and is said to be always associated with Brahma, the Creator and Siva, the Paśupati. In the historical period, this animal acquired prominence and King Aśoka, perhaps the first conservationist of the recent past, proclaimed in his first Giernar Rock Edict (U-11-12) not tounnecessarily salughter antelope/deer, peacock among other animals (Hultzsch-1991). Whatever the reason, the fact lies that the antelope was the most sought after animals during the Palaeolothic and Chalcolithic times where they are extensively depicted in the cave walls and in pottery of the respective periods.

Antelopes have been painted on Chalcolithic pottery in both stylistic as well as in realistic manner. They are shown either in frieze or single, body filled with dots or hatchings and sometimes totally in linear representations,

*Archaeological Survey of India, Excavations Branch-I, Nagpur.

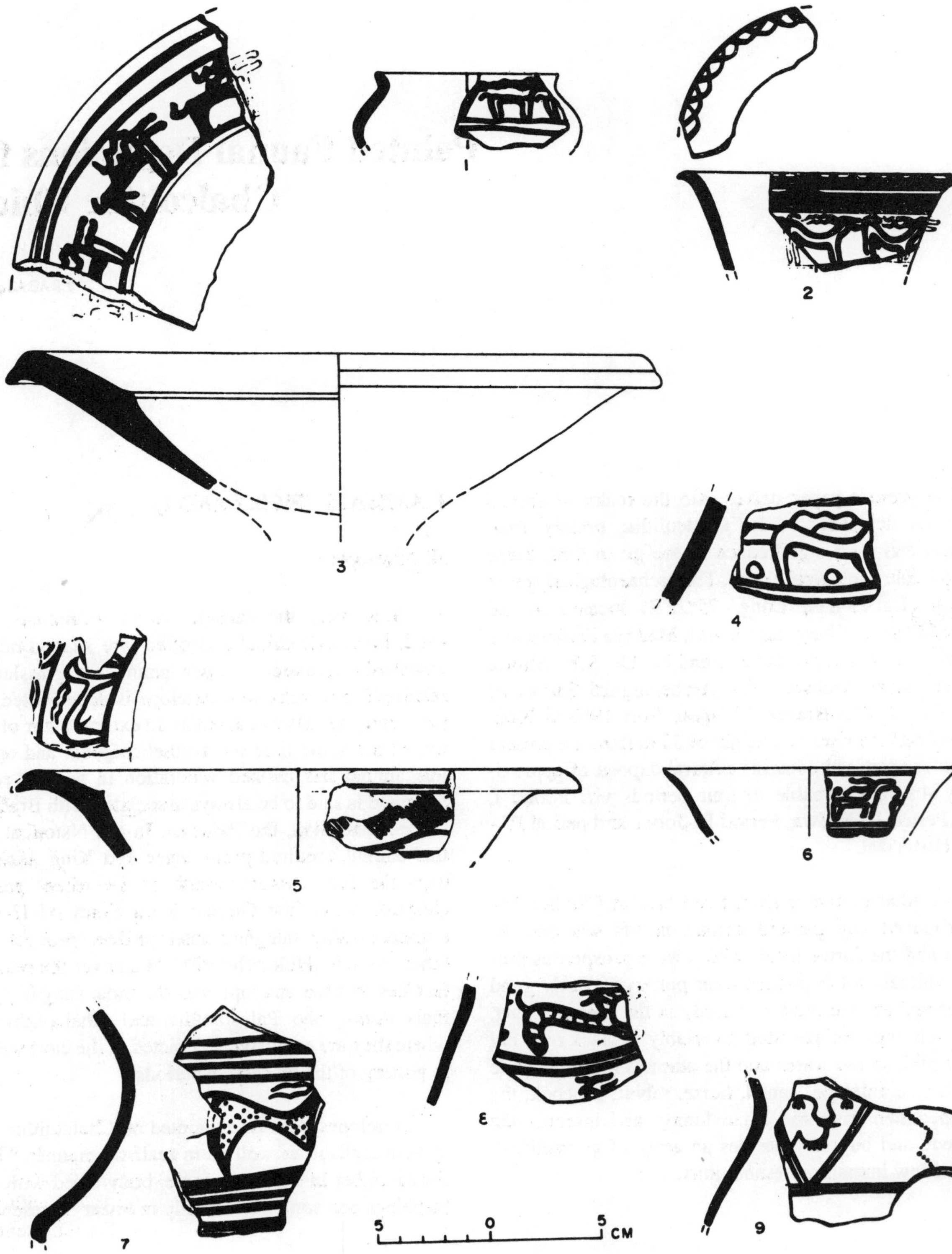

Fig. 1: Antelopes on potsherds from Chichali.

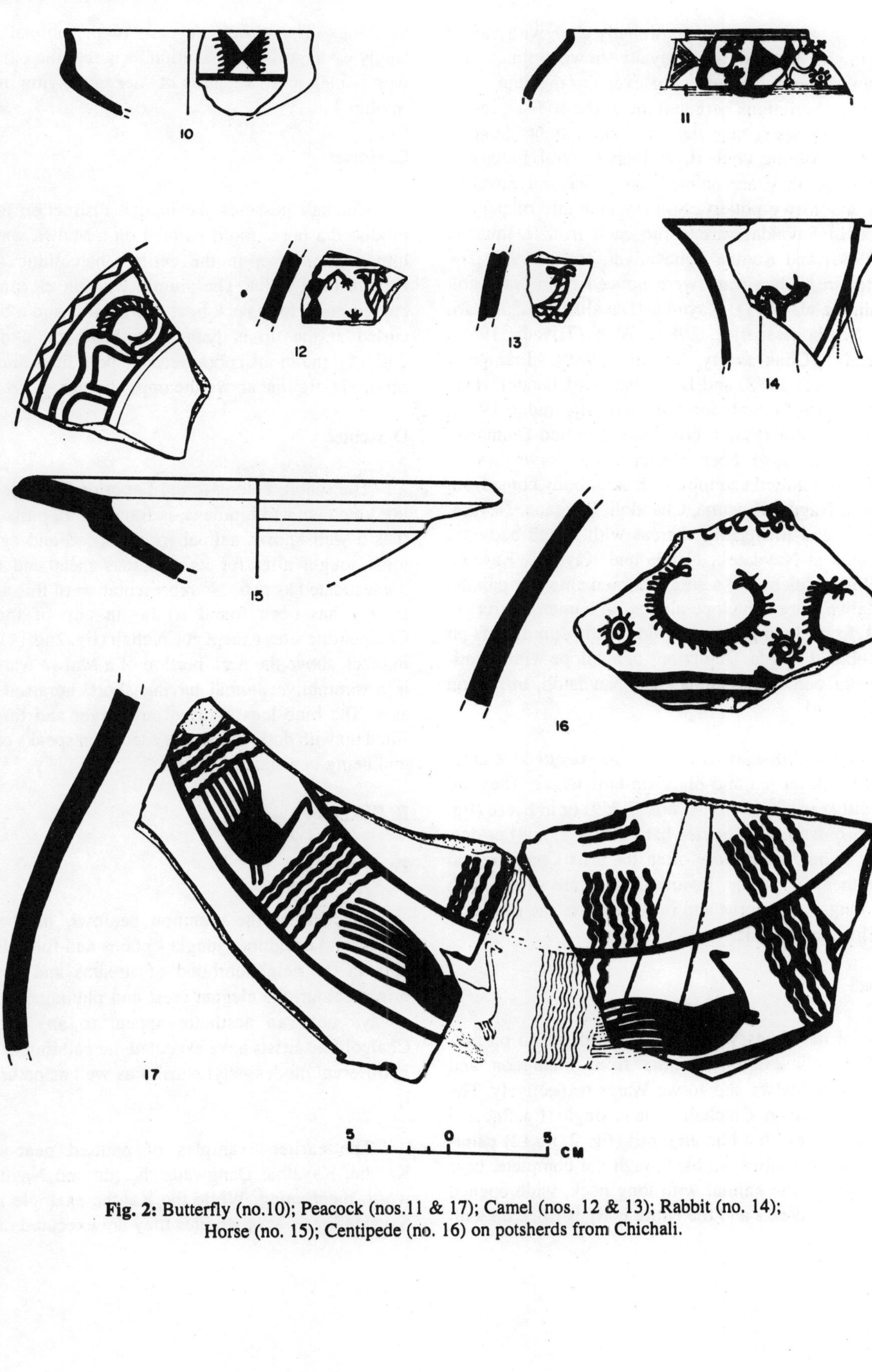

Fig. 2: Butterfly (no.10); Peacock (nos.11 & 17); Camel (nos. 12 & 13); Rabbit (no. 14); Horse (no. 15); Centipede (no. 16) on potsherds from Chichali.

with one or two horns and occasionally alongwith Sun or human motifs. Interestingly, they are shown at times with prominent genitals. In toto, whatever the medium, with some minor variations here and there, the stylistic renditions of antelopes remain the same throughout the ages. In the Chalcolithic context, in both Central India and Deccan sites, they are painted exquisitely on Savalda, Malwa and Jorwe pottery. Solitary example of painted antelope in Savalda ware come each from Daimabad (Sali, 1986) and Kaothe (Dhavalikar, et al, 1990). The examples in Malwa ware were noticed from Navdatoli (Sankalia et al, 1971), Kayatha (Davalikar and Ansari, 1965), Nagda (Banerjee, 1986), Avra (Trivedi, 1962), Dangwada (Chakravarty, et al, 1989), Inamgaon (Sankalia et al., 1988) and Daimabad. At Chandoli (Deo and Ansari, 1965), Songaon (Deo and Mjaumdar, 1969), Nevasa (Sankalia et al, 1960), Inamgaon and Daimabad antelope has also been depicted on Jorwe wares. Examples of painted antelope with solid body come from Navdatoli, Nagda, Kayatha, Chandoli, Songaon, Nevasa, Dangwada and Inamgaon whereas with dotted body are represented at Navdatoli, Nagda and Kayatha. Kayatha has yielded evidence of a single horned antelope painted on a Malwa ware. Antelope alongwith human motifs are noticed from Inamgaon and alongwith sun motifs at Navdatoli and Nagda. Depictions of antelope with prominent genital come from Dongwada, Navdatoli, Inamgaon and Daimabad.

The Chacolithic artists of Chichali executed the antelope on black-on-red and black-on-buff wares. They are shown either in single (fig. 1, nos. 7 & 9) or in frieze (fig. 1, nos. 1–6 & 8), with bodies hatched fig 1, no8) or dotted (fig. 1, no.7). But very often the artists preferred to execute them in outline. Invariably they are shown with typical long, wavy horns and in some cases the genital is well delineated (fig. 1,Nos.3–5).

B. Camel

Camel motif has very rarely been depicted on pottery. The only examples come from Inamgaon and Daimabad on Malwa and Jorwe Wares respectively. The two specimens from Chichali - one in single (fig. 2no.13) and other alongwith a human motif (fig. 2, no.12) painted in black on Malwa wares, though not complete, bear the features of the animal with long neck, wide opened mouth, upraised ears and the entire body is filled up with hatchings. The posture in case of the animal depicted singly is suggestive of "motion" whereas the other alongwith human motif suggests of "accompanying in a dance rhythm."

C. Horse

Chichali posseses the unique distinction of having produced a horse motif painted on a Malwa ware sherd, hitherto unknown in the entire Chalcolithic levels of Protohistoric India. The animal with an elegant stance, curved back, long neck bent downwards and a bushy tail curled at the tip is painted in black on a dish (fig. 2,no.15). the motif is bordered by bold lines and another set of zig-zig line above the upper border.

D. Rabbit

The rabbit, belong to the Leporidae family and having long ears and hindlegs, is found in all parts of India. It is a well known animal for its speed and agility and most sought after for its delicious meat and are even domesticated as pets. No representation of this animal on pottery has been found so far in any of the known Chalcolithic sites except at Chichali (fig. 2no.14). Painted in black above the neck portion of a Malwa ware vase, it is a diminutive animal having short, upraised tail and ears. The hind legs as usual are larger and the body is filled up with dots. The entire execution speaks of the animal being in a state of "flight."

II. BIRD

Peacock

Peacock or the common peafowl, inhabits dense shrubs and deciduous jungle - plains and foothill; preferably in the neighbourhood of streams and rivers. The bright colour, the elegant crest and plumage of this bird always pose an aesthetic appeal to any artist. The Chalcolithic artists have executed the painting of this bird in different modes - stylistically as well as naturalistically.

The earlier examples of painted peacock from Kaothe, Kayatha, Dangwada, Nagda and Navdatoli are worth mentioning. While the Kaothe example is over a Savalda Ware, at other sites they are executed on Malwa ware. At the neighbouring site of Navdatoli peacock motifs are found in Malwa ware, cream-slipped ware, metallic ware and also in Jorwe ware.

At Chichali two specimens of peacock motifs painted in Malwa ware have been found - one on the belly portion of a thick red ware jar in frieze sandwitched between bold lines (fig. 2no.17). The intermittent gap between motifs have been filled up with suspended wavy festoons. Though no crest of the birds is depicted, the thick, unfurled plumage shown by seven by radiating lines bespeak the beauty of the bird and the aesthetic taste of the artist. The second specimen of this motif, also in frieze, found painted on a Malwa ware vase (fig. 2, no.11). Here the specimen is bit stylistic. The crest of the bird is shown with three "cross" marks emanating from the head in oblique fashion and the thick plumage is shown in the form of two triangles one within the other. The body of the peacock roughly in elongated triangular shape and is totally filled up. The types in the plumage are shown by small dots. Below the neck of the peacock is depicted radiating Sun.

III. INSECTS

The love for Nature, which fascinated and frightens as well, has led the Chalcolithic artists to portray its various elements with meticulous care and even insect like centipede and butterfly are found painted on their pottery.

A. Centipede

Navdatoli is the first site which has previously reported painted centipedes on black-on-red ware pottery. But from aesthetic point of view the specimen from Chichali on the same ware is more realistic (fig. 2 no.16). painted in black, on a thick red ware sherd the motif is in frieze (of which two are seen) and intervening space is filled up with radiating sun symbols. The body of the motif is half curled up and the legs, mouth and hind parts are perfectly delineated.

B. Butterfly

The only specimen of a butterfly painted in black on a pinkish red ware bowl comes from the Jorwe level at Chichali (fig. 2. no.10). Two solid convergent triangles form the wings of the butterfly. On the edge of each wing six radiating lines are executed. The motif rests above a bold line. The motif is not completed. Perhaps the artist has finished his work in haste failing to execute certain essential organs of this insect.

The faunal motifs, as evident from the Chalcolithic pottery at Chichali, mainly belonged to the Malwa and to some extent Jorwe period. the richness in the art form is no doubt indicative of prosperity which is clearly reflected from the material vestiges of the two periods. The construction of well defined mud structures with thatched roof and bamboo screens; vast array of antiquities in copper; microliths and objects of personal use like beads in semi-precious stones etc. in addition to a fairly good number of charred foodgrains viz. wheat, pulses and rice and good quantity of animal bones point towards a sound economy. The cultivation of rice testifies to a favourable climatic conditions with good amount of rainfall. The vastness of the faunal assemblage pained on pottery which comprises mainly antelopes and peacocks amongst others and the zoological remains thereof lends support to a favourable ecological set up during the Chalcolithic period.

So far as the stylistic rendition of the painted motifs at Chichali is concerned there are certain uniqueness. But for the peacocks and the butterfly all the motifs are drawn in line having hollowed body - with occasional hatching are in one specimen the body of an antelope filled up with dots in contrast to the evidences from neighbouring site like Navdatoli. The Chalcolithic site at Chichali flourished as a contemporaneus settlement of neighbouring Navdatoli during the hey days of the Chalcolithic period and the art style is in much refined form and the motifs bespeak themselves as the handiwork of perfect craftsmanship.

It is hard to ascertain he religious beliefs of any illiterate society. But there are certain elements which help the archaeologists to draw inferences based on parallels prevailing in the later periods. Example like the prominent genitals in antelops depicted on the pottery reflect some sort of a "libidual symbol" and hence be termed as an "epitome of fertility".

REFERENCES

1. Hultzsch, E, 1991, *Inscriptions of Asoka,*Corpus Inscriptionum Indicarum,Vol.I, New Delhi, pp.1–2.

2. Sali, S.A., 1986, *Daimabad, 1976–79,* MASI No. 83, New Delhi.

3. Dhavalikar, M.K., Shinde, V and Atre, Subhangana, 1990, *Excavations at Kaothe,* Pune.

4. Sankalia, H.D., Subbarao, B and Deo S.B., 1971 *Chalcolithic Navdatoli, Excavations at Navdatoli,* 1955–57, Pune.

5. Dhavalikar, M.K. and Ansari, Z.D., 1965, *Excavations at Kayatha,* Pune.

6. banerjee, N.R., 1986, *Nagda - 1955–57,* MASI No. 85, New Delhi.

7. Trivedi, H.V., 1962, "Excavations at Avra", *Journal of Madhya Pradesh Itihasa Parishad,* Vol. 4, pp.13–14, Bhopal.

8. Chakravarty, K.K., Wakankar, V.S. and Khare, M.D., 1989, *Dangwada Excavations,* Bhopal.

9. Sankalia, H.D., Ansari, Z.D. and Dhavalikar, M.K., 1988, *Excavations at Inamgaon.,* Pune.

10. Eeo, S.B. and Ansari Z.D., 1965, *Chalcolithic Chandoli,* Pune.

11. Deo, S.B., and Majumdar, G.G. 1969, *Songaon Excavations,* Pune.

12. Sankalia, H.D., Deo, S.B., Ansari, Z.D. and Ehrhardt, S., 1960, *From History to Pre-history at Nevasa, Pune.*

Excavation at Ojiyana

B.R. MEENA & ALOK TRIPATHI*

The excavation at Ahar, District Udaipur, Rajasthan, by R.C.Agrawal' (Agrawal 1954–55) brought to light a culture whose moorings were not known. It revealed the existence of an indigenous rural culture in eastern Rajasthan. The site was re-excavated by Department of Archaeology and Museums, Government of Rajasthan and Deccan College, Pune in 1961–62.[2] The culture first time noted here was termed as Ahar culture. Since then a large number of sites of this culture have been reported during subsequent explorations in Banas valley of Rajasthan. During third-second millenium BC, this culture had spread in a large area of Rajasthan and Madhya Pradesh, from Ahar in the East to Eran in the West and Ajmer in the North to Navdatoli in the South. Due to the main concentration o,f this culture in the Banas valley (fig. 1) in Rajasthan it is also termed as the Banas culture (Ansari and Dhavlikar 1975).

Later, excavations at two other sites in Rajasthan, Gilund[4] and Balathal[5] brought to light many important facts about this culture. Although, all the three sites are located on the eastern margin or the nucleus zone of this culture, very close to each other, yet they show some different patterns.

Material evidence of the extension of this culture in central India have also been reported in various excavations like Eran,[6] Distt. Sagar, Nagda,[7] and Kayatha,[8] Distt. Ujjain, Manoti[9], Distt. Mandsaur; Navdatoli,[10] Distt. West Nimar etc. Despite these explorations and excavations, so far, very little is known about this rural culture.

Last year, Jaipur circle of Archaeological Survey of India decided to carry out scientific investigations on a site of this less known and less studied Copper Age culture of Rajasthan. Ojiyana, a site unusually located in the hilly region of District Bhilwara, far away from three earlier excavated sites, was selected for this purpose.

The site was discovered in 1980[11] and reported by R.C.Agrawal.[12] It was reexamined and studied by the first author[13] during the systematic survey of this region[14]. The excavation was conducted, under the direction and codirection of the authors from January to April 2000, at this site located at the northem boundary of the Ahar culture area. The main aims of this excavation were a) to know the cultural sequence of the site, b) to know the reasons for this unusual settlement of Ahar culture in this hilly area and c) to know there interaction with other contemporary cultures, if they had, being situated on the peripheral region.

Ojiyana[15] (Lat. 25° 53' N, Long. 74° 21' E) is a small village located about 30 km south west of Beawar and 11

*Archaeological Survey of India, 70/140 Patel Marg, Mansarovar, Jaipur 302020

km north of Badnor, on Beawar-Bhilwara road. The ancient site lies on the slopes of a small hill (Fig. 2) situated towards north west of the present village. The hill running from south west to northeast rises up to the height of about 523 m from MSL and comes to an abrupt end at the highest point at north east.

At a little distance, to the north of it, runs other hills. Low areas between these hills get flooded in rainy season and form `pools of various dimensions. Being the encatchment area`,quite large and under rocky surface, the water remains in these pools for a couple of months.

District Bhilwara consists of an elevated plateau. The ranges of Aravalli hills intersect the district at several places. The scattered and low hill ridges generally run from the southwest to northeast. The general level which moderately slope towards north east hills of Aravalli series are generally barren hills. Vegetation in the area is generally poor although small patches of wooded area exist in these hilly portions. The hillocks covered with scanty trees and bushes are not exploitable. Forest of Bhilwara falls under subsidiary edaphic type of dry tropical forests. The plains, south and east of village Ojiyana, with a few hillocks jutting out here and there, slopes towards river Khari, a tributary of river Banas, which flows about 14 km south of the site.Vast low area to the north of Ojiyana also receives water from hilly area. A huge reservoir has been created by throwing a bund some times in the past. This low earthen bund veneered by rubble, runs parallel to Beawar Bhilwara road. Over the centuries water running down from hill slopes has brought and deposited a thick layer of rich soil in lower areas. Chalcolithic people preferred this hillock skirted by low lying fertile land for their settlement.

This unusual location of the site on hill slope makes Ojiyana, unique among other sites of Ahar culture which flourished in river valleys. So far all other known sites of Ahar culture are found located in plains near the banks of rivers, mainly Banas and its tributaries. Some of the Ahar culture sites have also been found near the banks of Chambal and Narmada. Before excavation, the entire hill strewn with stones rolling down from the top was thoroughly explored and the northern slope of the hill was selected for the excavation. The site was systematically surveyed and a contour plan with 2m interval got prepared.

Initially four trenches, No. 1 to 4, measuring 5 x 5 m were laid in two rows on a comparatively flat area, near a rain gully, towards the seasonal reservoir and lower fertile area. Soon after removal of upper layers, structures of phase I and II were unearthed and further digging had to be stopped in these trenches. Later, six more trenches, No. 5 to 10, were laid down to slope, to the north of earlier trenches. Of these only four, No. 5 to 8, could be excavated down to phase IIb level. Digging in trench No. 9 and 10 not done except removal of uppermost loose soil, due to shortage of time.

The excavation revealed a thick cultural deposit and rich antiquities of Ahar culture. Natural soil could be reached in a small area between trench 3 and 4. The total deposit of Ahar culture at this site, about 7.5 m is, perhaps, maximum among so far excavated sites of Ahar culture. Antiquities found here include definite evidence of its relations with the Harappans and perhaps with other chalcolithic cultures. This single culture deposit is divided in three phases, on the basis of changes in structural activities as well as in pottery.

White painted black and red ware users came and settled down on the rock near the fertile land. Probably they were farmers and cultivated low land between hill ranges of Aravalli. In phase I thin mud floors were made right above the natural rock. Due to limited space no complete plan of any house could be unearthed but a thick debris of sun dried mud bricks makes it clear that the mud bricks were used as construction material. Thin bands of ash under the thick bands of water borne sand and collapsed debris of mud brick bats also suggest that the rain water, flowing down the hill slopes caused damage to these structures.

The white painted black and red ware, the most distinctive pottery of Ahar culture.,is present in this phase. Paintings in white were executed before firing so that some times only the impression of designs or negatives are left. Paintings are executed on exterior. Frequency of bowls, which are most recurrent type at Ahar,is comparatively less in this phase. White paintings are also executed on the interior of the bowls. The other important ware is black slipped ware. The main associated ware in early levels is medium to thick red ware of coarse fabric.l, Surface of these pots is generally rough and clay contains mica particles. The frequency of coarse red ware is

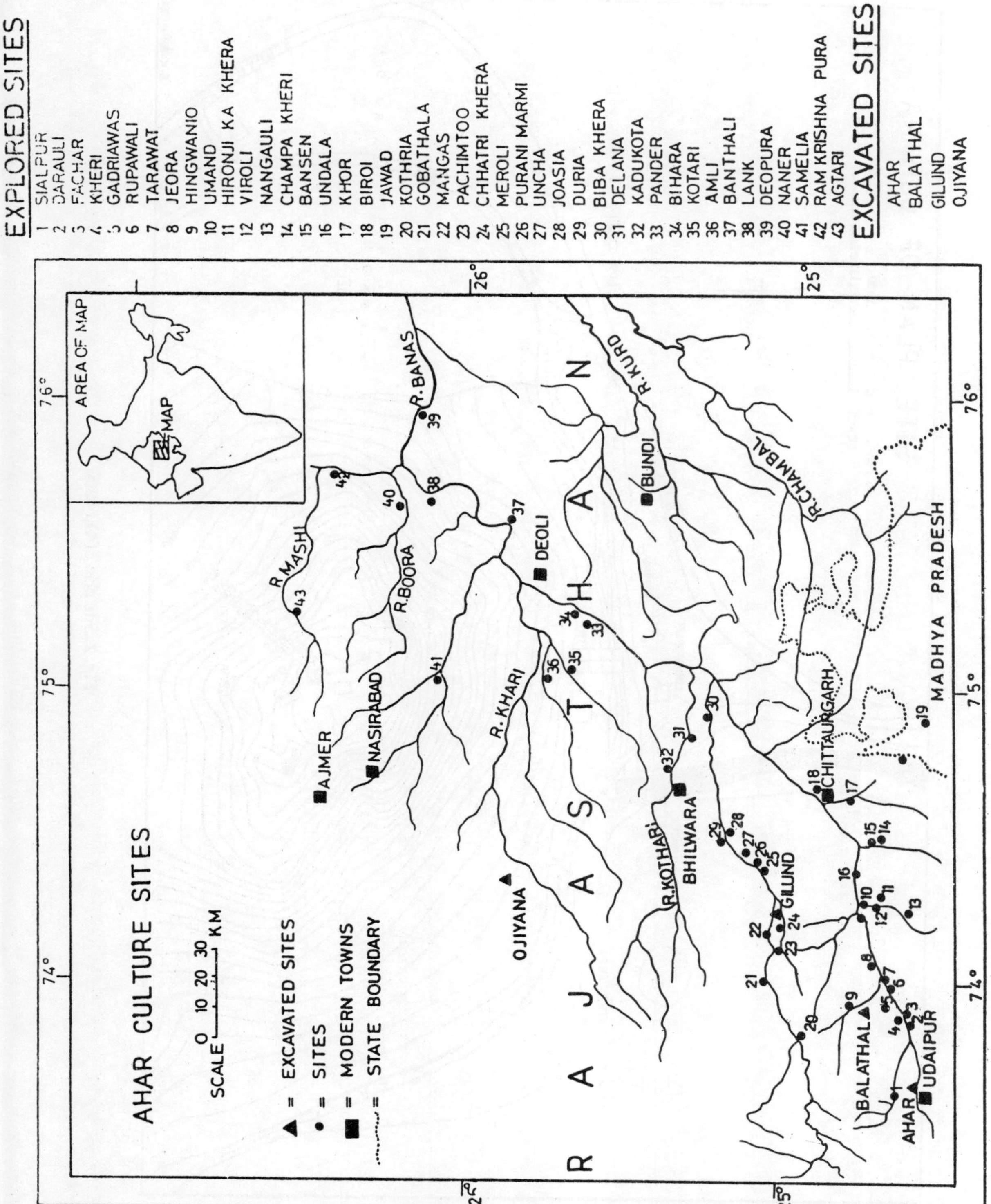

Fig. 1. Distribution of Ahar culture sites in Banas Valley.

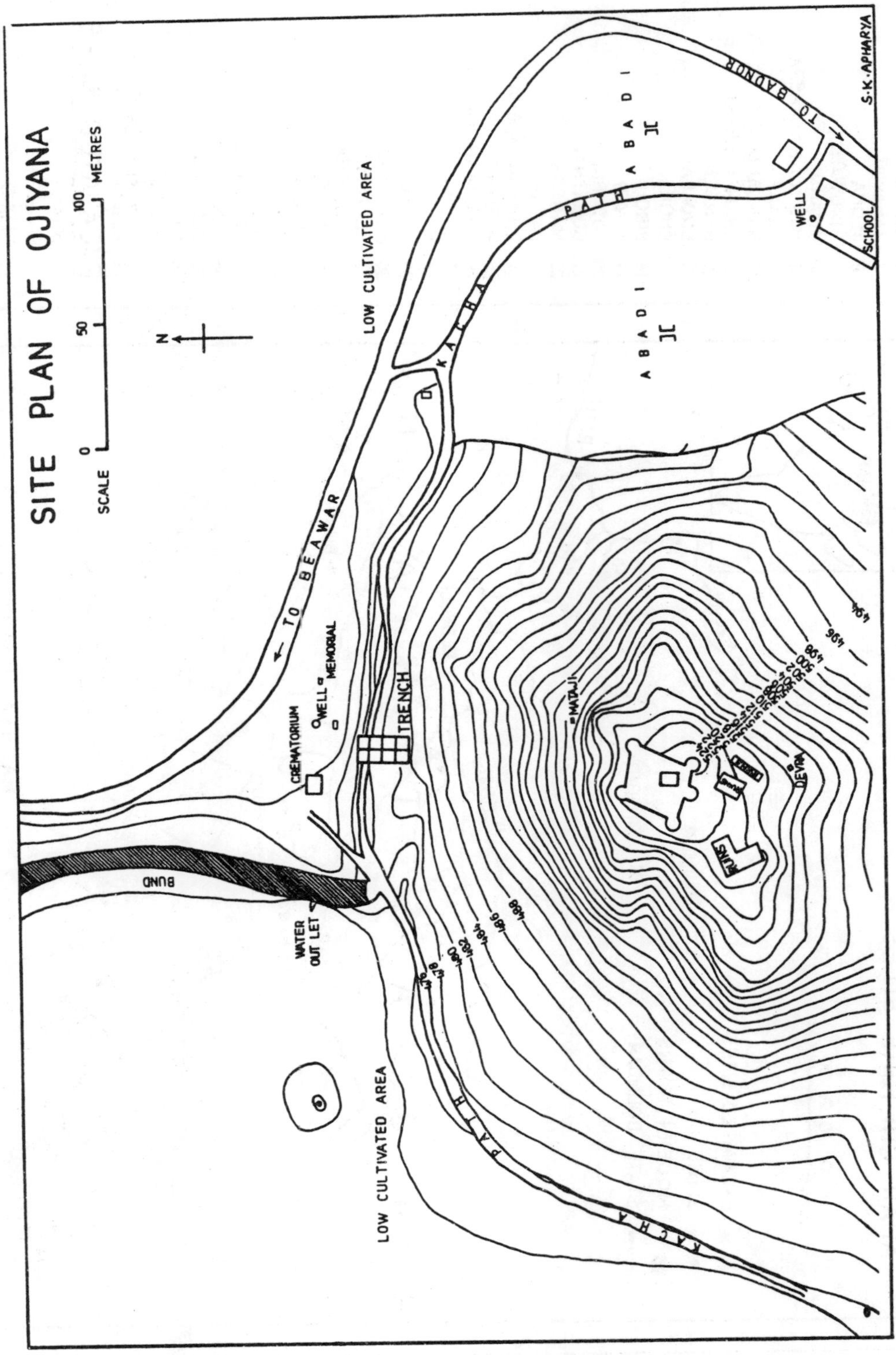

Fig. 2. Site plan of Ojiyana.

maximum which continue as the main associated ware in all the phases. Besides, a few sherds of black ware and grey ware were also found.

Phase II was the phase of prosperity which continued for a long period. It is further sub-divided in two structural phases IIa and IIb. In this phase big houses were built of stones. No complete plan of any structure of phase IIa is found due to limited area available for excavation. A thick stone wall of a granary was unearthed along the section facing south. The wall was nicely plastered with mud. The structure was destroyed in a devastating fire in which the plaster of the wall got baked. In this fire also got burnt the stock of wheat stored here. A large quantity of charged wheat was found on the floor of the granary.

Sometime after the fire another phase of building activity began. In phase IIb the thickness of stone wall was reduced and multi-chambered houses were built. A big house complex was unearthed in this phase (P1. 1). This house complex consists of a long narrow room, four chambers on a platform, an open courtyard in front of them and two rooms, all surrounded by a boundary wall. The house complex faces north. The floor of the long room is prepared by ramming small stones. This exceptionally long and very narrow room was probably used for storage. Its walls were plastered with mud and it had thatched roof. Along its northern side were made four chambers divided by mud brick partition walls. These partition walls of single brick thickness are made in stretcher bond. Two of the chambers were empty where as the third was meant for keeping kitchen goods, utensils and for preparation of food like grinding grains, etc. A saddle quern is found in situ on the floor of this chamber. A rectangular stone was also kept next to it as a seat for its user.

The last chamber is the kitchen with three *chulhas* built in a row. These *chulhas* of small, medium and big size were made along the back wall. The ash was still preserved in *chulhas* and on kitchen floor. First two chambers were open towards courtyard whereas the third and fourth chambers were partially covered with mud brick wall and had a narrow opening. Towards north of these chambers is an open courtyard. It was surrounded by a boundary wall made of random rubble. Along the northern wall was constructed one long or two small rooms. The entrance to the complex is in the northern wall.

The black-and-red ware remains the distinctive pottery but a clear change in quality and shapes is noticed. Deep straight sided bowls are now found in good number. Narrow and high neck globular pots both, painted with white and unpainted are also present. Thick storage jars of red ware with applique designs (Pl. 2) are also found in good quantity. They seem to be made locally and contain large quantity of mica. Sometimes these mica nodules are quite big and suggest the clay was not sieved to remove these nodules and other impurities. Black slipped ware and coarse red ware remain, the main associated wares. Other associated wares are red slipped ware, tan ware, burnished and unburnished black ware. The pots are decorated with paintings, incision, pinching and applique designs. Black-and-red ware pots are painted with white whereas other techniques of decorations are used on medium to thick pots of other wares.

This phase is very rich in antiquites also. An exceptionally large number of terracotta bulls are found. They are both naturalistic as well as of stylized. These figurines present a great variety in shapes and sizes. Blocked legged figurines have prominent hump and long horns.White paintings on some of these bulls is noteworthy. With large quantity and great variety it can not be ruled out that Ojiyana was a main centre of manufacture of such figurines and bull cult was predominant here. These painted bulls not only throw new light on the creativity of copper age people of Ojiyana but also seems indicating towards influence or interaction with some other contemporary culture. They also reflect their beliefs. Most probably these paintings were of ritualistic nature and these bulls were the cult objects.The most outstanding discovery from this phase is terracotta cow figurines. It is noteworthy that the cow figurines discovered for the first time from chalcolithic levels in India.[16]

Another outstanding discovery is a big decorated Harappan bead of faience. Similar beads have been found at Harappa[17] and Mohenjodaro. Finding of this Harappan bead at Ahar culture site leaves no doubt that both the contemporary cultures had some interaction.

A small chopper (P1. 3) made of thin sheet of copper is an important antiquity of Ahar culture. Similar choppers of copper have also been found at Balathal, Kuntasi, Khurdi, Chithwari, etc.'[18]

A good number of beads of carnelian, faience, shell, steatite, stone and decorated beads of terracotta of various shapes and sizes are found. Bangles of copper and shell and a ring of copper are other noteworthy ornaments. Toy cart wheels with incised spokes, spindle whorls, hop-scotchs, pendants, sling balls are the main finds of terracotta. Saddle querns, mullers, hammer stones of quartz, ringstones etc. are some other antiquities of this phase.

Phase III is the phase of decline.[19] No complete plan of any house of this phase is unearthed. The floors in the houses were made of fine pinkish clay. Postholes on the thick floors show that the superstructures of these houses were made of wattle and daub. These houses got burnt frequently. Due to one such fire mud plastered over the reeds got baked. These lumps bearing reed marks,give definite evidence of superstructure of the houses of the last phase.The black-and-red wares continue in this phase also but the frequency got reduced. This black and red ware is different from the black and red ware of phase II. The carinated shallow bowl is the most distinct type in this phase. Other associated wares also continue but a sort of decline is marked in them also.

This region is rich in copper. The copper is found here as chalcopyrite, disseminated in schist and phyllites. Slag heaps found in Bhilwara district suggest that the copper was extracted in this region since antiquity. Besides copper, garnet, which was one time much reputed as a gem stone, is found in abundance nearby. TheAravalli schist contain crystals of garnet. Perhaps the mineral wealth of this hilly region might have been the attraction for copper age people of Ahar culture to settle down in this hilly area.

Acknowledgements

We are thankful to Shri R.C.Agrawal, excavator of Ahar, for his guidance and encouragement throughout. Thanks are also due to Dr.S.P.Gupta, Chairman of Indian Archaeological Society for examining the excavated material and offering his valuable comments. Authors are also thankful to the Director General and Director (Excavations & Explorations), Archaeological Survey of India for their valuable suggestions and encouragement and their colleagues namely S/Shri Kanwar Singh, Brij Raj Singh, S.C. Gupta, S.K. Acharya and V.K.Uppal of Jaipur Circle of Archaeological Survey of India for making this excavation a success.

REFERENCES

1. Indian Archaeology 1954–55-A Review, New Delhi, pp. 14–15.
2. Sankalia, H.D., Deo, S.B. and Ansari, Z.D., 1969, Excavations at Ahar (Tambavati) 1961–62, Pune.
3. Ansari, Z.D. and Dhavlikar, M.K., 1975, Excavations at Kaytha, Pune.
4. Indian Archaeology 1959–60 A Review, New Delhi, p. 41–46.
5. Indian Archaeology 1962–63 A Review, New Delhi, p. 18.
6. Ghose A. (Ed.), 1989, Encyclopaedia of Indian Archaeology, Vol.2, New Delhi, pp. 134–136.
7. Banerjee, N.R., 1996, Nagda 1955–57, MASI 85, Archaeological Survey of India, New Delhi.
8. Ansari et. al. 1975, op. Cit.
9. Indian Archaeology 1958–59 A Review, New Delhi..
10. Sankalia, H.D., Subbarao, B. and Deo, S.B., 1958, The Excavation at Maheshwar and Navdatoli 1952–53, Poona; Sankalia, H.D., Deo S.B. and Ansari, Z.D., 1971, Chalcolithic Navdatoli The Excavations at Navdatoli, 1957–59, Poona.
11. The site was discovered in July, 1980 and published in Hindustan Times of 3rd August, 1980, personal communication with R.C. Agrawal.
12. Agrawal, R.C., 1981, Recent Explorations in Rajasthan, Man and Environment, Vol. V, Pune, p.62.

13. IndianArchaeology 1984-85 A Review, New Delhi, p.68.
14. Meena, B.R., 1986, Recent Exploration in the valley of Khari and Mansi rivers Rajasthan: With Special Reference to the Chalcolithic Sites, Purattava, New Delhi, pp. 17–18.
15. In old maps of Survey of India, the name of the village is spelled as 'Ojena'.
16. Although H.N.Singh in his book 'History and Archaeology of Black and Red Ware' has mentioned cow at Lothal but there is no such finding reported by the excavator in his report.
17. Vats, Madho Sarup, 1974, Excavations at Harappa, Varanasi, Vol.I, pp. 404–405; Vol. II, P1. CXXXIII Fig. 9d, e.
18. Information supplied by Shri R.C.Agrawal.
19. Meena, B.R. and Alok Tripathi, 2000, Rajasthan main ek adwitiya tamrayugeen sthal Ojiyana, Rajasthan Sujas, Directorate of Information & Public Relations, Jaipur.

The Ancient City of Sravasti: its Significance on the Urbanisation of North India

TAKAHIRO TAKAHASHI, TAIZO YAMAOKA, FUMITAKA YONEDA AND AKINORI UESUGI*

General outline of the habitational history of Sravasti

Kansai University led by Professor Yoshinori Aboshi (now Professor Emeritus) and Professor Takahiro Takahashi conducted nine-seasons excavations at the ancient city of Sravasti (Maheth), which is located in District Sravasti, Uttar Pradesh (Figs. 1 and 2). Although the significance of the site was recognised as early as the 19th century by British archaeoologists and was augmented by a small-scale excavation by Dr. K.K. Sinha in 1959 (Sinha 1967), there has not been enough attention paid to the site thereafter. Kansai University, in succession to the excavations at Jetavana (Saheth) from 1986 to 1989[1], commenced an excavation from 1991. As nine seasons have been spent for excavations, the importance of the site was increasingly re-affirmed by the results of excavations, although the work remains small-scale as the site is considerably large. In this short paper, we shall draw attentions of scholars by pointing out several aspects of the site.

As broadly known, Sravasti was one of the ancient cities of Kosala Kingdom during the lifetime of Buddha. The great prosperity of the city is described plentifully in Buddhist texts, and the city is associated with Buddha in those texts. A well known story of the donation of Jetavana by Anathapindika, a wealthy merchant of the city, to Buddha testifies its economic prosperity which was maintained by a growth of trade.

The site is surrounded by an earthen rampart, the circumference of which measures 5.23km. The area which is demarcated by the rampart amounts to 160 hectares. The shape of the site shows a crescent plan, facing an old riverbed of ancient Achiravati.

Whereas brick structures of Period IV afterwards show upheaval of ground forming mounds; Most part of the site is found to be considerably flat evenly, where successive floorlevels seem to have been uniformly formed over the site through Periods I to III, as indicated by our excavation areas. By the time when burnt bricks were introduced to buildings in Period IV, wood was a dominant construction material in the city, without leading to the formation of mounds. The fact that prominent mounds are more visible in the southern part of the site than in the northern part of the site indicates that the southern part of the site remained habited until later times than the northern half of the site. This observation has been confirmed by excavations.

The excavations by Kansai University was conducted at four points viz. Areas A to D (Fig. 2). Area A was located around the Suraj Kund which was in the northern

Takahiro Takahashi, Professor of Kansai University (Art history); Taizo Yamaoka, Professor of Kansai University (Art history); Fumitaka Yoneda, Assistant Professor of Kansai University (Archaeology); Akinori Uesugi, PhD student of Kansai University (Archaeology). All are the members of the Joint Excavation Project at Sravasti of the Archeological Survey of India and Kansai University, Osaka, Japan.

part of the site; Area B was on the rampart to the east of Area A; Area C was to the south of Area B; and Area D was situated in the western part of the southern half of the site. By the excavations, comparative data on the stratigraphy of the site was obtained.

The excavations revealed six cultural periods, as described below. As no Carbon14 dating has been available so far, the dating of each cultural period is based on characteristic objects in each period mostly, pottery (Tab. 1).

Table 1.

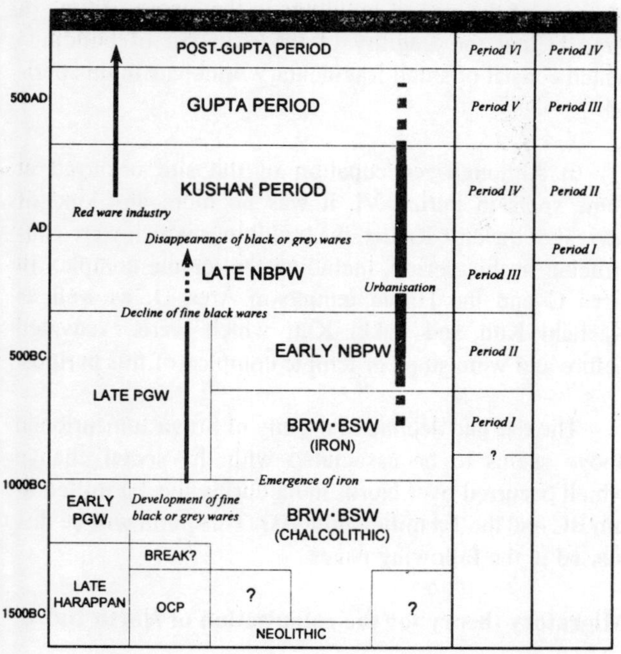

Period I	BRW/BSW Phase, the 8th to 7th century BC[2].
Period II	Early NBPW Phase, the 6th to 4th century BC.
Period III	Late NBPW Phase, the 3rd to 1st century BC.
Period IV	Kushan Phase, the 1st to 3rd century AD.
Period V	Gupta Phase, the 4th to 6th century AD.
Period VI	Post-Gupta Phase, the 7th to 10th century AD.

Period I, which is represented by BRW/BSW ceramics (figs. 3 and 4), is confirmed only in the lowest level of Area A. The cultural contents of Period II are observed in all areas, though there are some indications of time lag from area to area in the pottery types[3]; Area A produced more plentifully older types of NBPW (fig. 5), while other areas are represented by new types of NBPW, though both types are within the fine group of NBPW. Period III is also constantly found through all the excavated areas (fig. 7). Remains of Period IV is quite limited in Area A, but more plentiful in Area D in the southern half of the site. Period V is represented only in Area D. Period Vl, which seems to be an occupation after the decline of the city, distributed over the site, forming mounds here and there. As a matter of fact, the occupation of Period Vl is represented not by habitational buildings but by temple complexes as unearthed in Areas C and D.

The excavation at Area A yielded successive floor-levels from Periods I to III, showing a stable development of habitation. Period I is represented by only one floor-level, indicating that the occupation in this period was short lived. Period II, in which NBPW became dominant pottery, has several floor-levels, having in each level many pits containing pottery, ash, charcoal, and animal bones. What is noteworthy to state here is the existence of a working place of iron-tool-making, glass-bead-making, semi-precious stone bead-making and bone tool-making during Period III. The working place seems to have been maintained for a considerable period of time, as it is represented by several floor-levels. In Period IV, the habitational activity decreased its size to a great extent, and Period V witnessed a total desertion of habitation. In Period Vl, the area was resettled to some extent, but it was not a kind of urban character.

In Area B, which was laid across the earthen rampart at a point to the east of Area A, the excavation was aimed to confirm the stratigraphy and date of the rampart The excavation, has revealed that the rampart was constructed in Period III and was maintained until the end of Period IV. It seems likely that the rampart did not function during Period V, as there is no trace of maintenance on the rampart and no object assignable to Period V.

Area C is found to be extensively occupied in Period Vl, though the buildings of this period belong to a religious complex, not to urban settlement. It seems likely, judging from a limited excavation of layers below the remains of Period Vl, that this area was widely occupied in Periods III and IV as well, whereas the remains of Periods II are scarce and those of Period I is almost negligible.

The similar situation is found in Area D as well; the remains of Period II is limited, and there was vigorous activity in Periods III and IV; finally a brick-built Hindu temple was constructed in the area during Period Vl. It is much worthwhile noting that there was evidence of a long and vigorous occupation during Period IV; the accumulation of layers, reaching to about 3m in thickness with more than fifteen floor-levels. This is a clear contrast to the Area A where there was a limited occupation in Period IV. Besides, the occupation was maintained until Period V in this area, though decreasing its size through the lapse of time. There seems to have been a considerable decrease in the size of occupation in Period V leading to a total desertion of the area. The Hindu temple was constructed after the desertion of the urban habitation in this area in Period V, that is, the temple was not in association with the urban activity.

Comparing the results from four areas, several observations on the formation and the decline of the city can be pointed out.

1) The occupation at the site began in the northern half of the area, especially in Area A, in Period I. The first occupation seems to have been on small-scale.

2) In Period II, ranging from the 6th to 4th century BC, the occupation was spread over a much broader area of the site. Probably, in this period, most area of the site was occupied more or less, indicating that a great expansion of habitation occurred, coinciding with the development of the city.

3) The development of the city was stably in progress in Period III; the establishment of the city-structure was symbolised with the construction of the rampart which demarcated the area of the city from outside and which demanded a great deal of labour. It seems likely that the city came to its peak during this period.

4) In Period IV, there was a partial decline of urban habitation; there was a shift of densely settled area towards the southern half of the city, whereas the occupation in the northern half of the site came to be abandoned or to decrease its size.

5) Even in the southern half of the city, a considerable decline of habitation occurred in Period V, consequently leading to the total desertion of habitation by the end of this period. The process is quite visible in the decrease of the size of buildings in the elapse of time in Area D and the fragility of the structure of buildings which consist of small fragmentary brickbats in this period.

6) Although reoccupation of the site occurred at some spots in Period Vl, it was no more any kind of revival of the city. Rather, the buildhings which were constructed in this period, including the temple complex in Area C and the Hindu temple in Area D, as well as Kachchi Kuti and Pakki Kuti which were excavated before and were stupa or temple complex of this period.

The rise and decline of the city of Sravasti mentioned above seems to be associated with the social change which occurred over North India during the 1st millennium BC and the 1st millennium AD. This point will be discussed in the following pages.

Migratory theory for the colonisation of North India

It appears that the first occupation at Sravasti took place around the 7th or 8th century BC, judging from the cultural contents at the lowest level. The accumulation of deposits of Period II begins just over the floor of Period I which was on the natural soil, indicating that the occupation of Period I was not so long.

If we accept this date of the first occupation at Sravasti, what will be the focus of our discussion here? As a matter of fact, in the region along the Ganges River, the human occupation goes back to the neolithic stage during the 3rd and the later half of the 2nd millennium BC, except for Palaeolithic and Mesolithic human occupation, and a continuous cultural development occurred

Table 2.

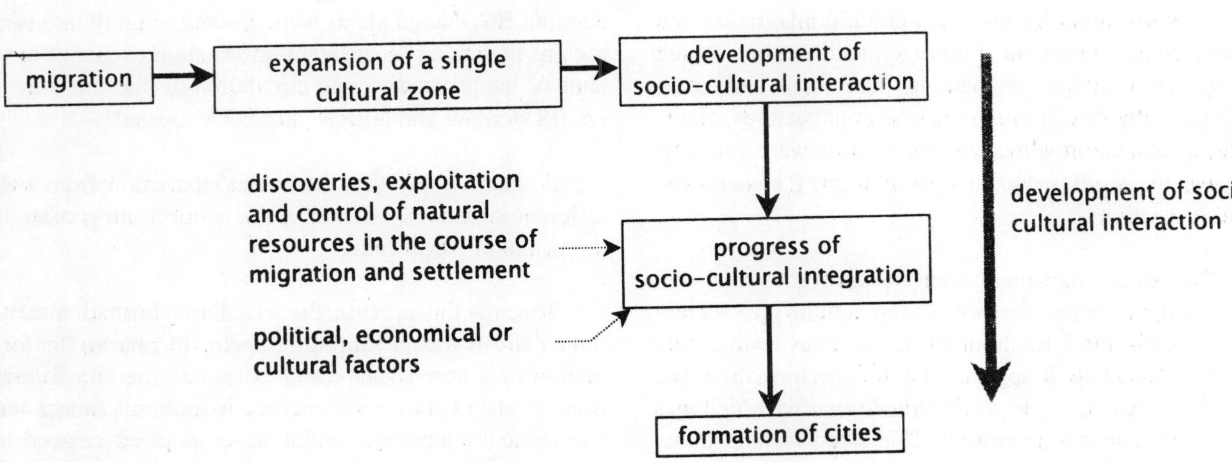

during chalcolithic and iron-using stages. Rice cultivation was adopted as early in the Neolithic stage, alongwith domestication of animals. On the basis of iron technology Ganga basin was able to develop its own cultural complex. In terms of cultural equipment, BRW was one of the most characteristic cultural traits in this region. BSW also appeared in the Chalcolithic stage along with BRW. As far as the ceramic industry is concerned, the development of culture in this region was linear in its course.

The important aspect of the Gangetic Chalcolithic and iron cultures is that they spread over the eastern half of Ganga plains during the Chalcolithic stage (fig. 8). This dispersal was extended as far as the doab region; this is testified in the excavations at Atranjikhera, Noh, Jakhera, Allahapur, etc. Although some scholoars argues that BRW at these sites came from Banas (Ahar) Culture in southern Rajasthan (Gaur 1969), we shall insist that the dispersal of BRW culture occurred from the lower middle Gangetic region, as argued by K.N. Dikshit (Dikshit 1969)[4]. By the analysis of pottery, the origin of BRW in the doab region should be placed in the east, not in the southwest. The excavations at Sringaverapura (78–84) by Lal and Dikshit also confirmed this hypothesis.

It seems likely from excavations at Neolithic sites in the middle and lower-middle Gangetic regions that the origin of BRW goes back to the Neolithic stage and that BRW developed through time, changing into fine ware during the Chalcolithic stage. On the basis of this observation, it can be argued that the Chalcolithic people using BRW occupied Gangetic plains during the later half of the 2nd millennium BC.

This expansion of BRW people seems to have continued in the early half of the 1st millennium BC. Besides, archaeological evidence attests the presence of iron by this time. It seems likely that the introduction of iron tools helped people to clear the vegetation which covered Ganga basin. It can be supposed that the settlement at Sravasti occurred around this period.

One of the noticeable results of the migration for the people may have been a discovery of various metal and mineral resources, which could have been exploited for, more importantly, trade. Some of the resources could have been found in rare availablility at limited localities, making them utilised as trading goods or prestige goods, the distribution of which might be controlled or limited by some kind of social class. Iron ore and semiprecious stones can be regarded as those among such resources.

Another important aspect of this expansion of people is the formation of a network which connected different regions in and around Ganga basin. As far as the content of material culture is concerned, the BRW sites have a cultural uniformity. From the 1st millennium BC, on the BRW/BSW sites formed a single cultural zone, sharing uniform cultural traits. This led the society form a continuous cultural interaction through network, creating a socio-cultural integration along Gangetic plains.

This socio-cultural integration through the maintenance of inter-regional network seems to have been one of the most influential aspects on the social transformation of North India. By the socio-cultural integration, the society came to need one or more regional centre/s, which might act as a knot connecting both local and inter-regional networks. Through these regional centres, natural resources, commodities and information were transmitted over the regions which were tied up by a socio-cultural interaction.

The social uneveness went towards the reinforcement of the function of regional centres to tie up a society and towards the formation of social elites with social power in a society. It appears that the city formation was one of the results of the social transformation which was backed up cultural integration. This socio-cultural transformation by social marked a major phase in urbanisation of the Gangetic baisn.

While the BRW/BSW- people were expanding over the eastern half of Ganga plains, another important factor of material culture, that is, PGW came to the scene around the same time. As far as our present knowledge of researches shows, PGW appeared in a few centuries of the later half of the 2nd millennium BC in the eastern Punjab (Joshi) 1993). On the basis of the excavation at Bhagwanpura, it seems likely that the PGW-using people lived in that region side by side with the Late Harappan people. The PGW-using people had a different cultural tradition from that of the Late Harappan, such as ceramic industry, and habitaional buildings of wooden huts.

Although the scale of settlements of the PGW-using people and the area in which they settled during this period are yet to be further excavated, the following some centuries of the 1st millennium BC witnessed an expansion of their settlements (fig. 9). With this expansion of their socio-cultural area, they came to have a contact with the BRW/BSW-using people. Some aspects of this cultural contact can be observed in the mutual influences on their ceramic industry and the formation of uniform cultural equipments; except for the differentiation of their fine ware industries.

PGW also formed another cultural interaction. The fact that the same form, shape and painted designs which were the results of the wide-spread exchange of information on the making technique indicates that an information net-work system existed in the PGW distribution zone as well. Thus, during the early half of the 1st millennium BC, Ganga plains were divided roughly into two regions in which two different information exchange systems of the production and circulation of the fine wares; i.e. BRW/BSW and NBPW, and PGW existed.

It seems likely that the social/interaction from two different directions resulted in the cultural integration of the whole of North India.

Through this process, the social transformation mentioned above was given more impetus to gear up the formation of a new social complexity, i.e., the city formation. As stated above, the increase in cultural contact and subsequent integration might have required centres to control and maintain the contact and the integration of the various regions.

This process of social transformation towards the city formation progressed to a greater extent during the middle of the 1st millennium BC, i.e., PGW/NBPW phase (fig. 1o). It seems that there appeared several cities in Ganga basin by this time, as testified by both literary and archaeological evidences.

Furthermore, the process continued towards the end of the 1st millennium BC; then the process came to its peak, fueled by the greater development of trade with Central Asia, West Asia, and even the Mediterreanean region through various channels of trade both on land and by sea. The great prosperity of the cities of North India has been attested by many archaeological excavations.

As stated above, the urbanisation of North India began with the activation of migration of people over North India, consequently leading to the constant socio-cultural contacts and integration between regions in North India. The urbanisation process reached to its climax with the formation of states and the great development of trade, which finally covered the whole of the subcontinent.

Urbanisation and formation of a city at Sravasti

Sravasti is not out of this urbanisation process caused by the socio-cultural integration. Immediately after the first settlement at the site, Sravasti became involved in the social transformation in North India, resulting in the expansion of the settlement during Period II. Rather, there is the most probability that the first settlement at this site occupied some position either in political or economic background of the North Indian society, as this site was located in a strategic point, which connected the Gangetic plain and the Himalayan region, and which was located on the main east-west route, *Uttarapatha*. It seems likely that the significance of Sravasti as a city should be sought as an eminent trading post in the northern tip of the Gangetic plain.

Based on a fact that cities played a siginificant role in forming and maintaining socio-cultural contacts and integration, it becomes quite clear that Sravasti was the largest centre of the contacts and integration of the southern foothills of the Himalaya. That is, Sravasti gave a cultural atomosphere of North India to this region, by assimilating itself to the culture of Gangetic plains. The fact that NBPW, a characteristic fine ware of North India, which was based on a skillful technique of modelling, surface treatment and firing and which seems to have signified an aspect of the cultural entity of North India, was abundantly found at Sravasti, indicates that Sravasti introduced informations of the techniques of production of NBPW immediately after its creation in the eastern half of North India and was a regional centre for the production, consumption and circulation of NBPW in the southern foothills of the Himalaya.

This constant cultural interaction with North India and North-west India was one of the most influential factors to the development of the city of Sravasti. That is, the impetus of the urbanisation was originated from the cultural interaction with other parts of Gangetic plains. This cultural contact can be attested in every aspect of material culture. More fundamentally, the socio-political and economic impetus for urbanisation was also trasmitted through the channel of cultural contacts in North India. After the first settlement at Sravasti set the trend for a cultural interaction with North and North-west India, until the decline of the city.

In relation to the cultural contact and interaction outside the BRW/BSW and NBPW zone, it is much interesting to note that there was a cultural amalgmation between the PGW distribution zone and the NBPW distribution zone. The evidence for this phenomenon can be found in two points; first, there were mutual influences between them in terms of forms and shapes of pottery; secondly PGW was imported into the NBPW distribution zone though in a much limited way. The former point became visible in the early few centuries of the 1st millennium BC after the PGW extended its distribution zone into the doab region from the eastern Punjab. Some forms of BRW were introduced into the PGW assemblage in this period. Regarding the latter point, discoveries of PGW have been reported from several sites in the NBPW distribution zone[5]. Although some of the sites are much dubious for their identification as PGW, the evidence from Sravasti clearly indicates that PGW was imported into this site (Sinha 1967). Besides, what would be interesting is that some specimens of imitation of PGW are discovered from Sravasti (RP1 124 in Fig. 4/5).[6]

They are slight different from genuine PGW in terms of shape, surface treatment, and firing, but have black painting on the surface. Since it is highly probable that whether they were made by local people, it can be suggested that some demand for the PGW or imitated PGW existed even in the NBPW distribution zone. This fact indicates the existence of an information exchange and a cultural interaction between the PGW and NBPW distribution zones.

Summing up the discussions above, it becomes clear that the whole North India became linked of information-exchange and trade, with subdivisions based on various aspects of material culture. This system accelerated the socio-cultural integration of North India.

Sravasti occupies a unique position in this exchange and interaction system. It is located on the border between the PGW and NBPW distribution zones and on the significant route towards the Himalayan region. In this term, Sravasti was a place to which various information and commodities were brought from various regions. It is strongly suggested that the cause for the beginning of the formation of the city should be found in this point. At the present condition of our knowledge, the cultural interaction with the Himalayan region is yet to be clear, but reaching up to the site of Kapilavastu, settlements in Ganga basins built up a stronghold for its cultural contacts with distant regions.

The decline of the city of Sravasti should also be considered in terms of the socio-cultural interaction and integration in North India. In general, it has been argued that the North Indian society faced an economical stagnation which was caused by the invasion of Ephthalite (White Hun) and by the decline of the Indo-Roman trade from the middle of Gupta rule on. According to the economic stagnation, the regional structucture of North India was forced to be changed and reorganised. The former widely integrated socio-economic entity was divided up into several smaller regional units. Thus, it is clear that a strong socio-cultural integration, which was based on a wide socio-cultural interaction, disappeared due to the decline of the economy. The economic decline caused a disintegration of the political unity as well.

As stated above, the decline of the city of Sravasti occurred around the 3rd or 4th century AD prior to the general decline of the urban society in North India. As a matter of fact, it becomes clear on the basis of the description of Fa-hien who travelled in North India in the beginning of the 5th century AD that the whole part of the region of the foothills of the Himalaya, like Kapilavastu, Kushinagara as well as Sravasti, had been already devastated in terms of population. On the basis of this fact, it can be supposed that the foothill region of the Himalaya started to decline in general, as early as the 4th century AD; this observation is reinforced by the archaeological evidence as well. The archaeological evidence from Sravasti accords with this regional situation.

On the basis of these evidences, it can be said that the urban society of North India came to be modified in part as early as the 4th century AD. It is probable that the disintegration of the society occurred due to some reasons, either political, economic or cultural. Sravasti was one of the cities which were devastated in this period. Based on consideration of the fact that the cities in North India were based for their existence on the role as regional centres to connect different regions; the factor which caused desertion of city should be searched for in the decline of the regional interaction. Since the excavations at Sravasti reveal that the habitation suddenly decreased its size in the later part of the Kushan Period, it can be supposed that some kind of factor to make urban inhabitants leave quite quickly occurred in this period. Such a sudden desertion of the city implies a large scale evacuation of inhabitants, not a gradual decrease of population. A picture which can be drawn by this situation might be that the inhabitants were forced to leave by a political power which controlled this city. This is a matter which has to be discussed later.

Tentative conclusion

In this short paper, we have attempted to discuss the formation of the city of Sravasti in terms of socio-cultural interaction and integration of Gangetic plains, starting from active migration of people along the region to the decline of the cultural integration which caused the devastation of the city of Sravasti.

In order to reconstruct the process of urbanisation in North India, the method of settlement archaeology seems to be quite useful. The detailed study of artefacts is also relevant, based on a hypothesis that any kind of artefacts were endowed with some socio-cultural codes, which enable us to reconstruct a given society by archaeological evidence. In order to trace the process of urbanisation, cultural interaction seem to be one of the most influential factors.

This paper is an attempt to draw some attentions of scholars to the study of artefacts from a viewpoint of socio-cultural interaction and integration which could be partly reflected in various attributes of artefacts, on the basis of the evidence from Sravasti. We would like to emphasise the necessity to interpret attributes of artefacts from some hypothetical perspective which is to be examined by further studies.

Acknowledgement

The authors would like to express gratitude to Dr. K.N. Dikshit who recommended us to publish this paper. We are also grateful to Dr. R.S. Bisht from the central office of ASI, and Dr. K.K. Mohammad, D.K. Ambastha, D.K. Singh, and N.K. Sinha from Excavations Branch III, ASI who assisted and advised us during the excavations at Sravasti.

NOTES

[1]A full report of the Jetavana Excavations was published in 1997 (Aboshi and Sonoda ea.,1 997).

[2]The absolutre dating for each period is determined based on the data from other sites.

Regarding the date of BRW/BSW, it is generally suggested that BRW/BSW appeared in the lower-middle Gangetic plains (present Bihar), and then dispersed westwards to the doab region. The authors of this paper believe that the BRW/BSW in the doab region were brought from the eastern region, not from the south, that is, Banas culture.

[3]On the basis of the typological analysis of NBPW, it can be suggested that those from Area A show older elements, and those from other areas have relatively later elements. The detailed discussion on the typology of NBPW will be made on another occasion. What we would like to point out here is that the later group of fine NBPW of Early NBPW phase shows elements which become more eminent in the Late NBPW phase. The earlier group consisted of elements which cannot be observed in the Late NBPW phase.

[4]Although the shapes of BRW in the doab is quite similar to that of Banas culture, the existence of dish in the doab region indicates a gap between the two. Rather, the origin of dish should be found in the BRW/BSW complex in the lower-middle Gangetic region. Typological study of BRW/BSW in the lower-middle Gangetic region shows the process of BRW/BSW from the lower-middle Gangetic region to the western regions.

[5]Although several pieces of GW from Kaushambi are said to be PGW (Sharma 1960), they are hardly identified with genuine PGW in terms of paintings, as far as we judge from the published photographs. Similarly, the sherds from Vaishali which are reported as PGW are also doubtful with their identification. Genuine PGW are confined in terms of its distribution to the upper-middle Gangetic region (doab regon) westwards.

[6]Beside with the illustrated specimen (RP1124), a limited number of imitated ware of PGW has been found from our excavation. All of them are from the stratum of Period II, that is, Early NBPW phase. Furthermore, some techniques of modelling which is peculiar to PGW are observable in some specimens of GW, similarly indicating the cultural exchange between the PGW and NBPW zone. No genuine PGW has been found from our excavation (though the earlier.) Excavation by K.K. Sinha yielded genuine PGW sherds from Sravasti.

BIBLIOGRAPHY

Aboshi, Y. & K. Sonoda ed., 1997. *Excavations at Jetavana (Saheth) - A Buddhist site in Uttar Pradesh (98689).* Kansai University.

Agrawal, D.P. & Ghosh, A., 193. *Radiocarbon and Indian Archaeology.* Tata Institute of Fundamental Research, Bombay.

Allchin, B. & R. 1982. *The Rise of Civilization in India and Pakistan.* Cambridge University Press, Cambridge.

Allchin, F.R. 1989. City and State Formation in Early Historic South Asia. *South Asian Studies*, 5: 1–16.

Allchin, F.R. 1995. *The Archaeology of Early Historic South Asia: The Emergence of Cities and States.* Cambridge University Press, Cambridge.

Chakrabarti, D.K. 1992. *The Early Use of Iron in India.* Oxford University Press, Delhi.

Chakrabarti, D.K. 1995, *The Archaeology of Ancient Indian Cities.* Oxford University Press, Delhi.

Dani, A.H. & Masson, V. ed., 1992. *History of Civilizations of Central Asia Vol. I The dawn of civilizaition: earliest times to 700 B.C.* Unesco Publishing, Paris.

Dikshit, K.N. 1969. A Note on the Problem of the Plain Black-and-Red Ware in Northern India, in (Sinha ed., 1969): 48–55.

Dikshit, K.N. 1973. The Allahapur Evidence and the Painted Grey Ware Chronology. in (Agrawal & Ghosh ed., 1973): 148–153.

Erdosy, G. 1985. The Origin of Cities in the Ganges Valley. *Journal of Economic and Social History of Orient*, Vol. XXVIII, part l: 81–109.

Erdosy, G. 1985. Settlement Archaeology of the Kausambi Region. *Man & Envirionment* IX: 61 80.

Erdosy, G. 1987. Early Historic Cities of Northern India. *South Asian Studies*, 3: 1 23.

Gaur, R.C. 1969. Nature of Pottery Complex of Black-and-Red Ware Phase at Atranjikhera, in (Sinha, 1969): 112–117.

Gaur, R.C. 1983. *Excavations at Atranjikhera*. Motilal Banarsidas, Delhi.

Gaur, R.C. ed., 1994. *Painted Grey Ware. Proceedings of Seminar on Archaeology held at Aligarh Muslim University, Aligarh.* Publication Scheme, Jaipur.

Joshi, J.P.,1993, *Exacavations at Bhagwanpura 1975–76 and Other Explorations & Excavations 1975-81 in Haryana, Jammu & Kashmir and Punjab*. ASI, New Delhi.

Lal, B.B. 1954. Excavation at Hastinapura and Other Explorations in the Upper Ganga and Sutlej Basins 1950–52.Ancient India, no.10–11: 5151, ASI, New Delhi.

Lal, B. 1992. The Painted Grey Ware Culture of the Iron Age, in (Dani & Masson ed.,1992): 421 440.

Lal, M. 1984. *Settlement History and Rise of Civilisation in Ganga-Yamuna Doab from 1500 B.C. – 300 A.D.* B.R.Publishing Corporation, Delhi.

Narain, A.K. & Roy, T.N. 1976. *Excavations at Rajghat Part I*. Banaras Hindu University, Varanasi.

Narain, A.K. & Roy, T.N. 1977. *Excavations at Rajghat Part II*. Banaras Hindu University, Varanasi.

Narain, A.K. & Roy, T.N. 1968. *The Excavations at Prahladpur.* Banaras Hindu University, Varanasi.

Roy, T.N. 1983. *The Ganges Civilization. A Critical Archaeological Study of the Painted Grey Ware and Northern Black Polished Ware Periods of the Ganga Plains of India*. Ramanand Vidya Bhawan, New Delhi.

Roy, T.N. 1986. *A Study of Northern Black Polished Ware Culture. An Iron Age Culture of India*. Ramanand Vidya Bhawan, New Delhi.

Sahay, S. 1969. Origin and Spread of the Northern Black Polished Ware, in (Sinha ed.,1969):146 154.

Sharma, G.R. 1960. *The Excavations at Kausambi (1957–59).* The Department of Ancient History, Culture and Archaeology, University of Allahabad, Allahabad.

Sharma, G.R. 1969. *Excavations at Kausambi 1949–50*. Memoirs of the Archaeological Survey of India, No.74, ASI, New Delhi.

Sinha, B.P. ed. 1969. *Potteries in Ancient India*. The Department of Ancient Indian History & Archaeology, Patna University, Patna.

Sinha, B.P. & B.S. Verma, 1977. *Sonpur Excavations (1956 and 1959–1962).* Directorate of Archaeology and Museums, Bihar, Patna.

Singh, P. 1994. *Excavations at Narhan (1984–89).* Banaras Hindu University, Varanasi.

Sinha, K.K. 1967. *Excavations at Sravasti, 1959*. Banaras Hindu University, Varanasi.

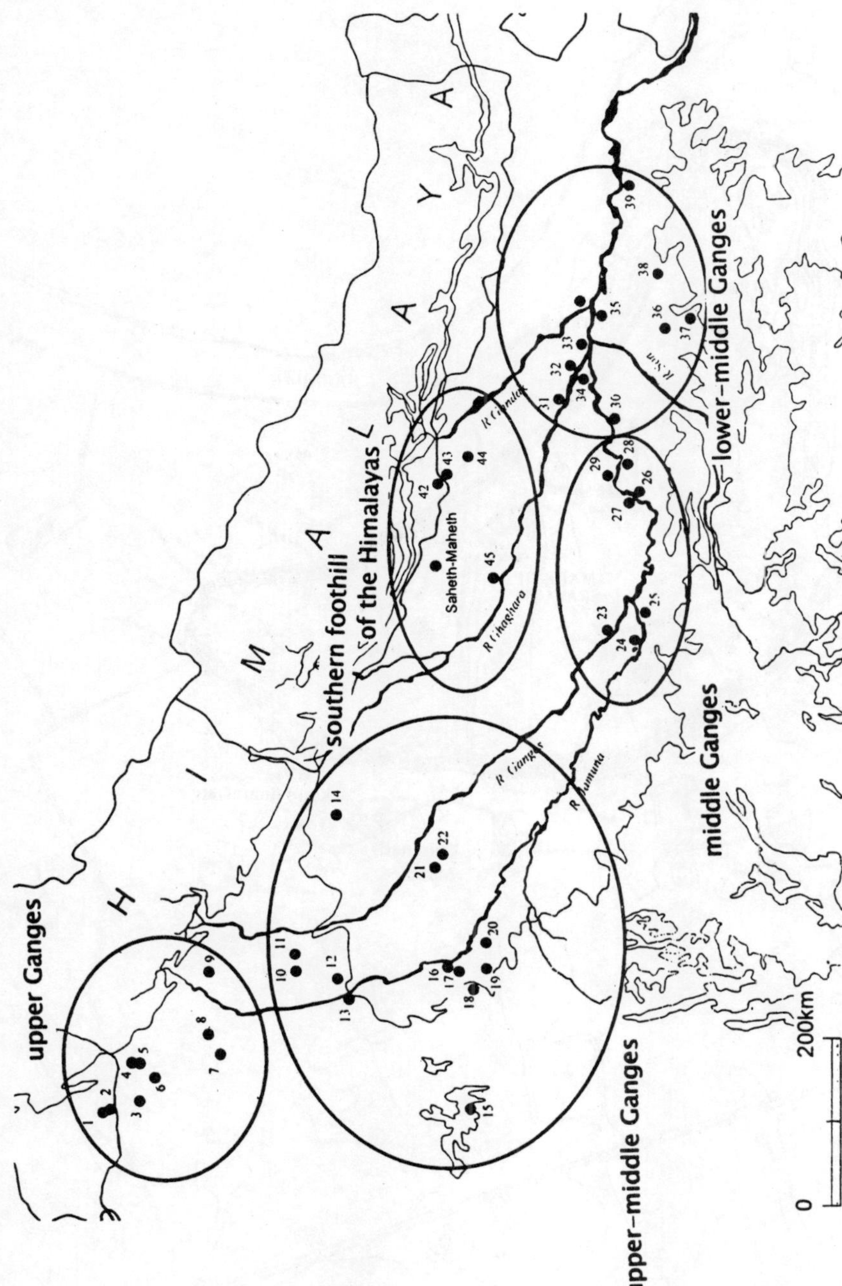

1 Nagar	10 Alamgirpur	19 Fatehpur Sikri	28 Prahladpur	37 Taradhi
2 Katpalon	11 Hastinapura	20 Batesvara	29 Masaon	38 Rajgir
3 Dadheri	12 Allahpur	21 Jakhera	30 Buxar	39 Champa
4 Rupar	13 Purana Qila	22 Atranjikhera	31 Narhan	40 Vaishali
5 Bara	14 Ahichchhatra	23 Sringaverapura	32 Manjhi	41 Saheth Maheth
6 Sanghol	15 Jodhpura	24 Kausambi	33 Chirand	42 Tilaura Kot
7 Bhagwanpura	16 Mathura	25 Bhita	34 Khairadhi	43 Piprahwa Ganwaria
8 Dhaulatpur	17 Sonkh	26 Sarai Mohana	35 Pataliputra	44 Sohgaura
9 Hulas	18 Noh	27 Rajghat	36 Sonpur	45 Ayodhya

Fig. 1. Ancient sites in Ganga Valley.

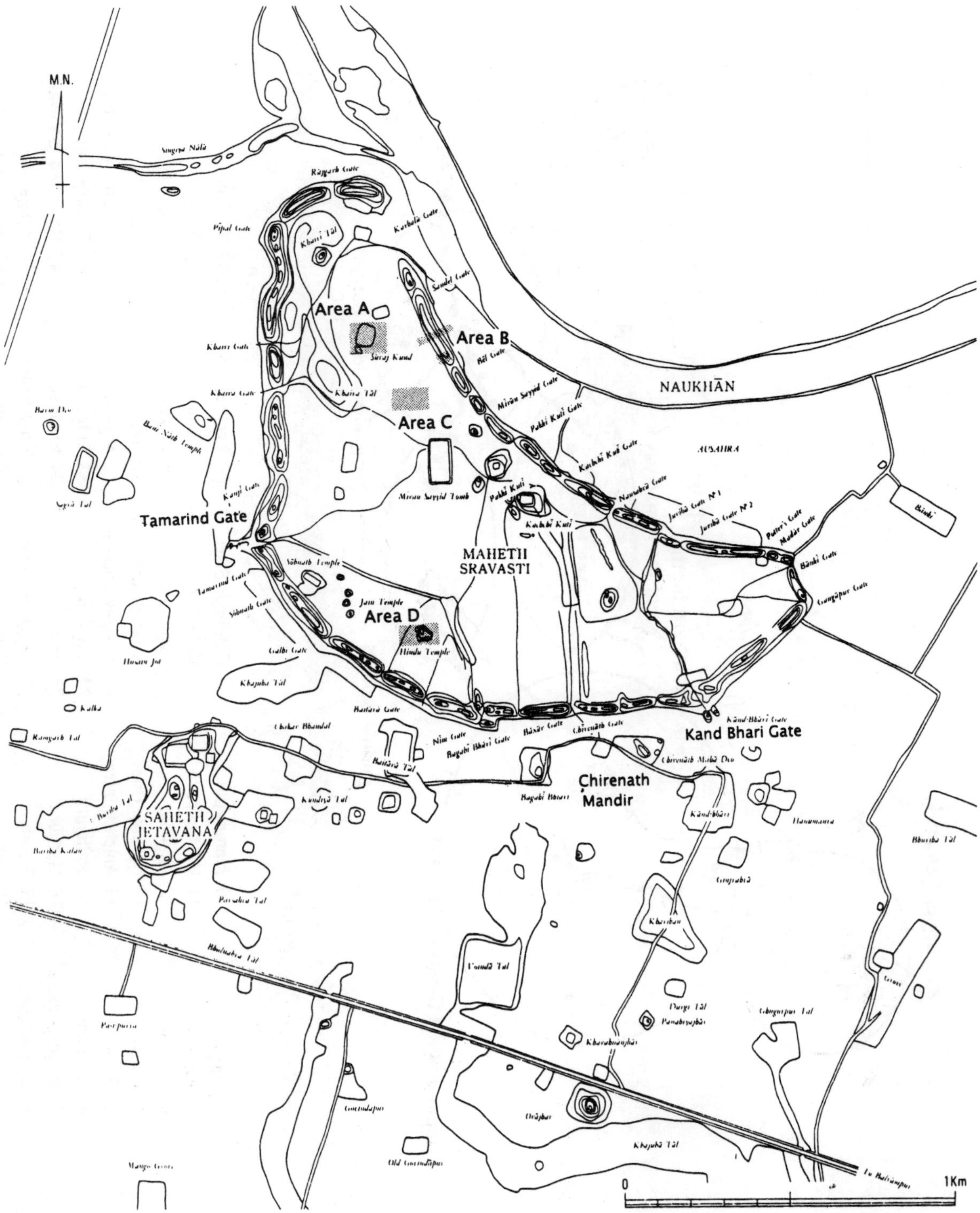

Fig. 2. Site plan Sravasti.

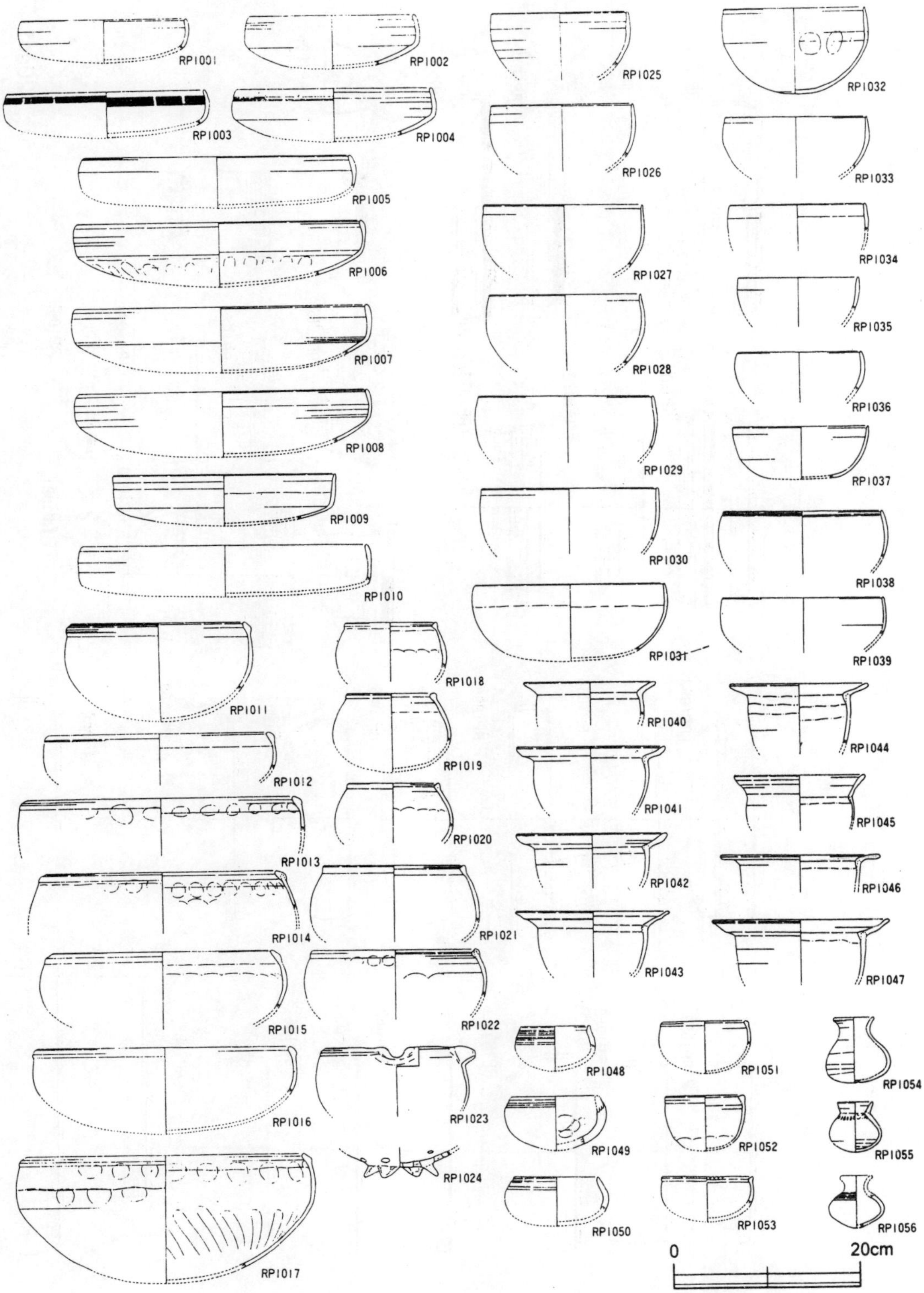

Fig. 3. Pottery-types - BRW/BSW - from lowest level of Area A.

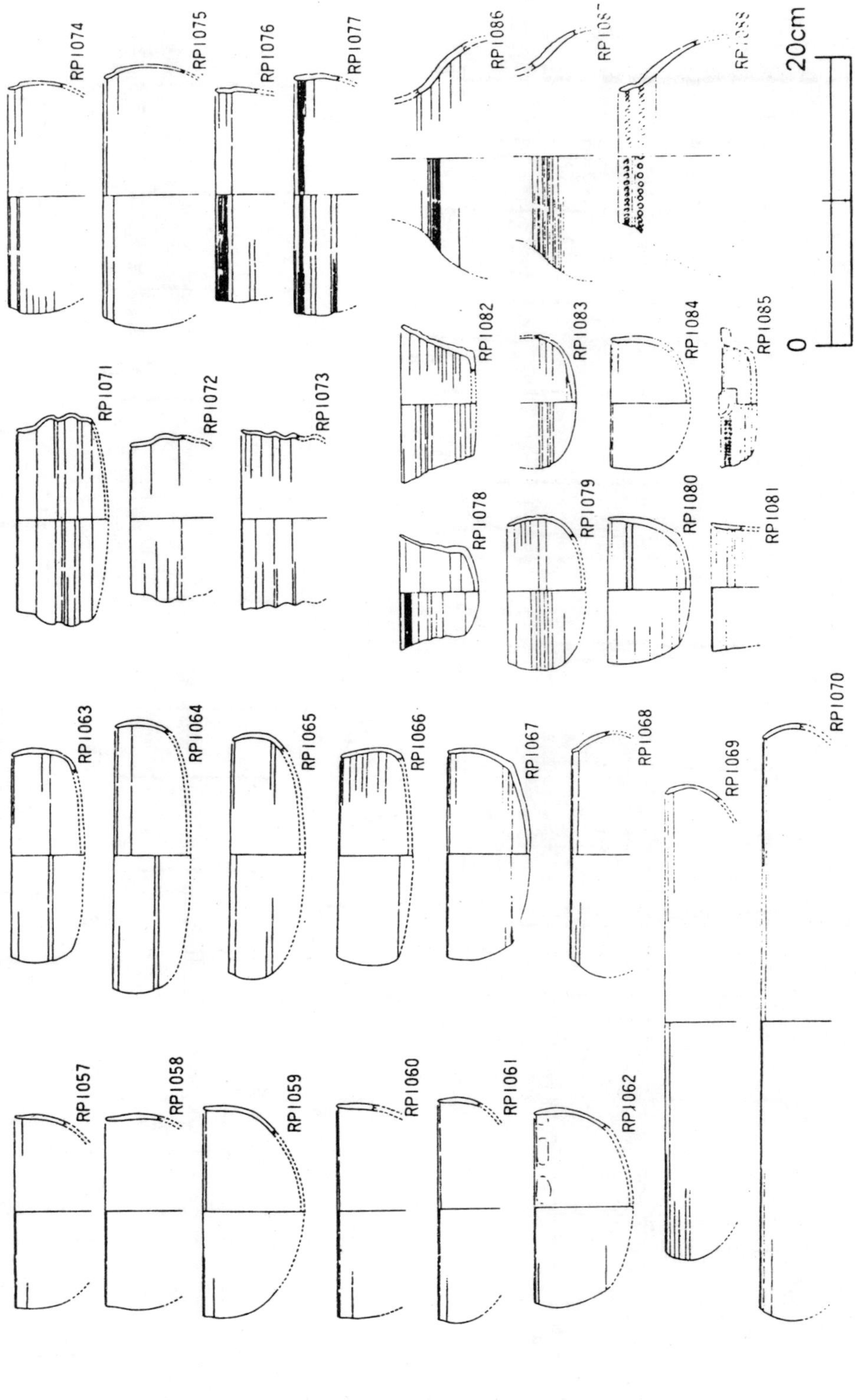

Fig. 4. Pottery types BRW/BSW - Lowest level of Area A.

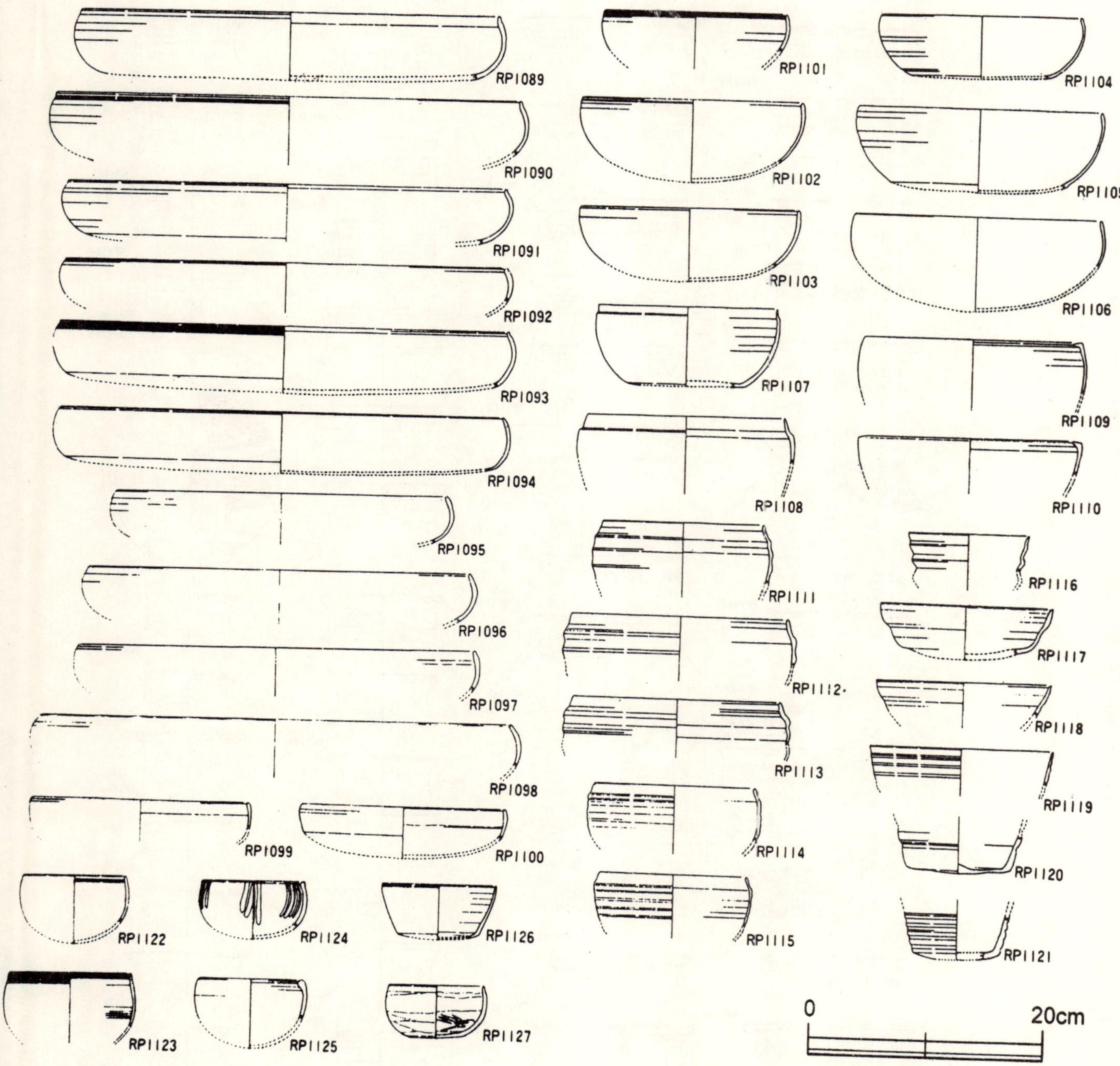

Fig. 5. Early types of NBPW from Area A.

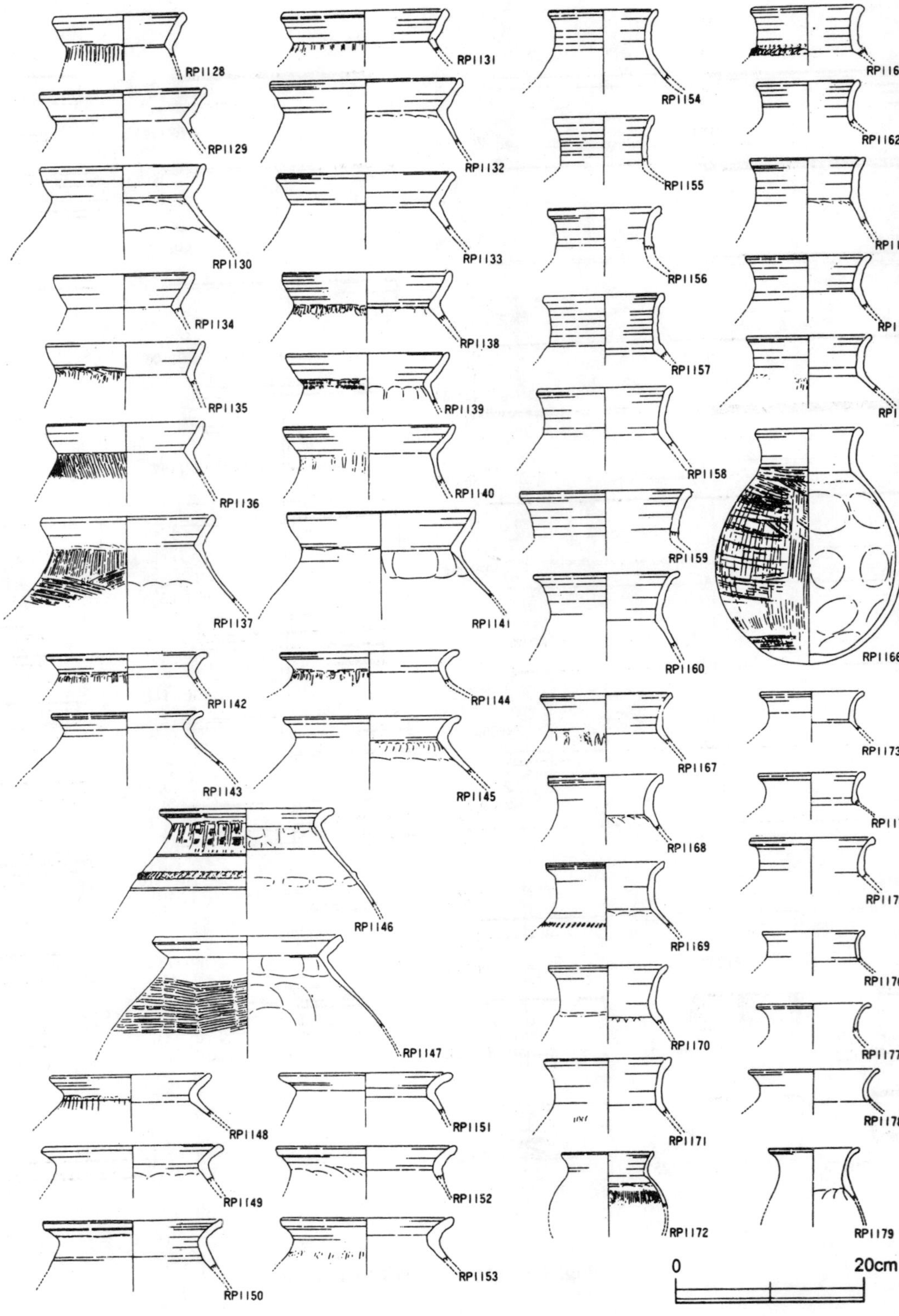

Fig. 6. Pottery fro Period III Area A.

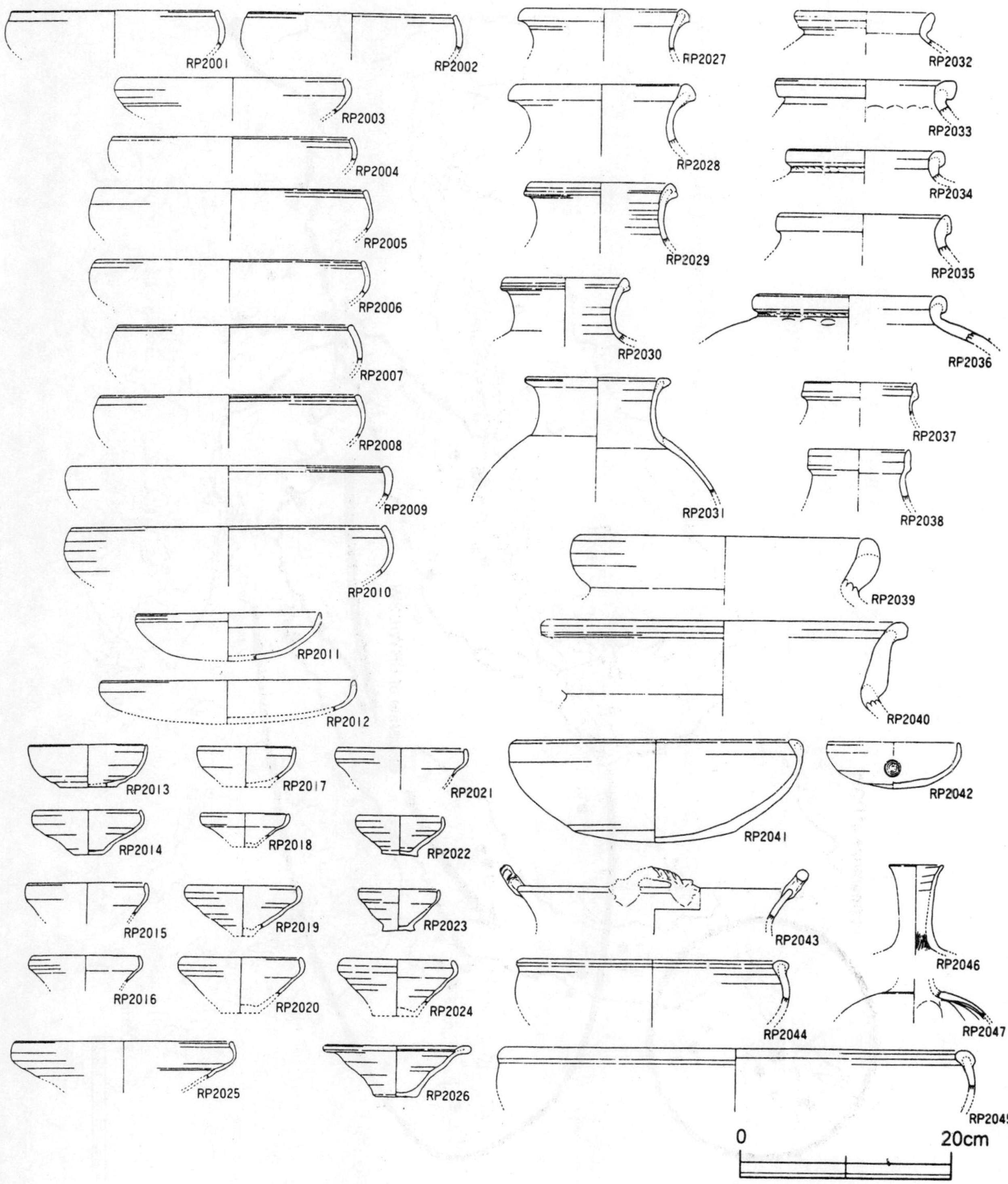

Fig. 7. Pottery from Period III from Area A.

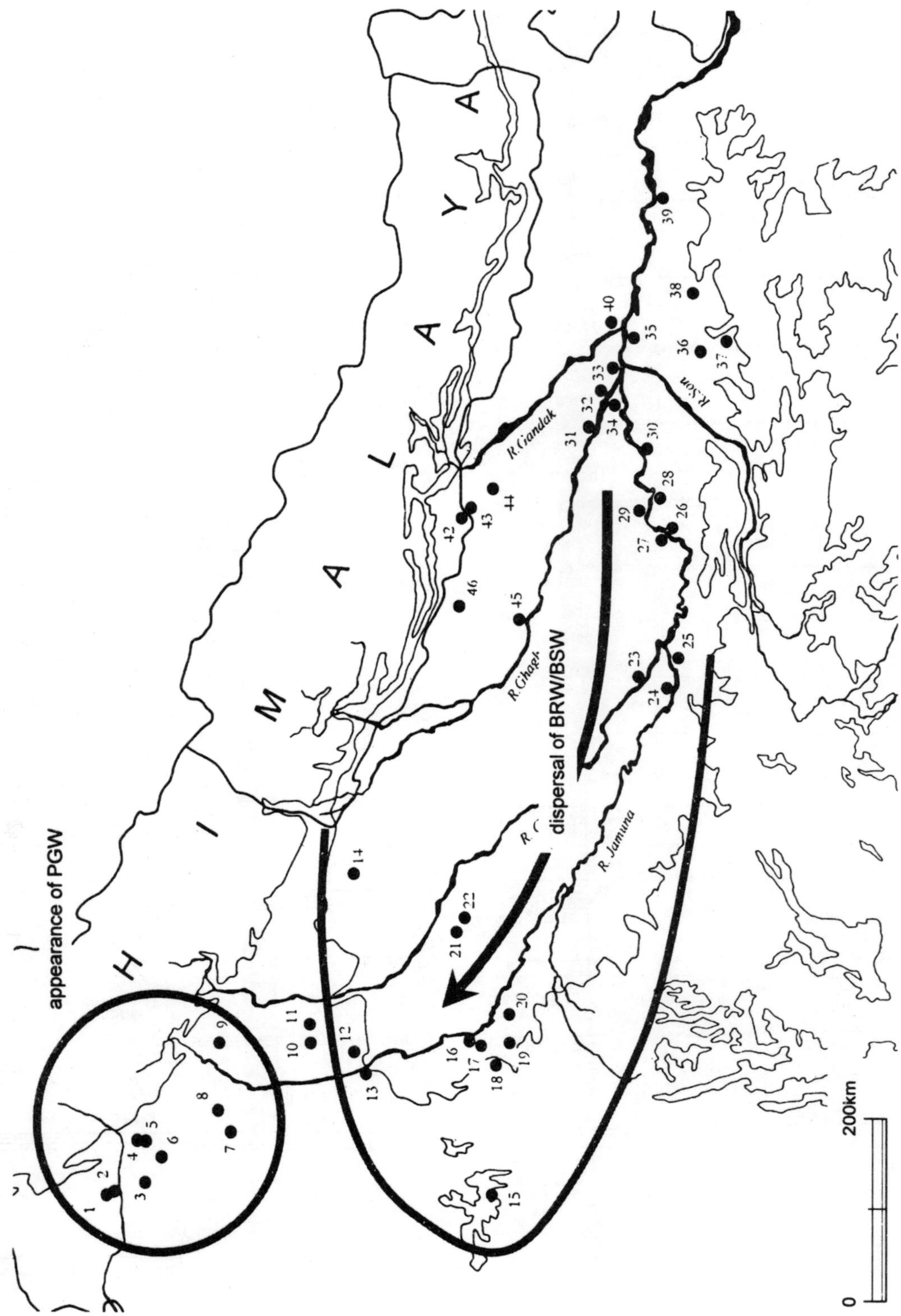

Fig. 8. Dispersal of BRW/BSW

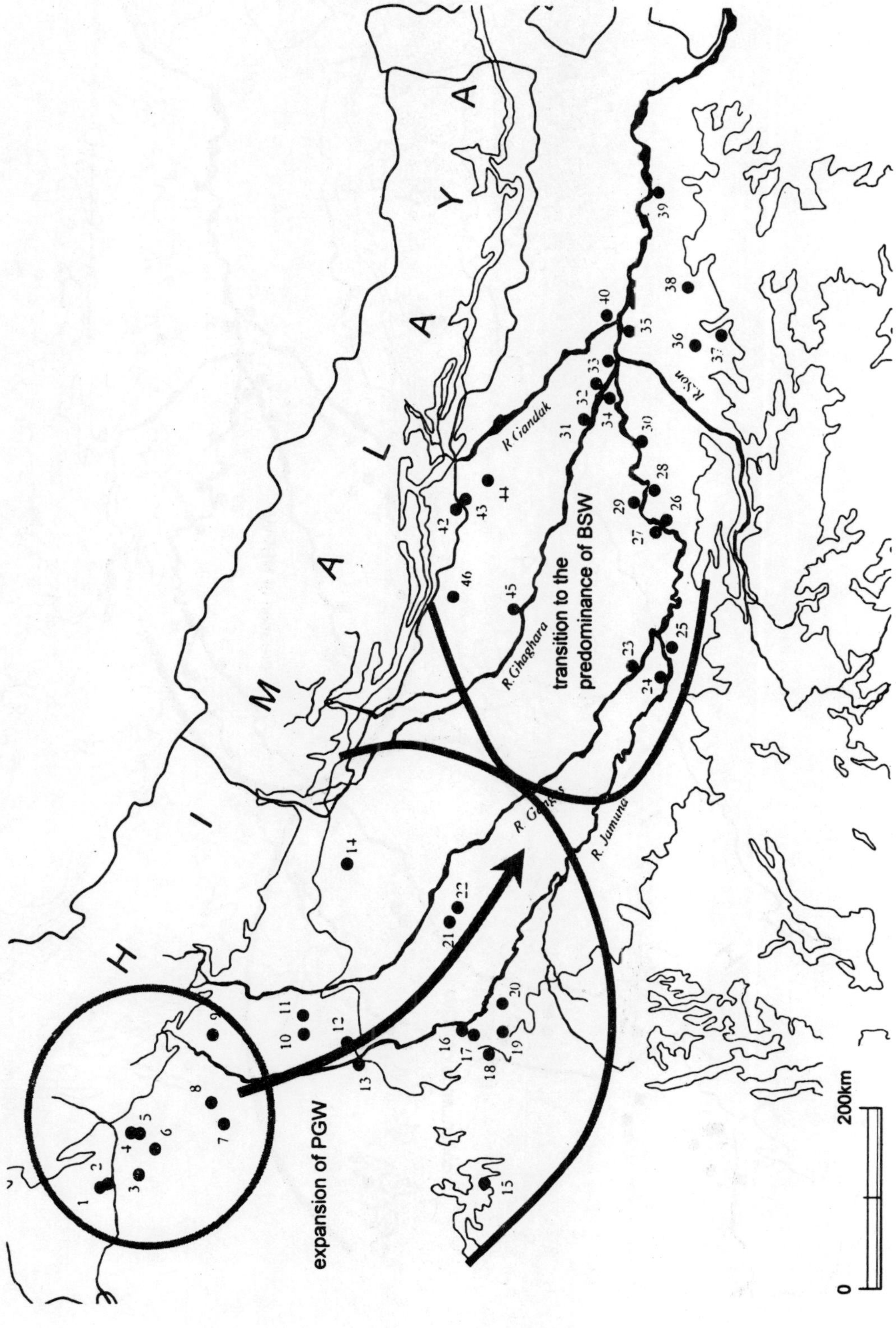

Fig. 9. Figure showing increase in the number of settlements.

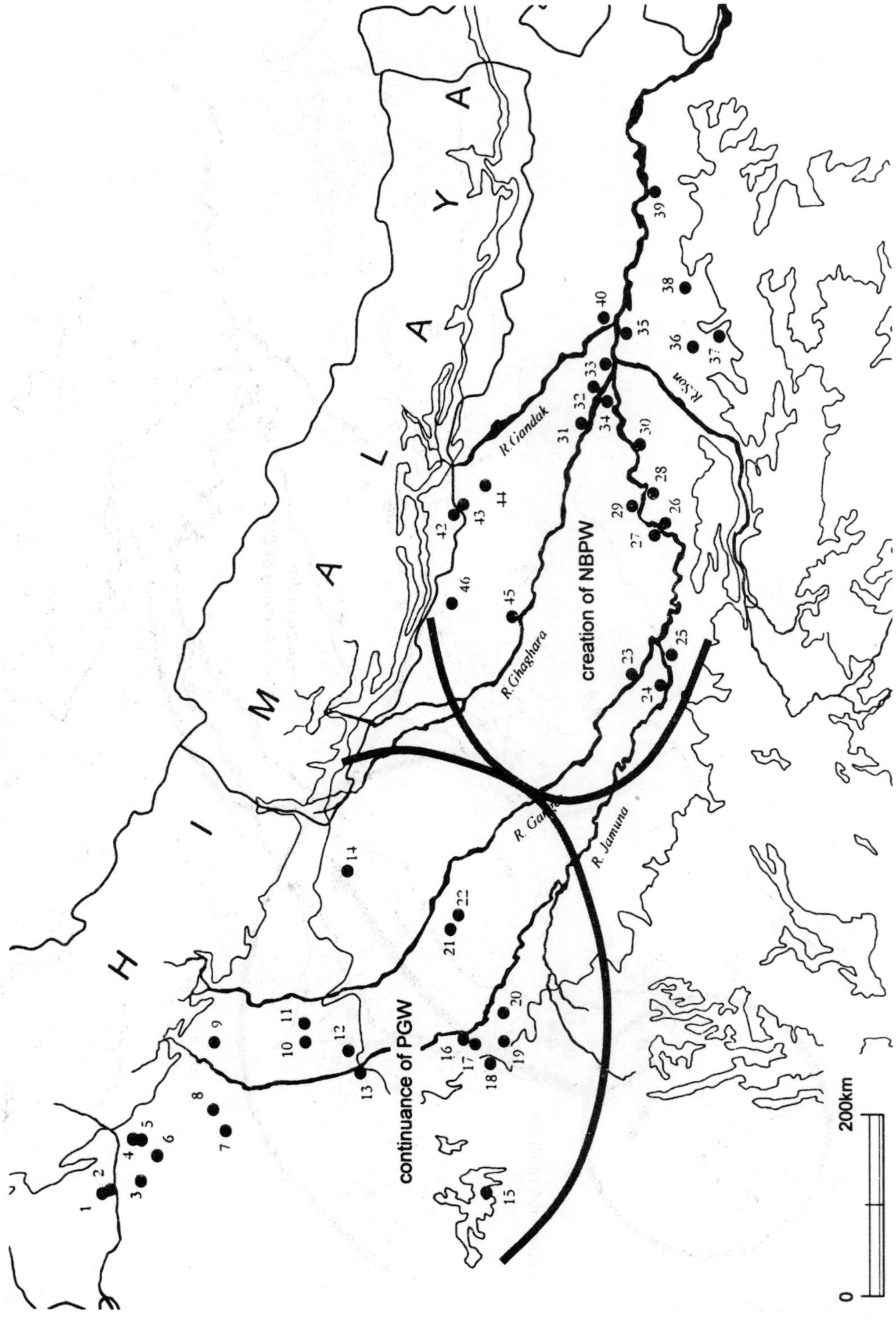

Fig. 10. Area of Creation of NBPW.

From Eastern Indian Ocean to the Yellow Sea Interaction Sphere: Indo-Pacific Beads in Yayoi Japan

SUNIL GUPTA*

In the protohistory of Japan, the Yayoi Period (300 B.C.– A.D. 250) represents a time of transition when foraging communities (1000 –300 B.C., Final Jomon Period) transformed into a fully agricultural society on the verge of 'state' formation (A.D. 250 –400, Early Kofun Period). The change was mediated from outside. In early 1st millennium B.C. migrants from mainland Asia introduced mass cultivation of rice and new agricultural tools into western Japan (Aikens and Higuchi 1982; Higuchi 1986: 121–125). From 4th 3rd century B.C., bronze and iron metallurgical technologies infusing through southern Korea were instrumental in creation of Yayoi material culture . The Yayoi landscape formed as farming villages rapidly spread from the 'core' area of northern Kyushu to most of Honshu between 300 to 1 B.C. (Kaneseki 1986: 317–333). By the beginning of the Christian Era, Yayoi Japan was a self-supporting society displaying innovations in agriculture, metal crafting and pottery making. A distinct funerary tradition emerged, characterised by jar burials and wooden coffins. Contacts with mainland Asia were now in the nature of long distance trade. High value commodities (bronze mirrors, iron tools) were sought from the old area of cultural borrowings, Korea and China. Together, the three regions formed what Barnes (1993: 208–221) calls the Yellow Sea Interaction Sphere (henceforth YSIS; fig. 1).

This notice discusses new evidence which shows that Yayoi Japan interacted (albiet indirectly) beyond the YSIS with another commercial sphere: the wide swath of territory from southern India to southern China which I choose to call the Eastern Indian Ocean Interaction Sphere (henceforth EIOIS; fig. 1). The evidence centers on the presence of Indo-Pacific beads in Yayoi tombs. The beads begin to appear on the Japan archipelago with the earliest YSIS imports. The term Indo-Pacific beads applies to a class of monochromatic glass microbeads (upto 5 mm diameter) cut and shaped from drawn glass (Francis 1990). Indo-Pacific beads have a long history of production in South and Southeast Asia (from 4th century B.C. to 12th century A.D.) and a wide distribution, occurring from the Swahili coast to Far East Asia (Francis 1990: 12–7; 1991: 28–43). The prevailing view is that Indo-Pacific bead crafting was pioneered in peninsular India around 4th 3rd century B.C. and the technology spread to Southeast Asia at the turn of the Christian Era (Francis 1991: 28–43; fig. 1). However, recent Indo-Pacific bead finds in Southeast Asia in levels dated to early 4th century B.C. call for a revision of the India-centric theory (Ian Glover: persn.comm). In any case, Indo-Pacific beads are diagnostic artefacts of the EIOIS.

Hundreds, and in many cases, thousands of Indo-Pacific beads have been found in Yayoi burials. Indo-Pacific beads are ubiquitous grave goods in Yayoi funerary contexts. Yayoi tomb-sites yielding Indo-Pacific

*Allahabad Museum, Allahabad.

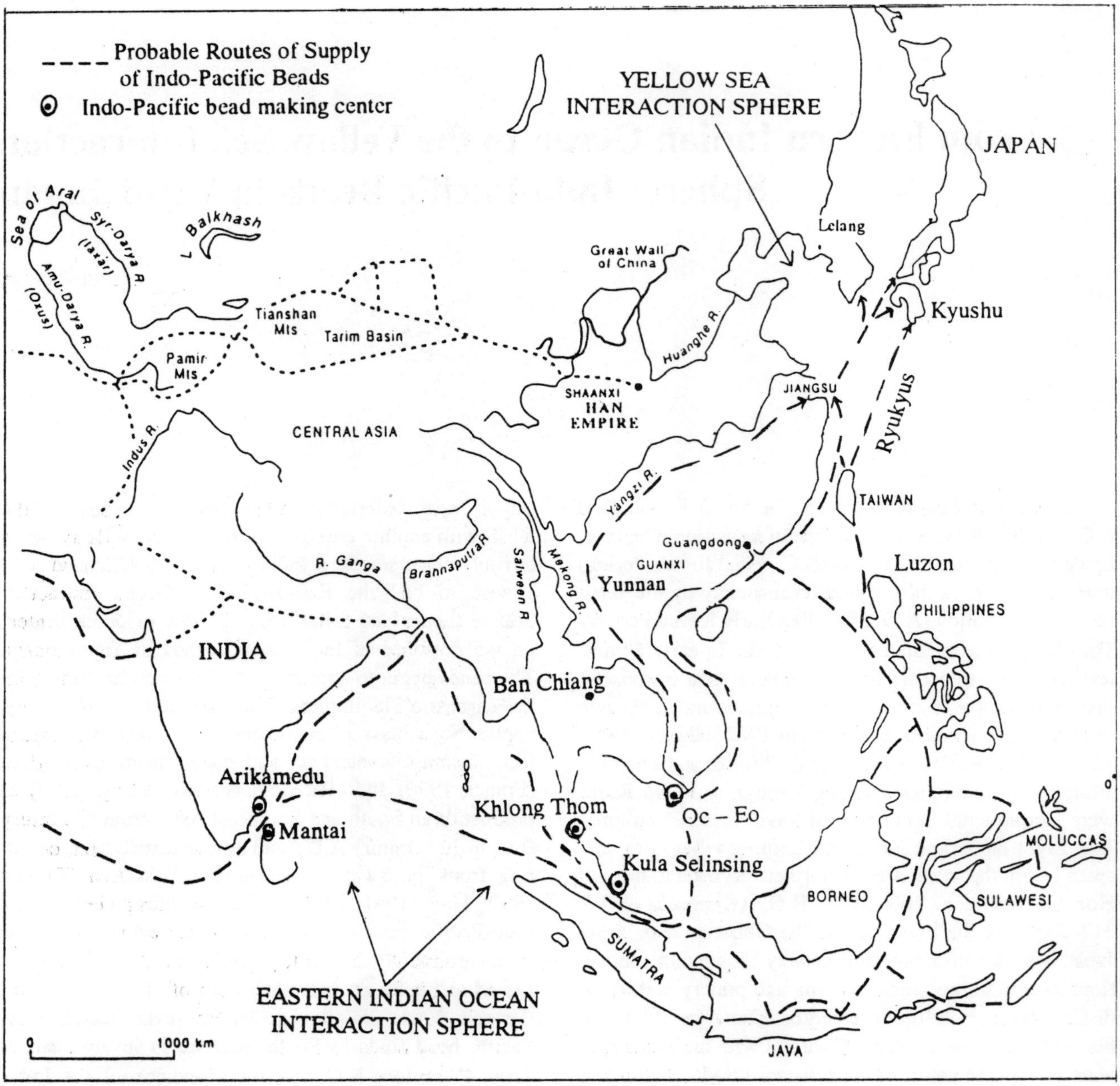

Fig. 1. Probable Routes of Supply of Indo-Pacific Beads from EIOIS to YSIS.

beads can be bracketed into three sub-periods: Early Yayoi (300–200 B.C.), Middle Yayoi (200–0 B.C.). and Late Yayoi (A.D. 0–250). In the Late Yayoi period, there is dramatic increase in number of burials yielding Indo–Pacific beads compared to Early–Middle Yayoi burials. Though Indo–Pacific beads have been studied for more than a century in Asia–Arica, the rich evidence of these microbeads in Japanese archaeological contexts is virtually unknown to the non-Japanese speaking audience. Within Japan, Indo-Pacific beads have been substantially documented and published, mostly in excavation reports of tomb sites. However, these records have remained unconsolidated and, therefore, largely uninterpreted. I have been studying Indo-Pacific beads in Japan as part of post-doctoral research on early contact and exchange between the Indian Ocean region and Far East Asia. My collaborator, Dr. Oga Katsuhiko of Kyoto University and I have created a preliminary database on Indo-Pacific beads deposited in Yayoi tomb sites. The salient parts of the database are specified below. Subsequent to introduction of the database, I shall discuss the information in context of early exchange and possible cultural interchange between YSIS and EIOIS.

The Database

The database was prepared by integrating information from published records, supplemented by our observations in the field. We have personally examined Indo-Pacific beads excavated from Yayoi and Kofun period tombs in a number of prefectural museums and archaeological institutes in Kyushu and Honshu. We believe our study tour exposed us to a fairly representative corpus of Indo-Pacific beads in Japan. Direct engagement with the artefacts allowed us to validate a 'cross-section' of the published sources and closely appreciate the evidence. The database comprises (a) map of Japan showing locations of Yayoi tombs containing Indo-Pacific beads (b) list of the sites plotted on the map with details of bead finds and (c) bibliographical sources. Fundamental to the database are locations of Yayoi period tomb sites containing Indo-Pacific beads. A total of 169 'microbead tombsites' are identified. By our estimate, the 169 sites represent 70 % of Yayoi period tombsites in Japan where Indo-Pacific beads have been found. Most of the sites are located on northwest Kyushu and southern Honshu. The greatest number of Indo-Pacific beads have been recovered from northwest Kyushu. This is the area of first Yayoi settlement and the place of dissemination of Yayoi culture to the rest of Japan (Kanascki 1986: 317–333). We have recorded a total of 50,180 microbeads for all three sub-periods. The Late Yayoi deposits are overwhelmingly greater. Our database shows 50,163 beads from 159 sites compared to 12 beads from 7 Middle Yayoi sites and 5 beads from 2 Early Yayoi sites. The quantification indicates substantial 'consumption' of Indo-Pacific beads in Late Yayoi times.

Far East Asian Bead Market

The database contributes to the closing of an information gap in studies of Indo-Pacific beads which, as explained above, had existed with regard to Japan. Equally important, the database makes it possible to establish the idea of a market for Indo-Pacific beads in the YSIS. The Far Eastern bead market is envisaged as a contiguous area of Indo-Pacific bead deposition comprising western Japan and southern Korea (fig. 1). The idea of market is given credence by the substantial quantum and spread of Indo-Pacific beads across Korea-Japan. In Japan, regularity of importation is indicated by occurrence of Indo-Pacific beads in all Yayoi sub-periods, with the Late Yayoi period registering a surge in acquisition. As pointed out, we have recorded over 50,000 beads in 169 sites. This makes about 300 beads per site with a spatial spread across much of western Japan. We can assume much greater numbers of beads than the average figure in use in Yayoi localities in the vicinity of the tombs. Deposition of Indo-Pacific beads in contemporaneous proto Three Kingdoms sites in Korea, though not quantified, seems to be comparable to Yayoi Japan. Lee (1993: 5–13), reviewing the evidence of early glasses in Korea says, 'A large part of the monochrome glass beads from Proto-Three Kingdoms and Three Kingdoms period sites in Korea probably belong to the Indo-Pacific beads category'. Holistically considered, the evidence suggests strong demand for Indo-Pacific beads in early Iron Age Japan-Korea and firmly conveys the 'idea of market'.

That Korea-Japan represent an import market is also indicated by absence of evidence for production of Indo-Pacific beads in either country. Glass micro beads of a certain kind were made at the Middle Yayoi site of Naguoka in Honshu. The beads were produced by drilling pieces broken from larger glass beads (see under KM..1997; persn. comm with Oga Katsuhiko). In Korea, glass beads were produced from clay moulds. The latter have been excavated in 1st 2nd century A.D. contexts in South Korea (Lee 1997: 19). However, these early glass beads of Korea and Japan are radically different in type and manufacture from Indo-Pacific beads which were 'cut' and shaped from drawn glass (for technique of manufacture see Francis 1991). Available evidence shows EIOIS to be the production zone of Indo-Pacific beads (fig. 1).

Finally, chemical compositions of glass beads found in funerary contexts in Japan–Korea indicate more than one source of supply. In compositional terms, four main kinds of glass beads have been identified in Yayoi and proto-Three Kingdom contexts: high lead, lead-barium, high pottasium and high sodium (for Yayoi - Early Kofun see Koezuka 1995; for proto-Three Kingdom see Lee 1993: 6–13; 1997: 14–23). A consensus prevails on broad geographical areas represented by the compositions. High lead and lead-barium glass beads have been sourced to middle and upper parts of China. Pottasium and high sodium beads, mostly comprising the Indo-Pacific type, have been related to the EIOIS (including southern China). These are the main fault lines of the debate, though discussions range within (for reviews see Brill 1993: 70–79; Glover and Henderson 1995: 141–169). Adopting an overview, we can say that Indo-Pacific beads relate to particular chemical schemes whose provenances cannot be extended further northward than southern China. Production areas of Indo-Pacific beads were thus far removed from YSIS, separated by the lead-barium and high lead glass zone of middle and upper China.

The correlation of compositional profile and territory with regard to Indo-Pacific beads reinforces the idea of the Far Eastern bead market.

Trade Routes

At the fringe of the eastern Indian Ocean region, two areas of bead concentration signify 'stages' in movement of Indo-Pacific beads from EIOIS to YSIS. One is southern China where thousands of Indo-Pacific beads have been found in Han period tombs in Yunnan, Guangxi and Guangdong provinces (Grover and Henderson 1995: 158–159). The other likely 'thoroughfare' is Phillipines, particularly the Luzon region in the north. Indo-Pacific beads are endemic to Phillipines, constituting 70% of all beads found between 1–1000 A.D. (Francis: www.the.beadsite.com; fig. 1). The routes by which microbeads may have been sent are envisaged as: (1) Mediated via southern China and moved through land and riverine routes to, in all likelihood, the Yangtze delta for onward shipment to Korea-Japan. A highway, built by the Ming Emperor in A.D. 69 connected mainland China with the outlying provinces of Sichuan and Yunnan on the upper course of the Yangtze and extended beyond to Southeast Asia (Hongfen 1998). The highway may have been used to transport Indo-Pacific beads (2) Ferried along the coast from Guangxi and Guangdong provinces to the Yangtze estuary. The southern China coast experiences both the Indian and Pacific monsoons and is near the north current moving towards Korea-Japan.

The littoral is also 'positioned' to receive maritime traffic from Southeast Asia. According to An Jiayao (quoted in Glover and Henderson 1995: 159) high potash glasses (including Indo-Pacific beads) found in Eastern Han tombs in Guangxi-Guangdong corroborate the Han dynasty records which say that Emperor Wu (140–87 B.C.) 'sent people to the Southern Sea to buy glass.' The archaeological record and maritime situation of southern China suggest it to be an important transhipment area for movement of micro beads from EIOIS to YSIS. (3) From Phillipines to Taiwan. Indo-Pacific bead have been found in jar burials from Luzon through Babuyan and Banates islands to the east coast of Taiwan (Solheim 1960: 115-148). From Taiwan two options *prima facie*: beads may have been moved along the Ryukyu chain to Kyushu and/or taken across the Taiwan straits to an entrepot on Chinese coast, the Yangtze estuary in all likelihood.

Indo-Pacific beads in the Yellow Sea Interaction Sphere

Of the four routes delineated above, three focus upon the Yangtze delta as the likely final staging area for Indo-Pacific bead exports to the Far Eastern market. The concept of a staging area on the Yangtze delta is in juxtaposition to the view that trade goods from China to Korea-Japan were mainly mediated by the Han Commandery at Lelang in northern Korea, the consignments arriving at the latter place via land routes traversing northern China and Manchuria (Higuchi 1986: 124; Barnes 1993: 209–214; Nelson 1993: 164–205). The Yangtze delta is also pivotal to a larger civilisational issue: introduction of rice cultivation into Korea-Japan. Higuchi (1986: 121–125) argues that rice cultivation was introduced simultaenously to southern Korea and western Japan in early 1st millennium B.C. from the Yangtze delta. His thesis is based upon evidence of common agricultural tool typology for all three interactive areas. Barnes (1993: 168–170) forwards the same basis to argue for a transmission through Lelang but leaves open the possibility of diffusion across the sea. In any case, consensus prevails on the lower Yangtze as original dissemination area. This technological diffusion and, subsequently trade, must have been supported at least partially by an early maritime network integrating the Yangtze delta, southern Korea and western Japan. The Chincse text *Sangouchi* (3rd century A.D.) describes a sea route from China to Wa (Japan) via Korea (Choi 1997: 5–13).

Indo-Pacific beads, distributed from southern Korea through Tsushima Island to north-west Kyushu indicate the maritime orientation of the *Sangouchi* (Fig. 1, 2). The concentrations of Indo-Pacific beads reported from southern littoral of Korea, specifically from stone lined tombs and jar coffins (Lee 1993: 5–13; 1997: 14–23), contrasts with the northern part of Korea where reports of Indo–Pacific bead finds in Proto-Three Kingdom contexts are lacking. Nelson (1993:183–191) reviewing evidence of grave goods in Han tombs in and around Lelang informs mainly of jade bead finds. Lee (1997: 14–23) is of the opinion that glass beads found in north western part of Korea (including Lelang) are of Chinese provenance. Similarly, the Ryukynan chain, though commercially active as indicated by the discovery of Chinese 'knife' coins dated to 2nd century B.C. at Okinawa (Meighan 1964: 3–13) does not seem to have been a regular route of microbead trade to Korea–Japan. Indo-Pacific bead finds in southern Kyushu, the natural landfall for those coming from the Ryukyus, are extremely meagre compared with those in north-west Kyushu (fig. 1). Compared to 58 sites yielding Indo-Pacific beads in north-west Kyushu, we have recorded only one such site in south Kyushu. Circumstantial evidence thus points to the Yangtze delta as the staging area of Indo-Pacific bead exports to the Far Eastern market. The elucidation of the early archaeology of this deltaic region will hopefully yield positive evidence.

Conclusion

Indo-Pacific beads stand out amongst the exotic assemblage of the Yellow Sea Interaction Sphere. The beads are aesthetically part of the Indian Ocean sphere. As Glover and Henderson (above) make it clear, there was little appreciation for Indo-Pacific beads in funerary culture of middle and upper China dominated by jade and ornaments of lead-barium glass. The presence of Indo-Pacific beads in Early Yayoi graves (small numbers but securely dated) points to long distance routes functioning between the EIOIS and YSIS as far back as 3rd century B.C. For Early Yayoi period, our database shows 1 cobalt blue bead from Yoshitake-Takagi site in Fukuoka Prefecture and 4 cobalt blue beads from Higashiyamada Ipponsugi site in Saga Prefecture (see under FK 1995 and SK 1995 respectively). As pointed out, there was dramatic rise in importation of Indo-Pacific beads in Late Yayoi period and still greater levels of acquisition in the Kofun period. The beads were accorded a 'high status' as grave goods in Yayoi society. Yayoi burials *containing Indo-Pacific* beads, especially jar burials, are close to 'Indo-Pacific bead burials' spread across the EIOIS, in particular Austronesian Southeast Asia (fig. 1). In this regard, the Yayoi people display a cultural affinity with regions beyond the Yellow Sea Interaction Sphere, hinting at cultural interchange.

Acknowledgement

I thank Prof. Yoshinori Yasuda for inviting me to work under the Environment and Civilization Global Program (ECGP) at the International Research Center for Japanese Studies in Kyoto. I am grateful to the trustees of the Japan Society for the Promotion of Science for granting me a Post-doctoral Fellowship to pursue my studies at the IRCJS.

REFERENCES

Aikens, M.C. and Higuchi, T. 1982. *Prehistory of Japan*. New York: Academic Press.

Barnes, G. 1993. *China, Korea and Japan: The Rise of Civilization in East Asia*. London; Thames and Hudson.

Brill, R.H. 1993: Scientific Investigations of Ancient Asian Glass, *Report of the Nara Symposium on Maritime Route of Silk Roads*. Nara: Nara International Foundation.

Choi, S.R. 1997.The Iron Age Culture in Southern Korea, *Korean and Korean American Studies Bulletin*, Vol.8, No.1/2 Spring/Summer 1997: 5 –13.

FK 1995. *Fukuokashi Kyouikuiinkai* 1995. Yoshitake Isekigun 8.

Francis, P. 1990. Glass Beads in Asia Part II. Indo-Pacific Beads, *Asian Perspectives*, Vol.29, no.1: 1-23.

Francis, P. 1991. Beadmaking at Arikamedu and beyond, *World Archaeology*, Vol.23, no.1: 28-43.

Glover, I.C. and J. Henderson. 1995. Early Glass in South and South East Asia and China in R. Scott and J. Guy (ed.), *China and Southeast Asia: Art, Commerce and Interaction*:141–169. London: Percival David Foundation of Chinese Art.

Higuchi, T. 1986. Relationships between Japan and Asia in Ancient Times: Introductory Comments, in R.J. Pearson (ed.), *Windows on the Japanese Past: Studies in Archaeology and Prehistory:* 121–125. Michigan: Center for Japanese Studies.

Hongfen, B. 1998. *Patchwork of Dali.* Yunnan: Dali.

Kanaseki, H. 1986. The Evidence for Social Change between the Early and Middle Yayoi, in R.J. Pearson (ed.), *Windows on the Japanese Past: Studies in Archaeology and Prehistory:* 317–333. Michigan: Center for Japanese Studies.

KM. 1997. *Kyotofu Maizoubunkazai Chousa Kenkyu Senta 1997*. Kyotolf Iseki Chousa Gaihou 76.

Koezuka, T. 1995. *Kodai Keisanen—Garasu no Kenkyu, Bunkazai Ronsou 11*. Nara: National Research Institute of Cultural Properties.

Lee, In-Sook. 1993. The Silk Road and Ancient Korean Glass, *Korean Culture*, Vol.14, No.4, Los Angeles: 6–13.

Lee, In-Sook. 1997. Early Glass in Korean Archaeological Sites, *Korean and Korean American Studies Bulletin*, Vol.8, No.1/2 Spring/Summer 1997: 14–23.

Meighan, C.W. 1964. 'Early Prehistory', in A.H. Smith (ed.), *Ryukyuan Culture and Society*: 3–13. Hawaii: University of Hawaii Press.

Nelson, S.M. 1993. *The Archaeology of Korea*. Cambridge: Cambridge University Press.

S.K. 1995. *Sagaken Kyouikuiinkai 1995*. Higashiyamada Ipponsugi Iseki.

Solheim, W.G. II. 1960. Jar Burial in the Babuyan and Banates Islands and in central Phillipines, and its relation to jar burial elsewhere in the Far East. *Phillipine Journal of Science* 89(1): 115–148.

The Early Historic Settlement and Subsistence Pattern in the Shetrunji River Basin, Bhavnagar District, Gujarat

ASHIT BORAN PAUL*

The study of settlement pattern in archaeology occupies an important place. The concept of settlement pattern is derived from geography. In archaeology its application is relatively-recent. It was Gordon R. Willey who was first inspired to undertake the study of distribution of sites by Julian Steward, an ethnographer (Willey 1953). An excellent definition of the term has been given by Willey. According to him settlement pattern is "the way in which man disposed himself over the landscape on which he lived. It refers to dwellings, to their arrangement and to the nature and disposition of other buildings pertaining to community life. These settlements reflect the natural environment, the level of technology on which the builders operated and various institutions of social interaction and control which the culture maintained. Because settlement pattern is, to a large extent, directly shaped by widely held culture needs, they offer a strategic starting point for functional interpretation of archaeological cultures" (Willey 1953: 1). It aims at finding out the manner in which human settlement are arranged over the landscape in relation to the physiographic, geographic and environment (Chang 1958).

The concept of settllement pattern was further developed (Adams 1961, 1965, Flanarry 1972, Renfrew 1972, Sanders 1965, Flamming 1971, Clark 1972, Trigger 1968, Chang 1962). In Indian context it is relatively-recent development. A number of scholars have carried out this type of work in India (Dhavalikar 1977, 1978, 1984, Dhavalikar and Possehl 1974, David Raju 1985, Shinde 1990, 1998, Chitalwala 1979, Paddayya 1982, Lal 1984, Erdosy 1988, Haque 1992, Bhan 1979, and Paul 1999). In the present paper an attempt has been made to study the settlement pattern in the lower Shetrunji river basin in Bhavnagar district of Saurashtra during the Early Historic period and is concerned with the working relationship between people and their technology and the landscape. The systematic explorations carried out by the present author have yielded 22 Early Historic as well as Harappan affliated sites.

The Area

The area of present study is confined to the lower part of Shetrunji river basin, i.e., in and around Padri and Hathab in Bhavnagar district. The district is characterized by a well-developed drainage system. The river, along with its tributaries, forms three groups of drainage system. 1) The Mandav group, 2) the Gir Girmar group and 3) the Shetrunjaya group. In the Gir Girnar group, the principal rivers are Shetrunji and its tributaries - the Shel and the Dattarvadi. The Shetrunji is the second largest river in Saurashtra with a total length of 180Km, of which

*Dept. of Archaeology, Jahangirnagar University, Savar, Dhaka.

92km lies in the Bhavnagar district. The river is fed by many tributaries, but in the Bhavnagar district it has only one tributary, the Shel. The river flows through Savarkundla Gariadhar Mahal, Palitana, Talaja and debouches into the Gulf of Cambay near Saltanpur Geologically, Bhavnagar district comes under the greater peninsula of the Indian subcontinent with basalt as the main rock formation. Numerous dykes and wide ranges of younger rocks such as aeolian and alluvial deposits are other geological formations of the district. The district is poor in metallic minerals, but other minerals are available. The topography of the district consists of coastal plains and the adjacent sand pits. The region falls in semi-arid zone and annual precipitation is between 500 to 800mm. The soil is fertile black cotton. The vegetation is mixed and dry deciduous types.

Size and Distribution of the Early Historic Settlements along the Coast and in the Lower part of Shetrunji River Basin

The ecological zones and many other factors like trade, political organization, warfare, religion and subsistence technology have affected the settlement pattern, distribution and their size in different ways (Trigger 1968). Out of the twentytwo sites, seven are located along the coast, eleven are located on the lower Shetrunji river basin and the rest of the settlements are away from the river (Fig.l). The main concentration of settlements are found on the Shetrunji river basin and most of them are multicultural sites. The extent and thickness of the habitational deposit varies from site to site (Table 1). Maximum sites are agricultural lands and few sites have preserved some amount of habitational-deposits in the form of mounds. Lithostratigraphically, the region is confined to basalt formation with some intrusive veins of chert, chalcedony, agate and calcite. The black cotton soil overlaps the lateritic deposit of about 5 m. Of the 22 two settlements, one falls in the category of below one (hectare) in size, 11 sites fall in the category of 12 ha. There are three settlements in the category of 3 ha. In the category of 45 ha, there are two sites. One settlement each in the category of 6 ha and 7.8 ha in the category of 25 ha, there are two settlements. There is only one settlement, which is more than 39 ha in area (Table 2; Fig.2 and 3).

Table 1. Sites: Their area and thickness of the habitational deposite

		Site dimension (Extent of occupational deposit)			
No	Site name	Length (M)	Breadth (M)	Thickness (M)	Area in Ha.
I	Bandi Rohil	300	100	3 00	3 0
2	Bhegali	200	100	1 00	‘ 00
2	Bhalar	200	100		2 0
4	Bharapur	300	400	2 00	12 0
5	Chopra	300	200	3.00	6.00
6	Dakana	300	400	1.50	12 0
7	Dantrad	300	150	1 50	4 5
8	Devalia	75	150	-	1.125
9	Gorkhi	300	150	1 50	4 5
10	Hathab	800	500	5 00	40 0
11	Ichhora	300	100	1 50	3 00
12	Katva	150	90	1.50	1.35
13	Khadsaliya	500	500	5 0	25 0
14	Padri	340	210	3.2	7.14
15	Pasti	38	75	1.00	0 285
16	Phulsar	200	100	1 50	2 0
17	Piparla	130	125	2.50	1 165
18	Shilavadar	150	200	2.00	3 0
19	Saltanpur	200	100	2 0	2.0
20	Thalsar	500	500	5 0	25 0
21	Timbana	150	75	10.0	1.125
22	Valavadar	200	75		I .5

Table 2. No. of settlements in respect of size (in hectare)

Total No of sites	Size (in hectare)	Total
22	less than 1 ha	1
	3 ha	3
	6 ha	1
	Beween 12 ha	11
	25 ha	2
	Above 39 ha	1
	Between 45 ha	2
	Between 78 ha	1
		22

Out of the twenty two settlements, ten are located on the bank of river Shetrunji Of the ten, six sites (Gorkhi, Timbana. Ichhora. Bandi-Rohil, Bhalar and Valavadar) are located on the left bank and four (Dantrad. Dalkana. Bhegali and Devalia) are located on the right bank. There is only one settlement (Sultanpur), which is situated on the river mouth of Shetrunji whereas four settlements (Piparla, Pavti, Shilavadar and Phulsar) are away from the river bank. Besides, there are seven sites (Padri, Chopra. Bharapur, Katva. Khadsaliya Thalsar and Hathab) which are located on the coast.

The above statistics confirms that the highest number of sites are between 3–12 ha followed by the sites of -3 ha. It is clear from the distribution of settlements, that maximum sites are confined to the bank of Shetrunji river.

Bruce Trigger (1968) has given a list of factors, which affect the settlement pattern. According to him, "the overall density and distribution of population of a region is determined to a large degree by the nature and availability of the natural resources that are being exploited. As long as areas with the soil, their economic resources and favourable climate are available, settlers tend to avoid areas that are naturally poor or where diseases or other dangers are common." The agricultural communities tend to settle on fertile land close to the rivers, whereas pastoral communities locate their settlements in the proximty of pasture land. The size, stability and duration of a settlement is obviously limited by the environment and the effectiveness of the subsistence technology.

Proximity to water: The Riverine Setting

The proximity to perennial source of water is an important feature of the settlement location. Riverine setting plays a vital role in the choice of settlements. Possehl (1980:85) has given importance to the riverine setting in a particular region to locate ancient settlements. According to him, "an obvious advantage to a riverine location is, reliable supply of water for human and animal consumption as well as for general domestic use. It would seem unlikely, however, that this alone could so unflexibly mould a settlement pattern in the environment. Ground water in Gujarat is readily available, even during the dry season (April and May), with fairly shallow wells" He also says that "another possibility is that the riverine location was selected because it afforded a potential for irrigation. Substantial increase over dry farming be expected from irrigated land in Gujarat As a rule of thumb the local farmers in Bhavnagar district expect irrigation to double yields which would materialize from the dry farming."

Of the twenty two sites, eleven are in the vicinity of the perennial source of water, seven are near the coast and rest of the sites are away from the perennial source of water. The Shetrunji river is sluggish in character and dries during the summer. At present it is observed that villagers or local people obtain drinking water during the summer by digging temporary wells in the river bed. Moreover, Bhavnagar is well watered. Along the coast, however, the water is brackish and charged with salt except where sweat water springs occur (Trivedi 1969). Such an opportunity could have been exploited by the Early Historic people too. Panini mentions that villages depended for their water supply on wells (kupas) to which were attached *nipanas* or water trough from which the cattle would drink (Agrawala 1953:141).

Soil and settlement

'Soil conditions are recognized to be one of the most important factors in the distribution of settlements' (Howston 1953: 99). On the other hand fertility of the soil is another important factor determining the location of human settlement, especially in the case of agricultural-cum industrial communities. The study region is in the black cotton soil area and maximum settlements are located on this soil. Possehl (1980: 53) also notes that the early farming communities in the western India are closely associated with the black cotton soil. A British agriculturist, who travelled in India in the latter part of nineteenth century, was very much impressed by the characteristics of black cotton soil. He made remarks about the soil in these words: "Black soil has wonderful power for absorbing water, and during rainy season it swells, so that the whole surface is raised. Although it continues to retain throughout abnormal amount of moisture, which is of great value to the crops grown on it. And, in short, enables cultivation to be practiced without irrigation, at the same time, in the dry weather, it loses a large amount of moisture, and shrinks in consequence. The shrinking is in all directions; consequently very deep and wide tracks are formed which make the land quite unsound and dangerous for riding. By the use of Dutch hoe-harrow, the cracks are filled and closed with the fine soil of the surface and by this means a regular circulation of soil is established. The cracks further furfill the functions of ploughing, by admitting air freely into the body of the soil. The objects of ploughing are attained, but nature is left to do a large share of the work, and, further, she provides the means by which man can successfully carry out the remainder of it. The plentiful supply of powdery soil is useful, not only for carrying on the circulation processes, but for closing up the cracks to present excessive evaporation of moisture from the body of under soil." (Wallace 1888: 180-181).

From the above statement it is observed that black cotton soil played a very important role in determining the settlement pattern of the Early Historic peoples who mostly practiced dry farming. Of the twenty two settlements, thirteen sites such as Bandi Rohil Bhalar Bhegaḷi Dakana Dantrad, Devalia, Gorkhi, Ichhora, Pavti. Piparla, Shilavadar, Timbana and Valavadar are located in the black cotton soil zone. The above mentioned sites could be agrarian settlements. From the available artifacts it can be said that the inhabitants of the above mentioned sites established their settlements to exploit the rich fertile land for producing food and might have supplied to the other settlement in exchange of other commodities. Apart from this, the site of Phulsar is very close to the sea. It could be identified as an agricultural and fishing settlement.

Of the fourteen settlements, one settlement called Bhalar played a very important role during the Early Historic period. When the present author explored the site, he found a fragment of pottery dish with green glaze on the inner side. It shows the contacts between the Persian Gulf and this study region, in the beginning of the Christian era. similar dish fragments of Bl Ware vessels have been found at the excavated Early Historic sites in the Persian Gulf (Paul *et al.*, 1997: 58, Fig. 28; Bernard *et al.* 1990, Fig. 4; Gupta 1997, Plate No. XXV b, c and d). Therefore, on the basis of this artifact, these settlements could be identified as trade as well as agricultural settlements, whereas another six settlements, such as Bharapur, Chopra, Katva, Khadsaliya, Saltanpur and Thalsar are very close to the sea shore, but do not seem to have played an important role in the overseas trade because the sites were not situated directly on the coast. Secondly, the Gulf of Cambay does not have natural ports because of silting problem. On the basis of ethnographic parallel and surrounding ecological conditions, it can be deduced that these settlements were established, for fishing purpose and inhabitants of these sites obtained food grain and other commodities from other settlements in exchange for fish.

Another ancient site, Padri is located in a shallow depression on a slightly elevated dune. In spite of the site being close to the coast, it doesn't appear to have played an important role in the external trade because the settlement was not located directly on the coast. The site is situated at least 3-4 km inland and the main intention of the occupants could have been cultivation. Therefore, the settlement appears to be have been a processing centre where the salt was extracted and then supplied to other settlements (Shinde 1992a: 79-86). Even today many families from the Padri and nearby villages are engaged in the manufacture of salt. Among the material mention should be made of two copper coins, similar to those issued by the Kshatrapa king Nahapan, two boatshaped terracotta motifs and one tortoise-shaped copper lamp. They indicate the overseas trading activity. Besides, an array of antiquities such as pottery, iron, copper, terracotta objects, beads of glass, semiprecious stones and shell bangles have been found.

Another settlement is called Hathab, which is located very close to the sea and covers an area of 40 hectare. Of the twenty two settlements, Hathab is the largest settlement in the study region. From the close observation of the location of site and surrounding ecology that it can be said the site could have been a regional centre (Fig.4). This site is also mentioned in the *Periplus of the Erythraen sea* as a port (Schoff 1912) during the Early Historic period.

The Early Historic settlements are distributed in a linear pattern in the Shetrunji basin. They form what Flannery (1979) describes as long strings of villages in "ribbon band fashion." Possehl (1980) has stated that the resources, especially fertile land and grass belts are evenly spread all along rivers. With growing population, acquisition of new land for agriculture is inevitable and people spread their activities to the other rivers basins. Flannery (1976: 177) has suggested that villages will be located on a particular river bank which affords the best catchment area with respect to mountain hunting and gathering pastures and metal and mineral resources. The formula for determining the spacing of settlements is based on the density of rural settlements. The average spacing between the two settlements is determined by dividing the total area surveyed by total number of settlements. In the study region there were altogether twenty two settlements. The average spacing between two settlements is 3.78 km. There are factors other than size affected the spacing of settlements. King (1961) has carried out spacing in Washington state and observed that the spacing of settlements was governed not only by the size of population but also by the economic potentialities of the area.

Subsistence Pattern

The locally produced cereals and domesticated animals could have met most of the food requirement of the Early Historic people in this region. The presence of direct evidence of faunal remains at the excavated site of Padri (Joglekar 1993) and other explored sites in this region and evidence of floral remains suggests that the people in this region practised a mixed food economy. The excavations at Padri have produced the direct evidence for the domesticated animals, such as cattle, sheep, goat as well as wild animals such as wild pig, wolf, jackal, antelopes and chital in the Early Historic level (Joglekar 1993). From this evidence it can be deduced that the Early Historic people in this region used domesticated animal for various purposes like dairy products and for meat. A number of fish bones recovered from the site indicates that fish was also included in their diet. No direct evidence for the cultivation of cereals and other food grains was found in the Early Historic level at Padri. But the presence of agricultural implements and cooking objects at the site suggests that agricultural products must have played an important role in their subsistence pattern. It should be mentioned, apart from Nagara and Somnath, no other Early Historic sites in Saurashtra has given evidence of cereal and other food grains. Excavations at Somnath have revealed four kinds of cereals.' At Nagara some chared seeds and grains consisting of Rice, Kodrava, Matha were found from the deposit of period I–II (IAR 1963–64:11; Mehta 1968:153).

Chronology

The extensivre explorations carried out by the author in the lower part of Shetrunji river basin, resulted in the discovery of 22 Early Historic as well as Harappan affliated sites. The cultural remains particularly ceramic assembloges from these explored sites have been compared with Padri material, which were obtained from proper strata and have been precisely dated The Red Slipped 'Ware, Red 'Ware and Grey Ware represent the Early Historic period at Padri The shapes include cups with tapering sides, globular jar/pot with out curved rim, deep dish and lids. This period of Padri can be dated to the beginning of 1st century B.C–A.D. on the basis of evidence like circular clay tablet with Brahmi script; a couple of copper coins similar to those issued by the Kshatrapa King Nahapana, two boat shaped terracotta motifs, figurines of Goddess Lajjagauri and structures of Goddess Lajjagauri's temple (Shinde 1992a, 1994 and 1998). This period can be chronologically correlated with Valabhipur period III phase I (Jairath 1986:344–46), Devnimori (Mehta and Chowdhary 1968:27), Shamlaji I and II (Mehta and Patel 1967:8) and with Nagara period III (Mehta 1960:27). As far as the present study is concened, in the Early Historic period the stratified ceramic assemblage of Padri provides a chronological index to the pottery obtained as a result of exploration from the Early Historic settlements. All explored sites have yielded more or less similar type ceramic assemblages including their forms and fabric as that of Padri However, it could be said that, all the explored Early Historic sites in this region are contemporary with the excavated sites of Padri and it can be dated to the beginning of the 1st century B.C.–A.D. on the basis of ceramic assemblage and other associated cultural materials.

REFERENCES

Adams, R.M. 1961. Changing patterns of territorial organization in the central highlands Chiapas, Maxico. *American Antiquity* 26(1): 341–360.

————1965. *Land Behind Baghdad: A History of Settlemnt on the Diyala Plains*. Chicago: Chicago University press.

Agrawala, V.S. 1953. *India as known to Panini*. Lucknow: Lucknow University.

Bernard, V.J., Gachet and J.F. Salles. 1990. Appostilles en

Marge de da ceramique des IVetv, in *Failaka 1986–88* (d' Yves Calvert and J. Gachet Eds.), pp. 241–284. Lyon: Travaux de la Maizon De L' Orient., Fig. 4.

Bhan, S. 1979. Early Settlemnt in Haryana: A study of Urbanization. *Journal of Haryana Studies.* Vol. VIII, Nos. 1-2:1–13.

Change, K.C. 1962. A typology of Settlement and Community pattern in some circumpolar societies. *Arctic Anthropology* 1: 28–41.

Chitalwala, Y.M. 1979. Harappan and Post Harappan Settlement Patterns in the Rajkot District of Saurashtra. In *Eassays in Indian Protohistory* (Agrawala, D.P. and D.K. Chakrabarti (ed.)), pp.113–121. Delhi: B.R. Publishing Corporation.

Clark, D.L. 1972. A provisional Model of an Iron Age Society and Its Settlement system. In *Models in Archaeology* (D.L. Clark ed.), pp 801–869, London: Methuen.

David Raju, B. 1985. *Neolithic Culture of Central Coastal Andhra, South India.* Unpublished Ph.D thesis, Nagarjuna University.

Dhavalikar, M.K. 1977b. Settlement Patterns at Inamgoan. *Man and Environment* 1: 46–5.

1978b. Settlemtn Archaeology of Inamgaon. *Puratattava* 8: 44–54.

Dhavalikar, M.K. and G.L. Possehl. 1974. Subsistence Pattern of an Early Farming Communities of Western India. *Puratattava* 7: 39–46.

Erdosy, G. 1988. *Urbanization in Early Historic India.* England: BAR International Series 430.

Flaming, A. 1971. Territorial patterns in Bronze Age. *Proceedings of Prehistoric Society* 37: 138–166.

Flannery, K.V. 1972. The Origins of Village as a Settlement type inf Mesoamerican and the near East: A comparative Study. In *Man, Settlement and Urbanism.* pp. 23–53 (ed. Ucko, P.J., R. Tringham and D.W. Dimbleby). London: Duckworth.

Gupta, Sunil 1997. *Roman Egypt to Peninsular India: Archaeological Patterns of Trade (Ist century B.C. to 3rd century A.D.),* Unpublished Ph.D Thesis, University of Pune.

Haque, M. 1992. *Pre and Protohistoric Settlement Pattern of the Middle and Lower Ganga Valley,* Unpublished Ph.D thesis, University of Poona.

Houston, J.M. 1953. *A Social Geography of Europe,* London.

IAR. 1963–64. *Indian Archaeoogy–A Review.* Annual Bulletine of the Archaeological Survey of India, New Delhi.

Jairath, V.K. 1986. *Archaeology of the Northern Part of Bhavnagar District, Gujarat State upto 15th century A.D.* Unpublished Ph.D thesis, M.S. University, Baroda.

Joglekar, P.P. 1994. A preliminary Report on the faunal Remains at Padri: A Harappan Site in Bhavnagar District, Gujarat. *Puraattaa.* 24: 35–39.

King, L.J. 1961. A multivariate analysis of spacing of urban settlements in the United States. *Annals of the Association of American Geographers.* 51:222–33.

Lal, M. 1984. *Settlement History and Rise of Civilization in Ganga-Yamuna Doabs (From 1500 B.C. to 300 A.D.).* Delhi: B.R. Publishing Corporation.

Metha, R.N. 1968. *Excavation at Nagara,* Baroda.

Mehta, R.N. and S.N. Chowdhary. 1966. *Excavation at Devnimori,* Baroda.

Paddayya, K. 1982. *The Acheulain Culture of the Hunagi Valley (Peninsular India): A Settlement System Perspective.* Poona: Deccan College Post Graduate and Research Institute.

Paul, A.B., B. Tripath and V. Shinde. 1997. New Archaeological Discoveries in the Lower Shetrunji River Basin, Bhavnagar District, Gujarat. In *Him-kanti: Archaeology, Art and History.* pp.53–63. (Prof. K.P. Nautiyal Felicitation Vol., B.M. Khanduri and Vinod

Naytiyal eds.), New Delhi: Book India Publishing Co.

Possehl, G.L. 1980. *Indus Civilization in Saurashtra. New Delhi:* B.R. publsihing corporation.

Renfrew, C. 1972. Patterns of population growth in Prehistoric Aegean. In *Man, Settlement and Urbanism.* pp.383–99, (es. Ucko, P.J.. R.Tringham and D.W. Dembleby).

Sanders, W.T. 1956. The Central Mexican Symbiotic region: A Study in Prehistoric Settlement Patterns. In *Prehistoric Settlement Patterns in New World,* (Willey, G.R. ed.), pp. 115–127, Viking Fund Publication in Anthropology No. 23.

Schoff, W.H. 1912. *The Periplus of the Erythaean Sea.* London: Longmans, Green and Co., Bombay and Calcutta

Shinde, V.S. 1984. *Early Settlement in the Central Tapi Basin.* Unpublished Ph.D. thesis, University of Poona.

1990. The Malwa Culture in Maharastra: A study of Settlement and Subsistene Patterns. *Man and Environment* XV (2):53–60.

1992a. Excavations at Padri-1990–91: A preliminary Report. *Man and Environment,* XVII (1): 79–89.

1992b. Padri and the Indus Civilization. *South Asian Studies* 8: 55–66.

1994a. Early Harappan phase in Gujarat with speical Reference to Padri. *World Archaeology* Unpublished vaolume, New Delhi.

1998. Pre-Harappan Padri Culture in Saurashtra: The Recent Disvoery. *South Asian Studies,* 14: 173–182.

Trigger, B.G. 1968. The Determinants of Settlement Patterns. In *Settlement Archaeology* (Chang, K.C. (eds.)) Palo Alto. National Press.

Trivedi, R.K. (ed.) 1969. *Gujarat State Gazetteers, Bhavnagar District.* Ahmedabad.

Wallace, R. 1888. *India in 1887.* Edinburgh: Oliver and Boyd: Twee dale court.

Willey, G.R. 1953. Prehistoric Settlement Patterns in the Viru Valley, Peru *Bureau of American Ethnology,* Bulletin 155, Washington D.C.: Smithsonian Institute.

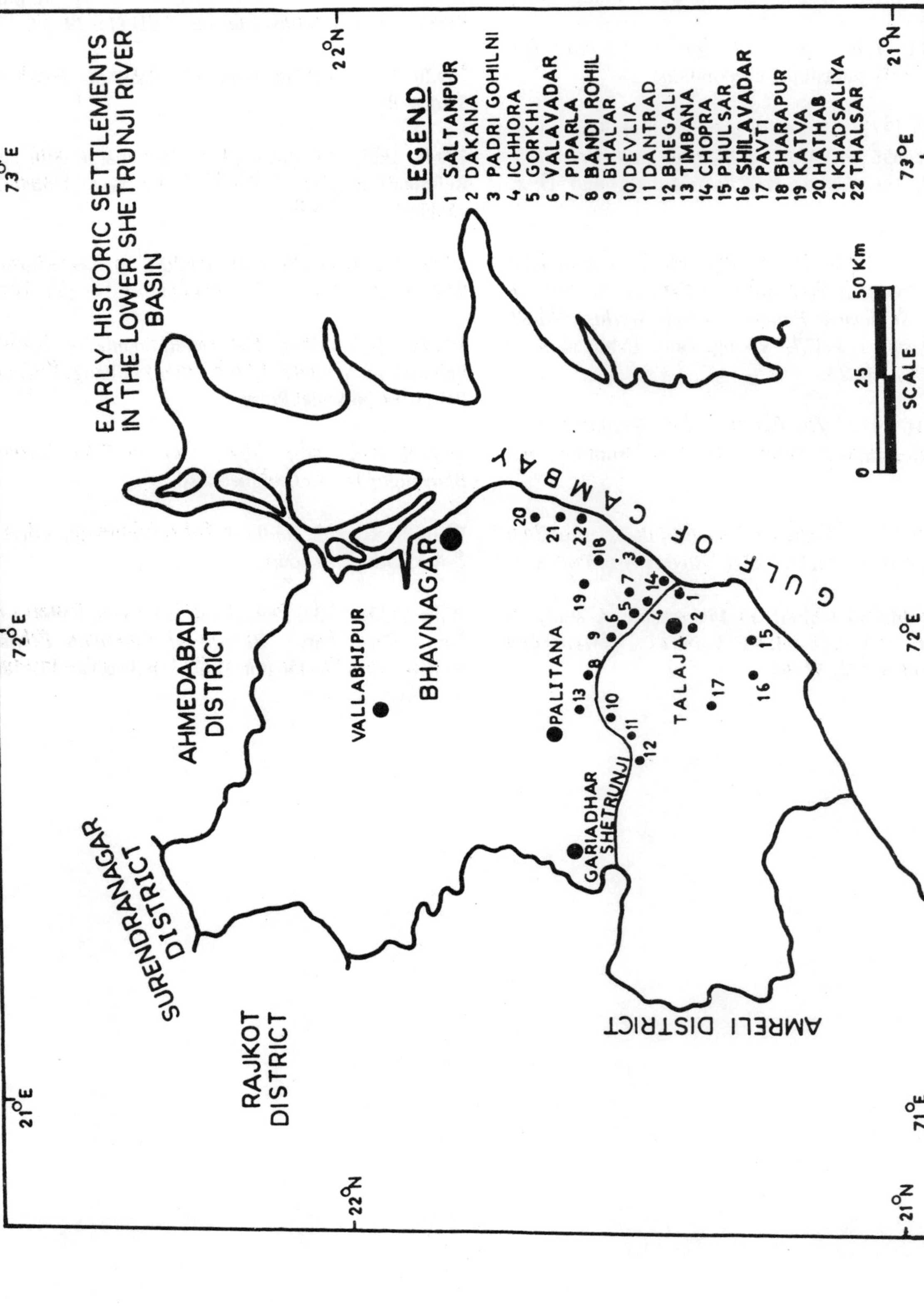

Fig. 1. Early Historic Settlements in the lower Shetrunju River Basin.

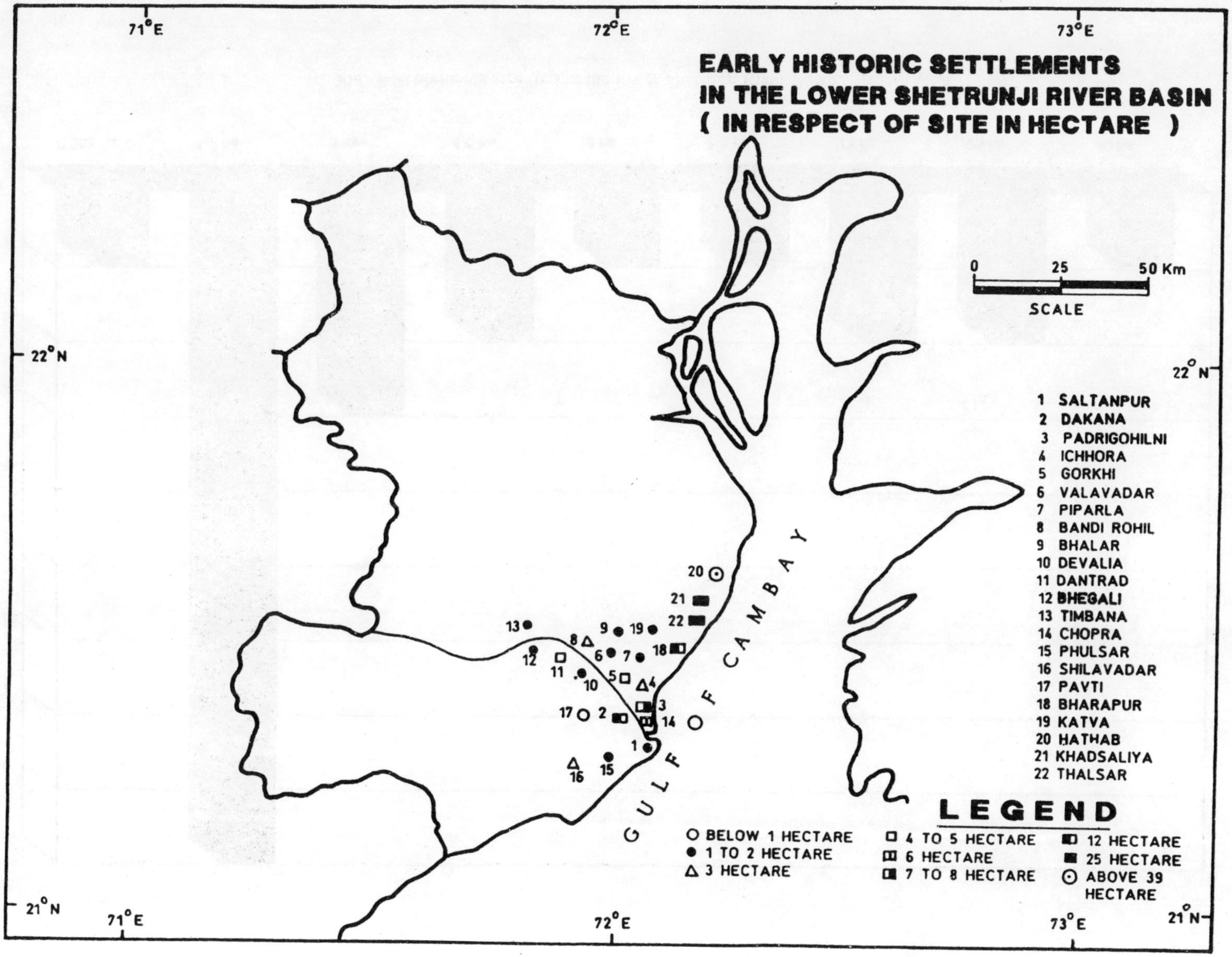

Fig. 2. Early Historic Settlemnts in the lower Shetrunji River Basin (In Respect of site in Hectare).

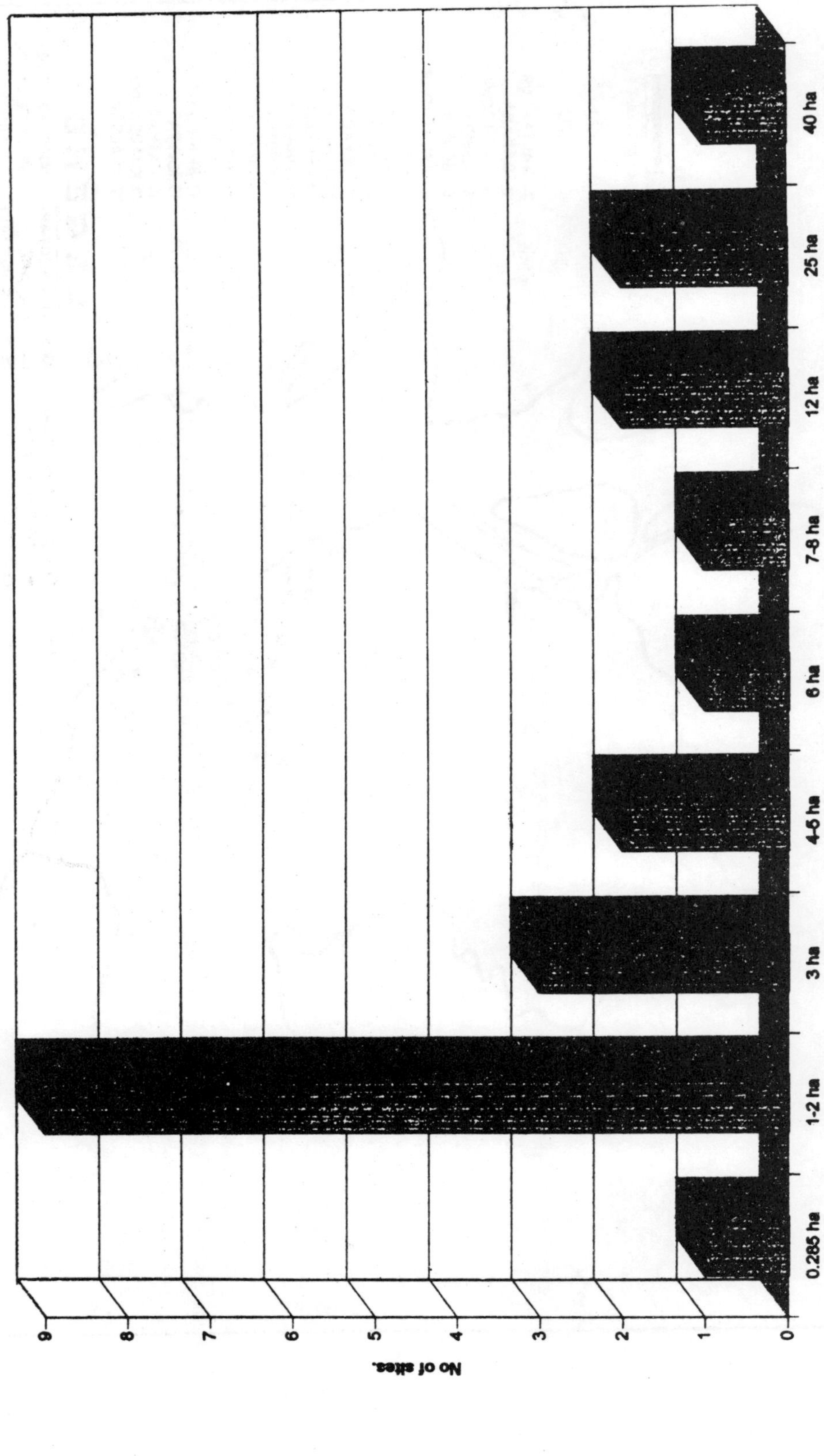

Fig. 3. Settlements size (ha) in the lower Shetrunji River Basin.

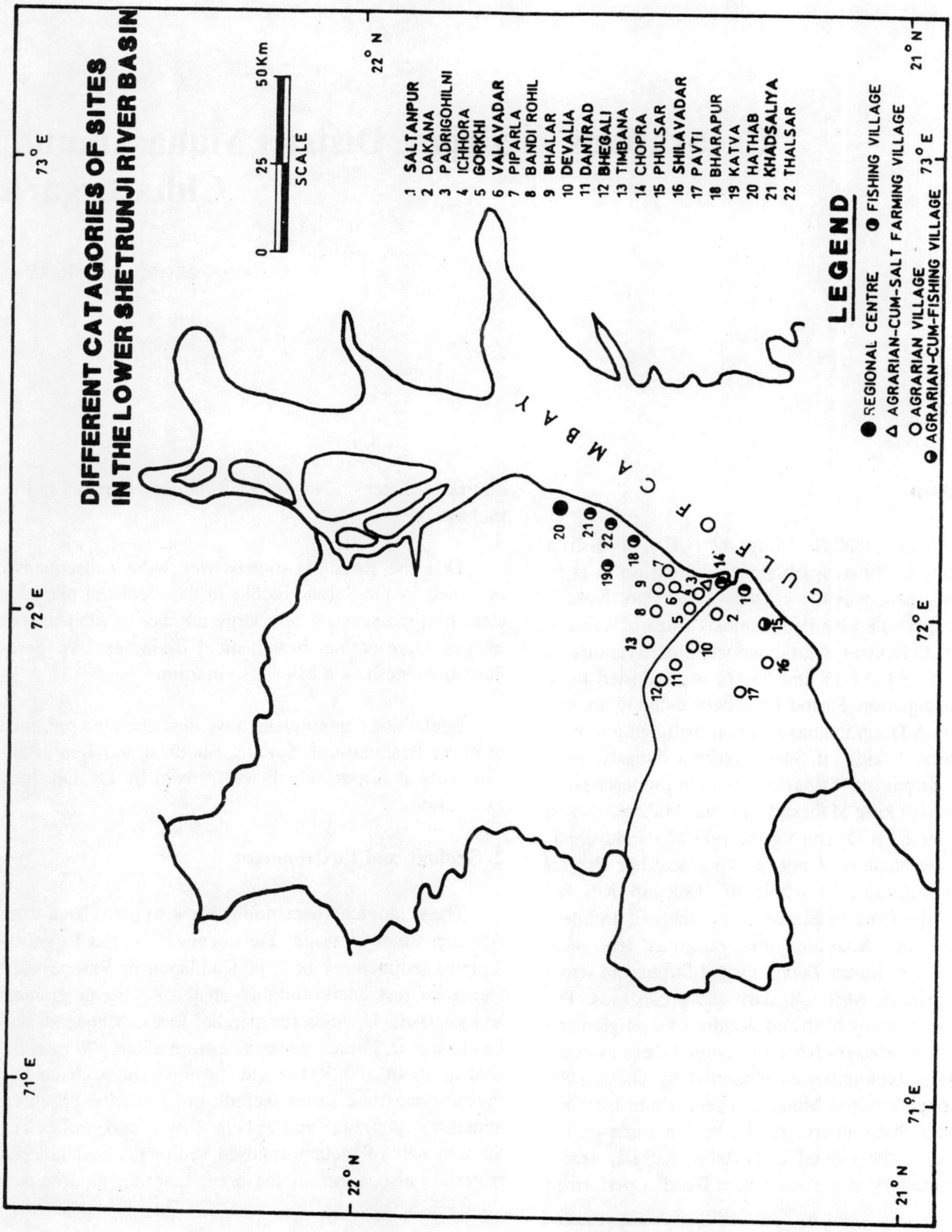

Fig. 4. Different catagories of sites in the lower Shetrunji River Basin.

Excavations at Sirpur, District Mahasamund, Chhattisgarh

JAGAT PATI JOSHI AND A.K.SHARMA*

I. Introduction

Sirpur, (Lat 21°20'N, Long 82°11'E), in district Mahasamund of Chhattisgarh state, situated on th right bank of Mahanadi, was the capital of Dakshin, Kosala, which was then ruled by Panduvamsis from 6th century A.D. Dr. M.G.Dikshit who conducted excavations at Sirpur in 1953-54, 54-55 and 55-66, has reported three periods of occupation. Period I has been dated to the end of 5th century A.D. on the basis of coin belonging to king Prasannamatra, a king of Sarabhapuriya dynasty. First mention of 'Sirpur' or 'Sripur' is found in the inscription of Sarabhapuriya king Mahasudeoraj and Mahapravararaj of 5th -6th century A.D. During the rule of Panduvamsis Sirpur was the nucleus of not only political but also art and literary activities in whole of 'Dakshin Kosala'. Attracted by the fame of Sirpur in the fields of architecture, art, literary activities and religious tolerance, Chinese traveller Hiusen-Tsang, visited Sirpur and wrote that the inhabitants were tall, dark and prosperous. The King was Kshatriya by birth and Buddhist by religion and very benevolent. Hiusen-Tsang discovered there as many as 100 Buddhist monasteries inhabited by about 1000 monks, belonging to the Mahayana sect. From his writings it is clear that emperor Asoka built a *stupa* on the southern end of the capital of Dakshin Kosala, near a Buddhist monastery at a place where Buddha performed a miracle. Later on Nagarjuna Bodhisattva stayed in this monastery.

That the Buddhist monasteries were subsequently occupied by the Saivite monks in the medieval period is clear by the existence of a large number of plaques and images representing Brahmanical divinities like Siva-Parvati, Ganesh, and Mhishasurmardini.

Beglar and Cunningham have described the presence of many Brahmanical, Saivite, Buddhist and Jain establishments at Sirpur, which was proved by Dr. Dikshit's excavations.

2. Geology and Environment

The geological formation in the area dates back from Archaen times to recent Pleistocene. The flat to gently dipping sedimentary beds of Cuddapah or Purana sedimentaries rest uncomfortably on the Archaean granites and gneisses. Uplands run parallel to the Mahanadi and lie close to it. These uplands rise from about 300 m at the foot to about 400-500 m., at the top. The archaen and Precambrian rock series include mica schists, phyllites, hematite, quartzite, basic lava flows and tuffs. The Satpura belt of metamorphosed sediments and igneous materials also accur in the area. Laterite, an iron-rich

*Former Director General, Archaeological Survey of India,
Former Superintending Archaeologist, Archaeological Survey of India.

vesicular dark brown or brick coloured mottled rock is often found capping the hill tops. The area is also dotted with sandstone and shells belonging to the upper Gondwana system of the Lower Cretacean period. There are extensive horizontal types of gritty and conglomeratic, quartzite and fine purplish sandstone with spots of green chlorite and pink to buff shales.

The Mahanadi rises in the Sihawa range and after collecting a number of streams, traverses the Mahasamund district in north-easterly direction but near Sirpur it flows in south-easterly direction with a deviation of nearly 23° east. Sirpur region falls in the trans-Mahandi Plain (north) in th drainage system of Chhattisgarh.

Sirpur region enjoys typical topical rainy climate with almost dry winters. The temperature varies from 19.8°c in January to 44.7°c in May. The area is fed by monsoon rains and gets about 140 cm of rain in a year. About 95% of the rainfall occurs between June and September-October. During the summer while the plains around Sirpur is extremely hot, the hills around are pleasantly cool. Sirpur is surrounded by low hills on the north-east to south-east which are mostly composed of sandstone formations with thick jungles. The area around Sirpur consists mostly of alluvial soils which are fine dark and deep. At upper level it is yellow sandy soil with some admixture of clay, light in texture and suitable for rice cultivation. It is locally known as *Matasi*. Below it lies very thick layer, 1.5 to 2.00 m of greenish fine sandy clay formed as a result of series of flooding and decomparition of organic material like leaves and vegetation of the thick forests. Floods in the floodplains of Mahanadi are recurring feature due to its low embankments and wide area.

Sirpur is surrounded on almost on all sides, particularly on its right bank with deep forests. These forest grow teak, *sal tendu*, *Bajasaal*, *sisham*, *mahua*, *barra*, *bahera*, *aonla*, *Kusum*, *char*, *palas*, *kahua*, *bel*, *bhilwan*, *ber*, *khair*, *karra*, *semal*, *kumhi*, bamboo etc.

The most common animals found around Sirpur are : Monkey *(Semnopithecus entellus)*, *kalmuha bendra*, Tiger, Leopard, Indian otter, mangoose, Jackal, the stripped hyaena, Indian fox, Indian sloth-bear, Indian bear, the *nilgai*, spotted deer and *sambhar*. In the villages cattle, sheep and goat ar common . Mahanadi and numeraus ponds and tanks in sirpur abound in varieties of fish. Jungle cock, peafowl, bush-quail, green pigeon and spurfowls are common in the area.

Apart from summer and winter crops of paddy, gram and wheat in summer months, on the sands of Mahanadi plenty of vegetable specifically water-melon is grown. Now-a-days water-melon is a major export item to as far of places as Nagpur by tempos and trucks and has become a major secondary source of income for the villagers. Another major export item is slate. Slate quarries in Mahanadi, supply the entire need of the slate slabs of the region.

3. Exploration/Excavation

The present exploration and excavation was conducted under the aegies of Bodhisattva Nagarjuna Smarak Sanstha Va Anusandhan Kendra, Nagpur and was directed by the authors who were assisted by Shri Jaulfiqur Ali, Kumari Reema Sobti, and Shri J.S.Dubey. Two potential areas on the eastern side of the present village to the south of Raikera tank, were taken up for the excavations. One numbered as SRP-2-2000 is located just outside the south-eastern end of the fortification while the other numbered as Srp-1-2000 is located inside the fortified area.

4. Pre-historic Period

From the Buddhist Vihara (RP-1-2000) right over the virgin soil at a depth of nearly 2.5 m below the present surface two Late Acheulian stone tools were recovered. These tools were recovered from the thick deposit of hard, greenish sticky clay. This is the first time that evidence of prehistoric period has been noticed from Sirpur. Both the tools have been made on quartizitic sandstone. One of the tools is a broken cleaver made on a flake. While the proximal half is broken, the distal half has a 8 cm wide sharp cutting edge. The secondary retouching on the periphery is clearly visible. It has been made on thick and reddish quartizite. The other tools are a highly rolled and encrusted hand-axe, 14 cm in length and shaped out of dark coloured quartizite.

The area around Sirpur abounds in rock-shelters and natural caves in the hills having escarpments.

5. Siva Temple (SRP-2-2000):- (Pls. I & II)

It is a west facing massively built stone and brick structure. The plinth i.e. upto the *Jangha* portion is built up of slate slabs, locally available from the quarries in and around Mahanadi. Though originally black in colour, due to fact that it remained buried under the soil for centuries, the outer surface has turned white due to leeching out of calcium carbonate. The *pancharatha* on plan temple, externally measuring 12.20 x 7.20 m (in the centre) consists of a. sanctum, 3.25 x 3.25 m internally, narrow *antartala*, measuring 3.50 x 1.60 m, a narrow *mukhamandapa* 1.50 m in width, preceded by a 5.75 x 2.9 m, internally, *mandapa*, which might have been approached by a flight of steps. The 1.30 m high slate slab plinh which is moulded consists of ten layers of slabs, over which brick superstructure was resting. The brick superstructure is available upto twelve courses of bricks measuring in size 40 (41) x 20 x 7 cm. The slate plinth of *garbhagriha* and *antarala* are caped by single layer of dressed rectangular lateritic blocks, measuring 1.70 m in length, 0.55 m in width and 20 to 22 cm in thickness, except he central wall of *grabhagriha*. No such laterite capping is available over the plinth of mandapa.

Mandapa: On outer side the *mandapa* is 8.0 m in length north-south and 4.15 m in width, east-west. The longer walls are 1.10 m in width while the shorter arms are 1.40 m in width. Though only three courses of slate slabs ar available, on the western wall of the *mandapa*, in collapsed condition, the inner wall consists of six courses capped by seventh course of thick slate slab. The inner wall is 1.05 m in width, while outer wall is 0.70 m wide. The southern wall is 1.30 m wide and the northern one which has virtually completely collapsed is only 0.80 m wide. On the south-eastern corner 4 to 5 courses of bricks are available. On the eastern wall four square pillar based made of lateritic blocks, two on the two corners while the other two in the centre, one of which is further capped by an octagonal lateritic pillar base, are available. The lateritic blocks and pillar bases were joined by iron dowells, which are available *in situ* also. The base of the *mandapa* is paved by sand stone boulders.

Antarala: In rectagular *mandapa* more than ten course of slate slabs and six courses of bricks are available on the inner side to the height of 2.10 m. On the outer side of *antarala* at the junction of *mandapa*, on northern and southern side atleast three flight of steps each, facing east are available. The steps are 35 cm in width and 50 cm in height each. On the outer wall of *antarala* both the central lateritic slab as well as the slate plinth slabs have vertical wide crack in the centre of the wall running east west.

Garbhagriha: At the entrance of *garbhagriha* two side projections on the slate slab plinth are available, making a corner of the brick superstructure. The square *garbhagriha* from inside is from outer side *pancharatha* on plan. The eastern back wall in 6.40 m in length and height of plinth is 1.50 m. having nine courses of slate slabs and three courses of bricks. The central portion of *ratha* is 1.00 m wide, followed by 0.95 m and 1.20 m wide *rathas* on either side, while on the northern and southern side they are 1.10, 1.0 and 2.05m. wide. On the southern side the extant height available is 1.65 m. with ten courses of slate slabs. The lowest course of the slate is of undressed slabs and projects outward slightly. The width of the walls is 1.15 m. The *grabhagriha* slate plinth is capped by two lines of single lateritic dressed slabs. Inside the square *grabhagriha* there is another square, slightly depressed area measuring 1.80 x 1.80 m. In the centre of this square is the *Yoni-peeth* having diameter of 1.80 m housing in the centre 1.20 m high black granite, polished linga. The girth of linga is 1.10 m. The bottom square portion of linga is 40 cm in height, followed by 40 cm high octagonal *Vishnu prabhaga* and 40 cm high *rudra-prabhaga* which is concave on the top. The central socket of *Yoni-peetha* is 45 cm x 45 cm. The linga displays *Brahma sutra* on western side.

Inside the *grabhagriha* another small linga and yonipeeth having makara mukha was also lying. While the linga is of granite, *yoni-peeth* is of white schist. The door of *grabhagriha* is 1.40 m wide with a laterite slab having width of 0.60m. On the northern side of the *grabha-griha* there is a covered drain of dressed lateritic hlocks. The drain is covered by wide schist slabs and leads to the tank on the north-eastern corner of the temple and inside the fortification of Buddha-Vihara (SRP-I). The drain runs below the eclosure wall. The drain has three layers of lateritic blocks capped by brick superstructure. With of drain in 0.50 m. Similar to th lateritic blocks capped by brick superstructure. Width of drain in 0.50m. Similar to the lateritic slab of *mandapa*, the central lateritic slab of *grabhagriha* door has also wide vertical crack running in east-west direction and in the same line as that of *manadapa* slab. These cracks have been caused as a result of severe earthquake, the picentre of which was in the west.

From this Siva temple site a large numbers of antiquities were recovered which include a white stone plaque with six armed 'Natraj' figure carved, head of 'Siva' in black granite, a small plaque on slate showing Mahisa surmardini, a terracotta mother goddess figurine, terracotta bulls with perforated solid wheels (such ones are even to this day being worshiped by the Hindu community during 'Pola' day which falls in 'Sravana' month of the long rainy season), a number of iron objects which include, sickle, dowells, fish-hook, pans, variety of nails, chisels, and knives.

The entire area where this Siva temple was exposed was in the form of a low mound, surrounded by fields on the east and west, extension of mound in the south and portion of fortification wall and tank on the north. The top layer, varying in thickness from 0.20 m to 0.70 m consists of black fine sticky clay with vegetal decomposed deposit and interspersed by stone pieces. This layer had mostly accumulated due to dumping of clay by the people from the adjacent fields and decomposition of subsequent vegetation growth. Layer 2 is almost uniformly thick with maximum deposit at the centre of the mound comprising fallen bricks and bricks-bats, at places with earth mortar intact.

The maximum thickness of this layer of superstructure debris is 1.85 m. In this layer except the debris of superstructure there is not a single foreign material which indicates that the whole superstructure collapsed at one time; another indication of destruction due to earthquake. Had the deposit been due to slow time spread crumbling of the superstructure, there would have been foreign elements including water and wind borne seasonal deposits.

Layer 3 is composed of greenish sticky, kankarey clay mixed with, at places with stone fragments. It varies in thickness from 10 to 30 cm. Layer 4 is again 25 to 30 cm in thickness and comprises of sandy clay with pieces of black stone.

Layer 5 is composed of greenish, sticky, kankarey clay in which the foundation of the temple has been laid. Nearly 30 to 35 cm of this layer was dug to lay the foundation. It is clear that top of this layer formed the working level and from this depth upwards brick debris have fallen on top of this layer and rest over it.

6. Buddha Temple *cum* Nunnery (SRP I-2000) (Pls. III & IV)

SRp-I area which on the surface contained debris of broken pillars, sculpture pieces and an image of headless monolithic Buddha statue, was partly excavated in an area of 700 sq. m. So far it has been excavated to the depth of 2.50 m and has yielded a west facing Buddha temple with a central *grabhagriha* housing a 1.45 high and 1.25 m broad (Knee to knee) monolithic Buddha image in *padmasana* posture and in *Bhumi-sparsha mudra*. The granite image has praavali on the back of head. To the east and west of central sanctum sanctorum two more shrines were added which occupied the two images of Bodhisatvas.

The plinth of entire complex was made of schist slab while the super structure was of bricks. Bricks used are of three sizes 1-42 x22 x 8cm., 2-36 x 20 x7..5cm and 3-29 x 23x 8.5 cm.

The construction activity was started at the depth of 2.80 m. from the present surface and consists of five layers. Layer 1 is nearly 5 cm to 15 cm thick humus and is composed of fine dark brown clay and decomposed vegetation. Being low lying area with stagnant water during rainy season and absolutely dry surface during summer,, both water and wind borne deposits are clearly visible in the section. Layer 2 varies in thickness from 30 to 50 cm. and is composed oc blackish brown clay layer has yielded most of the black ware sherds and fragments of glass bangles. The two copper coins belonging to Ala-ud-Din Khalji (A.D. 1296-1316) were also recovred from this layer alongwith terracotta animal figurines. Layer 3 varies in thickness from 40 to 65 cm and consists overwhelmingly of brick debris (fallen superstructure) indicating that it is at this time i.e. on top of layer 4 the entire super structure collapsed, as witnessed in Siva temple also. After a major and sudden fall due to heavy jerk, the remaining portion collapsed slowly. It is in this layer that the huge monolithic pillars have also collapsed. The direction of most collapsed members towards east due to sudden heavy jerk indicates earthquake with its epicentre towards west. The phenomenon is further corroborated by the horizontal straight line cracks on huge lateitic slabs which were used to cap the plinth level of the schist-stone wall and floor of the doors. Vertical cracks appear in the foundation walls and brick super structures (where ever remaining). Layer 5, 70 to 75 cm. thick is composed of greenish, hard sticky clay mixed with intervening deposits of slate pieces. Hardly any brick pieces could be seen in this layer indicating that while laying the foundation, only stone blocks for the foundation were stacked near the site of construction. On top level of this layer small thin chips are more conspicuous by their presence.

Layer 5 which has been excavated to the depth of 90 cm (2.80 m below present surface) is composed of greenish sticky clay lumps mixed with regular deposition of slate-stone pieces and sand stonenodules. In fact just at the top of this layer the slate stone pieces form a uniform, 5 cm thick capping layer. Such layers are uniformly deposited at regular intervals of 10 cm i.e. one layer of 5 cm thickness of slate stone pieces, followed by 10 cm thick layer of greenish clay indicating that after laying the foundation of slate stone dressed slabs upto the height of 90 to 95 cm, the entire dug up area was meticulously filled up with clay followed by stone pieces, then clay and so on, in order to make the ground strong and solid. In fact proper ramming was done after each deposit of clay and stone pieces by use of good quantity of water. As the whole area marked for construction was sunk deep instead of the traditional method of digging foundation trenches for individual walls, we do not get foundation trenches for individual walls except for the eastern end walls of *garbhagriha* where 'V' shaped foundation trenches for walls running in south-west-north-east direction could easily be demarcated. Filling material in these trenches consists of stone piece mixed with brick nodules. This indicates that as foundation wall went on rising in other areas, they went on filling and ramming the blank spots between the walls, whereas in case of eastern side the foundation trench was filled up after raising the superstructure, partly. In other areas the working level went on rising as the structural parts went on rising.

The foundation of stone slabs was raised upto 1m height as he capping stones of the foundation have not only the straight engraved lines, on both the lengthwise ends of the slabs, but also carry almost on each slab the masons marks in the form of a syllable of Brahmi words which consists of *Ka, Kha, Wa, Aa, Pa, T*a, etc. of which *Ka* is predominant. Other symbols like swastik also occur in many slabs.

The supporting evidence that the slabs heaving mason's marks and engraved lines were the capping layer of foundation walls is provided by occurrence of brick pieces column over each foundation, exactly of the same width (thickness) as that of the width of engraved lines. Such columns rise upto the bottom of layer 3 piercing through layer 4. It is on top of layer 4 and bottom of layer 3 that collapse happened as the pillars and brick debris are lying right over top of layer 4. As an example in southern and western area of *mandapa*, the lines engraved for the demarcation of the width of brick walls, are 1.10 m wide and exactly following this thickness is the impression of the brick wall in the section which is also 1.10 m wide, of course 5 to 10 cm. less at places, due to pressure of the adjoining filling. This impression is available upto the height of 90 cm to 1.0 m.

In the foundation of the *mandapa* walls first 2 to 3 layers of small stone (slate) pieces have been laid and then covered with big blocks of slabs upto this height (25 cms.). This first stage foundation is broadened by nearly 30 cm (15 cm on each side) and then the second level of foundation excepting the coping stone is laid. Between the coping slab and the big slab of first stage there are twelve courses of regularly laid, well dressed slate stone blocks (mostly rectangular blocks like bricks) rising to the uniform height of 65 to 68 cm. The engraved lines on the first and second stage of coping are in perfect straight line to the plumb.

In the foundation trench filling of eastern walls, pieces of stone and pot sherds could easily be seen. The presence of these pot sherds indicate that before the construction of this complex in 5th-6th century A.D., human existence predating this complex was in existence in Sirpur. The pot sherds are mostly of fine red slipped ware which is datable to 2nd–3rd century A.D. The foundation of the trench also contain pieces of charcoal and ash. The back wall of the *grabhagriha* is raised upto the height of 2.40 m. It consists of three tiers, in which three offsets are present.

In the foundation trench first a layer of big slab-stone blocks projecting out by 5 to 10 cm. from the above raised wall is put. Outside these slabs, nodules of stones have been arranged. Above this block eleven courses of dressed stone slabs have been raised capped by big blocks of stones. The first layer of blocks is nearly 10 cm, thick followed by 55 cm thick 11 courses, to be further followed by big blocks of nearly 15 cm thick. Over it again, eleven courses of dressed rectangular pieces. These courses are 58 cm high. The second rise is offset hardly by 1 to 2 cm. The second level is again capped by huge blocks of 12-13 cm thick stones, offsetting by 2 to 3 cm. Over it rises the third level of 9 to 10 courses of rectangular stones to the height of 50 cm. This level has been offset by 5 cm. Above this level another coping stone of big blocks has been laid which is 12-13 cm thick. Over it, rises 4 courses of smaller blocks to the height of 15-17 cm. Over this fourth stage is the coping stone of 12-13 cm thick blocks. The total height of wall, available, is 2.50 m.

The Buddha temple consists of three *grabhagrihas*, the central one being occupied by 1.45 cm high monolithic Buddha image whose head got severed and lay to the west of the torso nearby. Buddha in *Bhumisparsha mudra* and in *padmasana* portion is enshrined in the rectagular *grabhagriha* measuring 4.85 m north-south and 3.20 m east-west. Width of the schist slab walls of the plinth vary from 1.25 to 1.30 m. The door of the central *garbhagriha* is 1.32 m. in width where 0.46 m wide and 0.21 thick lateritic slab has been kept. This slab along with the wall on which it rests and the back wall of the temple behind the Buddha image have developed wide vertical cracks, apparently due to the shock of severe earthquake. As a result of this tectonic movement the huge statue of Buddha and some of the pillars have tilted towards east where as almost all the remaining pillars in the Vihara area have collapsed and broken into fragments. The fallen pillar in front of this *garbhagriha* is 2.15 m long, 0.44 m wide and 0.28 m thick. It has been carved with spiral motifs on the inner side. The brick super structure with thick lime plaster has collapsed towards east.

The other two subsidiary *grabhagrihas*, one each to the north and south of the main one, house the image of Bodhisattvas sitting over huge carved stone pedestal with figures of *sharduls* on the right and left. The *garbhagriha* on the north is 2.40 cm north-south and 1.80 m east-west with thickness of walls varying from 1.15 m to 1.30 m. while the one on th southern side is 2.40m north-south and 1.80 m east-west with thickness of walls varying from 1.25 to 1.40 m. The central sanctum sanctorum floor was raised thrice, the lowest being of plastered mud, followed by brick paved floor, the top one is plastered with lime plaster and pained with red-ochre solution making floral designs which have heavily weathered. The fact that the lower portions of earlier pillars inside the main *garbhagriha* have got embedded by the thickness of subsequent floors also indicate subsequent repair and renovations of the Buddha temple to which two more pillars were added by he side of the earlier two pillars.

In front of the *'grabhagriha'* a sixteen pillared *mandapa* of 10 x 8 m dimension has been exposed. The pillars which have all collapsed, are made of monolithic basalt and sandstone and are beautifully carved with *Ghatapallav, mithuna*-couples, *Chauri-dharinis* and scroll motifs. The *mandapa* is surrounded by a 2.10 m wide verandah on all the four sides. On three sides, leaving the eastern side which has the *garbhagrihas*, there are a row of rooms measuring 2.00 x 2.40 m inside. So far twelve rooms have been exposed. All open in their respective varandhas. On the south-western side the room near the entrance to the Vihara is also attached with a small store or office room, probably meant for the warden of the nunnery. On the north western side after the 3rd room there is a small corridor which had probably steps to go up. The room by the side of this corridor, to the west is bigger in size which was most likely the dinning hall. Almost all the rooms yielded a number of fragments of glass bangles in various colours with embossed designs. This indicates that the rooms were occupied by *'Bhikshunis'*.

One of the most remarkable and unique feature is the discovery of a huge iron-bell, 32 cm. long and 30 cm in diameter, from inside the main *garbhagriha*, and in front of Buddha image. This bell was recovered from the top of the last-floor level. On top of the body of the bell there is a welded hook for hanging. Probably this is the first bell of its kind to be recovered from a Buddha Vihara.

In all the three *garbhagrihas*, for out let of water, carved stone drains have been provided which shows that due to impact of Saivism at Sirpur Buddhist's have also started bathing the Buddha and Bodhisattva statues with water. Even from in front of the main *grabhagriha*, from the verandah covered drains flowed upto the northern and of the *Vihara*.

The entire nunnery complex was enclosed by a 2.5 m. thick dressed slate-stone fortification having sixteen bastions, measuring alternately 13 m and 30 m in diameter. In between the two bastions the length of the wall is 42 m and 30 m alternately. The 250 m x 210 m fortification or enclosure was on the south-western corner. On the south-eastern corner inside the enclosed area is located a beautiful tank where lotus still blooms and where the water from the *garbhagriha* of Siva temple was drained through a covered drain.t

From the Vihara beautiful image of Bodhisatvas, Manjushri, Avolokiteshwara, *Shardul*, *mithuna* couples, *chauari dharinis* and *ganas* were recovered, though in highly damaged condition. Other objects include, glass bangles, terracotta figurines, iron objects like nails of various shapes and sizes, door jambs, dowels, chisels, punnches, shaving razors etc.; a miniature four-armed sculpture on schist stone, a sealing with conch shell embossed on it, a stone amulet depicting a seated male figure with folded hands, a stamped pottery on black urnished ware. From the top level two round bilingual type billon (an alloy of bronze and silver) coins weighing 2.84 gms. each belonging to Sultan Muhammad Shah Alaud-Din Khalji, A.H. 708 (A.D. 1308-09) were recovered. The Arabic legends inscribed on the obverse in typical *Naskh* style of sultanate period, read-Sultan-ul Azam 'Alaud-Dunya Wad-Din'. On the reverse in the inner circle the legend in Arabic reads 'Muhammad Shah' whereas in the outer circle in Sanskrit is the title Shri Sultan Allaudin with date in Nagari figures 708, being the date of striking of the coin in Hizri era, which corresponds to A.D. 1308-09 This bilingual issue is commonly called *Jital*[1].

In both the structure i.e. Siva temple and Buddha temple *cum* nunnery a remarkable feature observed is the orientation of north-south walls from north-east to south-west deviating from the magnetic north by 23^0 towards east i.e.to *Ishan* direction. This is a deviation from normally practiced orientation of north-south, east-west. As far *Vastu-Sastra* the most sacred and auspicious direction for the religious buildings is north-east. Detailed examination of the Survey of India topo sheets of Sirpur area clearly show that at Sirpur Mahanadi flows from south-west to north-east and the centre of the bed of the river also shows exactly 23^0 deviation from the north towards east. Both the structures face towards the river just parallel to the flow line thus saving the walls the angular attack of the flood currents and moreover follow the topography of the area.

As the Buddha Vihara has so far been only partly excavated, further digging is likely to reveal more rooms.

[1]The coins were studied by the Epigraphy Branch (Persian and Arabic) of Archaeological Survey of India, Nagpur.

Mehrauli Iron Pillar Revisited

B.P.SINHA*

The Mehrauli Iron Pillar inscription was first brought to notice in 1834 by James Princep and was published in *JBBRAS* Vol. X by Bhau Daji and was later published by Fleet in 1887 (Fleet 1963)

Hardly any other Indian inscription has been a subject of intense controversy both about its contents and the issuer. In 1989 M.C.Joshi and S.K.Gupta collected and published the opinions of various scholars about the inscription expressed since its discovery in 1834. Here they have included extracts of my article on the Pillar published in the summeries of paper IHC1943. By the way this was my first research article.

To my mind, the only logical approach should be to examine the achievements of the king Candra in the inscription and then try to identify him with the known king of that name in ancient Indian history. What does, and does not, the inscription say about its hero '*Candra*'? Candra is credited with the following accomplishments : — (i) His enemies had gathered in Bengal and he defeated and forced them back; (ii) He crossed th seven mouths of the Indus and defeated the Vāhlikas; (iii) The southern ocean is still today being perfumed by the breezes of his powers; (iv) His glory even when he has left the earth is still lingering on the earth; (v) He ruled for a long time as lord-Paramount (*aikādhirājam*) on earth earned by his own strength. What the inscription does not say is also significant. There is not even a hint to the genealogy and dynasty of this King 'Candra', no allusion even to his father.

Now who is the King Candra in the ancient Indian history down to the 4th or 5th Century A.D. when the inscription was engraved on the pillar at the latest in view of its palaeography? Without entering into any long discussion about the identification of Candra with this or that king of India, we would refer briefly to some of the identifications proposed. Majumdar's view earlier (Majumdar, 1943 pp.179-83) that he could be Kanishka is not a serious proposition. A recent discovery of a Bactrian inscription of Kanishka found in north Afganistan clearly states that he started a new era, which clinches the issue; the only well known eras which he could start is the Saka era of 78 A.D. The palaeography of the Iron-Pillar inscription will on the other hand not makes it possible to place it in the 1st century A.D. and then Kanishka by no stretch of imagination be credited with 'perfuming the southern ocean'. The majority of scholars feel that Candragupta II was the 'Candra' of the inscription. But it is accepted by all that Candragupta II did not become the paramount ruler 'by his own strength'. He stood on the shoulders of Candragupta I, the 1st imperial Gupta ruler, and basked in the achievements of his father

*Retired Prof. of Ancient Indian History, Culture and Archaeology, Patna University, Patna.

Samudragupta. Candragupta's activities in the coastal south and in Bengal are not known to inscriptions and literature. Such so-called 'achievements' are, to say the least, speculative. Moreover, the most resounding success of Candragupta II over the Saka Satraps finds no mention in the inscription. Then the key statement about Candra in the inscription is that his glory even when he has left the earth is still lingering on the earth. This certainly suggests that Candra was a king of the remote past and not of recent times. Goyal has strongly pleaded that 'Candra' of the inscription is none other than Samudragupta (Goyal 1967, pp. 201ff). It is well argued that Samudragupta does certainly share the major achievements of 'Candra'. Majumdar later held that all that has been said of Chandra are applicable to Samudragupta (Majumdar 1971 p.234n). However, the claims of his defeat of the Vahlikas is certainly more speculative than real. That he went beyond the Punjab is most unlikely. But the identification has to be rejected on the ground that there is no evidence to show that Samudragupta was ever known as 'Candra', and Sastry (Joshi-Gupta 1989, p.86) has shown that the inscription clearly mentions 'Candra' as the name of the king (*Candrāhvena*).

Who is the 'Candra' then? We had suggested in 1943 that '*aikadhiraja*' Candra is Candragupta Maurya, and the Mehrauli iron pillar is set up by Candragupta II as a memorial to the great Candragupta Maurya who was the ideal and the model for the namesake Candragupta II Vikramaditya. The achievements attributed to Candra, the bygone king, admirably fit in with the known accomplishments of Candragupta Maurya.

The first great achievement of Candra was to successfully repulse in battle the united action of the enemies in the Vanga countries. It is clearly envisaged that the political revolution led by Candragupta Maurya with the advice of Canakya, resulting in the overthrow of the Nanda dynasty, caused serious convultions in the earstwhile Nanda's empire. We know from the Hathigumpha inscription of Kharavela that the Nandas had overrun Kalinga which appears to have later cut loose from the Nanda's apron in the troublous days of the Mauryan revolution. Kalinga, as we know was to be conquered by Asoka. Besides Kalinga, the Vangas also must have risen against the Magadhan imperialism and even posed a threat to the new Magadhan emperor Candragupta Maurya, who defeated them. From the Tibetan account we learn that Bindusara was the governor of Gauda for many years (Sarkar 1940). He must have assisted his father in resisting the Vanga revolt. The Vanga's rebellion against Candragupta Maurya may have another historical background. D.C.Sircar (Sircar 1983, pp.8-9) has argued that the Nandas originally belonged to the Vanga Country (*Gangaridae*). It was, therefore, natural for the people of the Vanga Country, a part of the Magadhan empire of the Nandas, to rebel against Candragupta who had uprooted the Nanda dynasty and captured the imperial capital, Pataliputra. The people living in the Vanga country (Deltaic region) appear to have taken offensive by forcefully moving into the Mauryan territory of Gauda (Western Bengal), and had to be repulsed. This is clearly borne out from the Meharauli pillar inscription (1st line - Fleet 1963, p.141), wherein "it is stated that he (Candra) kneeled (and turned back) with (his) breast the enemies who, uniting together, came against him." We have already seen that Bindusāra was the governor of Gauḍa. Tāranātha states, 'then Bindusāra, son of king Candragupta, ruled Gauḍa for 37 years' (Taranatha, p.130). This must have included the period of his governorship of Gauḍa under his father. It is very likely that after the defeat of the people of the Vaṅga country, the region came under the Mauryan rule. From the stone plaque inscription we know that the *Mahāmātra* has asked the officer of Puṇḍravardhana to replenish the store-house in apprehension of the implending scarcity for the use of the samvangīya people (Chattopadhya 1977, pp. 94-95). While some scholars see in it a special concern for a particular Buddhist sect; in our opinion, it may allude to the people of the Vaṅga. The inscription refers to the time of Bindusāra, who, on the advice of his father to propitiate the hostile Vaṅgas, tried to secure help for them during the last years of his father's rule when a terrible famine had broken out. Even if the inscription is ascribed to Aśoka, it is clear from this as well as referencee to the Chinese traveller's account of having seen Aśoka's stūpas at Samataṭa, Puṇḍravardhana and Karṇasuvarṇa. This would indirectly suggest that entire Bengal-Gauḍa and Samataṭa (Vaṅga) formed part of Aśoka's empire. Aśoka had conquerred only Kaliṅga, Bindusāra had merely crushed rebellions and so Chandragupta Maurya shouid be credited with the inclusion of Gauḍa and the conquest of Vaṅga.

For Candra, claim is made that he crossed the seven mouths of the Indus and defeated the Vahlikas. This achievement cannot be legitimately attributed to Candragupta II. There is no positive and even indirect evidence to deduce his forays in Bactria (Váhlika) or even in the Punjab. As a matter of fact, no Indian king of the name Candra can be attributed to have crossed the seven mouths of the Indus except Candragupta Maurya. It is he who expelled the Greeks from the northwest and liberated the country from 'Greek servitude'. He defeated the attempt of Seleucus to overrun the Indian provinces, and in the bargain obtained the territories of Afghanistan, Baluchistan, Makran, Herat and Kandhar. Seleucus certainly controlled Bactria as known from Justin, but as a result of this victory of Candragupta, must have lost its control to the Mauryan empire.

For Candra, the claim is made that 'the Southern ocean is still today being perfumed by the breezes of his powers'. That Candraguptaś empire included Deccan and south India down to Mysore is beyond doubt. Aśoka did not conquer it, but his inscriptions are found in the south. Bindusāra did not conquer the region. Tāranātha attributes to him only the supression of revolts of kingdoms between the eastern and western seas. It has been well observed. So, it seems that, "the revolting states were brought under his control, not all at one time". (Chattopadhyaya 1977, p.99). We know that Aśoka as a prince went to quell the rebellion in Taxila. So Candragupta's breeze of power definitely blew over the southern seas.

It is further claimed in the inscription that he ruled on the earth as 'a paramount emperor (*aikādhirājam*) earned by his own strength'. This credit can hardly be given to Candragupta II whose only conquest was of Malwa and Gujarat. He had inherited and not won the empire. Samudragupta was the first real paramount Gupta ruler ruling over north and south India as a result of his military campaigns described in the Allahabad Pillar inscription. But Candragupta Maurya had all by himself to conquer the empire and had extended its territories to the northwest down to Kandhar - the foot-hills of he Hindukush, the scientific frontier in the northwest. There appears to be no exaggeration in Plutarch's statement that 'Sandrocottus with an army of six hundred-thousand men overran and subdued all India'. This is confirmed by Tamil writers also who attribute Moriyar's capaigns with the help of their golden chariots into far south of the Peninsula (Chattopadhyaya 1977, p.90). This was all the work of Candragupta Maurya's geniosity as a military leader and empire builder. Mahāpadma Nanda's empire had collapsed due to the political turmoil during the reign of the last Nanda king -Dhanananda. Candragupta had to win it back by his own strength. The Mehrauli pillar inscription confirms this achievement.

It is claimed that Candra earned by the force of his own arms (*prāptena svabhujārjjitan*), the sole soveriegnty of the earth (*aikādhirājam kshitim*). It may of some signifícnce that while from Candragupta I onwards, the usual paramount title is mahārajādhirāja. Candra is '*aikādhirāja.*' It is very near to ekrāṭ assigned to Mahāpadma Nanda was the title of Mahārājadhirāja for Candra not used deliberately to make distinction between Candra and Candragupta II? We know that Candragupta Maurya is referred to as Candra in the *Mudrārākshasa* many time and Candragupta II is 'Candra' on the obverse of his coins. Only the imperial title thus could distinguish between them. It is possible to presume that the entire area over which edicts of Asoka prevailed were conquered by Candragupta with the exception of Kalinga (Sinha 1974, Pt. I, p.932). Basham rightly regards Candragupta 'the chief architect of the grestest of India's ancient empires'. Chattopadhyaya is of the view that "with the exception of the far south and the region east of the Brahmaputra all India, lay under the banner of the founder of the Maurya dynasty (Chattopadhyaya 1977, p.91). So all these make it clear that Candragupta Maurya won the large Indian empire by the force of his own arms - an achievement attributed to Candra in the Mehrauli pillar inscription. No Indian king of the name of Candra can rightfully boast of or be a king of the name of Candra, who can rightfully boast of or be credited with this memorable feat, before or after Candragupta Maurya.

Another significant suggestion may be considered. It is stated in the inscription that his achievements still perfumes the southern ocean (*adyāpyadhirasets*). It is further spoken of him that though the king has quitted this earth, his '*Kirti*', still lingers on the earth (*Kirkyashitasya kshitim*), and even now his victorious fame against his enemies still '*adyāpi*' remains on the earth (*Śeshaḥ kshitim*). All these certainly would lead one to infer that Candra and his victories over his enemies had occurred not immediately before the inscription was composed, but long before. We all know that paleographically the inscription cannot be placed long after Allahabad Pillar-inscription of Samudragupta and not much before the Bilsad pillar of Kumāragupta I of the year 96 (415-16 A.D.) Candragupta II would be too much near the time to which Candra is said to have earned the sole *rājyam (aikādhirājyam)*, when his fame was still (a matter of surprise) perfuming the southern seas.

It would be of some interest to take into account the *Mudrārākshasa* written in the Gupta age. Its theme is political revolution and intense diplomatic activities led by Cāṇakya and Candragupta's rule over the vast empire with its capital Kusumapura (Pātaliputra). Here Candragupta is called *'rājādhirāja'* (Act III, Act IV) nearer to *'aikādhirāja'* of the Mehrauli Iron-Pillar. The word *Mahārājādhirāja*, the usual title of the Gupta emperor since Candraguta I, is deliberately passed over. Reference to the rulers down to the southern seas, as his dependent vassals (Act III) reminds us of Candra's sway over the southern seas in the Mehrauli Iron-Pillar inscription. Then we have reference to the ladies of Gauḍadeśa as subserviant to Candragupta's army (Act V) in the *Mudrārākshasa*. It reminds us of Bindusāra governorship of Gauḍa as known from Tibetan sources.

When we proposed as early as in 1943 that the achievements attributed to Candra in the Mehrauli Iron-Pillar inscription are attributable to none else than Candragupta Maurya it was never claimed that the inscription on the pillar was inscribed in the time of Candragupta Maurya. That would be absurd in view of the palaeography of the inscription and the fact that any inscription, much less a sanskrit inscription, could never have existed anywhere before Aśoka, not much before Girnar inscription of Rudradāmana of the 2nd -3rd century A.D. The only plausible explanation is that Candragupta II Vikramāditya had this pillar set up to bring back to memory the heroic achievements of his name-sake, great predecessor Candragupta Maurya. It appears that Candragupta II had a sense of history. He was highly inspired by the career and achievements of Candragupta Maurya. And why not, like the Maurya emperor who has liberated the country of Greek servitude, Candragupta II had wrested western India from the rule of the Western Kshtrapas. It is not, therefore, unreasonable to ascribe to him the patronage of the drama *Mudrārākshsa* and its enactment in memory of the successful political revolution overthrowing the oppressive rule of the Nandas. Candragupta II himself had rescued the Dhruvaswāminī and the kingdom from the clutches of Rāmagupta and his mentors, the Sákas or the Khasas. The story related a work of the same dramatist Visākhadatta. The date of this author, as in the case of many authors is quite controversial. But the significant point is that the same author writes about the successful political revolutions by the kings of the same name but living at an interval of nearly 700 years. Almost the same feat is referred to by the composer of the Meharauli Iron-Pillar inscription when it attributes the conquest of India by the force of his own arms to Candra.

It is our plea that Candragupta II had good reasons to adopt Candragupta Maurya as his model and hero, and had arranged not only the composition of the drama — *Mudrārākshsa* to highlight the political revolution engineered by Cāṇakya and put into effect by Candragupta Maurya. Is it beyond the realm of possibility for Candragupta II then to highlight the political activities and conquest of the whole of India by his hero - Candragupta Maurya - in the Mehrauli Iron-Pillar inscription, which in a way he looked upon as supplement to the *Mudrārākshasa?* We support of the view of Jayaswal and others that Visākhadatta lived in the time of Candragupta II, and wrote about both political revolutions by Candra. The 6th century date for the *Mudrārākshasa* is suspected edBasham, puts a note of interrogation about it (Basham 1975, p.443). That the author was a great admirer of Candragupta II, is clear from the last verse (Act VII) of the *Mudrārākshasa* when he compares Candragupta with Vishṇu, particularly in His *Vārāha* incarnation stating that as the Earth had taken shelter behind His powerful tooth to be rescued from the difficult to be conquered, enemy (the nāgas), one is reminded of the powerful sculpture of *Vārāha* rescuing the earth in the Udayagiri cave of the time of Candragupta II. So, now the earth had found support on the powerful arms of Candragupta to rid herself of the oppression of the Mlecchas. Here Visakhadatta could easily mean both the Candraguptas (Maurya and Gupta) who in their own times freed the country from the servitude of the foreigners (*mlecchas* — Greeks and the Sakas). It may not be mere speculation to suggest that the *Mudrārākshasa* could have been composed after Udayagiri cave scultpure in bold relief was completed.

It is not claimed that the inscription was composed by the orders of Candragupta Maurya. Our contention is that the inscription records the historical achievements of

Candragupta Maurya as a memorial tribute by his name sake Candragupta II who remembered him by arranging the composition and eractment of the *Mudrārākshasa* written by the same author who by his *Devīcandraguptam* had put on record the political revolution by Candragupta II against the Saka and his brother Rāmagupta, who, we now know, on epigraphic evidence was the *Mahārājādhirāja* after Samudragupta.

Now the only question that remains to be answered is that how Candragupta Maurya could be contemplated to be a devotee of Vishṇu as the Candra of the Mehrauli pillar definitely is. It is known from the Jaina sources that Candragupta Maurya had turned a Jaina, had later abdicated the throne and as Muni Candragupta meditated on the Sravaṇabelagola hill in the south.

But it is qute resonable to assume that under Kauṭilya's guardianship he was a follower of Brahmanism. Magasthenese also speaks of the devotees of Vishnu and Siva, and not much about the Buddhists and Jainas. Magasthenes refers to Sourasenias of Mathura and Kṛshṇapura holing Heracles (Kṛshṇa) in high honour. Kautilya refers to *Apratihata ans Śri*, meaning Vishṇu and Lakshmi, as deities. He refers to Kṛshṇa and Kaṁsa also (Sinha 1976, pp. 170-172). Therefore, it is possible to hold that Candragupta Maurya, a follower of Brahmanism, worshipped Vishṇu. From Tibetan sources we learn that Kautilya continued to be the Chancellor of Bindusāra. It appears that change in religion could have been one of the causes that led to the difference between Kautilya and Candragupta who had to leave the throne for the life of a Jaina ascetic. In view of this it was quite in good stride for Candragupta II himself, a great devotee of Vishṇu, to record the achievements of Vaisnavite Candra on a *Vishṇudhavaja.*

So, Candragupta II got this memorial inscription engraved on the Iron-Pillar (*Vushṇudhvaja*) which may have had Garuḍa on the top (as Besnagar inscribed pillar) most probably in front of a Vishṇu temple. We learn from the inscription that it was set upon Vishṇupadagiri. Where should we locate this Vishṇupada hill? The pillar, as it stands today, is not on a hill though in a hilly region, but it has never been known as Vishṇupadagiri. Fleet's surmise thus has to be rejected. Then the Sircar's identification of Vishṇupada with the region round Kurukshetra, and Dasaratha Sharma's conjecture that the Vishṇupada hill be located in the Ambala district of Punjab (Joshi and Gupta 1989, pp. 168-69) lack any positive supportive evidence. As a matter of fact, Indian history and culture knows of only one Vishṇupada-hillock and that is in the Gaya town proper. We have no knowledge of any other Vishṇupadagiri or hill of that name in ancient Indian literature or epigraphy. Monier-Williams in his Sanskrit English dictionary (Willams 1899, p.999) mentions Vishṇupada as a foot mark of Vishṇu worshipped at Gaya. It has been well observed, "At all events there is not a single instance known to us where the footmarks of the Buddha are worshipped by the Buddhishts in the manner of the Hindu worship of Vishṇupada for the release of the departed spirits of their forefathers." There is no doubt that in the 4th Century A.D. there was a clear knowledge of the existence of Vishṇupada on the Vishṇupadagiri as known from the Mehrauli Iron-Pillar inscription (Fleet 1963, pp. 139-141).

Further, although V.A.Smith located it near Katra in Mathura, but it should be absolutely clear that there could be no Vishṇupadagiri at Katra near Mathura either. The Katra mound has been excavated and it has given a sequence of cultures from c. 600 B.C. to the Saka-Kushāṇa period. Remains of mud-fortification (Dhul-kot) were observed. Nothing from the excavations have shown that the mound had some prominent rock and was ever known as Vishṇupada. Nothing particularly important Gupta antiquities were observed in course of three seasons of excavations (*IAR* 1992-93; 1994-95, p.49; *IAR*, 1975-76, p.53ff.). As a matter of fact inscriptions of Candragupta II and Kumāragupta I are found at places in U.P. other than Mathura. Our point is that Mathura has not been associated with foot marks of Vishnu, and there is no Vishuṇupada hill at Mathura.

On the other hand, we find Vishṇu's step being associated with Vishṇupada from the time of Yāska or even earlier. Arunārbha states that the earlier conception of the Sun's movement as sunrise, noon and sunset, on the Meridian, were only planting of the Sun's foot on the mountains which were now being mentiones as terrestial *Samārohana Udayagirau* on Vishṇupada Gayāsirsa as hills in the city of Gaya which had become by the time of the Buddha a centre of Brahmanism. Later, the Vishṇupada hill became the centre of the Bhakti cult, and revered as a pilgrimage centre for the release of the departed souls. It is possible that something like a shrine was already there by the end of the 1st Century B.C., and Candragupta II erected the *Vishṇudhvaja*, probably before a Vishṇu's shrine on the Vishṇupada hill enshrining the foot-print on a rock representing the asura Gaya. Candra does not claim to build a temple. The ruins of the earlier temple may be beneath the present temple built by Ahalya Bai in the 18th Century. The name of the temple is derived from the foot-print of Vishṇu encased by the shrine. Some support for an earlier shrine may be had from ancient Brahmanical texts, such as Vishṇu and *Atri saṁhitās* referring the Vishṇupada as most *distinctive* object in Gaya along with Gayasirsha hill (*Brahmayonī*). The author of the *Atri Samhitā* recommends the pilgrims to have the darshan of the divine mace-bearer (Gadādhara) in Gaya. Buddhists also refers to Siva and Vishṇu temples in Gaya (Barua 1975, p.146). That as late as in the time of the Pāla king Nārāyaṇapāla (9th Century A.D.), a Vishṇu temple at Vishṇupada existed is borne out by the fact that an inscription of his time makes invocation to lord Vishṇu and dedication of a Vāsa for the pilgrims of Gaya. As a matter of fact, many temples arose in later Pāla period in the compound of the Vishṇupada temple. A temple at Vishṇupada before the 5th Century A.D. may be infered from a South-East Asian source. R.C. Majumdar (Kamboja inscriptions) says that a temple containing Vishṇu foot-print was buit by King Guṇavarman in Kāmbuja. This must have been inspired by such a temple in India proper; and wherelse in India the temple could be but at Vishṇupada hill in Gaya. A seal from Vaisali with the legend '*Sri Vishṇupada swāminārāyane*' shows that such a temple of Nārāyaṇa (Vishṇupada), epitomised by his foot-print was known to have existed in the 5th Century A.D. Nandalal Dey says that the present Vishṇupada temple was built by Ahalya Bai 'on the site of a more ancient temple'. The Vishṇupada was set up prior to Fahsien's visit (Dey, p.64). It could have come early in the time of Candragupta II or even earlier. The Gaya copper plate inscription of Samudragupta of the Year 9, may be an early forgery but the seal with Garuḍa figure and the legend is genuine. It shows the Vaishṇava inclination of Samudragupta. The inscription was found at Gaya and refers to Gayavishaya, which may be a genuine reference to Gaya as a Vishaya in the time of Samudragupta. So Gaya was becoming important in Gupta history at least from the time of Samudragupta who could be a devotee of Vishṇu. Did he build the Vishṇupada temple, we cannot say, but that his son Candragupta II set up the Iron -Pillar in front of an existing Vishṇupada temple on the Vishṇupada hill at Gaya brooks no deying.

I am aware of certain difficulties in accepting the hypothesis put forward. One is that ancient memorial or commemorative inscriptions are not generally found. Allan (Allan 1914, pp. XVIII) held that Candragupta-Kumāradevi type of coins were commemorative coins issued by Samudragupta. His main contention was the standard type of Samudragupta's coins 'is a close copy of the later coins of Kushāna type (Allan 1914, pp. LCV-LXVII). Altekar has tried to rebut the arguments of Allen and has held with other scholars like V.A.Smith that the Candragupta-Kumāradevī type of coins were issued by Candragupta I himself (Altekar 1954, pp. 20-23). But in our opinion, there is no conclusive evidence to explain the obvious fact that the standard type of Samudragupta's coins are copies of Kushāṇa coins and it is difficult to explain why after comparative originality in Indianising of the Candragupta-Kumāradevi coins, Samudragupta would revert to almost slavish imitation of later Kushāṇa type. We may also refer to the Eran Posthumous Pillar inscription (Fleet 1963, No. 20, pp. 91-93). This is clearly a memorial inscription to commemorate the memory of King Goparāja and his queen who became a sati with him on the funeral pyre. So memorial coins and inscriptions are not unknown in ancient Indian history.

A more serious difficulty is whether it is possible to suggest that Candra in the inscription means both Candragupta Maurya and Candragupta II Vikramāditya. In this connection we may refer to the Mandasore inscription dated in the Mālava Year 493 and 529 (Fleet 1963, No. 18, pp. 84 ff.). This long inscription refers to the building of the Sun temple by King Bandhuvarman in M.E. 493 (437-438 A.D.). It then goes on to say that in course of long 36 years time, under other kings, the temple fell into dispair, and it had been repaired again in M.E. 529. And this (long) composition is the work of Vatsabhaṭṭa. It has been expressly stated that Kumāragupta was ruling. We have argued (Sinha 1953, pp. 70-71) that it is clear from the phrase (Kumāragupta was ruling the earth, i.e. in A.D. 473, when the temple was repaired after many kings has passed away in the meantime. Now who was the king who was ruling when the temple was built? Clearly, kumargupta I who ruled from *c.* A.D. 415-455). So, here King Kumāragupta though mentioned once represents two kings of the same name, one in whose time the temple was built, and the other when the temple was repaired. Bandhuvarman was a feudatory king under Kumāragupta I, while, when the temple was repaired, the corporation is only mentioned and not the feudatory ruler because of change in political situation at the time. Many kings intervening between the building and the repair of the temple could be Kumaragupta I, Purugupta, Skandagupta, and even Ghaṭotkacagupta. We argued that the Mandasore inscription dated in the Mālva era 473 and 529 refers to both Kumāragupta I and Kumāragupta II (Sinha 1993, p. 113), though the word Kumāragupta appears only once. In the same way the Mehrauli Iron-Pillar inscription's Candra refers to both Candragupta Maurya and Candragupta II.

Can the Mehrauli Pillar Inscription be reinterpreted as such? The memorial part of the inscription ends with the phrase '*svabhujārjjitam*' and then the operation part of the inscription begins stating that Candra erected the pillar Vishṇudhvaja on the Vishṇupadagiri 'and the use of the word 'ca' after '*svabhujārjjitam*' makes the break.

It is clear that Candragupta II had set up the inscribed Iron-Pillar at Vishṇupadagiri in Gaya. But the pillar now stands in Mehrauli in Delhi. About the exact position of the pillar in Mehrauli, Fleet observes—"The actual position of the column is in a slight depression, with rising grounds on both sides: a position which hardly answers to the description of its being on a 'giri' or a hill .... lays it quite open to argument whether this is the real original position of the column or whether .... it was brought to where it now stands from some other place (Fleet 1963, pp.140-141). It is immaterial that finally Fleet favoured its being now in its original position. This position cannot be defended, archaeologically and historically.

Candragupta II's foray into the northwest, as far as Gilgit, becomes very suspicious. But Candragupta Maurya's reaching Vāhlika is much more possible. Seleucus who ruled over Syria and the country including Bacteria (North Afghanistan) and Herat and Baluchistan as successor of Alexander, had advanced into India across the Indus in the west but was defeated by Candragupta Maurya, who obtained as a result of the victory not only a Greek princes? but the provinces of Kabul, Kandhar, Herat and Baluchistan. We do not know where the decisive battle took place. However, taking into account the geography of the cited provinces, it is not unreasonable to believe in Candragupta as a sound military strategist pushing Seleucus down to Bactria (Vāhlika), and forcing him to cede the provinces, which may or may not have included Bactria. He was interested in only securing the northwestern region down to Kandhar and Bactria as a defence-outpost against any future Seleucidan or later adventurers into India. Cangragupta did not press up to Syria, the seat of Selecus empire which he could very well have done after the resounding victory in Bactria, because he was not on an aggressive imperial compaign as a matter of fact no Indian emperor before or after him set his eyes beyond the Indian territory and its borders. As a matter of fact all the three major military achievements of Candra of the Mehrauli Iron-Pillar (up to line 5), are most reasonably atrributable to Candragupta Maurrya than to any other king bearing the name of Candra. To us, the phrase *'adyāpiadivasyate'* in line 2, suggest a considerable lapse of time between the actual achievements and the recording of the exploits. And the statement that though he has left this earth for the land (paradise) which he has won by his action but his fame still (*adyāpi*) remains on this earth (the memory of his fame) also reinforces the idea of his having departed long before the time of the recording of the inscription. If by 'Candra' only Candragupta II was to be meant there is no reason why he or his successor had not recorded his genealogy or some specific distinction for the remarkable achievments to be recounted in his name. But as the great achievements are referred to his ancient predecessor Candragupta (Maurya), whose genealogy is not even known today, and was not known even in the 4th-5th Century A.D. and so was not given in the record. So, the position we hold is that the inscription belongs to the 4th-5th Century A.D. and the operative part, that of setting up Vishṇudhavaja on the Vishṇupadagiri belongs to the credit of Candragupta II, who as a form of memorial to his great predecessor, recorded it in the laudatory verses (1-5) the achievements of Candragupta Maurya.

The inscription is generally believed to be posthumous and line 2 says that the king was dead and had gone to the heaven. But this refers to Candra who is credited with the military achievements and not necessarily to the Candra who set up the pillar on Vishṇupadagiri. It is therefore, possible that Candragupta II himself had put up the pillar with the inscription. This is quite reasonable. Candragupta II had built a Jaina temple on the

Vaibhāragiri at Rājagṛha, he had also built the Mahābodhi temple at Bodh Gaya in Magadha, the centre of the Gupta empire. Then how could the *Paramabhāgavata* Candragupta forget his own *ishṭadevatā* in Magadha? So he set up the Vishṇudhvaja with the Garuḍa on the capital. The Garuḍa may have been lost in the transportation from Vishṇupada (Gaya) to Meharauli (Delhi) or was destroyed by the iconaclast Muslim ruler who built the Kutub complex by after destroying Hindu and Jaina temple structures. They just could have left the pillar with the inscription which they certainly could not read. But an interesting point referred by S. Sankaranarayan (Joshi and Gupta 1989, pp. 171-179) is worth mentioning. "A good deal of intellectual exercise has been done by way of interpreting the expression *'mūrtya' karmmajitāvanim gatavātaḥ'* (line 3). King is dead and interpreting '*mūrtya*' in the sense 'in bodily form' it is argued that as no one can go with one's body to the heaven, this expression must be taken as indicative of the fact that the King was alive at the time of the composition of the edict on the verse indicates that Candra had abdicted and was living as a mendicant *murtya* is *divya murtya* (heavenly body). We known that Candragupta Maurya had abdicated. And, therefore, in my opinion Candragupta II Vikramaditya himself set up the inscribed pillar on Vishṇupadagiri and we are disposed to agree with K.C. Chattopadhyaya (Joshi and Gupta 1989, p. 169) that there is much similarity in the style of the Mehrauli and Udayagiri inscriptions, and both the inscriptions might have been composed by Virasena. Sava (who had come from Pātaliputra and Candragupta to Malava, and was his minister. Candragupta II could have trusted his Magadhan minister to compose this intricate inscription and who might have been well-versed with achievements of Candragupta Maurya. This expression must be taken as indicative of the fact that the entire verse indicates that Candra had abdicated his thrown and was living as a mendicant. If there is any sense in this interpretation, then it admirably suits Candragupta Maurya who had abdicated the throne and become a Jaina mendicant as gleaned from the Sravanabelgola inscription.

Cunningham (CASRI) declared 'there are no existing remains that can be assigned with certainty to the old Hindu city of Delhi'. V.A. Smith (1897, pp. 1ff) observed , "there is absolutely no reason to suppose that any buildings of the 5th Century, from the beginning of which the pillar certainly dates ever existed on the spot." The pavement, according to him, in which the pillar stands is the 11th Century structure which was covered over by a layer of rubbish due to destruction by Qutbuddin or Altamash. Smith is certain that the pavement does not, like the pillar, date from the 5th Century A.D. M.C. Joshi (Joshi and Gupta 1989, p.135) is of the view that no structural remains of the Gupta period are noticed here or have been reported earlier except the Iron-Pillar itself. As a matter of fact, opposite the pillar on the west within the prayer hall or elsewhere in the mosque one could observe old stone columns, decorated or otherwise, some of them in situ, date not before the 9th century or so. The Archaeological Survey of India accepts that the pillar was brought to Lalkot Delhi from somewhere else (Y.D.Sharma, Archaeological Remains, Monuments and Museums, pt. II, p.248).

Our point is that Candragupta II set up this Vishṇudhvaja (Mehrauli Iron-pillar) before a temple of Vishṇu on the Vishṇupadagiri at Gaya. The pillar was not set up by Candragupta Maurya and so all arguments of Gopals about the palaeography and state of iron technology in the Mauryan times (Joshi and Gupta 1989, pp. 124ff) are unnecessary exercises. About the validity of Candragupta Maurya's victory over the Vaṅgas, it can be said that it is based on better evidence than that credited to Candragupta II. It should be borne in mind that the Meharauli inscription refers not to the aggression of Candra against the Vaṅgas, but to the repulsing of the aggressive attempt by the united Vaṅgas (peoples) to uproot Candra. D.C. Sircar, as we have shown, argued for the Nanda's original home being in Deltaic Bengal, and if so, it is logical to argue that the Vaṅgas had good reason to lead an aggression against Candra (gupta) who had uprooted the Nandas. The victory over the Vahlikas also can be more reasonably attributed to Candragupta Maurya than to Candragupta II. The Hunja inscriptions referreing to Devasri Candra (Vikramaditya) are shown by S.K. Gupta to belong not to Candragupta II Vikramaditya but to a later local king, the date 143 is referred to in the Harsha era (Joshi and Gupta 1989, pp. 159 ff). And about Candragupta's suzerainty over the southern seas much less said than better. There is no evidence of Candragupta Vikramāditya by the force of his own arms reaching the southern seas. As a matter of fact, only tangible memorable conquests that he made were of the Western Kshatrapa (Saka dominion of Malava and some parts of Gujarat) and that is not at all even hinted in the Mehrauli Iron-Pillar inscription. The plea that these conquests were made after the inscription was engraved on the pillar is clearly fallacious as the inscription is according to the author posthumous one, and so if Candragupta II's successors have recorded the greatest achievement, the conqust of Malwa by his father must have been a part of the inscription.

Thus, there appears to be no solid evidence at all to identify Candra of the Iron-Pillar inscription with Candragupta II. And no other king bearing the same name except Candragupta Maurya foots the bill totally.

So the question that boils down simply is when and who got this pillar (*Vishṇudhvaja*) from Vishṇupada removed and reset up in Delhi, presumably before a Vishṇu temple?

In this connection we may have to consider the history of Delhi. As is well known the city of Indraprastha was set up by Yudhisthira after burning of Khāṇḍava forest and driving away of the Nāgas. It is certainly intriguing that after the Mahābhārata war, Indraprastha appears to have become an obscure territory. The excavations at Purana Qila (the old Indraprastha site) yielded some Painted Grey Ware sherds and Northern Black Polished ware sherds in the limited excavated area. Delhi appears to be, in post-Harsha period, a part of Hariyānaka territory. This is known from some inscriptions of the 14th century (Ray 1936). Delhi was also known as Yoginipura as mentioned in Batihagarh stone inscription dated V.S. 1385 (=1328 A.D.). According to bardic tradition Anangapāla Tuar (Tomara) founded Delhi in V.S. 792 (736 A.D.) (M.C.Joshi in Joshi & Gupta 1989, p. 135 and note 2) and established the Tomar Dynasty (Ray 1936, DHNI. II p. 1145). The Delhi Museum inscription of the time of Muhammad Tughlaq dated in 1328 A.D. says "There is a country called Haryana, a very heaven on earth; there lies the city called Ḍhillikā built by Tomaras". Ibn Batuta also observed that Delhi is the old city built by the idolators (Ray 1936, note 2, p. 1145). Cunningham makes an unequivocal statement, "The Tomar family is admitted by all the authorities to have been established by Anangapāla I in V.S.792 or A.D. 736. The same date is given in another era on the Iron-Pillar at Delhi, as Sam 418 Raja Tunwar Ādi Anang. Taking this date as recorded in the Gupta era it will be A.D. 418+318=736" (Cunningham 1967, p.81). Did Anangapāla in 8th Century knew that the pillar is of the Gupta period? Amir Khusru, the contemporary of Alauddin Khilji (A.D. 1300) says that Anangapāla I was 'a great Rai who lived five hundred or six hundred years ago, that is between A.D. 700 and 800 Elliot III, 565). The Palam Basti inscription dated in V.S. 1337 (A.D. 1280) says that the land of Hairyānaka was first enjoyed by the Tomaras, and then by the Chauhanas. Thus, it is clear that Anangapāla I (Tomar) in the 8th Century A.D. carved an independent kingdom of Delhi in Hairyānaka territory. It is very likely that he got the Vishṇudhvaja set up by candragupta II of the Vishṇupadagiri (Gaya) transferred to the new city he had founded. The political situation in northern India in the Post-Harsha period was very confused. The Chinese and Tibetan invasions had occurred, and the political condition in Magadha was very unstable. We cannot be definite as to who were ruling. The later Guptas who maintained some semblance of authority had passed out by A.D. 725 when Jivitagupta II passed away. We had observed, "But the end of the later Gupta dynasty did not only mean the eclipse of Magadha, at least for sometime to come. Worse than that it heralded an era of anarchy and confusion in the Gangetic valley, and Magadha and Bengal suffered most (Sinha 1953, p.312). It was in this volatile situation when one after another invasions were coming and in the west the Pratihāras had not yet consolidated their position, that Anangapāla who may have come on a pilgrimage of Gaya, removed the Iron-Pillar to his new city. He could have been a devotee of Vishṇu as most of his successors were, as can be inferred from the coins of Ajayapāladeva, Kumārapāladeva, who had four-armed Lakshmi figure on their coins. (Cunningham 1967). Anangapāla could have built a temple of Vishṇu before which the Vishṇudhvaja (Mehrauli Iron-Pillar) was resetup. Çunningham had noticed the inscription of Anangapāla dated A.D. 736 on the iron-pillar. The city's name Dhillikā may have become popular because the reset Iron-Pillar was somewhat loose (dhilā) and the city became Ḍhillikā. Cunningham refers in detail to legend concerning it (CASE I, pp. 170ff). It is well documented that the Tomars of Ḍhillikā and thè Chauhanas of Sakambhari had long history of hostilities between them, and Visāladeva-Vigraharāja IV of the Chauhana dynasty, according to the Bijolia inscription of his so Somesvara, conquered Ḍhillikā and Āskā (Hissar) from the Tomars in A.D. 1163 (Majumdar, Vol. V, 1966, p. 52). It appears that after Anangapāla I, the Pratihāra king Bhoja established his sovereignty over Delhi and Haryana region and

Tomaras were their feudatories. A fragmentary stone-inscription of Bhoja was found incessed on a small piece of stone built on the 9th step inside the Pandvon Ka Kila (Purana Qila)- vide Rajputana Museum Report (1924, p.8). But with the end of the reign of Mahendrapāla, Pratihara power began to decline and during this time the Tomaras regained their position as independent kings of Delhi region about the beginning of the 10th century A.D. In the 11th Century Anangapāla II was a ruler of importance and he with a view to counter the offensive of Muslim rulers of the Punjab, appears to have built the Lalkot and the Delhi gate. Anangapāla II issued coins which have a figure of recumbent humped bull. So, he was a Saiva while most of his predecessors and successors were Vaishṇavas. Anangapāla II's inscription appears on the Iron-Pillar. But it does not claim that the pillar was set up by him. As he had built the fort, he preferred to get his name inscribed on the pillar as his ancestor Anangapāla I's inscription was there on the pillar. So, Anangapāla I of the Tomara dynasty who founded Dhillika (Delhi) had brought the Iron-pillar from Gaya. Anangapāla I, the founder of Delhi, to impress on the people his prowess and devotion, and to have a unique object of veneration in his new city (now Mehrauli) hauled down the pillar from Vishṇupadagiri and carried it to Delhi largely by boat on the Phalgu flowing below the Vishṇupada via the Punpun the and *sone* to the Ganga and Yamuna to Delhi. Heavy Aśokan Pllars have been removed by Feruz Tughlaq to Delhi.

REFERENCES

Allan, John 1914. *Cataogue of the Coins of British Museum Gupta Dynasties and Sasanka,* 1914 London.

Altekar. A.S. 1957. *Coinage of the Gupta Empire.* Varanasi: Numismatic Society of India.

Barua, B.H. 1975. *Gaya and Bodh Gaya,* Books I & II 1975, Varanasi.

Basham, A.L. 1975. *The Wonder that was India,* Varanasi.

Chattopadhyaya, S. 1977. *Early History of North India.*

Curringham, a. 1967. *Coins of Medieval India from 7th century down to the Muhammadan conquests,* reprint, Varanasi.

———1977. *Archaeological Survey Reports,* Calcutta.

Dey, N.L 1927. *The Geographical Dictionary of Ancient and Medieval India.* London.

Fleet, G.F. 1963. Corpus Inscriptionous Indicarum, Vol. III, 2nd Edition Varanasi.

Goyal, S.R. 1967. *A History of the Imperial Guptas* Allahabad.

IAR - Indian Archaeology. A Review.

Joshi M.C. and S.K. Gupta 1989. *King Chandra and the Mehrauli Iron Pillar,* Merrut.

Majumdar, R.C. 1943. *JRASB* (L) IX , pp.179-83.

Majumdar, R.C. 1966. *The History and Culture of the Indian People* Second Edition.

Ray, H.C. 1936. *Dynastic History of Northern India* Bombay, India Vol. II, Calcutta.

Sarkar, S.C. 1940. *Journal of the Bihar Research Society,* Patna.

Sircar, D.C. 1983. *Aspect of the Cultural History of Ancient Bihar,* Patna.

Sinha, B.P. 1953. *Decline of the kingdom of Magadhia* Patna.

Sinhe, B.P. 1974. *Comprehensive History of Bihar,* VAI, Pt1, Patna .

Sinha, B.P. 1976. *Readings in Kautilya's Arthasastra,* Delhi.

Smith, V.A. 1897. *Journal of Royal Asiatic Society* pp.ff. London.

Williams, M. 1899. *Sanskrit to English Dictionary.*

Excavation at Mansar, Distt. Nagpur, Maharashtra—1997-2000

JAGAT PATI JOSHI AND A.K.SHARMA*

Under the aegies of Bodhisatva Nagajuna Smarak Sanstha Va Anusandhan Kendra, Nagpur, excavations at Mansar (Lat 2°24'N Long 79°17'E) located 40 kms north-east of Nagpur, have been carried out for the last three field seasons (1997-2000).

Mansar attracted the notice of archaeologists from 1928. Amongst the early references there is an article by TA Wellsted entitled 'Notes on the Vakatakas of the Central Provinces and Berar and their country, 4th to 8th cenury A.D. in the *Journal of the Bombay Asiatic* society in 1935 mentioning the remains of Asvamedha and other antiquities found during mining operations. He also mentions of Buddhist monastery near Mansar. The site was protected as a site of national importance in 1935.

Work Done So Far

The site earlier excavated by the University of Nagpur and found some very impressive brick structures in the flat area of th site now named MNS-I. A few years back, Archaeological Survey of India found the remains of some ancient structures in an area which is now called MNS-2'. These excavations have revealed the presence of a brick temple complex built up in three phases. Structural remains from the complex include live size clay human and animal figures. The present excavations have been carried out in the mound locally known as Hidimba Tekdi has been named as MNS-3

Exploration

The exploration carried out (by us) in the area have yielded stone tools right from Early Stone Age to Late Stone Age. The Early Stone Age tools (Pl. 1) which have been shaped out of quartzitic sandstone and crystalline quartz, found in the seams of granitic deposit comprise of hand-axes, cleavers, choppers, scrapers etc., mostly belong to Late Acheulian period. The Middle Stone Age tool kit comprising of smaller hand-axes, points, cleavers, scrapers etc., are mostly on quartizitic material. Majority of the tools of these periods are digging and cutting tools, pointing to the fact that the Early Man at Mansar was predominantly dependent on vegetarian food rather than on hunting. The Late Stone Age tools both geometric and non-geometric ones, have been shaped out off crystalline material such as quartz, chert, chalcedony and agate. These comprise of triangles, points, trapeze, lunates, burins etc. In the hillocks few rock shelters and caves have been noticed which were probably used by the Early Man of Mansar.

Along the bank of the present Mansar lake few megalithic cairn circle have also been noticed. Probing

[1]Indian Archaeology 1994–95 A Review, p. 56.

done by Dr. S.N. Rajguru in May 2000, showed that prior to the formation of the Mansar lake (ancient Mansarovar) a stream flowed from east to west.

Period -I, Circa 200 BC to 250 AD

Digging in the eastern peripherial and the central areas of MNS-3 gave the evidence that the early settlers of the area of the historical period decided to build a *Stupa* following the natural contour of the hill. The early *stupa* also found in the central area was having extant four to five courses of bricks measuring 48x25x8 cm in size. This earliest *stupa* (stupa-1) wa having a dia of 8 m. Not much could be said about its superstructure as its three sides were superimposed with massive later structures which could not be removed. This *stupa* was later enlarged by using bricks of the size 42x22x7 cm (stupa-2) Pl. 2. It was increased by making brick boxes filled with earth and small boulders, a technique of building *stupa* also found at Pauni. The present available height thus achieved was 2 m in the peripheral area and 3.6 m in the central area of the *stupa* boxes. The approximate dia of the *stupa* is 14 m.

It has a brick *pradakshiina path* around it and a rectangular projection is also available in the eastern side. The stupa has been given support on the eastern side with a stone-rubble revetment having 8 to 9 courses of boulders. A fragment of a soap-stone relic-casket along with a lid fragment has also been recovered from the peripheral area of his *stupa*. On the north-eastern side there is another brick-structure which has been badly damaged.

Another stupa (Stupa-3) roughly roundish in shapes of undressed boulders having a dia. of 11 m with an extant height of 2.70 m. has 7-8 courses of undressed stones. It has a Pradakshina path of 1 m wide which has been built right over the northern wall of the last box of the stupe-2. This stupa came into disuse along with stupa-2.

On the north-eastern side of the central area an oval Chaitya built in two phases having a pedstal on the northern side and an entrance on the western side was exposed. It is 8 m long in the north-south and 5.50 m wide in east-west.

After an accumulation of 1.25 m deposit, at the end of the Satvahana period and beginning of the Vakataka period two sacrificial altars, one in the shape of a *syena-chiti* and the other a *Kurma Chiti*, made of bricks have been exposed. The *syeennachiti* which is in the north was made after smashing the cross-walls of he earlier *stupa* which has gone out of the use by that time making the ground levelled.

In the *syenachitis*, figure of a Purusa made of lime has been found sacrificed with his head smashed (Pl. 3)). The head of the figure is oriented towards west, whereas the legs are put towards east. A *vedi* in the chest portion with a hole for fixing a *yasti* over it was made and an earthen lamp was found kept nearby. Two pots have also been kept near the knee region of the figure which lies on his right side with an iron snake kept near his left toe, looking towards the human figure.

The entrance to the *syenachiti* and *Kurmachiti*, is 2.90 m in width with three flight of steps. The lower two lying in the centre of 0.80 m in width. The entrance has two side arms. While exposing the entrance it was noticed that it was blocked at a later period with a brick wall, which later on collapsed, all at a time, due to a sudden jerk apparently caused by tectonic movement that might have occurred, as per this evidence, after the performance of *Purusamedha Yajna* and before the construction of the top most *stupa* i.e. some time between 4th and 6th century A.D. All the bricks have fallen in brick-on-edge position with mortar in between remaining intact. The eastern outer wall of the two *chitis*, exposed also display same triangular method of construction technique as has been witnessed in constructing the inner side of the *Chitis*.

Adjoining the *Kurma-chitis* in the southern side there is a stone-staircase comprising of eight steps leading towards a small *havanȧ kund*, a lime kiln and a square shrine made of bricks which apparently appears to have been a Saiva shrine as there is a hole for outlet of water. Stratigraphically, it appears that the sacrifice was made at the end of the Satvahana period and beginning of Vakataka period. A whitish layer seals the sacrificial alters and other associated structures.

Period-II (Circa 250 to 500 A.D.)

During this period, on top of he mound, a magnificent temple with plinth of dressed sand stone blocks and supper structure of bricks was built by the Vakatakas. This temple with two phases of construction has yielded many fragmentary sculptures having impressive head dress and bedecked with jewellry. These are in the best traditions of the Vakataka art.

The temple facing east consists of a large *mandapa* and a *garbhha-griha*. In the centre of the western wall of the sanctum sanctorum their is a brick platform. Major part of the temple complex is concealed under the walls of the later stupa. The side entrance in the north is 0.90 m in width and comprises of five courses of dressed rough grained whitish sand-stone. North-south width of the temple is 12.60 m. In order to strengthen the norhern and southern slopes of the hillock massive pitching walls were raised to an extent of 60 m on each side, using huge boulders. Due to this pitching the temple complex would have looked like a fortress.

This temple appears to have been built either by Pravarasena I (275-335 A.D.) or by his son Rudrasen I (335-355 A.D.) as Manser was the Devekulsthanam of the Vakatakas, which has been proved by further evidences described later. Incidentally the rose coloured, fine grained sand stone sculpture of a sitting deity, now housed in the National Museum, New Delhi and identified as Siva-waman by late Dr. C.Sivrammurthy, was recovered in 1970 near the south-western end of this temple. This statue was probably installed in the main temple by Pravarasena II (420-455 A.D.) who declared the Devakulsthanam of Mansar as Pravarpur in honour of his illustratious great grandfather Pravarasena I and the temple as that of Pravareswara. Probably while carving this image Pravarasena II wanted to elevate his great grandfather to the status of god, hence named the temple as Pravareswarasya. This was observed and commented upon by the well-known archaeologists Shri Krishna Deva.

On the eastern side, in the central line of the structures, an impressive staircase has been exposed for approaching structures built in different periods keeping its length and height increased through the centuries (Pl. 4). The staircase also shows the evidence of the use of temple material in the stage of its renovation and enlargement during the time of the last *stupa.* This period has yielded a copper coin of Vishnukundin Dynasty and belongs to King Mahendra Verman of 5th century A.D.

Further dig on the north-western, south-western and western slopes of th site MNS-3 revealed a sizable temple complex belonging to Eastern Vakatakas. It is quite evident that the Siva shrines exposed so far, belong to two phases. Taking advantage of the massive retaining walls built of dressed and undressed stone blocks and of bricks measuring 46x27x7 cm were apparently raised to make a flat platform on the top of the hill for the construction of a temple and later a *stupa*. Around the temple in the first phase the shrines were mostly constructed on the northern side where two natural caves exist. One of the cave was also converted into a shrine by laying bricks on the floor and plastering it with lime plaster and then applying over it red-ochre paint, while the other cave was used as a meditating chamber by constructing concave brick walled approach. The shrines were built over fluted bases with sharp angles making octagons. Over these octagons simple rectangular shrines were raised, each having a nich facing north for the diety and having an approach from either the east or the west. Right from the bottom of the octagonal base a straight staircase led up to the outer side of the shrines and later on to the cave shrine. The foot of this staircase had a brick built semicircular *Chandrasila*, where as two narrow staircase lead to the cave shrine apparently to maintain one way flow of devotees. In order to close the roof of these staircases, triangles and inverted triangles have been used in the construction. The walls and the steps were well plastered with lime plaster, also using lime concrete for strengthening the surface of the steps. Red sand-stone sculptured pieces mostly belonging to Saiva cult have been recovered from these shrines.

On the western and southern side a row of Siva shrines built of bricks were exposed. These shrines built in three terraces are approached by flight of steps. So far three rows of flight of steps have been exposed. Out of total 16 shrines exposed six have Siva lingas, one each resting over a square brick pedestal having a *pranala* on the northern side whereas in some only pedestals are present. The pedestals have been made out of chiseled bricks. None of the Sivalinga is associated with any stone circular *Yoni-pitha.* However most interestingly one of the shrine itself has been built in the form of a *Yoni-pitha* with the *linga* kept in the centre of th shrine over a brick pedestal. (Pl V and VI)

Vertically all the shrines have been built in the form of 'lotus buds' by adopting the triangles and inverted triangles (equilateral). Method for raising petals that ultimately close into a pointed end making the close roof of the *Sikhara* has been adopted. The evidence clearly show that the whole complex was plastered with lime mortar. At the base of these shrines, on the southern corner of one of the steps a burnt wooden *Yupa* was found, apparently for offering sacrifices to the deities. The triangles, particularly on the outer side of the *Jangha* portion of the first row of shrines, make a human face. Almost each shrine has an approach either from the east or west, with some having a small *'mandapa'* and a small semicircular or triangular *'kund'* for water storage near the steps. In one of the shrines the linga has been kept over a square brick pedestal just below the natural rock inclined.

On the south-eastern corner at the base of the steps two square *havan kunds*, with brick linings were exposed in front of the Siva shrines. The larger *havan kund* is having two rows of brick linings, outer 3.0x3.00 m while the inner one 1.35x1.35m. The outer lining have two *pranalikas* on each side having a width of 0.20 m. Thickness of the lining walls is 0.85 m. The inner square is built around a outcrop of rock. Just in front of the *hawan-kunds* to the north, a shrine has been constructed to house a 'Swayambhu' diety-which is a huge natural rock.

On the southern side to the east of the *havan kunds*, a man made cave, by the side of the huge natural granitic outerop was dug and its side walls were lined with bricks to a depth of 1.5 m in corbelled arch fashion to close the top. On the western side of this cave brick steps were laid to go down the cave.

A large number of fragmentary sculptures and architectural members of temples, mostly of red sand-stone, have been recovered from the debris sealing these shrines. The sculpure display superb craftsmanship in delineation of the facial, physical features as well as the decorations.

The sculptures mostly Saivite images, particularly belonging to Tantric cult, are well delineated. Sulptures of Siva-Parvati, Uma-Maheswar, Ganas, Lajjagauri, a *Khinara* (Pl. 7), Lakshmi with an attendant (Pl. 8) and structural fragments are noteworthy. A good number of inscriptions on structural fragments in typical Eastern Vakataka style box headed Brahmi have been recovered. An earlier inscription datable to 2nd century B.C.has also been recovered. The inscriptions are mostly prayer hymns in Sanskrit. A number of iron objects were also recovered. Base of an earthen jar having eleven holes on fine slipped red ware was found from one of the shrines.

The most noteworthy find is the factory site of clay sealing on the north-eastern corner, just at the base of the northern row of shrines. The baked clay sealing bear the legend in box-headed ***Brahmi*** character, reading *'Pravareswarasya'*, (fig 1) referring obviously to 'Pravareswara deva Kulsthanat' referred to in the well known copper plate inscription from Pandhurna. The main shrine was obviously the devakul temple, the dynastic temple of the Vakatakats renovated by Pravaresena II (420-450 A.D.) in memory of his great grandfather Pravarsena I. Incidentally the Pandhurna copper plate mentions its issuance from Pravareshwāra Devakulsthanat or Pravareshwara temple which has now been unearthed at Mansar (ancient Pravarapur). The additions in IInd phase were carried out probably by Prithvisena II, who was a known devout Saivite.

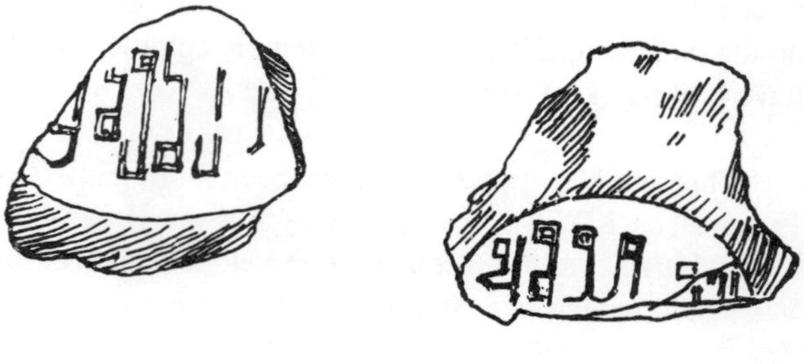

Fig. 1. Age copy of the inscibed sealing.

Apart from a number of sealing that bear the legend *'Pravareshwarasya'* and *'Shri Jaivirdhi'*, some sealings depict elephant, the animal that appears to have been of great importance to the 'Eastern Vakatakas'.

The 'lotus bud' pattern of shrines discovered at Mansar display superb example of *Vastukala* and construction of shrines without any regular Sikhara or tiered (Peedha) roof, as the ends of top petals joined and made the simple Sikharas of the shrines.

Further on the western side, on the foot of the Siva shrines, a huge hall measuring 9.60 x 9.60 m with attached verandah, 8.0 x 1.60 m and a corridor on the southern side leading to the main entrance of the cave shrine, was exposed. While constructing these structures of bricks, the huge granitic outcrop on the north-eastern side was not disturbed. The southern and eastern walls had two projections and were decorated with mouldings in the entire length.

To the north of the *Purshamedha*, at a higher level, abutting the northern wall of the boxes of the earlier *Stupa*, a stone *Stupa* built of semi-dressed stones was exposed. It has a diameter of 13.0 m and is enclosed by a 1.10 m wide *pradakshinapath* of bricks measuring 42x22x7cm in size. The inner side of the Stupa has been strengthened by providing two stone walls, running in east-west direction. On the eastern side stupa elevation is available to a height of 2.10 m having six courses of semi-dressed stones.

To the east of the grand steps and amphitheatre, on a levelled surface a *vihar*, made of bricks was exposed upto twelve courses. It comprises of atleast nine rooms measuring 2.20 x 2.20 m each, on the north, south and east, which have been created by partitioning an earlier 12.50 x 12.50 m hall. In between the two rows of rooms, 8.00 m long east-west and 2.30 m wide, north-south, open space leads o a 7.00 m long east-west, and 2.10 wide, north-south, prayer hall. Bricks, used in the construction of this *vihara* are 30 x 22 x 7 cm in size.

A silver coin of western Kshatrpa king showing Swami Rudrasena III's bust on the obverse and on the reverse a *chaitya* with inscriptions reading Maha Kshtrapasa Swami Rudradaman Putasa Raja Maha Kshtrapa Swami Rudrasena 21 Saka (348-378 A.D.) was recovered from the surface.

Period III (Circa 500 to 700 A.D.

During this period after the Vakataka activities ceased, particularly keeping in view the commanding position of the hill, the Buddhist's finally built a *Stupa* - 4 (Pl. 9) having 24 brick built boxes with a central box filled with rubble and stones. It is having a diameter of 18 m and steps on the eastern side. This large *stupa* was built at the top and remained in existence till the end of 7th century AD. This *stupa* was also associated with an oval *chaitya* on the south eastern side which was built over an earlier *chaitya.*

While exposing the boulder foundation of the upper most Stupa, on the south-eastern corner, at the depth of 1.00 m below surface, fragments of an earthen relic casket is made of micacious clay with an additional coating of mica on the outer surface. A copper coin of Bahmani king of 14th century has also been found from the top layer.

Purani Marmi: A Late Ahar Culture Settlement in Chitaurgarh District, Rasjasthan

R.K. Mohanty, Anup Mishra, P.P. Joglekar, P.K. Thomas,
Jeewan Kharakwal and Tama Panda*

The Site

The ancient Site of Purani Marmi (25° 06' N: 74° 25' E) was discovered way back in 1957–58 by K.N. Puri (*IAR* 1957-58:43-45) in Chitaurgarh District, Rajasthan. The site is situated on the right bank of the river Banas in the Rasin Tehsil. The present village Nai Marmi, or simply as it is called Marmi, is situated half-a-kilometer southeast of the ancient settlement. Regular bus services are available from Chitaurgarh as well as from Udaipur to this place.

The people of Marmi are aware of the ancient settlement and recollect that due to recurring heavy floods about two centuries back Purani Marmi was abandoned and the people shifted to the present location.

The ancient settlement is located on the undulated loamy, sandy-silty soil deposited by the river on its right bank. The river has cut the extreme northeastern part of the mound. Because of its topography the habitation has been spread over a larger area forming several mounds intercepted by shallow rain gullies. The mounds are about 20–25m above the present river-bed. Though the site spread over an area of about eight hectares, it is not continuous. Again different localities within the site were inhabited at different period starting from Chalcolithic of Medieval period. The southern part of the mound was mostly occupied during Early Historic period, which on the surface has yielded Early Historic pottery, burnt-bricks, fresh water shells and iron slag (Hooja 1988:210; Misra *et al.* 1993). A sporadic scatter of Ahar pottery could be found in the entire site. However, a sizeable habitational deposit of the Chalcolithic period along with the concentration of Ahar pottery was observed in the northeastern side of the mound. This part of the mound has been dissected by a number of rain gullies filled with washed out Ahar pottery.

Topography and Environment

Both the present and the ancient settlements are located on an undulated shallow basin resulting out of a low hill range to the northeast of the settlements on one side and flash flood deposits of once very active river on the other. In this particular place, the river is about 600m wide, which meanders and cuts deep into the right side of the bed near the mound. Even in lean seasons water is available till March-April as was noticed during 1999–2000 field trip to the site. Though, Mewar experienced very low rainfall in this season and most of the deep wells dried up, yet some water was retained in the river near the ancient settlement. Even little digging on the river-bed could provide water throughout the year.

The area beyond the left bank is plain that support

*Department of Archaeology, Deccan College, Pune-411006.
[1]Institute of Rajasthan Studies, Udaipur, Rajasthan.

shrubs, thorny bushes like *khejri (Prosopis spicigera), babul(Acacia arabica), neem (Azadirechta indica)* and variety of grasses. The vegetation around the hills and the land surrounding the settlement on either bank of the river provides substantial pastureland for domesticated animals, like cattle, sheep, goat and camel. The situation must have not been very different during the period when the Aharian people moved to this place some three thousand and five hundred years back.

The land surrounding the site has sandy loamy soils with patches of black soil. The average rainfall in this region is about 800 mm and mostly precipitates during the rainy season. However, during November-December it rains sporadically, which helps the winter crops. Now-a-days, with extensive use of well irrigation, a variety of crops are grown throughout the year. The important ones are maize, *sorghum*, and pulses like *tur*, mustard, linseed, wheat, cotton and sugarcane.

The condition that probably induced the Ahar culture people to settle at this place could have been the vast tract of pastureland on either bank of the river. The river action most probably had been subdued, i.e, no more heavy floods causing damage to the right bank by depositing sand and silt was experienced. On the other hand, probably the river retained sufficient water to last for the whole year. As it seems, during this period more of the Ahar culture sites were coming up very close to the riverbank (Misra *et al.* 1993), which were earlier often prone to heavy flooding. In other words, the precipitation during this period had declined causing riverbanks inhabitable and also mushrooming up of settlements around natural depressions and lakes, which could retain enough water to sustain the entire year round. This phenomenon could be observed especially in all the excavated Ahar culture sites in Mewar (Sankalia *et al.* 1969; *IAR* 1959-60:41-46; Misra *et al.* 1995: 57-80; Misra *et al.* 1997.: 35–59; Misra 1997: 251–273)

Aim of the Study

During past eight years, while excavating at Balathal, it had become an annual pilgrimage to visit Marmi with trainee students. The attraction was its location, the environment, the exposed mound due to tilling in some parts, the top of which was strewn with the terracotta stylised bull figurines that we had found in large number in our first visit to the site. Earlier explorer (Misra 1993, Hooja 1988; 210) have also reported it.

The pottery samples collected in our every visit to the site were compared with that of Balathal, which indicated that they belong to a very late period of Ahar Culture. Another interesting point was that the previous authors had focussed only on the bull figuriness collected from the site. However, nothing was known about the cultural materials, life style of the people and the relative chronology of the Chalcolithic phase at this site.

As usual during our excavation at Balathal in this year the site was visited in the first week of March 2000. It was really disappointing to see the entire mound 'under farming'. The government has granted the land to the economically and socially backward farmers of the village. These farmers have levelled the mound by using bulldozer and have left no trace of the ancient settlement. Wells have been dug at several places for irrigation. Only the north eastern part of the mound, where the village cemetery is located, has been spared. It covers an area of 40 m x 10 m. In order to recover, whatsoever, the available data, a rescue operation was undertaken.

Salvage Excavation

The section of the mound near the cemetery was available for an intensive investigation. Section scrapings at two places were carried out to understand the nature of deposit and their cultural contents. One scraping of 1 m x 5 was undertaken at the extreme western part of the mound facing the river and other, 1 m x 5 m, was on the southern side opposite to the recently levelled field.

The total deposit of the mound at the north western end and southern side was 1.70 m and 1.50 m respectively. It comprised of five layers. The top layer was of two to three centimetres in thickness and had mixed pottery of Ahar and Early Historic period. The layers 2 to 5 belonged to the Ahar culture. The site has a thick deposit of alluvium about 4-5 m above the riverbed. The erosion and deposition of cultural material on the slopes had made the earlier archaeologists to estimate the cultural deposit to about six metres (Misra *et al.* 1993). The layers were distinguished on the basis of the nature of soil, i.e., texture and colour, while the cultural material did not show much variation except for a few varieties of pottery were either fell out of use or could not be recovered from a small collection. Unlike Ahar, Balathal and Gilund the entire exposed sections or even the levelled ground did not show any kind of structural activity either on stone or mud bricks. We could hardly gather any information about the Chalcolithic structural remains at the site.

The Cultural Remains

The cultural material recovered from these two scrapings yielded a variety of ceramics, a large number of terracotta bull figurines, animal bones, a long barrel agate bead, a few fresh water shells and a fluted core.The stone tool assemblages of Ahar culture has been reported from some of the sites (Misra 1964; Sankalia *et al.* 1969; Hooja 1988; Misra *et al.* 1995; Misra *et al.* 1997). The amount and characteristics of these stone tools do not suggest that it was an integral part of the lifestyle of the Aharians, as observed at Balathal and Marmi in particular. Probably, the tool came into the context either with the solid brought to the site from a Late Stone Age locality near to the site, or such sites existed there itself prior to the Chalcolithic settlements. It is also possible that these people had contact with the Late Stone Age inhabitant of the region. The terracotta bull figurines are similar to the finding that has been reported earlier from Marmi (Misra 1993) and Gilund (*IAR* 1959–60; 41–60). They are well compared with the bull figurines reported from the Kayatha excavations (Ansari 1975).

Chalcolithic Ceramics of Marmi

There are four types of wares, broadly divided into two groups, i.e., (1) medium fine/coarse and (2) coarse, present in the Chalcolithic ceramic assemblage of Marmi. The medium fine group comprises Black-and-Red ware and a few Red Slipped ware. While the coarse group comprises Thick Red Slipped, Coarse Red and Grey Slipped ware.

In comparison to the Aharian ceramic technology, the technology at Marmi seems to be very degenerated type. Mostly the wares are coarse with lot of sand used as degraissants. The clay has not been carefully kneaded in order to achieve the so-called 'well-levigated' state. The vessels are mostly made by hand. The bigger size of vessels has been achieved by commonly used dabbing method. Slipping and decorating processes are very poor. Other than a few Black-and-Red ware, most of the wares are undecorated. Appliqué designs and incised decorations, in which the Aharians were the pioneer, are scarcely noted on the pottery of this site. The firing techniques remain as usual, though the vessels are poorly fired. There are three types of firing techniques used by the potters, (1) open firing - for Red ware, (2) closed firing - for Grey ware, and (3) inverted firing - for Black-and-Red Ware. The wares along with their shapes and forms are described below.

Medium Fine/Coarse Ware

Black-and-Red ware

This ware comprises bowls and is made by hand or by wheel. The clay used for this ware is mixed with lots of coarse sand. The bowls in the beginning (lowest level) have outwardly projected rim and are decorated in white pigment on the outer surface. The designs are simple geometric and executed on a black background, such as criss-cross lines, series of oblique lines and dots. In the later part of the Chalcolithic period the bowls have simple or featureless rim. Some have tapering tip. In this time, the black portion of the ware is confined to the inner side and the outer part is completely red or dull red in colour. So, the decorations are only made on the inner surface. All the bowls are convex-side with wide mouth and round bottom (fig. 1.1–4).

Thin Red Slipped Ware

A few fragments of Red Slipped ware with thin cross-section have been noted in the ceramic assemblage. The ware comprises small bowls with flared or out-turned, short rim and convex sides. These bowls are entirely slipped with a dark or dull red slip. On some fragments cordon designs are made on the shoulder. The cordons, at times, have been cut with narrow intervals. These bowls are wheel made and fired at a high temperature (fig. 1.10–11)

Coarse Wares

Thick Red Slipped Ware

Thick Red Slipped ware is the major ware that comprises about 50% of the total ceramics. However, it recedes radically towards the end of the Chalcolithic culture giving rise to the number of Coarse Red and Grey Slipped wares. It also becomes extremely coarse and crude. Thick Red Slipped ware is a typical Aharian ware. In this site, the ware has a better fabric in the beginning. It comprises mostly high-necked big jars. These jars are slipped with a dull red slip from the tip of the rim to the shoulder. The lower portion is unslipped and is rusticated. The jars are made in two parts, the upper neck and rim portion and the bottom part, which has been dabbed to increase the size. A ridge followed by incised designs separates the slipped and unslipped portions. The designs are simple geometric, such as sets of oblique lines arranged alternatively. A horizontal line abounds the designs. The big jars have thick body. The rim is thick, out turned or beaked with flat or pointed top. The neck flares downwardly (fig. 1.5–7).

The small pots have high straight or concave neck. The rim is simple everted or out turned. The body does not have any decorations, but is entirely slipped. The bottom is round.

A few fragments of dish-on-stand are present in this ware. It includes a complete hollow stem of 10 cm. It has two prominent appliqué ridges at the proximal end. The distal end flares out and forms the base or stand (fig. 1.12). The stands are simple inverted funnel type. They have concave profile and splayed out base (fig. 1.8-9). The dish-on-stand has a better fabric and is well baked in comparison to other shapes of Thick Red Slipped ware. It is completely slipped with a dull red slip.

Grey Slipped ware

In the beginning the Grey Slipped ware is represented by a few fragments. However, later the number increases to 25% of the ceramics. In appearance Grey Slipped ware is identical to the Thick Red Slipped ware. The vessels of this ware can be divided into two parts, an upper slipped and lower unslipped/rusticated body. The decorating patterns are both incised and appliqué, such as cordons, ridges, and incised and cut designs. The popular shapes are narrow-mouthed, high, straight or concave necked jars, concave necked globular handis, small pots and dishes-on-stand (fig. 1.13-16).

The high-necked, narrow-mouthed jars are medium to small in size. These are decorated with cordon designs on the neck and shoulder. The necks are cylindrical. The rim is simple everted or flared. The waist is also decorated with cordons and some have closely spaced cut marks.

The *handis* have wide mouth with short concave neck and flared out, simple rim. These are decorated with cordons at the waist. The small pots have round body and are similar to handis.

The dish-on-stand has a short, thin and solid stem. It is decorated with spiral cordons from top to bottom. The length of the stem is six centimetres. The base fragments are inverted funnel-shaped.

Coarse Red Ware

The Coarse Red Ware is another major ware that comprises about 30 to 40% of the total ceramics. The percentage increases towards the end of the Chalcolithic Culture while the percentage of Thick Red Slipped ware decreases. The ware is very coarse in texture. It comprises a variety of deep pans and basins (fig. 1.17–18). These vessels are unslipped, but have smooth inner surface and rusticated outer surface. They are hand-made or moulded on a similar baked vessel. The rims are simple, thick, rounded, and beaked with flat or pointed top. Some have under-cut rim. A few of them are decorated with cut marks and oppositely placed set of the oblique lines at the top of the rim (fig.1.17). The soot marks on the outer surface indicate their use in cooking.

Ceramics of Marmi in Relation to Balathal

The Chalcolithic ceramic assemblage of Balathal has been divided into two major phases (I and III)apart from a transitional phase (II) that lasted for a short time. The Phase I and III, beginning and mature phase in order, have two sub-phases each, such as Early (Ia and IIIa) and Late (Ib and IIIb) (Mishra 2000). The ceramics of Phase-I and III of Balathal has been briefly described here for a comparative study with that of Marmi.

The Phase I pottery at Balathal has been divided into five wares, *vis.*, a) Red, b) Black-and-Red, c) Grey, d) Reserved Slip and e) Buff. The Red ware has two categories, 1) fine and 2) coarse. The fine category encompasses Sturdy Red ware and Perforated ware, while the coarse category includes Thick Red Slipped and Coarse Red wares. In general, the characteristic features of these wares are - (i) these are made mostly on slow wheel and are also moulded by hand; (ii) occasionally decorated with simple incised designs and (iii) prevalence of a painted tradition. The red slip is as thin as a wash. Thick Red Slipped ware has rustication on the outer surface but does not have incised decoration. Some of the Thick Red Slipped ware potsherds bear red painted decorations. A Sturdy Red ware is present that tallies with Tan ware of Phase III in terms of the fabric. It, however, does not have the unique shapes of Tan ware. The Reserved Slip ware, Painted Buff ware and Black-and-Red ware represent the exuberance of the pottery tradition of this phase. The common shapes found in the pottery assemblage of this phase are jars of various sizes, bowls, dishes and dishes-on-stand and basins. Besides, cooking pots and pans are also present.

Phase III is characterised by the development of a wide range of pottery types, complete disappearance of the Sturdy Red ware and a change in Reserved Slip ware in quality and quantity. However, Red ware and Grey ware continue having more evolved new shaped. Introduction of a variety of lids with animal figurine handles, pots elegantly decorated with incised lines and pots with thick ledge below the rim are important. Coarse Red ware, that was one of the major wares in the previous phase (i), sharply recedes in number. Thick Red ware, Tan ware and Chocolate Slipped ware appear for the first time. Perforated ware and Painted Buff ware still occur in this phase. Shapes vaguely resembling Harappan types, such as dishes, dishes-on-stand, basins and jars have been more prominent in this phase. However, these vessels are mostly undecorated and have highly burnished surface. An over all maturity in the technology, multiplication of vessel forms and improvement in the standard of living of the people is clearly noticed in this phase. The ceramic assemblage of this phase exhibits clear Aharian characteristics. This pottery phase of Balathal can be compared with that of Period I (Phase la, b and c) and Ahar.

The ceramic assemblage of Marmi does not represent any fine variety of Aharian wares, such as Tan, Chocolate slipped, Thin Red ware and the dishes, dishes-on-stand and basins of Tan/Chocolate Slipped ware do not figure in the ceramics of Marmi, let alone the intricately decorated Reserved Slip ware of Balathal.The Black-and-Red ware of Balathal has been seen changing its shape and form from wide-mouthed carinated bowl of Phase I to convex-sided bowl of Phase III through a humped or shouldered bowl of Phase II. However, Marmi represents another type of shape, i.e., straight-sided and round-bottomed deep bowl, which is peculiar in the Ahar Culture.

From the above perusal of the ceramic assemblages of Marmi and Balathal, it is apparent that there is radical difference between them. A severe deterioration of the ceramic technology and manufacturing ability of the potters of Marmi with respect to the poor standard of the people is envisaged. So, the ceramics of Marmi indicate further devolution and modification of the pottery types represented by Balathal and Ahar. Thus, they can well be put into another Phase (IV) of Ahar Culture. It would not be out of place to note here that such type of ceramics have been obtained from the upper levels of Gilund. The surface collection of pottery from Gilund in our several visits to the site since 1993–94 during the excavations at Balathal confirms the existence of such a phase. This phase can be called as the decline phase of Ahar Culture.

Faunal Remains

The faunal material collected from two section scrapings comprised a total of 545 skeletal elements. Of these, 356 were identifiable, while 189 (34.79%) could not be identified even to the genus/family level. This collection revealed presence of domestic as well as wild animals and mulluscan shells. The domestic species are *Bos indicus* (Cattle), *Bubalus bubalis* (Buffalo), *Capra hircus* (Goat) and *Gallus domesticus* (Fowl). The collection has some bones that possibly belong to *Ovis aries* (Sheep), but due to absence of clear distinguishing markers on them have been identified as of sheep/goat. Wild Animals include *Axis axis* (Chital) and *Antilope cervicapra* (Blackbuck). The two freshwater molluscan species are *Lamellidens* sp. and *Viviparus* sp.

The species found at Marmi are comparable to those at other Chalcolithic sites in the region (Table 1). Among the domestic animals, cattle, buffalo, sheep and goat seem to have been present almost at all the sites. It is interesting to find that black buck is also highly ubiquitous. Marmi showed presence of 9 species out of expected 22 at the Chalcolithic sites in the region. This expected count is from Balathal, and it is on two considerations - Balathal

Table 1 Species found at Chalcolithic sites in Rajasthan

Species/Sites	MRM	BTL	TVT	AHR	Obiquity
Bos indicus	+	+	+	+	1.00
Bubalus bubalis	+	+	+	+	1.00
Capra hircus	+	+	–	+	0.75
Ovis aries	+	+	–	+	0.75
Gallus domesticus	+	+	–	–	0.50
Canis familiaris	–	+	–	+	0.50
Bos gaurus	–	+	–	–	0.25
Boselaphus tragocamelus	–	+	+	–	0.50
Antilope cervicapra	+	+	+	–	0.75
Tertracerus quadricornis	–	+	–	–	0.25
Cervus sp.	–	+	–	+	0.50
Axis axis	+	+	–	–	0.50
Sus scrofa cristatus	–	+	–	+	0.50
Herpestes sp.	–	+	–	+	0.50
Lepus sp.	–	+	–	–	0.25
Pavo cristaus	–	+	–	–	0.25
Turtle/Tortoise	–	+	–	+	0.50
Lamellidens sp.	+	+	–	–	0.50
Parreysia sp	–	+	–	–	0.25
Viviparus sp.	+	+	–	–	0.50
Indoplanorbis exustus	–	+	–	+	0.50
Freshwaterfish	–	+	–	+	0.50
No. of species	9	22	4	10	–

MRM: Marmi - Joglekar (unpublished observations)
BTL : Balathal - Thomas and Joglekar 91996) and Joglekar (on-site observations)
TVT : Taravat - Joglekar (unpublished observations)
AHR: Ahar - Shah (1969)

was quite extensively excavated for a number of seasons and the faunal identification is based on modern archaeo-zoological techniques. Though the collection from Taravat is from the surface, it has provided a useful point for comparison.

Cattle bones were most abundant at all the four sites. Measurements of available cattle bones suggest that perhaps at least two (medium-tall) types of cattle existed during the Chalcolithic period in Rajasthan (Table 2). Qualitative observations of cattle from Taravat also indicate that they were of tall type. Shah (1979) in her report on cattle at Ahar has suggested that both "longhor" and "shorthorn" cattle existed. Although, she has not indicated about possible size, her observations match to the findings at Balathal. As it has been pointed out, the measurements fall well within the range of present-day "Malwi" cattle breed that is common in Udaipur, Chitaurgarh and other districts of Rajasthan (Thomas and Joglekar 1996).

Table 2 Estimates of cattle height

Site	Cattle height (in cm) based on astragalus
Marmi	107.54
Balathal	96.77, 99.11, 110.98, 115.15, 135.99*

*Based on metatarsal

Discussion

The decline of Chalcolithic culture at Balathal and the abandonment of the site have been attributed to severe water scarcity (Mishra 2000) for which the people were rendered to resettle near the perennial water-bodies. A closer observation of the settlements in south eastern Rajasthan reveals that a number of major sites, like Balathal, are located near the large reservoirs. However, during the late Aharian phase such sites have been deserted. As a result, settlements like Taravat and Purani Marmi have come up in this regions. The unlashing climatic situation has reinforced the people to change their adaptation and now the area, which was once inaccessible due to the active flooding of the river, has been occupied. It tells that around last quarter of the second millennium B.C., the rainfall was erratic. The flash flood of the river was restrained, but had enough water to support small settlements are comparatively smaller in size and the habitational deposit is, by and large, less than two metres. On the contrary, the bigger sites, which were strategically situated near the riverbanks, such as Gilund, have sustained the cusp of the climatic fluctuation.

The recent work on Holocene climate of western Rajasthan reveals that around 4800 B.P. there was abrupt fluctuation in the south western monsoon and the region was experiencing inadequate rainfall and a dry phase was prevailed (Enzel *et al.* 1999). The lakes were getting desiccated and were dried out by 2430 to 2160 B.P. However, the eastern part of Aravalli might have witnessed a better climatic condition during this period in comparison to the western part.

The situation in the western and north western Gujarat is quite unequivocal. From the researches carried out by several scholars in Gujarat, it is apparent that during the late Harrpan times the settlements were shifted from the hinterlands to the perennial water resources. The settlements are clustered around the water-locked areas amidst the stabilized sand dunes (Bhan 1992). These settlements are smaller in size, less populated and have low-level infrastructure (Desai 1985: 103). Such settlements are suggested to be temporary and associated with pastoral economy (Bhan 1989). The situation is quite matching with that of south eastern Rajasthan. Some to such late Harappan sites, e.g., Ratanpura (Bhan 1989), Jokha (Mehta *et al.* 1971), Dhatva (Mehta *et al.* 1975) and Rangpur (Rao 1963), have also revealed contacts with the Ahar Culture and Malwa Culture, which establishes contemporaneity and greater mobility of the people.

At Marmi, the faunal remains suggest that it was mostly cattle pastoralism along with sheep-goat herding. A few wild animals were also hunted. Considering the limited area from where the bones were collected the quantity of bones are very high. The dependence on domesticated fauna is higher at the site in comparison to more agriculturally oriented phase in the culture. Therefore, it may imply that the economy was more inclined to a pastoral mode of life. The large number of tarracotta bull figurines found at the site, if it had any thing to do with the socio-cultural and religious aspect of the people, do not show any significant impact on the nature and amount of cattle bones recovered in the faunal assemblages. However, they (bull figurines of both stylised and naturalistic types) certainly emphasizes on the vital role of the cattle in the society.

Settlement pattern of Ahar culture suggests that the sites locâted near water bodies were getting deserted around 3500 B.P. and moving towards more perennial water sources. Misra (1967) has suggested a general chronology on the basis of pottery typology from his explored site in Berach basin, that the "sites on the western fringe of the (Ahar) cultural zone show earlier wares, while those lying on the eastern edge of the explored area show later features, such as the absence of Tan Slipped and Thin Red wares, paucity of decorative patterns and the presence of painted red sherds" (Misra 1967: 196). His observations probably holds good, when Marmi is viewed in that light.

The observations made from the pottery assemblage of Marmi suggest a degenerated phase of Ahar Culture. Some of the typical Aharian was, such as Thin Red, Tan, Chocolate Slipped, Buff, Reserved Slipped and Perforated wares are absent in the collection. The pottery becomes micaceous towards the end of the culture, particularly the Coarse Red ware. The evidence from Gilund unequivocally corresponds to the above observations (*IAR* 1959–60:41–46). It is, therefore, not unlikely that the settlement like that of at Marmi was established when the condition at the site like Balathal was inhospitable. However, the technological and typological gap between the Marmi pottery and the Early Historic pottery of the region is far apart. This suggests lapse of a big gap of time between them. A technology lapse scale of ceramics from Chalcolithic to Early Historic can be helpful to determine a relative time bracket between them.

it is clear from the above findings that Purani marmi represents a hitherto unknown Phase (IV) of the Ahar culture. As far as the date and duration of the settlement is concerned. further investigation on this phase and some absolute dates are required to confirm the place of Purani Marmi within the chronological framework of Ahar culture. The calibrated radiocarbon dates indicate that chalcolithic period of Ahar began around 2580–2170 B.C. and continued until 1500 B.C. or later (Allchin and Allchin 1982:262). Taking into account the uncalibrated date from Ahar, Sankalia had suggested that the beginning of Chalcolithic culture could have been around 2100 and continued till 1300 B.C. (Sankalia *et al.* 1969). However, a series of dates available from Balathal excavation suggest a long span of occupation during Phase III. It can be firmly placed between 2900–1500 B.C. (Misra *et al.* 1997; Misra 1997). Two dates available from the upper part of the Phase I. i.e., from OE layer 23 (PRL. No 1933-577±100), and HX2 layer 18 (PRL. No. 1928 = 455±180), when calibrated gives date around 4500–3300 B.C. Considering the terminal dates available from Ahar and Balathal, at present, it can safely be suggested that the settlement at Purani marmi came up when Balathal was already deserted around 1400–1500 B.C.

REFERENCES

Ansari, Z.D. and M.K. Dhavalikar 1975. *Excavations at Kayatha*. Poona: Deccan College.

Bhan, K.K. 1989. Late Harapan Settlements of Western India with Special Reference to Gujarat, in J.M. Kenoyer (ed) *Old problems and New Perspective in Archaeology of South Asia,* Madison: Wisconsin Archaeological Reports 2:219–42.

Bhan, K.K. 1992. Late Harappan Gujarat. *Eastern Anthroplogist* 45: 173–93.

Desai, A. 1985. *Special Aspect of Settlement Pattern: A Study of Narmada Command Area of Mehsana District, Gujarat*. New Delhi.

Mehta, R.N., S.N. Choudhury, K.T.M. Hegde and D.R. Shah. 1971. *Excavation at Jokha.* Baroda Archaeological Series 11.

Mehta, R.N., S.N. Choudhury, K.T.M. Hegde and D.R. Shah. 1975. *Excavation at Dhatva.* Baroda Archaeological Series 12.

Rao, S.R. 1963, Excavation at Rangpur and Other Explorations in Gujarat. *Ancient India* 18–19:5–201.

Enzel, Y., L.L. Ely, S. Mishra. R. Ramesh, P. Amit, B. Lazar, S.N. Rajaguru, V.R. Baker, and A.Sandler. 199. High-Resolution Holocene Environmental Changes in the Thar Desert, Northwestern India, *Science,* 284: 125–127.

Hooja, R. 1988. *The Ahar Culture and Beyond-Settlements and Frontiers of 'Mesolithic' and Early Agricultural Sites in South-Eastern Rajasthan c 3rd.–2nd* Millennia B.C., BAR International Series 412. Oxford, Enland.

IAR: Indian Archaeology: A Review, Annual Publication of the Archaeological Survey of India: New Delhi (1959–60:41–46).

Mishra, A. Chalcolithic Ceramics of Balathal, District Udaipur, Rajasthan. Unpublished Ph.D Thesis. University of Poona.

Misra, V.N. 1967. *Pre- and Prtoto- History of the Berach Basin. South Rajasthan.* Deccan College, Poona.

Misra, V.N., V.S. Shinde, R.K. Mohanty and Lalit Pandey 1993. Teracotta Bull Figurines from Marmi: A Chalcolithic Settlement in Chitorgarh District, Rajasthan. *Man and Environment,* XVII(2): 149–152.

Misra, V.N., V.S. Shinde, R.K. Mohanty, Kurush Dalal, Anup Mishra, Lalit Pandey and Jeevan Kharakwal 1995. Excavations at Balathal: their contribution to the Chalcolithic and Iron Age cultures of Mewar, Rajasthan. *Man and Environment,* XXII(@): *35–59.*

Misra, V.N., V.S. Shinde, R.K. Mohanty, Lalit Pandey and Jeewan Kharakwal 1997. Excavations at Balathal, Udaipur district, Rajasthan (1995–97), with special Reference to Chalcolithic Architecture. *Man and Environment,* XX(1):57–80.

Misra. V.N. 1997. Balathal: A Chalcolithic Settlement in Mewar. Rajasthan, India: Results of First Three Seasons' Excavations. *South Asian Studies* 13: 251–273.

Sankalia, H.D., S.B., Deo and Z.D.Ansari 1969. *Excavations at Ahar, (Tambavati).* Pune: Deccan College.

Shah, D.R. 1969. Animal Remains from Excavations at Ahar in *Excavations at Ahar (Tambavati)* (H.D. Sankalia, S.B. Deo and Z.D. Ansari Eds.), pp. 237–245. Pune: Deccan College.

Thomas, P.K. and P.P. Joglekar 1996b. Faunal Remains from Balathal, Rajasthan: A Preliminary Report, *Man and Environment* XXI (1):91–97.

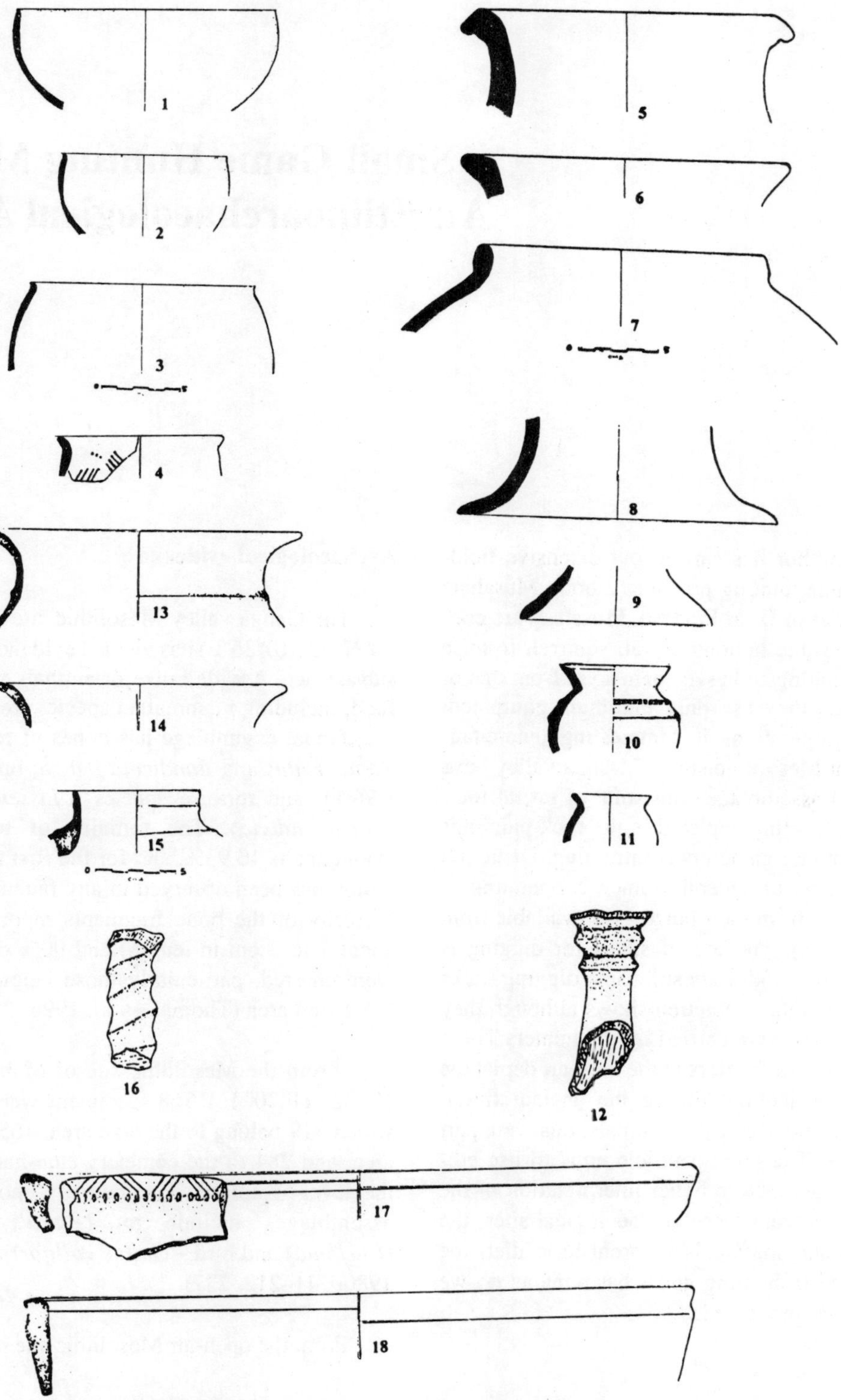

Fig.1. Chalcolithic Ceramics of Marmi: 1–4 Black-and Red ware, 5–12 Red Slipped ware, 13–16 Grey Slipped ware and 17–18 Coarse Red ware

Small Game Hunting Musahars: An Ethnoarchaeological Approach

SHAHIDA ANSARI*

The present author has carried out extensive fieldwork on small game hunting practices among Musahars of Allahabad district of Uttar Pradesh. Musahars are connoisseur in small game hunting of rat, squirrel, tortoise and birds. Their hunting style sets them apart from that of other hunters since they use only minimum equipment during the hunting operations. It is interesting to note faunal assemblages at Mesolithic sites of Ganga valley have yielded the faunal assemblage consisting of rat, tortoise and birds. The rat hunting depicted in the rock paintings at Jaora of early hunter-gatherers is intriguing. Depiction of an elaborate scene of several women cooperating in catching rats (fig. 1) from their burrows is available from (Neumayer 1993: 78). The use of sticks for digging is intriguing as Musahars today are still using digging sticks for rat hunting. The other depiction shows although they hunted big game, rats were carried by the hunters.These illustrations (fig.1) of rat hunters in the rock-art depict the type of hunting carried out during the ancient times. Although there was no scarcity of animals, rats were part of their usual diet. The present article aims to use ethnoarchaeological approach to better interpretation of the small game remains from these archaeological sites, the role played by small mammals in prehistoric diet, the technique involved in hunting and what remains do we expect after they are processed.

Archaeological evidence

The Ganga valley Mesolithic site of Damdama (26° 10' N; 82° 10' 36"E) has yielded evidence of animal-based subsistence. A wide range of animals were exploited for food, including mammalian species from elephant to rat. The faunal assemblage has bones of rodent species like *Rattus rattus* and *Bandicota indica*; birds (*Gallus gallus* 8.96%); and tortoise species (*Lissemys punctata* and *Chitra indicia*). The remains of tortoise bones at Damdama is 10.93%, and for the first time such a distribution has been observed in any faunal sites from India. Majority of the bone fragments reported were tiny (of about 1 to 3 cm in length) and 90% of these fragments were charred, particularly those belonging to the main habitation area (Thomas *et. al.* 1996: 258–259).

From the Mesolithic site of Mahadaha (25° 29' 2" N.; 82° 11' 30" E.), 768 specimens were examined out of which 319 belong to the lake area, 165 to the butchering area, and 284 to the cemetery-*cum*-habitation area from the level-Mesolithic Geometric without pottery. These assemblages include rat (*Rattu's rattus*) tortoise (*Chelonia*) and bird - *Gallus galliformes* (Sharma *et. al.* 1980: 211–212, 227).

From the open-air Mesolithic site of Sarai-Nahar-Rai

*Department of Archaeology, Deccan College, Pune.

(25° 48' N; 81' E) the animal bones were found from two locations i.e., hearths and floor area. Those recovered from the hearths were in different stages of roasting with extensive soot on them. The faunal assemblage from the level-Mesolithic with Geometric microliths are without pottery, contained bones of tortoise (*Chelonia*) of roasted and partly roasted variety, found from hearths. There were dorsal plates and the shells of these reptiles.

Study Area and the People

Ethnographic fieldwork was carried out among the Musahar settlements of Allahabad District (24° 47' and 25° 47' N; 81° 9' and 82° 21' E.) of Uttar Pradesh. The Musahars i.e. rat catchers are also called *Banmanus, Banraja, Gonr, Mushera* and *Musaha.* Their traditional economic activity is collection and sale of medicinal roots and herbs, wild honey, preparation and sale of leaf plates, collection and sale of gum, live lizard (*goh*), lighting of brick kilns, field labourers, rearing silk worm and carrying palanquins (Crooke 1896: 12–13, 36–37). But nowadays, they are working as palanquin bearers, labourers in brick kilns, and agricultural labourers. Some are involved in piggery (Singh 1993: 969–970).

During the fieldwork it was observed that Musahars have varied type of settlement style. Some stay in mango or mahua plantations of the village head or of a influential villager. Here they prefer to stay just under these huge trees, which protect them from seasonal severities. They make no hutment of any kind during their stay. These Musahars supply leaf platters and cups to the villagers and local markets. Therefore, only few can be accommodated in a particular village (4 to 5 families only). Usually they prefer to stay near the field as they get leaves to make leaf plates. Here field rats not only provide them with meat but also the grains from their holes. Sometimes they are especially called upon to clear the rat menace from the agricultural fields.

The other Musahars settlements are mainly on the outskirts of villages, mostly near the agricultural fields. They make temporary huts of straw and nearby wood/branches. They work as agricultural labourers, stonecutters and also make leaf plates and cups. About 7 to 8 families stay in such type of settlements. Some Musahars stay in villages in groups in mud houses. These are partly well off and own land and are involved in agriculture. Here 15 to 20 families stay in a settlement. But it is interesting to note that rat eating is a delicacy and relished by all.

Small Game Hunting

According to Musahars they eat 36 types of small and big animals including snakes. They never kill monkey and cow. They domesticate pigs for consumption and sacrificial offerings.

It is more often that the small game hunting is preferred to the big game hunting as it is less laborious and saves time. They usually carry out hunting while gathering leaves from nearby forest area.

Rat Hunting

A peculiar type of rat hunting practice sets the Musahars apart from that of the other rat hunters like Irulas, Bondos and Yanadi. When approached for rat hunting they enthusiastically took the task after the day's tiredness of working as part time labourers in the rice field, they immediately took all the items required for hunting. Rat hunting is actively participated by men, women and children alike. The tools used during the hunting operations are:

1. Multipurpose tool '*khanta*' has iron head hafted in bamboo. It is generally used for digging, cutting, hunting and selfprotection.
2. Iron tool '*Gahdala*' is used during digging and burrowing.
3. Digging tool '*Pharua*' has a handle and broad blade.
4. Sticks of various length and sizes.
5. Bucket for water.

Two to ten people hunt the rats i.e., *mus* depending on the quantity required. First and foremost is locating rat holes and to make sure that the rats are in. They excel in differentiating the rat holes than those of other burrowing animals. Generally the rat holes are near or in the agricultural fields. The average diameter of a burrow varies from 15–20 cm and some are 2 m deep. Every burrow includes surface openings, feeding tunnels, nesting chamber, and food cache. Feeding tunnels are parallel to surface, while storage chambers are usually found at greater depths than feeding tunnels. Sometimes there may be as many as 7 to 10 adult as well as young rats in a single hole. Besides this they also take out the grains collected by the rats in the rat hole. The best season for rat hunting is when the grains are ripe and threshing of grains starts.

After tracing the rat hole a man starts digging the hole with *khanta* and the other man simultaneously pours water with the bucket after the feeding tunnel is clearly visible. This whole process is to scare the rat inside the hole. The water suffocates the rat and it tries to escape from other outlets. Meantime the accompanying children occupy the outlets of the rat holes and wait with sticks in their hands. Now when the rat tries to escape, a hit of the stick kills it or they catch them with bare hands.

In the other situation when the rats do not escape and dies inside, the hunters dig (using *Gahdala*) them up. Musahars prefer field rats to other types. They never eat house rats as according to them the house rats stink and don't taste good. Many Musahars keep the rats by captivating it in small pots for later consumption and these pots are generally placed/ buried in one corner of the house.

After the rats are caught preparations for roasting starts. An adult rat may attain a length of 30 cm, including the tail. If the kill is of two or three rats they roast it there on spot, and eat it, otherwise bring them back to the settlement. They collect twigs and dried leaves from the surrounding area and choose a dry area to roast the kill. When the fire is lighted they start roasting the rat, by holding the ear and the tail with both hands. This is done for about 5 to 6 minutes during this time the rat is fumed around several times and this process makes the body stiffen and all the hairs on the body burns. Now the rat is removed from the fire and the body is rubbed with dried leaves or with sharp sticks for removing the burnt hair.

The second step is to break the rodent tooth (incisor), which works like a sharp blade. The cook cuts open the belly and removes unwanted body parts. Again fire is lighted and inner body is roasted. Sometime this is not done as it depends on the type of taste they prefer to have. The kill is equally distributed among all. From the ear to the tail every part is consumed and nothing is spared. The waste body parts, the tooth (incisor) and the burnt twigs remain behind.

The most important part of rat hunting carried out by Musahars is minimum use of tools. No small blade or knife is required to cut the rats (tooth i.e. incisors are sharp enough to carry out the task). After ten days the site was again visited to check the remains, and it was noticed that the wind had blown away the twigs and ash and just an ashy appearance remained with a rodent tooth (incisor). It is the remains of rats kept in the pots for later consumption, which were due to some reasons never consumed, are the only evidence of rats from the Musahars house, buried in the ground. It is worth mentioning that the hearth at Mahadaha and Sarai-Nahar-Rai, from the hearth loose blackish ash was obtained (but charcoal was conspicuous by its absence), suggesting that for roasting flesh only twigs, grass or leaves were used (Sharma *et. al.* 1980: 99).

Squirrel Hunting

Men and children hunt the common striped squirrel i.e., *Sciurus palmarus*, Children use catapult for hunting while men use sticks to kill them. To hunt a squirrel at least four men are required. When men are hunting only the adolescent boys are allowed to accompany them, the reason that squirrels run very fast and hide away on slight noise.

Firstly trees are searched for squirrels, if they are sighted, one among them climbs the tree and the others stand about 2 to 3m away on three sides. Each knows well his area for chasing the animal once it is on the ground. Now the man up in the tree starts shaking the branches and simultaneously makes loud noises to scare the animal. This takes some time as the squirrel jumps from one branch to other very fast; the idea is to tire the animal. Once the animal comes down the man nearest to it runs towards it and gives a blow by using stick. One hit and the animal faints. It is then picked the legs are broken it is because the animal is smart to fool the man by acting dead and often runs off. They never kill the animal completely till they start the fire for cooking.

The other type of squirrel hunting is when about 15 to 20 men accompany. In this, group of trees or trees in a row are selected. For example if there are about 6 trees in a row, then six men climb on the individual tree and the others surround the trees, the same hunting technique follows as described above. But the only difference is that large number of squirrel can be caught by this technique.

The procedure of roasting is similar to that of rat. The only difference is that it is very rare that the squirrels are taken back to the settlement, and is always relished soon after the hunting is over. Equal distribution is done for all; from ear to tail every thing is consumed. Nothing is spared except the waste body parts, the rodents tooth (incisor), and the burnt twigs. In one instance the squirrel was pregnant, the babies were removed and placed on green leaves and were disposed in water, but the adult was consumed.

It is interesting that none of the Mesolithic sites of Ganga valley has yielded the evidence of squirrels in the faunal assemblage. The probable reason is that the hunted squirrel is never taken back to the settlement and eaten away from the settlement soon after the hunting operation is over.

Tortoise Hunting

Musahars catch freshwater slow moving reptiles i.e., tortoise *Chelonia.* The tools required to remove tortoise from underground are the digging sticks and *khanta.* Generally young boys and women catch tortoise from nearby ponds and lakes by hand, and bring it back alive to the settlement.

The placement of hearths of Musahars is always outside the hut, in open. It is only during rainy season the hearth the built inside. Firstly, they light the wood and twigs in the hearth and wash the tortoise. The body of tortoise remains within shell and the neck, limbs and tail outside the shell but when are caught they hide inside the shell and it is very important to kill them before roasting and are thus placed near the flames. Due to warmness the tortoise brings out the head, which the women immediately breaks the neck with the hands.

The reason for roasting is to loosen the body from the hard outer bony shell. After roasting the inner layer the bony plate is opened by hand. Once it is open the flesh is removed. This is then cooked with oil and spices.

The outer shell and the bony plates are placed on the roof of the huts to dry, which is later powdered and eaten during the ailment of stomach problems. The scatter of large quantity of discarded bone and shells were seen inside the old hearths, behind the huts, and nearby settlement.

The tortoise (*Lissemys punctata* and *Chitra indica*) remains from Damdama were 10.93% and 90% of these fragments were charred, particularly those belonging to the main habitation area. From Mahadaha evidence of tortoise (*Chelonia*) shells mainly comes from the lake area, butchering area and the cemetery-cum-habitation area. From Sarai-Nahar-Rai the animal bones were found from two locations i.e., hearths and floor area. The bones of tortoise (*Chelonia*), found from hearths were of roasted and have partly roasted variety. The contents were the dorsal plates and the shells.

The ethnographic work carried among Musahars helped in understanding why the faunal assemblage were either found in the hearth or in habitation area and the placement of hearth outside in open:

1. The placement of the hearth is always outside the hut because the food preparation requires lot more roasting, which gives smoke and burning of flesh smell. (The placement of hearths at Chopani-Mando is outside the floors (Sharma *et. al.* 1980: 40).

2. They often place hearth wherever suitable for roasting, generally direction of wind is kept on mind while cooking. The tortoise is roasted in the hearth and thus the remains are left in the hearth. They also consume roasted tortoise without further preparation, resulting to the leftover scattered near hearth. These shells are reused for fire.

3. When new hearths are made the old hearths are left with the remains of tortoise and other charred animal bones.

4. The hearth if cleared, the bones and shells are usually thrown behind the hut.

5. They also bury these shells in rice fields as it attracts filed rats.

Bird Trapping

The men and young boys generally trap all types of birds available in the area except vultures, eagles and owls. The birds are either hunted for consumption or for sale in the local market. Though they work as labourers in the fields they do not get much time for bird hunting but whenever they do get an opportunity they go for bird catching. Some of their favorite birds mentioned during the survey were collected, further literary sources (Ali: 1996) were referred for their English, scientific and local name (Table 1a, 1b)

The methods described below, however, are the ones that are currently adopted by Musahars in the study area and they serve to illustrate the ingenuity with which exploitative activities are adapted according to the peculiar habits of various birds. The techniques followed for birds trapping are as follows:

Net

To trap the bird they spread a net made of thread with 0.615 m x 0.615 m dimension between the two big trees. The net is spread at least 0.2 m above the ground. They then spread grains to lure birds, when the bird comes and sits on it to eat the get entangled and are caught in the net. Later they are removed by hand and placed in a bag and carried to the camp, but a few are consumed then and there itself if the bird's quantity is more.

Gummed Bamboo Stick

They apply gum (of *Acacia arabica* Willd.) to the bamboo sticks, which is available in the nearby area and jungles. The sticks of about 0.30 m lengths, to which gum is applied and then is, placed in between the branches and leaves of any fruit bearing tree. As soon as the groups of birds come to the tree to eat the fruits they are entrapped. These are later removed. Birds, which are to be consumed, are kept separately and the others are kept in the cage, which are later sold in the market

Catapult

Firstly small stones or pellet are collected to use in the catapult. Once hit by the pellet the birds faint, which are then collected.

Well

In this method birds which sit in a well for its coolness, like pigeons are trapped, About 4 to 6 people surround and simultaneously cover the well with net from the top to which gum is rubbed. Then noise is made to scare them, which leads them to fly upwards. In this process they get entangled and are caught due to the gum applied to it. Net is overturned and the birds are removed.

Birds caught in big quantity and big sized birds are generally brought to the camp, otherwise they are consumed then and there. Birds are brought alive to the settlement. Firstly twigs and grasses are collected and fire is lit, meanwhile other men strangulate the birds by twisting the neck. Immediately feathers are removed, as it is easier when the bird is warm. Now the bird is roasted, after which the abdomen is cut with a sharp stick or knife. The waste parts are removed and thrown away. The bird again is roasted from inside. Small birds are always roasted and consumed but elaborate cooking follows for large birds.

It is interesting to note that besides beak, feathers, waste body parts and ash nothing remains at the site everything else is consumed. But when big birds are cooked and consumed the leftover bones are thrown in the hearth or behind the hut.

The evidence of bird species (*Gallus gallus*) is from Damdama. It is interesting to note here that *Gallus gallus* is regarded as the ancestor of all domestic breeds of fowl (Ali 1996: 125).

Division of labour

The division of labour is according to age and sex. Men do more strenuous work while women attend to delicate and simple tasks and children do the lightest work. Small game hunting as food quest demands different contribution. Following table shows the work carried out by them:

The faunal remains at Damdama indicated that large species were preferred for some time and then the preference shifted to smaller animals. In general, about 23% of the identified bones belonged to aquatic (reptiles, mollusca and fish) and avian species. The cyclical trend observed in the resource management is interesting. The exploitation of one class of the mammalian resources for a longer period of time, thereby depleting it to such an extent that other alternatives such as the aquatic and avian resources had to be chosen to furfill their food requirements (Thomas *et. al.* 1996: 261). It was noticed among Musahars that they prefer small game hunting more often

Table l a Game birds of Musahars

No.	English name	Scientific name	Local name
1.	Barheaded goose	*Anser indicus* Lathum	Kareyee hans, hans
2.	Black breasted or rain quail	*Coturnix coromandelica* Gemlin	*China bater*
3 .	Black partridge	*Francolinus francolinus* Linn	*Kala teetar*
4.	Bustard quail	*Turnix suscitator* Gmelin	*Bater*
5.	Common or grey quail	*Coturnix coturnix* Linn	*Bada baser*
6	Common Indian sand grouse	*Pterocles exustus* Temminck	*Kuhar, bhat teetar*
8.	Common peafowl	*Pavo cristatus* Linn	*Mor, mayur*
9	Crow pheasant or coucal	*Centropus sinensis* Stephens	*Mahoka*
10.	Common snipe	*Gallingo gallingo* Linn	*Chaha*
11.	Greyleg goose	*Anser anser* Linn	*Rajhans*
12.	Great Indian bustard	*Choriotis nigriceps* Vigros	*Sohan, hulna*
13.	Grey partridge	*Francolinus pondicerianus* Gmelin	*Safed teetar*
14.	Hoopoe	*Upupa epops* Linn	*Hudhud*
15.	Indian myna	*Acridotheres tristis* Linn	*Desi myna*
16.	Jungle bush quail	*Perdicula asiatica* Latham	*Lowwa*
17	Jungle crow	*Corvus macrorhynchos* Wagler	*Kala kowwa, jangli kowwa*
18.	Koel	*Eudynamys scolopacea* Linn	*Kwal*
19.	Lesser florican	*Sypheotides indica* Miller	*Barsati*
20.	Painted snipe	*Rostratula bengalensis* Linn	*Ragehaha*

Table lb Birds caught for the sale

No.	English name	Scientific name	Local name
1.	Blue rock pigeon	*Columba livia* Gmelin	*Kabutar*
2.	Red munia	*Estrilda amandava* Linn	*Lal*
3.	Red turtle dove	*Streptopelia tranquebarica* Herman	*Seroti*
4	Roseringed parakeet	*Psittacula krameri* Scopoli	*Tota*
5.	Spotted dove	*Streptopelia chinensis* Scopoli	*Chitroka*

Men	Women	Children
Hunting small animals including rat and squirrels.	Processing and cooking	Hunting rat and squirrel
Roasting	Catch turtle in in pond Processing and cooking	Catch turtle in ponds and lakes
Bird trapping. Roasting	Processing and cooking	Bird trapping with net
Birds selling in local market	-	-

than the big game hunting, as it requires less energy and tools. They have knowledge to how much the animals are to be hunted otherwise they will be extinct and create harm to the ecology. The Mesolithic man must be well acquainted to how much the animal has to be exploited, which invariably left them with the option of exploring new food resources from time to time. But it is interesting that the animals are seen either in less or more percentage from all the layers leading to think that the Mesolithic man was experimenting due to the scarcity of stone tools and that might be the reason why every second or third bone in Damdama was a worked bone, if not a well-made tool.

Conclusion

Small mammals like rodents do represent a potentially rich food source. However, despite dietary potential afforded by small mammals they are generally assigned minor significance in archaeological interpretation. The evidence of prehistoric diet can very well be seen from the Mesolithic sites of Ganga valley which included bandicoot rat *Bandicota* cf. *bengalensis*, porcupines species Hystrix indica, tortoise *Lissemys punctata* and *Clhitra indica* and birds *Gallus galliformes*.

Every part is consumed in case of these small animals thus, are likely to leave few archaeological traces. Less quantity of bones does not mean they didn't consume small animals. The bones recovered from the sites of small animals certainly contribute to our knowledge that these were consumed but how much each species contributed to the diet of the Mesolithic people is difficult from the amount of remains recovered, which is hardly anything. The point should be taken into account that why is that they consume such small animals in their diet, which demands more energy but fewer yields, and how nutritive they are if consumed. It was observed that small animals suggest relatively high edible meat to live weight ratio. However, despite the dietary potentials afforded by small animals, they are generally assigned minor significance in archaeological interpretation and are constantly overshadowed by larger animals, as these small animals remains can be an important indicator in reconstructing the prehistoric diet. This study shows the inclusion of rat bones at site, showing their dietary habits, besides rat holes provide them grains for consumption. Mesolithic man may have explored these possibilities and started collecting wild grains.

The placement of hearth is of archaeological importance. Among the Musahars the placement of hearths helps in understanding why they are placed outside as mentioned earlier. Roasting is always carried out in open and rarely in hearth. The animal bones are scattered near the site and hearths similar to excavated sites. Thus, it can be said that this study has largely helped in understanding the significance of small animal remains and how ethnographic studies can help in understanding them.

Acknowledgements

The author wishes to thank Prof. V.N. Misra, who has always been a sole inspiration to carry out ethnoarchaeological work in Ganga Valley and for giving constant encouragement. Dr. P P. Joglekar for his valuable suggestions and comments, Rampalji, Sarita didi and A. Kanungo for accompanying me during fieldwork.

REFERENCES

Ali, Salim 1996. *The Book of Indian Birds.* (Salim Ali Centenary Edition). Bombay Natural History Society. Mumbai: Oxford University Press.

Crooke, W. 1896. *The Tribes and castes of North-Western Province and Oudh.* Vol. III, Calcutta: Government of India.

Neumayer, E. 1993. *Lines on Stones, The Prehistoric Rock Art of India.* Delhi: Manohar Publishers and Distributors.

Sharma, G.R., V.D. Misra, D. Mandal, B.B. Misra and J.N.Pal 1980. *From Hunting Gathering to Domestication of Plants and Animals: Beginning of Agriculture,* Allahabad: Abinash Prakashan.

Singh, K.S. 1993. *The Scheduled Castes.* Vol, II: 969–971. New Delhi: Oxford University Press.

Thomas P.K., P.P. Joglekar, V.D. Misra, J.N. Pandey and J.N. Pal 1996. Faunal Evidence for the Mesolithic Food Economy of the Gangetic Plain with Special Reference to Damdama in *The Prehistory of Asia and Oceania, Colloquium XXIII, Bioarchaeology of Mesolithic India: an Integral Approach* (Gennadii E. Afanasev, Serge Clenziou, John R. Lukacs and Maurizio Tasi Eds), pp 255–266. Forli Italia: A.B.A.C.O. Edizioni.

Fig. 1. Depiction of rat hunting and hunters carrying rats from the rock painting, Jaora.

Copper Objects from Dihor: Archaeotechnical Studies

PRANAB K. CHATTOPADHYAY*

In West Bengal a number of Chalcolithic sites were discovered and excavated by the Archaeology Departments of the Universities and the State and the Central Governments. Amongst the sites Dihor is one of them. The site (23° 08'N, 87° 86'E) is situated at the confluence of the Darakeswar and the Kana nadi (dried bed of the former), 6 km north of Vishnupur in Bankura district, West Bengal. Late Manik Lal Singha of Vangiya Sahitya Parishad, Vishnupur, discovered the site in 1974. He discovered a large number of Neoliths tools from this site along with three hundred cast copper coins of different shapes, etc. A number of ancient villages were discovered which yield the runs in the surrounding localities.

Late Professor Anil Chandra Pal and his colleague of Calcutta University conducted three sessions of excavations during 1983–84, 1984–85 and 1990–91. The first Chalcolithic level in Bankura district was established. Two distinct cultural divisions of Chalcolithic and Early Historic periods were identified.

Metallic Finds

From the three sessions of excavations fragments of copper-bronze objects, comprising antimony rods, fragment of a bangle, a spool of copper wire, etc. were found from period I, i.e. Chalcolithic level. In Early Historic level along with other objects the cast copper coins, (sqaure and round) were recovered. These coins were in circulation in West Bengal from c.4th century B.C.

The cast copper coins of these varieties have been found in Early Historic phase that have been observed at Baneswardanga (Period III), Bangarh, Bharatpur (Period III) Chandraketugarh (Period II), Dihor (Period II), Kotasur (Period II), Mahisdal (Period II), Mangolkot (Period III), Pakhanna (Period III), Pandurajar Dhibi (Period IV), and Tamluk (Period II).

Analysis

The detials of the copper-bronze objects that were selected for analysis are included in Table-1. The objets are shown along with the original specimen number, layer from which they were collected, locus and the date of excavation.

A. *Round cast copper coin:* One side of it bears a symbol of an elephant and the other side that of a *Chaitya*. It was made of a metallic core with patina - a complex salt of chloride, oxide, sulfate or hydrated oxide of copper.

B. *Rectangular cast copper coin:* This coin was highly corroded and brittle. Faint symbols appeared which

*Visiting fellow, Centre for Archaeological Studies and Training, Eastern India. 92, Rajendera Prasad Avenue, Durgapur 713205.

TABLE - I

Sl. No.	Spec. No.	Object	Layer	Locus	Date
A	DR 38	Round cast copper coin	2	3.96 x 1.32 — 40 cm	18.03.84
B	DR 45	Rectangular cast copper coin	3	0.57 N1	01.03.84
C	DR 4	Copper Bangle	4	0.65 M	14.03.84
D	DR 27	Copper Wire	6	2.88 x 3.18 — 1.65 m	28.03.84

recognize that the obverse bore that of elephant and the reverse includes the tree in railing.

C. *Copper Bangle:* A unique fragment of a bangle the shape of an arc, about 29 mm in length and 3 mm in diameter in cross-section. Its external surface was engraved with grooves. Projecting the arc, it appeared that its internal diameter was about 60 mm. The specimen was covered with blackish green patina. A small portion was cut off for analysis.

D. *Copper wire:* This was a very important pattern of a spool of wire. The cross-section of the wire was oval irregular size of 2.45 x 1.65 mm. About 20 mm in length of the specimen was selected for different observations. After removal of greenish patina the core became 2.15 x 1.35 mm in size.

Methodology of Analysis

The objective of this study was to examine the constituents of the metal pieces and the trace elements present. From the analysis of trace elements there is some possibility to locate the source of the copper along with the probable identification of ore-mineral. Since the quantity of specimen was very small simple spectrochemical method was applied. A large hilger Watts Spectrograph performed this. The selected spectral region was 2700–4400 Å, RU being the standard. In Table- 2, semiquantitative presence of the major constitutions are given. Al these four specimens are confirmed with copper as base element. The qualitative presence of elements together with the rave elements is indicated as follows. All the four specimens are found to be same in quality. Elements present are Ag, Fe, As, Pb, Bi, Cu, Sn, Ni, Al, Mg and Si. Elements absent are Sb, Zn, Mn, Co, Au, Cr, Mo, Zr, W and Ti.

To determine the probable ores from which the metal had been extracted for manufacturing the artifacts Friedman Et. Als (1966) method was applied. The relative probability of occurrence for the three types of ores (i.e. I-native, II- oxidized and III-reduced type) is also included in Table-2.

Metallurgy

The specimen B and D had been selected for metllographic studies. One small piece was taken from each of the specimens and was fixed in polystyrene mounting.

TABLE-2

Sp	Ag	As	Fe	Bi	Pb	Sb	Sn	Ai	Si	Zn	Normalized Probability %		
											I	II	III
A	0.02	0.10	0.005	0.1	0.50	0.2	6.0	0.1	0.1	0	2.41	70.74	26.64
B	0.02	0.05	0.005	0.1	0.05	0	5.9	Tr.	0.1	0	0.44	88.01	11.54
C	0.02	0.10	0.005	0.1	0.20	0	9.0	Tr.	0.1	0.5	1.27	37.33	61.39
D	0.02	0.50	0.50	0.1	0.50	0	0.8	0.1	0.1	0	5.09	62.92	31.99

After careful polishing with emery papers of increasing fineness and finishing with diamond cloth the specimens were observed through an NEOPHOT-10 metallographic microscope.

The specimen B (rectangular cast copper coin) was found with greenish black matrix with grains of copper. This clearly indicates the intergranular corrosion - specially formed in cast copper coin and this represent its dendrite characteristics.

The specimen D (Spool of wire) was found with a relatively cleaner surface. Throughout the length of 15 mm only one inclusion was noticed. Its nature and colour appears to be $Cu\text{-}Cu_2O$.

Etching: This is the process of revealing the structural details by preferential dissolution. The etching of ancient copper specimen is an art. Generally these specimens do not respond to the traditional etching processes. With reagents lots of experiments were made and the best response was obtained. A few ferric chloride crystals were directly dropped in a watch glass containing ammonium hydroxide and mixing straight with hydrogen peroxide and then a little distilled water was added. A reaction immediately starts with the evolution of nascent gasses. The mounted specimens were swabbed with cotton. After washing thoroughly with absolute alcohol and drying the specimens become ready for observations, through microscope. By alternately polishing and etching several times the true structure of the metal was revealed.

As mentioned earlier in Table-2, except the wire, other three objects are intentionally alloyed. The spool of wire with this low amount of tin and lead are probably without any alloying. There is every possibility of natural contamination from ore body or flux. On the other hand, because of non-availability of supply of alloying elements the metal smiths failed to make the proper alloy. Whereas, for making the bangle or other ornaments, the metal smiths of Dihor used 8 to 10% tin which is quite satisfactory in case of true bronze, or better *alpha-bronze.*

Process metallurgy; When the working on a metal takes place, say forging, the force applied to it tries to change its shape or deformed it. The process of deforming a metal below the 'recrystallisation temperature' is called 'cold working.' The said temperature varied from metal to metal. It has no connection of our common sense hot or cold. Similarly, the meaning with 'hot working' is processing above that temperature. When a metal is cold worked its strength and hardness increases but at the same time the metal becomes brittle due to the development of high internal stresses. 'Annealing' is the process to reduce the hardness and to relieve internal stresses.

The figure represents the photomicrograph of the copper after etching. This is shown at a magnification of 250 X. The structure is different from that of the cast structure containing dendrites. The structural details have been revealed and a polycrystalline metal is shown with grain boundaries. A polycrystalline solid is composed of many grains. These are oriented at random and are well separated by gain boundaries. The structure as shown in figure is termed as "twins". This is especially evident in copper and some other metals. A crystal is twinned when one portion of the lattice is a mirror image of the neighboring portion. The twin is generally of two types. One of them is called - 'annealing twins'. In Pl. 1 the microstructure of the same is shown which was revealed at a magnification of 250 x.

From this observation it appeared that the spool of wire was made by means of cold forging and subsequently the metal was annealed at a higher temperature. In this figure some scattered minute particles are also seen. These are the inclusions mainly of $Cu\text{-}Cu_2O$, appearing greenish in colour and also a few spherical black particles that are lead. From this it is inferred that moderate poling was performed.

The microstructure of the coin is made of a structure of cast dendrites. (Pl. 2, 100x) For casting, small earthen moulds were used. In case of cast cooper coin the metalsmiths used the similar manufacturing techniques that were practiced in northern part of the country. Pure copper was perhaps not used for manufacturing cast coins. Alloying with tin and lead was practiced. The knowledge in making cast copper coin with 5 to 7% tins and 4 to 5% lead was matured enough.

Source of Cooper

The probable source for copper for A, B and D was from malachite-azurite minerals. The source for C is perhaps from chalcopyrite. But this specimen was very small in quantities and that high amount of tin was added to it, so there perhaps some statistical error might have occurred.

Agrawal analyzed some Indian copper ores. His findings on the trace elements with regard to Singhbhum, Rakha copper ores (samples P-56, P-57, P-58and P-188), Rajasthan (P-98) and Gujarat (P-189) may be compared with the trace elements in Dihor specimens. It is found that absence of Ag,As, Sn and Bi along with the presence of Ti and Mn differentiated it with Singhbhum chalcopyrite ores. On the other hand, the presence of Zn, Mn, Co and Sb and absence of Bi in Rakha ores totally differentiated it with Dior coppers. The same has differentiated in with the copper ores of Rajasthan and Gujarat.

In this part of West Bengal a few ancient copper mines/workings had been explored by the Geological Survey of India. The important ones are as follows. Particularly at Bankura district, Chhedapathar and Tamakhum (22°53'N, 86°45'E), from Purulia, Beldie (23°03', 86°18'), Biramdi (22°05N, 86°12'E), Kharindwara, Punda (22°59', 86°40'), Ranganigora and Tamakhun, (22°59', 86°36') are well known and, the last but not the least, source is from Gohalbaira (22°39'N, 86°43'E) of Medinipur district. Unfortunately, no analysis of this group of ores is available.These small pockets produced small quantities of copper since the Chalcolithic period. Since there is much work to be done in future the exact identification is incomplete at present.

Conclusion

It may be concluded from the present study that the metalsmiths of Dihor were conversant with forging of cooper, wire drawing and annealing from the Chalcolithic period. Subsequently, they learnt the technology of alloying and bronze making. The people of Chalcolithic Dihor were agriculturists. Their copper-tool kits were meager. From these studies it was found that they also knew adding tin and lead to copper to reduce the melting point and better fusibility required in case of manufacturing of cooper coins in Early Historic period. It may also be mentioned that in specimen D the presence of sodium was noted. Like similar copper artificals' of this region, it is possible that the smiths used borax as a flux. Iron was introduced in Early Historic period.

Acknowledgements

The author is thankful for the supports provided to him by Late Dr. A.C. Pal of Calcutta University, and last not the least to Mr. S.K. Banerjee, Dr. S.K. Bhattacharjee, Mr. D.J. Desair and Mr. Kanhaia Lal of Alloy Steels Plant and Dr. B.R. Guha and Mr. M.L. Dutta of Central Mechanical Engineering Research Institute, Durgapur. Without their support this paper would not been produced.

BIBLIOGRAPHY

Agrawal, D.P. 1971. *The Copper Bronze Age in India*, Delhi: Munshram Manoharlal.

Agrawal, D.P., R.V. Krishnamurthy and S. Kusumgar, 1978. 'New data of the copper hoards and the Daimabad Bronzes' *Man & Environment* 2: 41–46.

Friedman, A.M. *et al.* 1966. Copper artifacts: correlation with source types of copper ores', *Science*, 152 (3728): 1504–1506.

I A R 1983–84, p. 92–93, *1984–85*, p. 92–95.

Mukherjee, B.N. 1991. Coins in Pre-Gupta Bengal,' in *Studies in Archaeology*, papers presented in memory of P.C. Dasgupta, pp. 281–308, (ed.) A. Dutta, Books and Books, New Delhi, .

Pal. A.C. 1992. 'Dihar: a Chalcolithic site,' *Pratna Samiksha* 1, 101–106.

Excavation at Bisokhar, Distt. Ghaziabad, (U.P.) 1999

The site at Bisokhar lies in one of the cultivated fields in the village Bisokhar (Lat. 28°51' 15 N", Long. 77°35' E.). In a chance discovery, some beautiful sculptures in sand-stone, and lintel, door jambs etc. of a Hindu temple of Pratihara period were found in June 98.

With a view; (i) to study the actual nature of the structures, if nay, at the find spot of the sculptures, (ii), to find out any other related material of the temple the Excavation Branch-II, New Delhi of the Survey under the direction of the author examined the temple remains and the site in August 98 and carried out excavation.

The excavation revealed a step-well (Pl. 1), a circular type burnt earth structure (fig. 1) and some other architectural remains from the loamy deposit. It seems that the other structural evidence, which were under a metre from present ground level, the villagers in June, 98, completely destroyed for agricultural operations and no plan of the temple as such could be traced out.

The exposed step-well has 24 steps with an average rise and tread of about 20 cm and 25 cm respectively. The height of rise was maintained by brick-lining below stones. The available total height of steps is about 6.30 m and total available length with the wall is about 8.80 m. The 1.5 m. broad steps have a 80 cm. wide brick-retaining wall on both sides. The lower 24th step with side retaining wall is connected with the well having a dia 4.5 m.

Most of the steps are made off locally available *kankar* stone slabs. However, later on, some of the steps were replaced by the slabs of the disused temple remains. In this series 9th, 10th, 13th, 16th and 24th steps are fully or partly replaced. The 9th step is of red sand stone slab with decorated Kinjaraksha type design. The lime concrete plaster was used to seal the corner joints and other steps for water tightening.

A profusely carved porch pillar adorned with th pillar *Kirtimukha* capital and Ghatapallava at the middle was found fixed in a re-used position as an eastern side door jamb for a small passage of the size of 1 m x 1.54 m and was closed later on. It seems that due to heavy water thrust the step-well as well as temple was damaged. Later on, step-well was repaired by the readily available material at the site i.e. temple remains, brick-debris, have been found used. The architectural pieces of the temple were reused as per the requirement of the stones in the present available step-well at a later stage. When the area of step-well was filled up it appears that the well-shaft was raised and used by the people.

From the loamy deposit over the lower steps, two fallen arcthtectural pieces, the first one is door lintel and other one lies a pillar, were collected. The fragments of decorated bricks were also collected from this area.

In the eastern side of the step-well, remains of a circular type burnt hearth was unearthed. The outer and inner diameter are 1.80 m and 1.5 m. respectively. The available height of structure is about 3 to 5 cm. According to the villagers from this place pure ash was scooped out in a huge quantity in June 98. This structure at the site was popularly named as Hawan Kund.

About sixteen architectural fragments are found from the temple site at Bisokhar. Out of these, three door lintels, three door jambs, two porch pillars, two pillasters, one Ganesh panel, two Krishna Lila panels, one decorated slab, one lotus medallian and one pranala (part of a drain) with other plain slabs are found. Amongst these, one door lintel decorated with various incarnations of Vishnu (Dasavataras i.e. Matasya, Kurma, Varaha, Narsimha, Vamana, Parasurama, Rama, Balrama, Buddha and Kalk. The door jambs are ornamented with Makarvahini Ganga, or, Kurmavahini Yamuna at the lower portion, and, profusely carved porch pillars decorated with *kirtimukhas* and *ghatapallava* designs, Krishna Lila panels bear the scenes of Dadhi-Manthana, Putanavadha, Yamalarjun Uddhar, Shakatasuravadha, Dhenakasur vadha, Kaliya mardan, raising of Goverdhana parvat etc. (Pls. 2-3).

An unique Ganesha panel shows seven four armed images of Ganesha in sitting posturess.

The step-well was a part of the temple of the 9th century A.D. The sculptures found from here are one of the finest examples of the Pratihara sculptural art. Possibly, this step-well was used for taking water for worship and also to take holy bath at the temple site. It appears that even after the temple came into disuse the step-well continued to be is use for a considerable period of time.

Madhu Bala

Superintending Archeaologist
Archaeological Survey of India
New Delhi

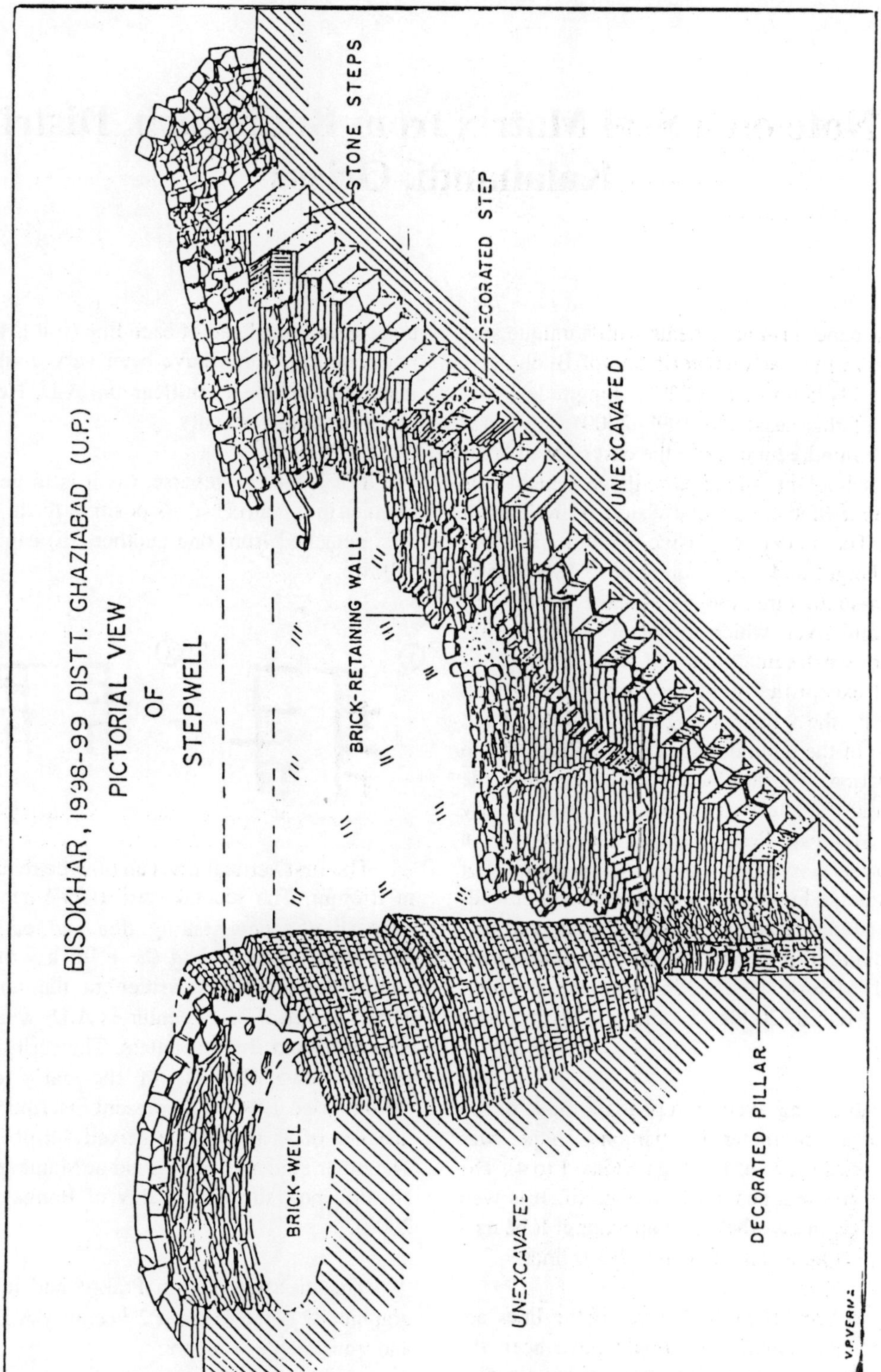

Fig. 1. Bisokhar, Distt. Ghaziabad (U.P.) Pictorial View of Stepwell

A Note on a Seal Matrix from Budhigarh, District Kalahandi, Orissa

The present paper primarily deals with a unique seal matrix found from the Early Historic site of Budhigarh, (19° 3'N and 21° 5'N latitudes and 82° 20' longitudes) during the course of this season's (1999–2000) fieldwork. The site lies five hundred metres to the east of Madanpur upper primary school in Madanpur village which falls under the Rampur-Madanpur subdivision of Kalahandi district (fig. 1). The mound, extensive in nature, is about three metre in height and covers an area of 1000 x 500 metres in north-south direction, is situated on the left bank of the Rahul river, which ultimately joins the Tel river further downstream. Most of the mound has remained intact except the middle portion where a path has been made by the villagers to go to the Rahul river. Another portion of the mound close to the village shrine is under cultivation. The artefactual evidence from the site indicates that the site was occupied from the Early Historic to the Medieval Period. The site has revealed a rich ceramic industry, terracotta, an enormous quantity of cast and punchmarked coins, iron implements in considerable number, faunal remains, brick structures, and lavish use beads made of precious and semiprecious stones (Mohanty and Mishra 1999; Mohanty *et al* 1999; Mohanty and Mishra 2000a, b and c; Mishra and Mohanty 2000).

The seal matrix, engraved on a pendant made of red jasper is about a centimeter in diamond shape, was unearthed from the surface of Budhigarh (Pls. 1 to 4). The proximal end of the seal bears a flower motif. It is well polished, attractive and aesthetically appealing. It bears a legend in reverse. The legend consists of two lines.

According to Prof. B.N. Mukherjee if the lines are taken as written horizontally, as should have been the case, no sensible reading is possible. Moreover, a continuous serif at the head of each line (if it is taken as written horizontally) would have been very unlikely in Brahmi inscription of the 1st millennium A.D. Hence the legend has to be read vertically.

The legend in reverse, (as it is to be incised in this manner in a matrix) (i) its positive form, (ii) and the letters, detached from one another (iii) can be arranged as follows:

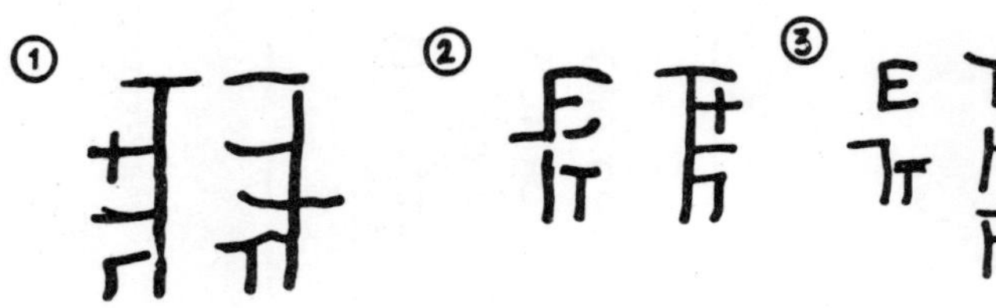

The first vertical line can now be read as *jaña* written in Brahmi. The second vertical line can be deciphered only as *ḍha peta*, taking *ḍha* and *pe* (=*pa* + 'e) as Kharoshti letters and *ta* (*ta* + '*a*) a written in Brahmi. Hence the legend is written in the now well known Mixed-script of early centuries A.D. which consisted of Kharoshti and Brahmi letters. The script was in popular use in lower Bengal in the early centuries A.D. (Mukhe-rjee 1990). The present inscription is the second instance of writing in the Mixed Script found in Orissa. The other evidence was found at Manikapatana, an Early Historic port site on the Bay of Bengal (Pradhan *et al.* 2000).

The inscription is in Prakrit and it can be palaeographically dated to *circa* 2nd century A.D. It can be read and translated as follows:

Text.

l.1 – *Jaña*
l.s – *ḍhapeta*

Sanskritised Version

l.1.2. *yajña – sthāpeyitā*

Translations

(A) founder or establisher or sacrifice

The seal matrix belonged to a person who was a patron of Brahmanical sacrifice. The perforation in the top region of the matrix, may suggest that it was used as a pendant of a string garland. It was probably worn by the owner, who used the matrix whenever necessary. This also indicates how Brhamanical religion had infiltrated into the upland region of tribal principality.

Acknowledgements:

The authors are grateful Prof. B.N. Mukherjee, who deciphered the script. We would like to thank Nabin Meher, Ganesh, Majhi and Singh who assisted us in our fieldwork. The first author is grateful to ICHR for a fellowship.

REFERENCES

Mishra, Baba and P. Mohanty 2000. The Tel River Valley Civilization (From Prehistoric to Medieval), in *River Valley Cultures of India* (K.K. Chakravarti & G.L. (Badam) Eds.). Bhopal: Indira Gandhi Rashtriya Manav Sangrahalaya.

Mohanty, P. and Baba Mishra 1999. Beads from Archaeological Sites from Kalahandi District, Orissa, *Beads Study News Letter* 34: 14–15.

Mohanty, P., P.P. Joglekar and Baba Mishra 1999. A note on the Study of Faunal Remains of Early Historic Sites of Kalahandi District, Orissa. *Puratattva* 29: 120–131:

Mohanty, P and Baba Mishra 2000a. From Stone Age to Early Historic: Recent Archaeological Discoveries in Kalahandi District of Orissa, In *River Valley Cultures of India (K.K. Chakravarti & G.L. Badam Eds.).* Bhopal: Indiara Gandhi Rashtriya Manav Sangrahalaya.

Mohanty, P & Baba Mishra 2000b. The Early Historic Archaeology of Kalahandi District, Orissa, in *New Perspectives in Eastern Indian Archaeology* (G. Sengupta and Panjha Eds.). New Delhi: Munshiram Manoharlal Publishers.

Mohanty, P. & Baba Mishra 2000. Early Urbanization in Kalahandi district of Orissa. *Marg* (Special Issue-Orissa: The Enduring Tradition).

Mukharjee, B.N. 1990. Kharoshti and Kharoshti-Brahmi Inscriptions in West Bengal (India). *Indian Museum Bulletin.* XXV:

Pradhan, D., P. Mohanty and J. Mishra 2000. Manikapatana: An Ancient and Medieval Port on the Coast f Orissa, in *Archaeology of Orissa* (K.K. Basa and P. Mohanty Eds.), pp. 473–494. New Delhi: Pratibha Prakashan.

Deccan College
Pune

Pradeep Mohanty and Baba Mishra

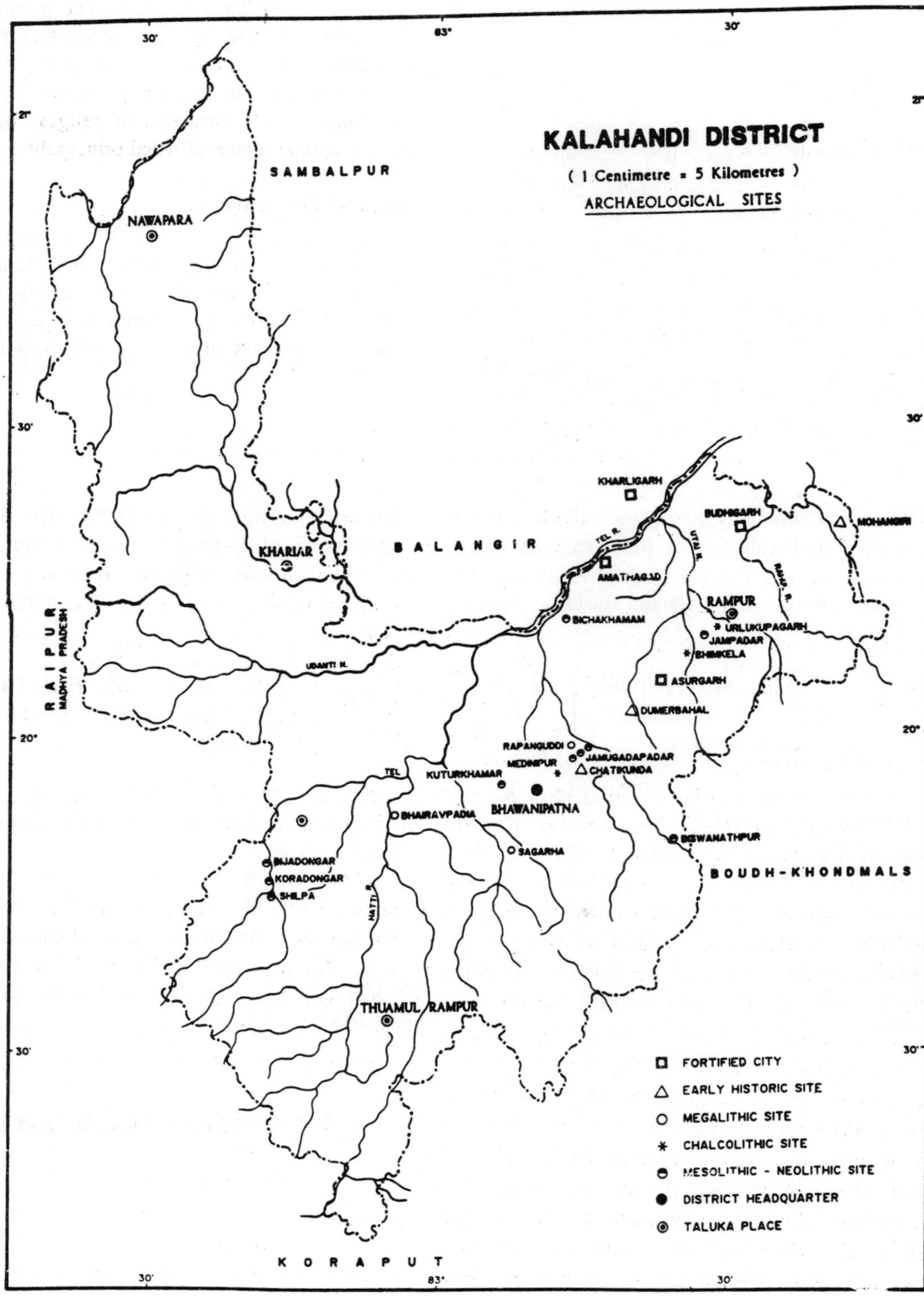

Fig. 1. Map of Kalahandi District.

Unveiling the Ancient Trade Route of Paratewadi

The recent discovery of the 'Gothe' cave (Mulsi Taluka, Pune district) is an important discovery. It sheds new light on the ancient trade route of Pratewadi in Maharashtra with the other trade routes such as Nameghat and Borghat.

The village Paratewadi is located on westward boundary of Pune district (Taluka Mulsi, 74 km from Pune city). Paratewadi is situated near the valley of 'Kundalika' river which flows through the 'Sinarkhind', i.e., pass of Sahyadri mountain range. For entering the valley, there are nearly seventy rockcut step, descending in the Konkan region. At the beginning of these steps, there are two watertanks on both sides of steps. After descending forty steps there is another watertank and after furthermore thirty steps, the footpath goes to right side of the valley. By entering 100m down in the valley, there is another watertank. The footpath goes vanishing in the jungle after this watertank.

The rock-cut steps, tanks and the geographical location of Pratewadi signifies it as an ancient trade route; as similar as other trade routes in the Sahyadri range like Naneghat and Borghat which travel from Konkan region to Desh region.The 'Kundalika' river, passing from Pratewadi, runs down to Bhira, Roha and it finally ends in the Arabian sea at Chaul. Chaul is a well-know trading port city of ancient Indi-Roman trading circuit which flourished from the second century B.C. onwards.

In Konkan region, there are many rock-cut caves such as Chaul, Ramdharana, Thanale, Khadasamble, Gomashi and Kude-mandada which are dated from 1st century B.C. to 2nd century A.D. In the parallel lines of these caves, there are many contemporary caves on the Deccan, such as Bhaje, Karle, Patana, Bedsa, Shelarwadi with other minor rock-cut caves at Telbaila, Ghanagad, Kailasgad, Tikona. Therefore the rock-cut steps of Paratewadi - connecting the Konkan region to the Deccan plateau - are considered to be contemporary to the above mentioned rock-cut caves.

By the study of the geographical features of this area and the peculiar placement of these caves, we can reconstruct the ancient trade routes as under:

1. Chaul > Thanale caves > Waghajai pass > Telbaila ? Barpe village.

2. Chaul > Khadasamble caves > Kivani pass > Tikona > Barpe village.

3. Chaul > Gomashi caves > Paratewadi > Barpe village.

All these three routes meet at Barpe village and travel towards Bedsa caves via Tikona fort, which further meets the main route from Borghat. This route connects Junnar and Paithana (ancient 'Pratishthana'), the capital of the Satavahanas.

To complete this route the proper evidence from Pratewadi was not available earlier. But the discovery of 'Gothe caves' solved this problem and the missing link of this ancient trade route are clear now.

The village 'Gothe' is located 7 km away from Paratewadi. At the west side of Gothe village there is a huge waterfall. The natural cave hides behind this waterfall. This natural cave was further turned into rock-cut cave manually. Due to the loose rock bond, the walls had collapsed, but originally with the seven Viharas, the cave is measured as 108 ft x 25ft x 7 ft. The presence of chisel marks on the roofs and the left wall signifies the cave as manmade rock-cut cave. The six Viharas are measured as 14ft x 16ft x 7ft and the only one small Vihara is measured as 11ft x 4 ft x 7 ft. In the third Vihara, there is a 'Shayanasana' - i.e., Rock-cut bench (6ft x 2.5ft). Due to the mud in the cave, only 10 inches of the bench is exposed from the surface level. Besides these remains, the remains of mudfilled rock-cut watertank on the left side of the cave was found.

Behind the Mulsi dam, there is a small pass which joins the Tikona fort with the Bedsa caves. The recent discovery of Gothe cave now links the Bedsa caves with the Paratewadi route.

This discovery makes the ancient trade route much clear and definite. Even the placement of 'mana' cave (village Mana, Mulsi Taluka, near Nnjawadi Infotech Park), which has a single Vihara dated to 1st cent. A.D., was not clear with reference to this trade route earlier. But now, due to finding of the Gothe cave, we can link up the Mana cave with Gothe cave > Kailasgad ? Mana cave ? Shelarwadi cave. This link proves that Mana cave was also on the Paratewadi trade route.

Deccan College
Pune

Vikram Marathe

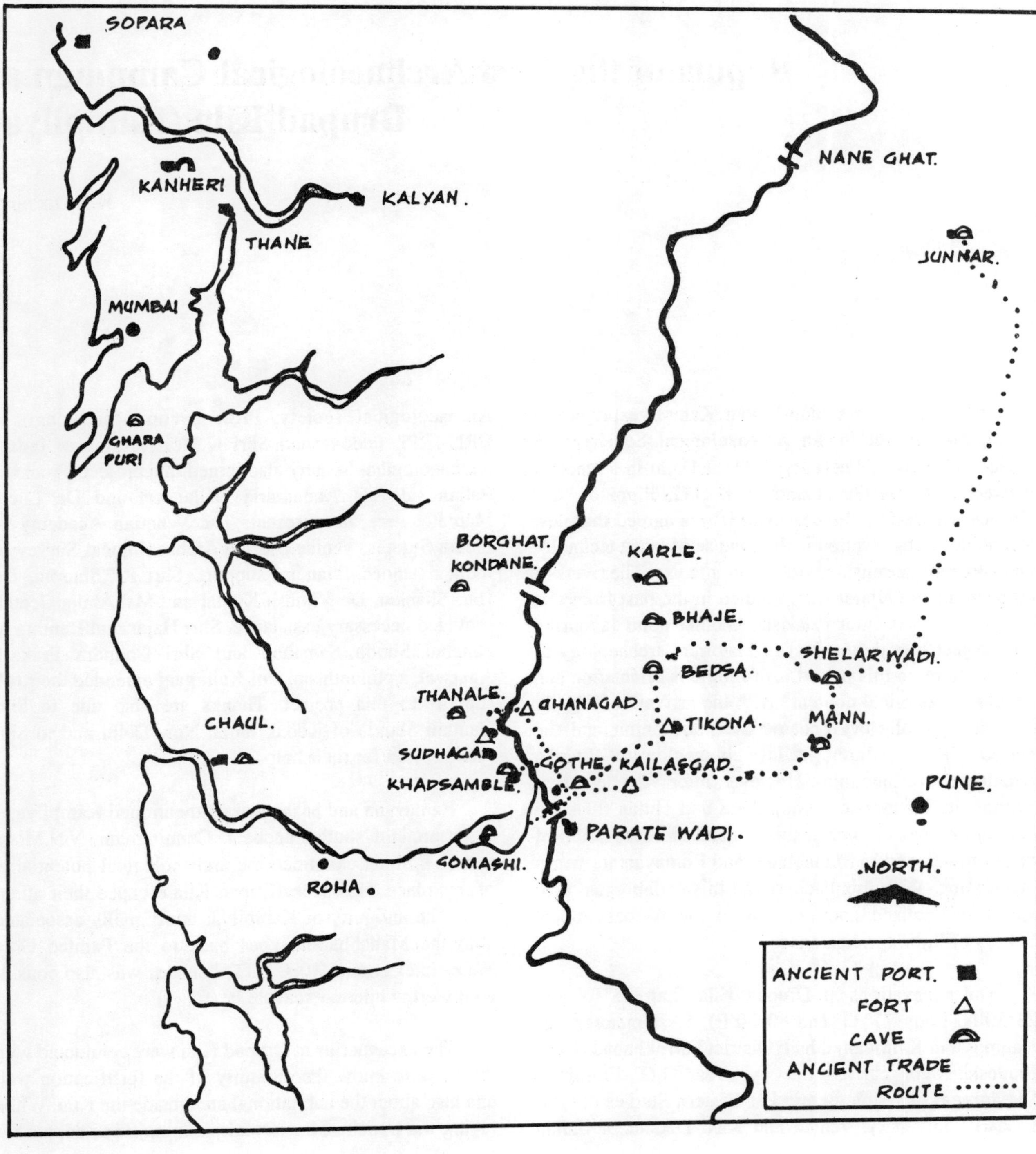
SOPARA
KANHERI
KALYAN.
THANE
MUMBAI
GHARA PURI
NANE GHAT.
JUNNAR.
BORGHAT.
KONDANE.
KARLE.
BHAJE.
SHELAR WADI.
BEDSA.
THANALE.
GHANAGAD.
TIKONA.
MANN.
CHAUL.
SUDHAGAD
GOTHE.
KAILASGAD.
KHADSAMBLE.
PUNE.
PARATE WADI.
GOMASHI.
.NORTH.
ROHA
ANCIENT PORT.
FORT
CAVE
ANCIENT TRADE ROUTE

Fig. 1.

Report of the First Archaeological Campaign at Drupad Kila (Kampilya)

K.N.Dikshit*

The birth of this Indo-Italian Kampilya project in collaboration with Indian Archaeological Society took place on 1st day of February, 1999 at Delhi in a meeting between Dr. S.P. Gupta and Prof. G.G.Filippi of 'Ca' Foscari' Univesity, Venice where it was agreed that new techniques of excavation including use of latest technologies like remote sensing will be put into use. The rivers of Rajasthan and Gujarat were studied in the past from this angle but not of Uttar Pradesh. Another point favouring this project was the neglect of historical archaeology as the literature on this period is of religious orientation and devoid of historical content. With the arrival of Wheeler in India, protohistory became the main ambit and the period after the Indus valley civilization to Buddha remained terra incognito. However, after Wheeler excavations at Hastinapur, Atranjikhera and Hulas filled up the chromological gap. In this context the excavation of places mentioned in Mahabharat and Ramayan are worth mentioning. With this background this collaborated project was finalised and referred to the Archaeological Survey of India for clearance.

The excavations at Drupad Kila (Lat. 26°30' and 28°30'N, Long 77°33' and 80°00'E), 5 kilometres from Kampilya in Kaimganj tahsil, District Farrukhabad (Uttar Pradesh) were carried out by Prof. G.G. Fillipi of Department of Indology and Far Eastern Studies of 'Ca' Fascari' University, Venice and K.N. Dikshit of Indian Archaeological society. Prof. Bruno Marcolongo of CRN-IRPI, Padova and Shri K.M.Srivastava of Indian Archaeological Society also joined this project. From the Italian side Dr. Annamaria Dallaporta and Dr. Lucio Marcato were also present. The Venetian Academy of Indian Studies, Venice and the Archaeological Survey of India extended financial support. Shri R.P.Sharma, Dr. Hari Shankar, Dr. Vijnesh Kumar and Ms. Anuja Geetali provided necessary assistance. Shri Hajarimal Banthia of Panchal Shodh Sansthan and Shri Chandra Prakash Agarwal, a philanthropist of Kaimganj extended their full support to this project. Thanks are also due to Shri Gautam Shukla of Kodak India, New Delhi and to Shri Pukhraj Jain for their help.

Ramayana and Mahabharata mentioned Kampilya as the capital of south Panchala. Cunningham, V.N.Misra and K.K.Sinha examined the archaeological potentiality of this place. However, Drupad Kila escaped their attention. The antiquity of Kampilya, traditionally associated with the Mahabharata, goes back to the Painted Grey Ware times around 1000 B.C., hence it was also considered worthwhile to excavate it. (fig. 1)

The excavations at Drupad Kila were conducted with the view to know the antiquity of the fortification wall and also about the habitational area inside the Kila. While laying the trenches, horizontal planning was adopted for

*Former Joint Director General, Archaeological Survey of India.

the co-relation of different localities inside the Kila.

The locality KP/dk-1 was identified for excavation as it was found about 4 metres above the surrounding plain and about 1200 metres in circumference. The trenches laid on the top of the mound revealed in ZAI Qd2 and Qd3 five structural phases. The earliest wall of burnt brick, running in east-west direction, was found cutting the base of compact earth which may have been mud-platform raised over the natural soil which is yellowish and sandy in nature. Further digging was done to ascertain the thickness of compact earth which was found about 1.54 metres thick. However, it requires further confirmation. The ten courses of the wall, about 0.65 metre in thickness may be the foundation cut in the compact earth, whereas four courses were noticed above the compact earth. The thickness of the wall is 1 metre and it runs 22 metres in length in trench XA1 and XA2. The wall has two structural phases. The size of the bricks available in this construction were 35 X 25 X 5 centimetres. This wall which met another wall at north-west corner was destroyed by the rains.

In one of the quadrants just over the compact earth, five slabs (average sizes 1.45 X 0.26 X 0.21 metre) of kankar lime were found resting in the corner of the trench. One more such slab was found covering one of these slabs. To reach this level the debris noticed on the top of the mound was cut upto the depth of 1.05 metre. At a distance of 1.5 metre from these slabs, a regular deposit of burnt brick-bats was again noticed at the depth of 0.30 metre below the surface. The formation of these brick-bats is about 1.64 metre in length and 1.58 in breadth. In the adjoining quadrant remains of three more structural phases were noticed.

A regular deposit of brick-bats, resting on debris was found running parallel to the east-west wall at the height of about 1.30 metre. The terraced nature of this structure indicated the possible presence of a temple which may be earliest in date in this region, but this could not be confirmed this year (fig. 2). Further work is required to trace interconnection of the walls.

In one of the adjoining trenches A2Qd1 on the southern side of these structures, just 0.50 metre below the surface, three fragmentary architectural pieces of kankar lime belonging to a temple of 9th-10th century A.D. were encountered.

Another locality KP/dk2 was taken up to correlate the fortification wall with the strucures of the adjoining mound. A trench across the fortification wall (3.84 metre in width at this place) revealed two regular burnt brick courses over the compact earth. The brick sizes were 31 cm in length and 5 cm in height. Above these, brick-bats in regular courses were present. The extant height of the wall was 0.62 metre. On the eastern side of this wall, the trench was taken to 0.70 metre deep. It was also noticed in the section that a portion of compact earth was found destroyed by the rains. The exact height of the fortification wall and its construction which may have started during or after the occupation of Drupad Kila, could not be ascertained. As the work was of limited nature the structural phases of wall will be studied by putting more cross trenches at intervals.

In the same line perpendicular to the fortification wall leaving the distance of about 20 metre in trench ZA1 on the western side of the mound a broad area was exposed. Again at this place above the compact earth a wall of burnt brick, brick-bats platform and regular alignment of brick-bats walls was noticed. To ascertain the thickness of compact earth an area was selected for deeper digging. No antiquity, potsherds were encountered from 0.98 metre deposit of compact earth. In one of the quadrants a wall of burnt bricks was found having twelve extant courses cut in the compact earth. The potsherds found in the digging correspond to Kushan level. Iron objects were also noticed on the other side of this mound. A burnt brick wall with corner were found about 0.50 metre below the surface. The level of these structures is about 1 metre higher from the structures noticed on the northern side which are resting on the compact earth.

The locality KP/dk3 was selected about 200 metres south of dk1. Trenches were laid here to encounter the earliest habitational area inside Drupad Kila. As this area was higher from the surrounding plain as such it was selected for excavation. Three tenches A1, B1 and XA1 were laid. The thickness of habitational deposit encountered at this place was 2.80 metre although we went to the depth of 4.10 metres cutting the natural soil. A number of burnt brick structures from top to the bottom in the same cardinal alignment were encountered at different levels. In all seven layers divided into two phases were noticed.

The earlier phase represented by 1 metre thick deposit from layer 7 to 5 ranged in date from c 200 B.C. to 100 A.D. The pottery noticed was post NBP. Structures of burnt brick were encountered including the floor levels. The presence of pits in this phase indicated that the first settlers at this side cut the natural soil for different purposes possibly for the construction of houses. No sherd of NBP, grey ware or any other associated red ware was present at this place. The majority of pots were of medium fabric in red as well as in grey. The earliest layers, 7 to 5, are compact in nature whereas from layer 4 to the top these are loose in nature. All the layers are full of brick bats and in pits even complete bricks were found. Most of the structures had 3 to 4 extant courses and there was not marked difference between the structures of two phases except that in later phase earlier bricks were found reused. The sizes of bricks is 31X21X5. In the upper phase the time bracket assigned ranged from c 100 A.D. to c 400 A.D. and the material was of mixed nature. Burnt brick structures dominated the scene (fig. 3).

The pottery found in excavation was all wheel made and the fabric ranged from medium to thick. As noticed at Hastinapur or Atranjikhera the pottery is treated with wash and occasionally with slip. It also indicated sprinkling of mica. The sherds are basically plain red but grey pottery was also found. The characterstic pot in grey ware is a vase with an oblique shoulder, sharply carinated body and rounded base. The pottry of this group is generally un-painted but occasional sherds having paintings were not altogether absent. Besides this stamped or impressed or incised pots were also found. The characterstic shapes are sprinklers spouted pots, variety of jars and other miniature pots. Storage jar is also present.

The pottery from upper phase was not much different from lower phase except that a few new shapes made their appearance. The earlier pottery continued in later phase (fig. 4 + 5).

The excavation yielded a total number of 81 antiquities made of stone, terracotta, iron, copper, shell and semi precious stone. These included terracotta object-dabbar, fragmentary animal figurines and ghat shaped beads, beads of banded agate and glass bangles. Iron objects in the form of nails, knives and other non-descript forms were found (fig. 6). A fragmentary decorated right leg of a lady in stone and a human leg placed on pedestal in terracotta were also encountered. Copper objects are corroded. One Panchala coin was also found from the surface.

The construction of the Drupad Kila was perhaps necessitated because of insecure condition after the collapse of stable political structure of the Mauryas in northern India and also as safeguard against the advancing Indo-Greek and Indo Parthinians including Kashanas. In northern India between Taxila and Ahichchhatra there was no other fortified township. Kampilaya was also fortified as it was situated on the trade route. A. Ghosh has rightly remarked that with the centralisation of power under Magadha from the 5th to 3rd century B.C., the need for local defences was less pressing than in the following centuries (c 200 B.C.-100 B.C.) The defences at Kausambi, Rajghat, Patna, Ujjain, Eran were originally embankments of flood protection in NBP period but later converted into ramparts in the late NBP/Kushan period. The construction of massive burnt brick structures testify to the development of defence architecture in India.

However, in the absence of earlier settlement of PGW and NBPW at Drupad Kila the excavated data though inadequate can not be considered in isolation. It revealed a cultural synthesis covering the periods of Panchalas, Kushanas and Guptas. From the results of the excavation, it appeared that the capital was shifted to Drupad Kila near Jijauta village after the destruction of Kampilya by the fury of Budhi Ganga or the old course of Ganga towards the end of the NBPW period.

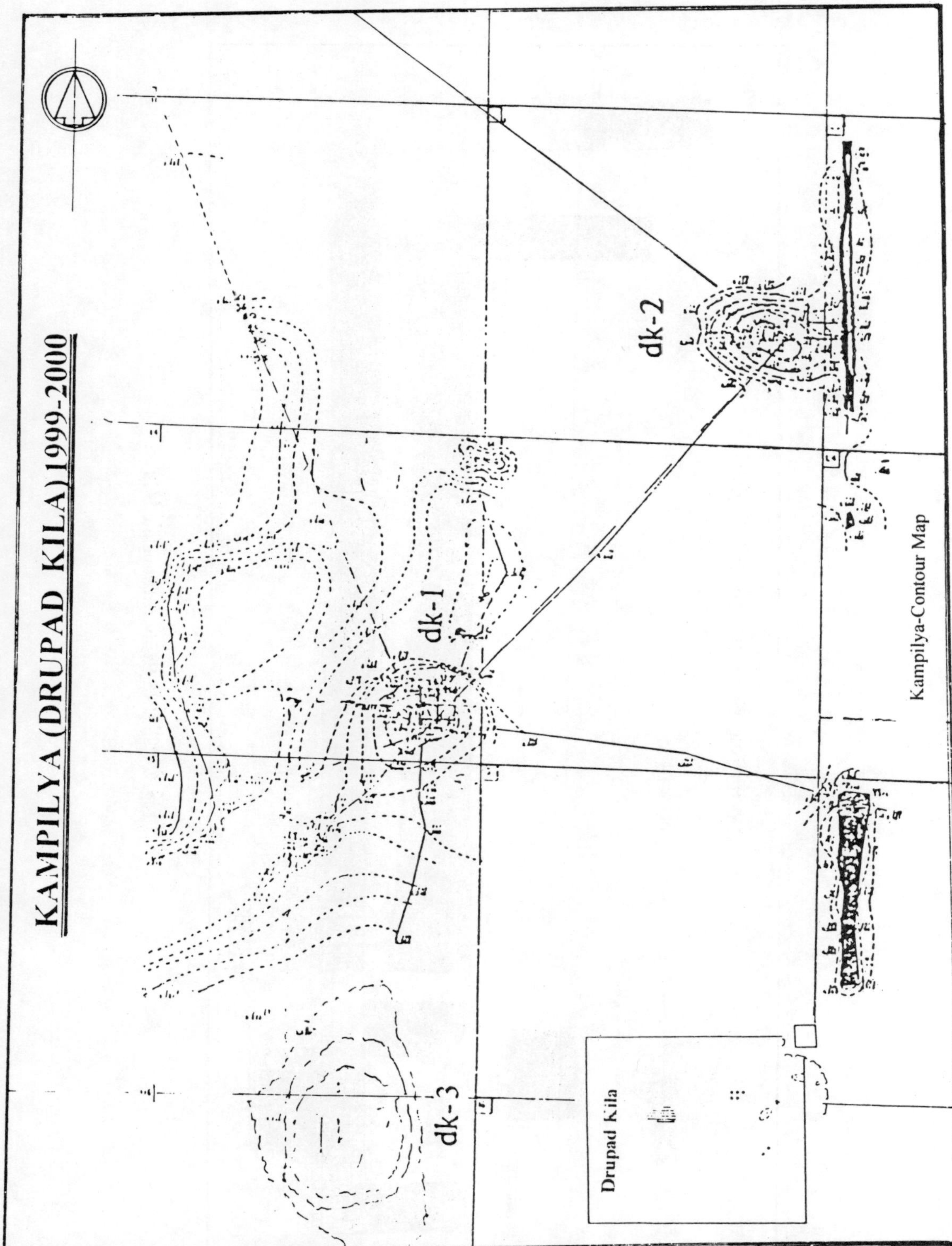

Fig. 1. Kampilya-Countour Map.

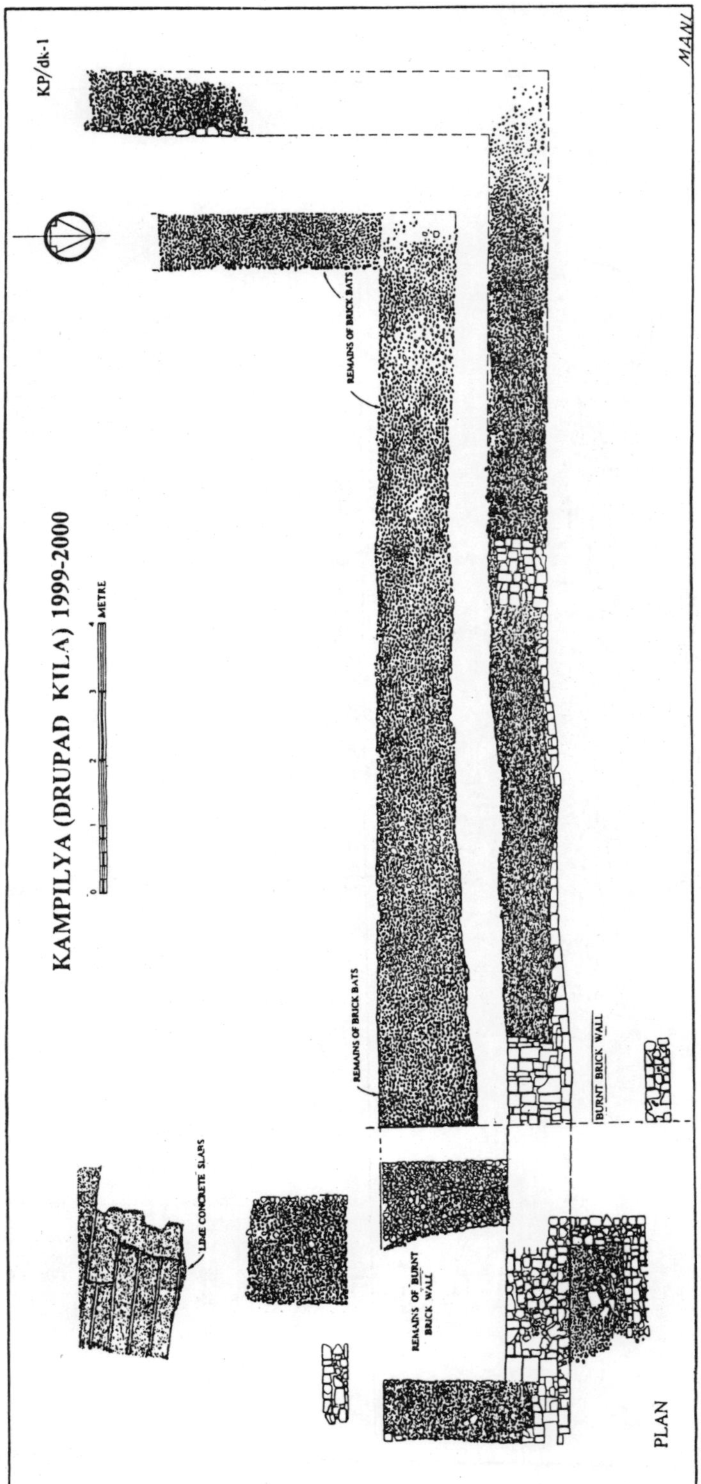

Fig. 2. Kampilya-Excavated Structure Plan

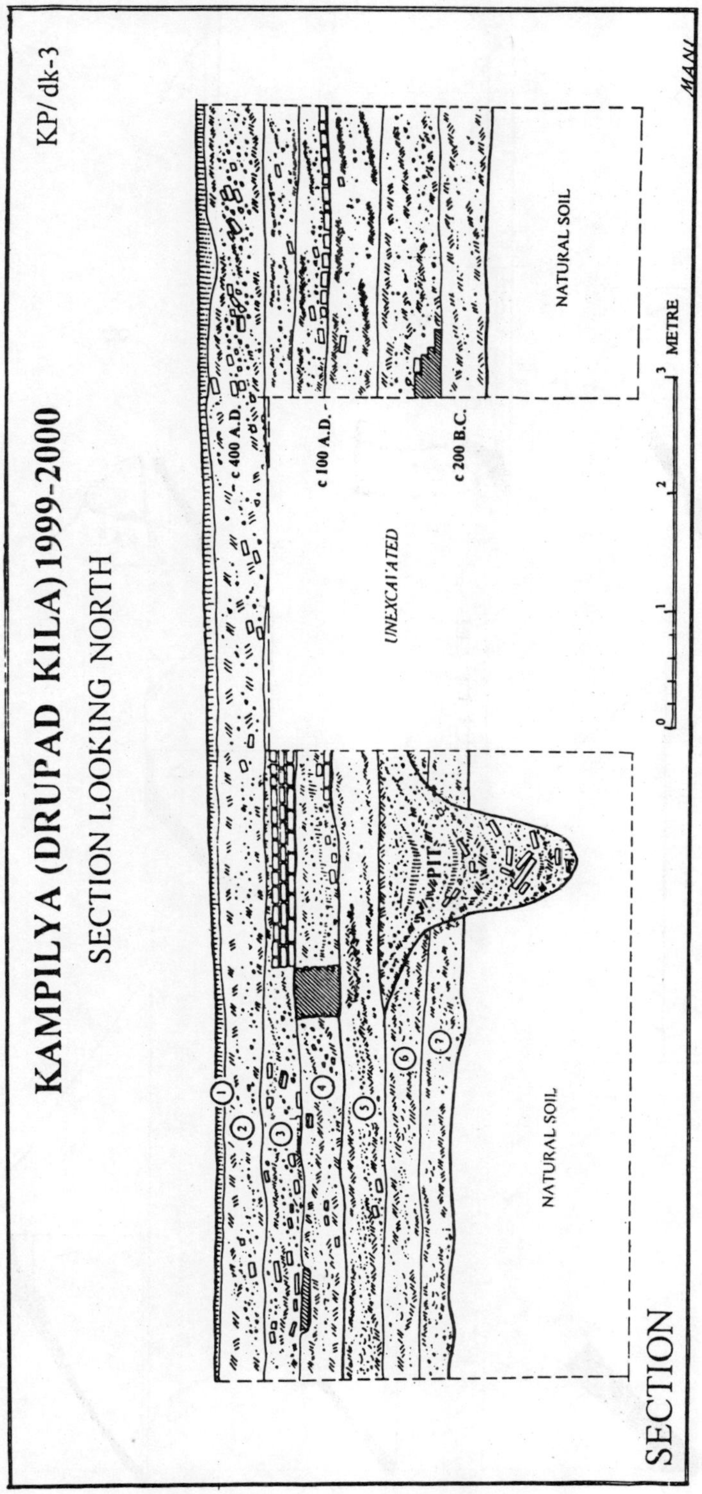

Fig. 3. Kampilya-Excavated Section

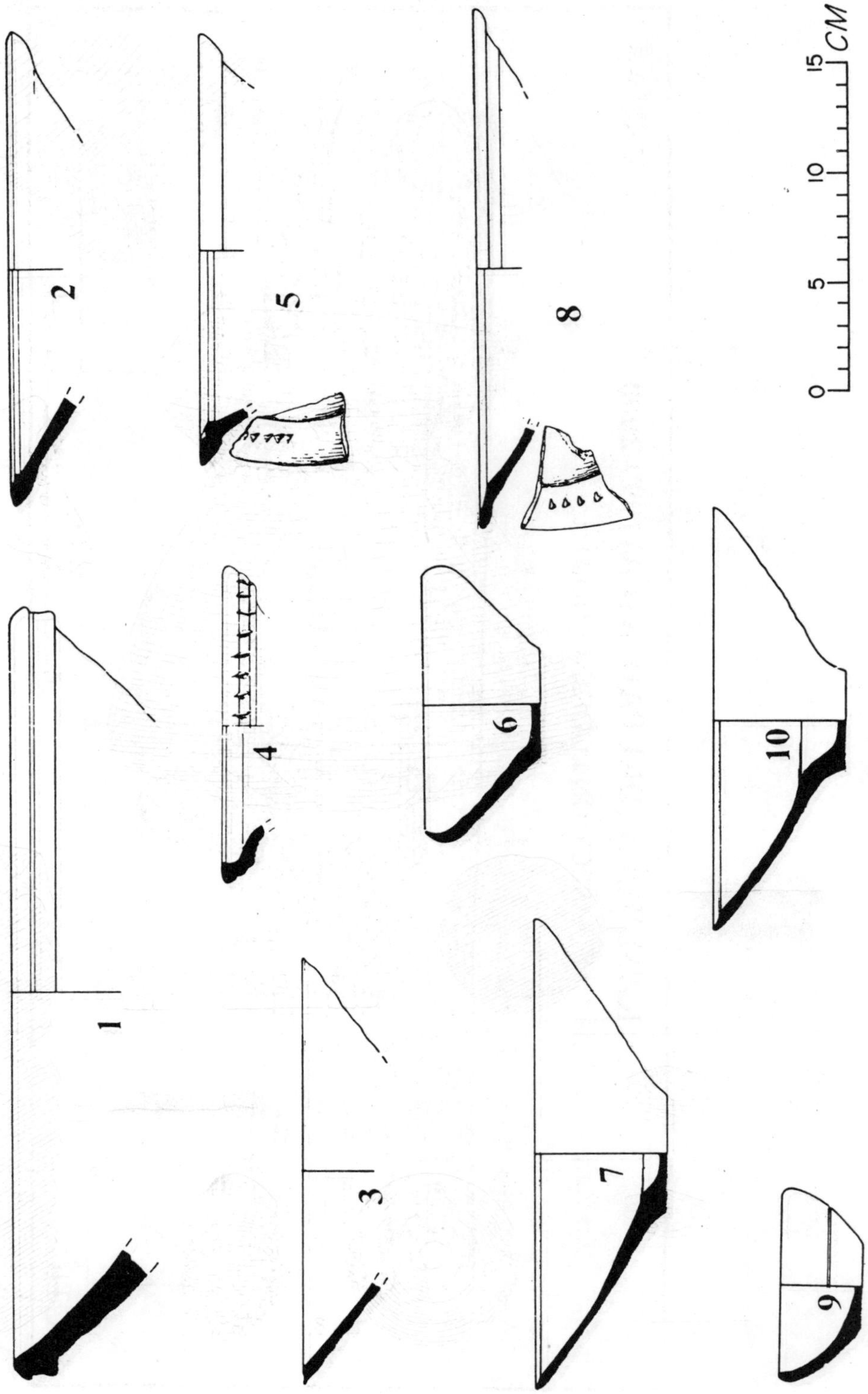

Fig. 4. Kampilya-Pottery

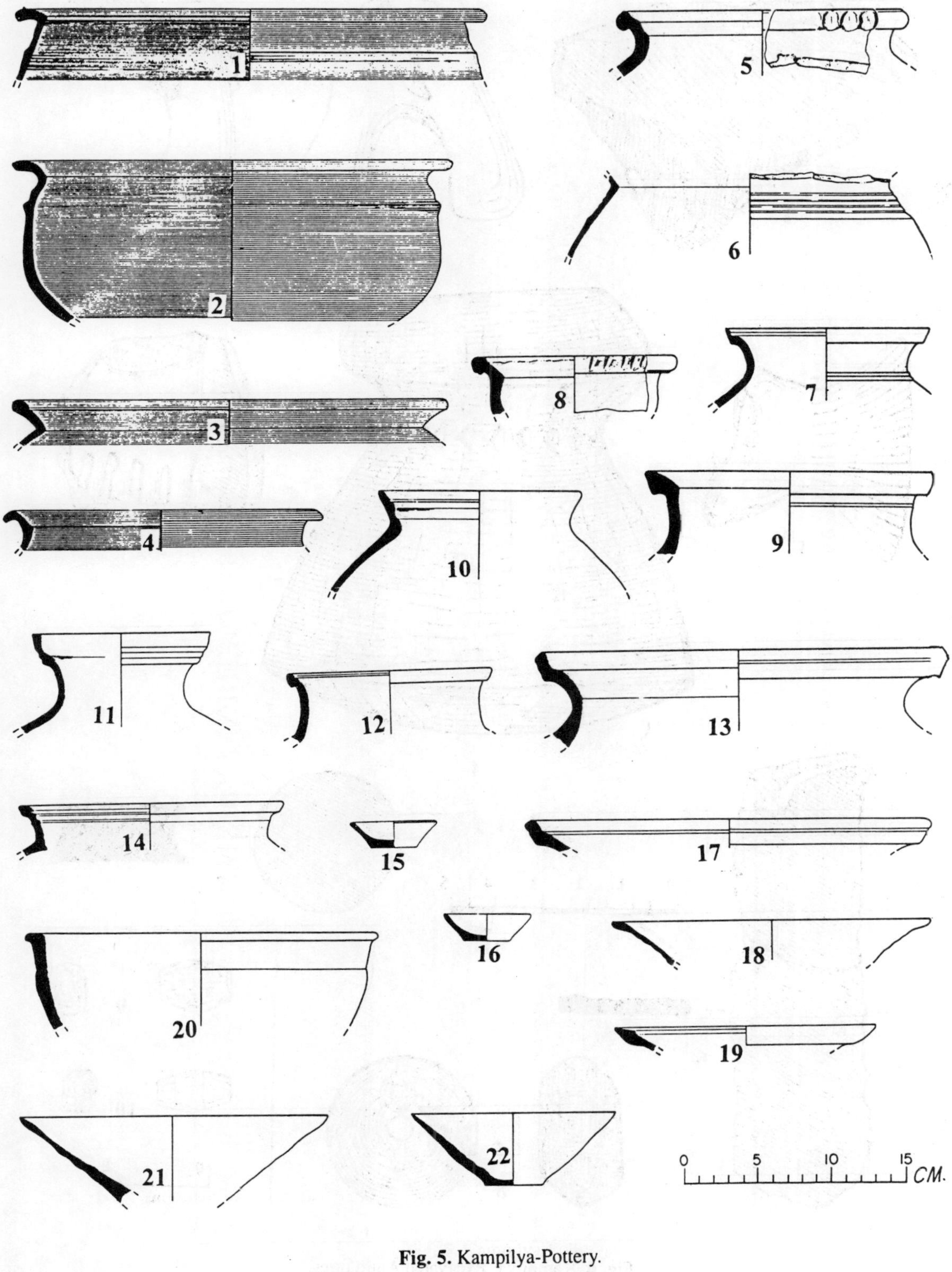

Fig. 5. Kampilya-Pottery.

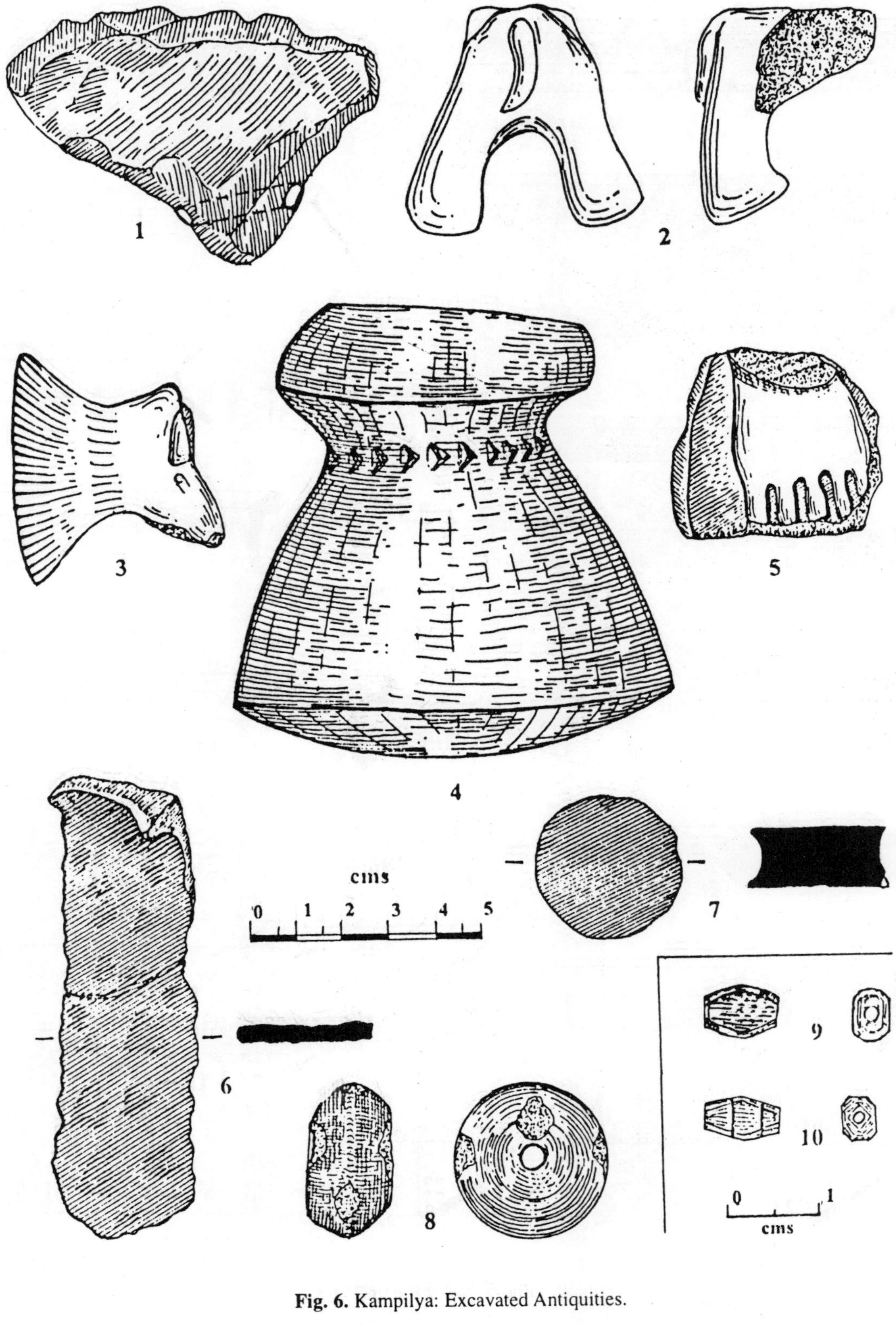

Fig. 6. Kampilya: Excavated Antiquities.

BOOK REVIEWS

N.Jha and N.S Rajaram, *The Deciphered Indus Script : Methodology, Readings, Interpretation.* pp. xxviii + 269 with photographic illustrations, tables, appendices, bibliography and index (Aditya Prakashan, New Delhi, 2000) price Rs. 950/-

This is a collaborative work of two scholars, N.Jha and N.S. Rajaram, the former an orientalist and Vedic scholar and the latter an engineer who is also a noted mathematician and computer scientist. They have put their heads together and pooled their expertise to decipher the Harappan script and read and interpret their legends and devices. Arguing against the theory of Aryan invasion and the late dating of the Vedic literature they have assigned a date before 2100 B.C. for the late Vedic literature when the Harappa civilization was at its peak in India. It is admitted that the planning of the major Harappan towns like Mohenjadaro, Harappa, Kalibangan, Lothal, Surkotada and Dholavira followed some prescribed geometrical rules which according to the author were inspired by the contemporary *Sulbasutras*, which deal with the details of the shapes, sizes, proportions etc. of the multiple varieties of sacrificial altars.

The main thrust of the book is to show that the Harappa civilization was one with the Vedic civilization and flourished during the later Vedic period which the authors date as early as *c.* 3000–2100 B.C. To quote the authors, "The language of the seals in Vedic Sanskrit, with a significant number of them containing words and phrases traceable to the ancient Vedic glossary *Nighantu* compiled from still earlier sources by Yaska. The language is less archaic than that of the Rigveda, and correspond closely to that of the later Vedic works like the *sutras* and the *upanishads*".

The authors regard the writing on the seals as generally syllabic which they have tried to decipher in a few cases with the help of palaeography of Brahmi and the old West Asiatic scripts like the Aramaic, Phoenician and Himyaritic. Thus letters *ka, ga, ra* and *ma* (the last with changed direction of projecting strokes) are directly adopted from Brahmi, while the vowel *i* and constants *cha, ja* to *thâ, bha* and *va* also partly resemble Brahmi letters. The authors have postulated more signs than one, known as homophones and polyphonies for most of the consonants, viz. *ka, ga, ja, ta, da, na, pa, ba, ya, ra, va* and *ha,* while only one sign has been postulated for all vowels appearing as initial signs. The entire alphabetical subject taken to be written as *akārānta* but also read with other *mātras* (vowel endings) to suit the Vedic vocabulary. The signs are actually written as *rama* but read as ṛāma, ramā or roma as required in the relevant context. Again for the reading *hutaṁ sama* they would actually write *hata ma sama*. Further, a few simple strokes indicating numerals, viz I, II, II, II have been given phonetiic value, e.g. *da* from *dvi* (ii) *ta* from *tri* (IIII) and *pa* from *chatur* for III.

The above are some of ten devices adopted for reading the writing on the Harappan seals. Though most of the signs have been assigned phonetic value hypothetically, it has to be admitted in all fairness that the authors have been quite consistent in their reading, though one may not approve of their method of decipherment.

The book is planned in three Parts of which Part I deals with the socio-cultural and literary *milieu* of the Harappan Civilization which is identified with the later Vedic. The language of the Indus seals and its grammatical formation are regarded as later Vedic while the script is post-Rigvedic.

Part II is concerned with the methodology of decipherment and interpretation and is illustrated by the reading and meaning of a few of the highly significant seals, such as the Pasupati seals; Tiger seals and the one showing seven goddesses in a row below an enshrined deity.

Part III provides actual reading and detailed explanations with full references of published seals. Thus on pages 189-213 the authors have read and listed 375 words mainly from the *Nighantu* and *Nirukta*, citing full references. These include such familiar words used also in later Sanskrit literature as *agni, indu, avi, soma, artha, Isvara, reta dasa, rupa, kavi* and *anga*, etc. The list also includes such proper names as Pipru and Kutsa (Vedic sages). Akrura (Krishna's brother), Plaksha and Plakshagra (source of the river Sarasvati), Yadu (a famous ancient tribe), Yama, Aryama and Vrtra etc.

Further, as many as 108 seals referred to in I. Mahadevan's concordance (pp. 224-238) are taken up for reading and explanation. These provide a peep into the contemporary society, its religious beliefs and everyday life. Two seals record Rama's greatness, one his magnanimity in treating everyone as equal and the other his threat to the recalcitrant ocean. Some seals refer to other deities like Rudra, Vishnu, Varuna, and the twin gods Nasatau. Seals also record six *Agamas* and *Śravani* (popular festival of *Rākhi*).. Many seals refer to horses and their keepers, while a few allude to floods (some dangerous ones). [The notable inscribed signboard in bold letters from Dholavira has been read as *mad-dvidhaḥ rāga vedhāsvaiḥ sahaśradhā* and interpreted to mean I was a thousand time victorious over greedy raiders desirous of my wealth of horses (p.152).] Geographical features and regions referred to include Madra, Vatsa, Suvastu (the Swat) the Seven Waters (Saptasindhu) and Dvaitavana, while peoples mentioned are the Purks and the Parsus (Persians). One seal records Brahmi (was the Harappa script also known as Brahmi?) Also noted are miscellaneous seals alluding to rich merchants, a merchant charging excessive interest, craftsmen of sorts (one named Ravi), an angry mother-in-law, besides ṣuch cereal and household provisions as barley and *ghee*.

The authors assign 3100 B.C. as the date for the Mahabharata and Krishna. We shall examine the validity of such high antiquity for the Mahabharata little later, but first we have to take note of the interesting explanation which the epic provides for the oft recurring unicorn and the magnificent bull designs occurring on the Harappa seals. While the magnificent bull (*vrshamuttamam*) stands for Dharma (right eousness) the unicorn represents the Vedic deity Vrshakapi or Varaha who rescues on his single mighty horn the Earth and the Vedas, sunk in the deluge. Yeh another name for Vrshakapi is Trikakuda, standing or three-bodies figure, which is also frequently seen on the Harappa seals. It will thus be seen that according to the epic the designs of bull, unicorn and the three-bodied figure are symbols of deep religions significance. It is noteworthy that bull continues to be a most popular design on the historical seals and bears obvious cultic Saiva significance.

Coming to the proposed date of 3100 B.C. for the Mahabharata, this is indeed mind-boggling even for the Mahabharata war, leave alone the text of the epic which is a pure product of post-Paninian classical Sanskrit.

According to the well-established archaeological record 3100 B.C. is assignable to the early phase of Harappa which conformed to incipient chalcolithic culture, much antedating the discovery of iron. It is unbelievable that such a sanguine and eventful war, wherein practically all the kingdoms of Northern and Central India are said to have participated, could be fought without iron and steel weapons, when according to the archaeological record the antiquity of iron in India cannot be pushed beyond 1400 B.C. Moreover, the geographical horizon of the Mahabharata extended far into Eastern India and included Magadha with capital at Girivraja (Rajagriha) whereas we know from the Brahmana literature that Eastern India beyond the Sadānīrā (Gandak) was Aryanised quite late and that Magadha before the Brahmana period was a cursed land, unfit for Aryan habitation and Vedic sacrifice. Interestingly enough even the late phase of the Harappa Civilization is known to extend not beyond the Hindon (Distt. Meerut) near Delhi. Further, the epic presents a scenario of large forests existing side by side with sophisticated capital towns like Hastinapura and Mathura with all the amenities and complexities of urban life which came to be known in India Not before the Mauryan period (4th century B.C.) Such an early date as 3100 B.C. is, therefore, not possible for the epic unless we completely ignore the evidence of history and archaeology. What may have actually happened is that a tribal war, not unlike the Rigvedic Daśarājña, was fought between two contending branches of the same tribe during the Brahmana or Sutra period and the same was joined in by tribal allies on both sides and its memory survived as a floating tradition, which was recorded sometime between 400 B.C. and A.D. 400 or an epic of smaller size known as *Jaya* and later twice enlarged as *Bharata* and *Mahabharata* with added poetic embellishments and concomitant exaggerations at each stage.

To conclude. The learned authors have presented a mixed fare. While part of it, based on unverified tradition deserves to be ignored, there is much in the book that needs careful attention, especially the method of decipherment and the consequent readings and their interpretations along with the symbology of the images depicted on the seals.

Krishna Deva

Ram Sharan Sharma, *Advent of the Aryans in India*, Monohar, New Delhi-1999 Rs : 95; pp.130; maps 9:ISBN 81-7304-289-6

Over the period of a decade interest of scholars in the Aryan problem has been revived all over the world. In addition to the linguists, archaeologists, ethnologists, anhopologists and historians have shown equal enthusiasm in locating the Aryans. In India, we come across the word *'Arya'* or the superior ones. Whether they were indigenous or migrated into the land of the 'Sapta Saindhavadesa' or from somewhere outside is being debated afresh. Indologists working earlier on the Eurocentric hypothesis advocated that the Indo-European speaking groups with their special language, racial features and culture migrated to different parts of the world including India from some part of Europe or adjacent region of Asia. It was premised that the urban civilization of th Harappans was of Dravidian origin and was destroyed by the invading Aryans. However this hypothesis has been challenged by scholars due to heavy concentration of Harappan sites in the Sarasvati basin - the most revered river of Rigvedic times. Presence of horse-bones and terracotta figurines of horse, firealtars etc., in Harappan culture have forced scholars to review the civilisational dimensions afresh. Now it is being argued that the Harappans were Aryans. Sharma's *Advent of the Aryans in India* which is being reviewed here aims in marshalling arguments to counter this hypothesis. It is second in the series following his earlier work *Looking for the Aryans* (1995).

The subject has been dealt with a thoroughness typical of Prof. R.S.Sharma. He has made use of all possible sources to drive the points home. It is a well researched piece of work substantiated by as many as nine maps, charting the routes of Aryan migrations, folk-movement, dispersal of languages and people (Dravidian, Indo-Iranians, Indo-Aryans etc). The archaeological sites in Central Western Asia that have been examined range from 5th mill. B.C. to the 1st mill. B.C. The book has been divided into four chapters with a brief 'Summing up' in the end.

Chapter one is 'Markers of the Aryan Culture'. The main sources for the study are Rigveda, Zend Avesta and Homer's Illiad and Odyssey along with the cognate terms found is the proto-Indo-European languages. Homer's epics, even though much later than the other two have been used because they are the earliest Greek texts representing the tradition of the European society of Copper-Bronze Age. The distinctive features of the Aryan life identified are temperate climate use of horse, presence of spoked-wheels the practice of cult of fire, *'soma'*, characteristic disposal of the dead, sacrifices etc. Attempt has been made to trace (and show a diffusion of) these cultural features in Eastern Europe, Central Asia and the spatially-linguistically related regions close to Pakistan and India, like Afganistan, Iraq, Anatolia, and Greece. Horse receives special attention besides 'war chariot' and 'spoked wheel'.

Horse is the a key factor associated with the Aryan way of life. In Rigveda it is the most frequent mentioned (215 times) animal; after this, it is *'go'* (176 times) and *vrisabha*, (170 times). Tiger and rhinoceros do not find mention in Rigveda, though they appear frequently on seals of the Indus sites. Sharma attributes this to the 'Central Asian influence on the animal world of the Rgveda'. The occurrence of horses (bones and figurines) are shown to be a relatively later phenomenon in Harappan civilisation. Besides, he argues that India was never the region known for horses.

War chariots, the other important marker of Aryan culture, have been mentioned frequently in the Rigveda but not found on Harappan sites. One comes across only solid wheel carts right from the early levels of the civilisation. On the other hand, they show up right from 3000 B.C. in southern Russia. The spoked wheels are found in 2300 B.C. context in Iran and North Caucasus region. A potsherd from Banawali in Haryana bears depiction of 'a canopied cart, and wheels' said to be spoked; to Sharma's these are only 'decorations showing parallel lines- numbering 17. They may not be called spokes.

Special reference has been made of 'pit dwelling', 'birch', 'fire cult', 'animal sacrifice', 'horse sacrifice', *'soma', 'swastika'* etc. All these have been shown not only to be in vogue outside India but also in earlier contexts. For example, fire altars (even though not exactly similar to Vedic ones) and animal sacrifice were found in Ukraine in 40000-3000 B.C. (p.24). Horse sacrifice was prevalent in Eastern, Central, and Central Asian region. In Ukraine, western and northern Europe, and also in Caucasus there are cemeteries (with more than one horse, (at times) in 4th-5th mill. B.C. (pp.25-26). The region of Caucasus is supposed to be the home of Indo-European languages. It includes eastern Anatolia and northern Mesopotamia that is also a centre of early domestication of horses, the favourite Aryan animal.

Chapter II is entitled 'Was the Harappan Culture Rigvedic and Saraswati based?' The focus here is to undo the premise put forth by scholars like S.P.Gupta in his significant work, *The Indus-Saraswati Civilization'*; Bhagwan Singh's work on the subject entitled *The Vedic Harappans* has not been mentioned. Similarly, Malati J: Shindge's (1977) Book, *The Civilised Demons: The Harappans in Rgveda*, has also been totally ignored. In Sharma's view, the large number of sites on Sarasvati-Hakra (700 against 100 in Indus zone), do not belong to a homogenous cultural phase. Instead, they belong to diffrent phases of the Harappan civilisation. This assumption is based on a survey of Haryana conducted by R.C. Thakran. He has located 55 pre-or Early Harappan, 117 mature-Harappan and 581 Late Harappan sites. Mughal's survey of Hakra shows 40, 174 and 50 sites respectively belonging to the three Harappan phases. This declining number of Late Harappan sites on Pakistan side of the river is supposedly due to some kind of movement from the upper reaches towards the Haryana side at that point of time. It is manifested in a higher concentration of sites in the latter region. Additionally, some of these sites are also said to possess Cemetary H related material indicating thereby new traits. "In this sense these sites on the dry bed of Hakra may contain Aryan elements also" (p.34). The statement that 'Harappa and Mohanjodaro may be equal to hundreds of Harappan sites in the Ghaggar-Hakra zone" (p.34) about sums up he position held by the author of the book. The significance of Dholaivira is rejected because it is far away from Sarasvati. He asserts, however, hat even if more sites come forth in future, there is no justification in redesignating the culture after the river Sarasvati as it is only "a tributary of th Indus". (p.35) which is not a fact.

Sharma has even gone a step ahead and identified Sarasvati with the (Avestan) Harkhavati or the Helmand in Afghanistan because the present Sarasvati-Hakra cannot fit in the description of *'Naditama'*. However, this assumption does not hold water in view of the recent remote sensing data that shows Sarasvati as a mighty river. There are many European linguists like Witzel who think that Iranization of the names is a later phenomenon, therefore, there is little justification of this identification by Prof. Sharma.

Sharma does not agree with the early dates of Rigveda (3500 B.C. as proposed by Lal and others on astronomical grounds, p.37). Similarly, the Rigvedic *'purs'* in his opinion are nothing but 'clusters of dwellings'. Thus, not agreeing with identification of Rigvedic people with the Harappans, he propounds migration of the Aryans in the Sarasvati basin at a later phase of the Indus civilisation. That the Rigvedic people ventured into a long distance sea trade is equally unacceptable to him, even though they might have been familiar with sea as a number of settlements are found on Makaran coast and Persian Gulf.

Chapter III is 'Linguistic and Archaeological evidence for Aryan Arrival'. Rigveda mentions *mrdhravac* spoken by Dasyus and Panis, the enemies of Aryans. Sharma deals with the languages spoken in and around the Indus region and says Brahui belonged to a family of Northern Dravidian. It is supposedly related with the Elamite language that was prevalent in South Iran, Afghanistan and Baluchistan. Some scholars also indicate a presence of 'Dravidian-speaking people in the Indus valley' that survives till the present day in some form in NWEP and Kashmir. He further argues that Dravidian element is present in the language of Oraons in Chhota Nagpur, the Dhangar tribe in Madhubani and Western Chapran (N.Bihar). Thus there is a 'fairly strong evidence for the presence of the pre-Aryan substratum in th Indo-Aryan languages'. Gujarat was th route adopted for migrations by the Harappans as indicated by survivals (almost till 1st mill. B.C.) of the culture in this region. Trautmann and Southworth view Marathi and Maharastri Prakrit to be an extension of Dravidian language. This explains the Harappan element in Maharastra (Daimabad is one example in the case).

The other point put forth by the author is, Dravidian loan words in Rigveda. In view of M.Deshpande, and Parpola these are important as they show some contacts. Renrew regards spread of language due to elite dominance. In the cultural *milieu*, the arrival of the Aryans may be traced in archaeological remains in Periano Ghundai in Zhob river, Pirak the reviewer has been wrongly quoted as saying that the grey ware of Pirak is similar to the Painted Grey Ware, Gumla and other grave sites in valleys of Gomal, Swat etc., as seen in the use of horse, practice of cremation, etc. These features are said to be akin to Andronovo culture of North Central Asia. Similarly,. it has been argued that the Swat cemeteries show material that may be related to Iran and the Caucasus. Dani thinks that the Grave Culture people destroyed Harappan settlement of Gumla on the Indus that is not far from Gomal valley, identifiable with Rigvedic Gomati. Such evidences in Swat (Rigvedic Suvastu), Gomal (Gomati) Zhob (Yavyavati) indicate arrival of Aryans in this region sometimes in the first half of 2nd mill. B.C.

Chapter 4 deals with 'Migration from Central Asia'. Presence of Aryans in the region of Central Asia and their migrations from this region towards Iran and India has been traced with the help of archaeological data. Andronovo culture extending over an extensive area with a time bracket of 5000 B.C. to 2000 B.C. is argued to be similar to the material culture of the Rigveda and Avesta. In all there are five maps in this chapter to support his contention. The non-Vedic linguistic element is traced in several remote parts of India (Dravidian words in ethnic groups residing in the Ganga plains) to prove displacement of Harappans from the primary zone.

Seals have been used as evidence to distinguish the Harappans from the Vedic people. The author points out that the most important animals on these seals are unicorn and rhino. Both ar unknown to Rigveda. The Sanskrit words for these animals, he further asserts, have non-Aryan roots.

Summing up, one wonders why a senior scholar like Sharma fails to take into account some well researched works by Indian scholars. While he makes frequent references to Russian and other European scholars who continue to advocate the old theory of Aryan migration from outside India advanced during the colonial times, he chooses to ignore the very significant work of Malati Shindge. Similarly, omission of any reference to Bhagwan Singh's voluminous work, representing he other view point (that the Harappans were Aryans), also appears to be deliberate. Rejecting all these alternative positions as prejudiced account of 'Hindu fundamentalists' is not academically tenable nor is it in keeping with Sharma's academic temper. Underplaying the significance of recent archaeological evidences from important sites like Dholavira, Rakhigarhi, as also of Banawali, Kunal etc. are equally disconcerting. Evidences from these sites, e.g. animal sacrifice at Rakhigarhi well formed fire altars at Banawali, Rakhigarhi, Kalibangan horse bones from Surkotada, Ropar, Kalibangam, figurines horse from Mohenjodaro, Lothal etc, spoked wheel from Banawali etc. indicate that the two cultures may have more elements of similarity and familiarity with each other than has been hitherto believed. They call for a fresh look at the issues involved and this can hardly be done by ignoring well researched works of Indian scholars like B.B. Lal or S.P. Gupta Bhagwan Singh, Malti Shengde and others. However, this fresh examination should be free of cultural and ideological bias. History must not be used as tool for fighting ideological battles. Only then we will be able to tell the true story, or to reveal the *itihas* i.e. *it-ha-as*, or so it has been -the traditional Indian concept of history.

Vibha Tripathi

Satyendra Kumar Jha, *Beginning of Urbanization in Early Historic India*, Novelty & Co. Tarabhawan, Ashok Rajpath Patna 1998 Rs. 550 p.325; Fig. 21; illustrations 5, ISBN : 81-86931-13-9

In a dialectic web Satyendra Kumar Jha has successfully interwoven the archaeological, historical and literary sources to trace the beginnings of urbanization in Early Historic India. The Early Historic urbanization has had the attention of scholars for decades. The book under review is the latest addition to the list of publications on this theme, an outcome of a sustained research undertaken by the author. In the 'Foreword'. The author aims to revise the older paradigms and comes up with new constructs. He has indeed succeeded in fulfilling this aim. He exhibits a deep understanding of the subject, discussing with characteristic thoroughness the processes and the imminent emergence of city in the Mid Ganga Plain (MGP), the foci of the investigation.

The work is based on the Ph.D. dissertation of the author dating back to 1988. However, it has been thoroughly revised, reviewed, enlarged. A postscript has been added. Fresh data from the excavations conducted in recent years have been taken into account. The time-bracket spans over a millennium. The researches underline the divergent stages of growth of culture in the Ganga Plain—from Neolithic through Chalcolithic to the Iron Age and the emergence of cities.

The book has been divided into five chapters. The first chapter is introductory. It deals with existing theories on urbanization. He has reviewed them critically—right from Gordon Childe to the most recent author and then formulates his own hypothesis. The variability of contentions held on a theme like urbanism show that there is still scope to work on it, especially in the context of the Ganga Plains. It also underlines the fact that every region has its specifics and, therefore, should be evaluated independently. Jha does not seem to be making any pretentions about universalizing his assumptions. He has focused his attention to th specific area of the Ganga Plains; to be more precise to the Middle Ganga Plain. Together, the two sections of th book, i.e., the introduction and the postscript, set the temper for the ensuing discussions.

The next chapter (Ch.II) is entitled 'Technological Base of Urbanization". Technologies like metallurgy—iron and copper ceramic and agrotechnologies have been treated en defuse. Maximum space has been allocated to iron technology because of its association with urbanization process. Against the general assumption he tries to demonstrate that iron technology, right from its early levels, is employed into production mechanism. He underplays the concept of saliency of war-hunting tool-types. The detailed, phase-wise break-up of iron objects from Atranjikhera and several other sites help such a construct. To be precise, 21.48 per cent of tools may be classified as war and hunting weapons while 42.96 per cent have been placed under the class of household or carpenter's tools. These include nails, rods, champs bar-rods, hooks, needles, knives (that could serve other alternative functions too) along with the carpenter's tool-like, chisels in good number. Instances have been given from other sites like Taradih, Sonpur, Koldihwa, Narhan, Rajghat in MGP as also from lower Ganga Plain like Mahishdal, Hatigra, Barudih, etc. wherefrom chisels,. knives, borers, etc., have been unearthed from the early levels (Black-and-Red ware phase). More recently, agricultural implements have also been forthcoming from sites like Jakhera (ploughshare and hoe from Proto-PGW/early PGW phase. Ganwaria also yields a ploughshare though in a slightly later context. Besides, sickles, hoe (Chirand has yielded a socked variety), axe, etc., prove utilization of iron in agricultural sector. He discusses 'the twin factor', i.e. 'the availability of rich iron ores in the proximity of the lower-middle Ganga Valley and the necessity of iron implements' for cultivation of the characteristic soil of the region. Using both literary and archaeological evidence he comes to the conclusion that PGW culture of western UP appears to be making an earlier use of iron implements in agricultural sector than the contemporary BRW using pre-NBP phase in Lower Ganga Plain (LGP). The presence of ploughshares at Jakhera (proto-PGW-PGW phase) and Alamgirpur are important indeed. Sickles, hoes, etc., have been reported from contemporary levels from a large number of sites. On the contrary in the MGP the number of agricultural implements is much smaller, viz. Rajghat has the richest tool repertoire (total 136 objects)) having the only type-sickle that is 3 in number (pp.110-113). Thus he deducts "The present postulate of linking iron's role with agricultural surplus...... in the eastern parts of the Ganga Valley should not be emphasised too much" (p.113–114). One may not agree with this but what is significant here is that Jha has forcefully demonstrated his case of dynamic role of iron in the production mechanism as shown in the statistical data above from almost the earliest phase of introduction of iron in the Ganga Plains.

Copper and iron-copper object juxtaposition in typological exclusively have ben discussed. Alloying technique and its impact on the end-product along with the analytical data have been incorporated that add further value to this discussion. In addition resource zone for various minerals/metals have also been considered. Even the mining practices have been brought into the purview of examination. It is indeed a difficult if not an impossible task, at the present state of our knowledge-especially in the case of early settlements of this region, of objects like bar-celts for mining—a bold attempt in the absence of doubtful evidence. The Arthasastra has been made use of to build up a case for mining practice at his juncture.

Chapter III on 'Settlement-pattern and Demographic Features' is a thorough study incorporating the available literature on this subject. Two studies on the subject by M.Lal and G.Erdosy, both based on U.G.P. have been critically examined and used. The disparity of their approach and discrepancies therein have been highlighted. But in the absence of well defined or better models of settlement pattern-studies suited to the Indian conditions he tries to come up with models of his own using literary data also. In the absence of a thorough work on spatial distribution settlements, however, his constructs would remain at best 'tentative', on admission. Demographic features have been worked out on the basis of Blanche's suggestion of interrelationship between increased rainfall and population density. By adding margin to the data provided by Lal and Erdosy, Jha draws a demographic profile of MGP. The rainfall in UGP is 80 cm per annum while it is 122.6 cm per annum in MGP. Therefore, the population density should be higher in the latter zone (according to the theory of Blanche).

Reconstructing the settlement pattern in the area of study is indeed a well nigh impossible because of the shifting drainage system of the region. In large cases the surface contours have been almost totally obliterated. Even Pataliputra, the Mauryan capital, has undergone topographical changes because of changes in river courses around this place. A number of graphs and tables have been drawn up in support of his arguments. Jha has overcome the constraints of archaeological evidence by further substantiating with literary and historical accounts (like those of Megasthanes) wherever available. Using such sources he draws out plans of Kumrahar palace and fortification plans at several sites. Arthashastra helps him work out inter-spatial population flow and settlement hierarchy. The terms like *ghosha* (a pastoral settlement), *grama, mahagrama* etc. while indicating their status in the hierarchy also suggest their functional position. It may be worthwhile looking into such gradations in the archaeological context. A planned work to locate such evidence archaeologically, through exploration and excavations, would have added immensely to the merit of this work.

The last chapter on 'Chronology and Diffusion' situates the beginning of urbanization process in the UGP in view of an early beginning and the comparative prosperity of sites like Atanjikhera and Jakhera at the pre-NBP level (during PGW phase). Secondly, he comes to the conclusion that the origin of NBP should be looked in the UGP rather than in Bihar, since NBP, he argues, is an extension of PGW ceramic tradition. This has been argued on the strength of radiocarbon dates as well as relatively early techno-cultural growth discernable in the UGP. Though this is forcefully putforth, he may not find many takers. Because, firstly, there is no consistency in C_{14} dates to support the early dates for NBP in UGP. Secondly, the dispersal of ceramic cultures has a very complex pattern. Thirdly, the associated cultural assemblage, especially red ware, at more westerly sites like Hastinapura goes against its being an early NBP centre. Lastly, the smaller finds like tarracotta, *ghata*-shaped or arecanut beads, discs and figurines, etc. all show some kind of contact between the two zones from the first half of 1st millennium B.C. itself. Interactions must have led to similarity in cultural material between PGW and NBPW. The two also overlap in most of the sites. Interestingly, the break up of different objects at Atranjikhera clearly demonstrates a decline in material culture around NBP times. Jakhera presents a similar picture. There appears to be a shift in cultural foci from west to east around this juncture. Perhaps the emerging socio-political power of the middle Ganga zone was shaping it as an 'area of attraction' quite for some time before the actual rise of Magadhan imperialism.

Difference of opinions are key to a healthy academic debate. That apart, the arguments put forth by Jha have a force. Besides some minor shortcomings like the chart of iron objects has been wrongly placed and there are some errors in printing here and there, the book is a welcome addition to the increasing study on urbanization in India. The language is clear and crisp but the style becomes a bit laborious at times. The treatment of the subject is thorough. The author deserves to be congratulated for producing this excellent book.

Vibha Tripathi

Muhammed Abdul Nayeem, *The Rock Art of Arabia*, Hyderabad Publishers 10–2–5/8/1, A.C. Gaurds, Hyderabad-500 004, India, 2000 A.D., pp. i to xxxi + pp. 527, illustrations1271 + 23 maps. Price not given.

The present work undertakes comprehensive study of the Rock Art of of the Arbian peninsula as a whole, comprising the states of Saudi Arabia, Oman, Qatar, United Arab Emirates and Yemen.

The rock art has been treated as branch of archaeology providing us a glimpse of the material culture of the past without conducting scientific excavations. This art basically represents the personal expressions of the Artist about his environment, daily life, ideological and religious expressions, socio-cultural activities, depiction of nature's creations like animal and birds, internal and cultural influences both from internal states of Arabia and neighbouring countries. The author has also demonstrated, that the rock art had a gradual evolution from schematic to naturalistic and then it degenerated. The illustrations also give pictorial narratives which communicate certain incidents, such as hunting, fighting, battle scenes, important and memorable feasts etc. Epigraphs, ethnic information, and tribal marks are brought into focus incidentally.

The book consisting seven parts, part one is introductory and general in nature. Part 7 is synthetic and conclusive dealing with human and animal representations and their mutual associations, mythological and ritual scenes, geometrical designs, hand and foot prints, tribal signs (*Wusum*), Astral object mainly sun, style and techniques and ethnography of the people. Some affinities with internal states and neighbouring countries like north Africa and Europe have been brought to light. Parts two to six deal individually in detail with the component countries of Arabia, namely Saudi Arabia, Qatar, the United Arab Emirates, Oman, and Yemen. The book is concluded with chronological Index, general bibliography and index.

The chronological time bracket of the Rock Art of Arabia ranges from Epi-Palaeolithic period to the Pre-Islamic period. Several archaeological, and, extra archaeological factors have been taken into account. The archaeological factors and lithic artifacts, pottery found in exploration, and, also as a result of soundings at Rock Art sites. The other factors are patination, geo-morphological and environmental studies, flora and fauna, typology, stylistic peculiarities, superimpositions of figures engraved, and, tools and weapons.

Periodisation is as below

Period			
1	Epi-Palaeolithic	-	10,000–6000 B.C.
II	Neolithic	-	6000–3000 B.C.
III	Chalcolithic	-	3000–2000 B.C.
IV	Bronze Age	-	2000–1000 B.C.
V	Iron Age	-	1000-0 B.C.
VI	Pe-Islamic	-	A.D. 1–622
VII	Islamic Period	-	A.D. 622–todate

The art has numerous parallels in neighbouring countries. The animal figures in profile and "the heads on plan found commonly in Arabian Art" are also recorded from north Africa., Syria, Palestine, Jordan etc. The exaggerated long horns of bovids have parallels in north African rock carvings. The author has stated that female figures of Jubbah have parallels with palaeolithic figure of Europe and female figuring of Saudi Arabia have parallels in Nubia and Germany also.

The book, an outcome of several year's of research and inspection of far-flung sites of different states of Arabia. This ia a formidable task achieved singly bringing to light several hundred petroglyphs. A few tribal signs have been recorded from Qatar along with the characters of ancient Arabian script. The word "write" also means 'to draw to engrave'. This implies that all the rock painting and other engravings of Arabia are a form of writing, which the ancient man has left for the posterity. Without these rock drawings of writing, culture which has been defined as "communicable intelligence "would not exist. The rock drawings of Saudi Arabia, which date to Epi-Palaeolithic period (100000–6000 B.C.) depicting human and animal figures in various forms and walks of life, and engraved writing, communicate the culture of the ancient people. It is a pictographic or picture writing in a rudimentary form. From this stage, the use of signs and symbols have developed which are an embryo-writing. The signs, symbols, lines, geometric forms etc. used in tribal marks are ideographic writing. The individual symbols are called ideograms. After ideograms, the next development was a phonetic script."

A number of line-drawings, photographs, charts and tables, histograms, illustrate the contention of the scholar. The author has also endeavoured to make it as comprehensive as possible so far as Arabia and individual states are concerned. Generally and individually, the author, besides explaining his own work, discussed earlier studies, ancient environments, art regions, terminology and techniques, methodology and contents of the Art and. chronology with tables.

It is a useful and scholarly contribution for understanding the rock art of Arabian peninsula.

R.P. Sharma

Suchitra Khanna 1999. *Dancing Divinitics in Indian Art*. Sharda Publishing House Delhi. pp 170 Figs 134. Rs 1750.

In the realm of performing arts, dance has a singular position. It underwent a long course of development which has been reviewed, discussed and interpreted by a number of scholars. Indian dance has its foundation in Bharata's Natyasastra. A number of monuments in India have been generously embellished with sculptures which are in turn the matic representations of a rich literary tradition as well as dance *karanas*. They have been examined from varied perspectives by contemporary art historians. In the present work, Suchitra Khanna attempts to explain the reciprocal development of dance and sculptural art in India between 8th and 12th centuries A.D.

The book has eight chapters. In the first Chapter, the author traces the development of dance from Saskkrit and Prakrit sources. Examining a vast corpus of Vedic and Puranic literature, she discusses and enunciates the essential components of *rasa* dance. The etymology of *natya*, its unfolding through literature and its development as a calssical art form are discussed in the second chapter. The author, however, is concerned more with functional aspects of dance and less on its development from a historical view. The depiction of the art form in preview and protohistoric periods and its delineation from Sunga to Gupta periods are reviewed in the third chapter. The efflorescence of the art form in temple art during the Pallava, Chola and Chandella periods is vividly portrayed in the fourth chapter which is introduction to the focal theme.

The fifth, sixth and seventh chapters discuss at length sculptural representations of Shiva, Vishnu, Devi as well as subaltern deities from various places and museums. Sculptures in bronze and brass are less in relations to those in stone. The iconometry of dancing images holdings various attributes are explained in the literary context. Shiva occupies the prime position among dancing images, and quite a few terrestrial manifestations such as Kalarimurti, Bhairava and Gajasamharamurti are discussed. Images of Vishnu are comparatively few and is represented mainly as Krishan and Mohini. Devi is represented either as Parvati or as one of the Saptamatrkas. The images of Ganesha and Skanda have also been considered in this aspect.

Subaltern deities such as *Yakshas, Gandharvas* and *Apsaras* are also highlighted in the work. The author has stressed on the importance of multi-handed dancing images in relation to double-handed images, since the latter are a rare phenomenon in Indian art tradition.

The text has 3 tables, 134 figures, a glossary, bibliography and an index. It is a well documented source book for scholars interested in performing arts.

B.S. Hari Shankar

Neeta Yadav, *Ardhanarisvara in Art and literature.* D.K. Print World (P) Ltd. Delhi pp. 255, Figs 20, Plates 88. Rs 1800.

Ardhanarisvara or the androgyne deity marks its explicit presence in Kena Upanishad and has become a unique concept, eulogised in literature and depicted in art. Neeta Yadav in her work attempts to explore the conceptual development of Ardhanarisvara and examines the socio-cultural fabric that nourished it in terms of iconography and aesthetics.

The author presents the origin of Saivaite symbols and images and argues that the cult is pre-vedic and non-Aryan from the two postulations of Stuart Easton and John Marshall. She traces the origin of Saivaite cult to Indus civilization and its development under Kushanas, Satavahanas, Nagas and Pratiharas in ancient India.

The second chapter discusses iconography of Ardhanarisvara prescribed in classical treatise, *agamas* and *puranas*. She refers to the bifurcation of the cosmic concept and its terrestrial manifestation as the androgyne deity. The features and attributes of the composite dual gender is explained in this chapter.

The third chapter deals with Ardhanarisvara represented in sculptural art from various places such as Mathura, Gudimallam, Ellora, Badami and Kanchi and the collection from museums and temples.

In the fourth chapter, Ardhanari in literature is dealt.

An study from the aesthetic perspective is given in the fifth chapter. The Sankhya theory. symbolism of Hermophrodie, reciprocity of Advaita school and Ardhanarisvara concept, the contribution by classical poets and the influence of Pratyabhigna system of Kashmir Saivism on the androgyne deity are discussed.

The sixth chapter is a discussion of the socio-religious environment conducive for the development of the Ardhanarisvara concept. The author analyses the history and synthesis of cults.

Tantricism is reviewed in the seventh chapter and the eight chapter is conclusion.

The text is supplemented by 9 maps, 20 figures 70 plates, a glossary, bibliography and an appendix. The book is useful not only for scholars of art history, but for everyone interested in ancient India.

B.S. Hari Shankar

R. Krishnamurthy. *Non-Roman Ancient Foreign coins from Karur in India*, Garnet Publishers, Chennai 2000, pp. i-viii, 145, 6 maps 10 plates, text illustrations, bibliography and detailed index price: Rs.600/-

Krishnamurthy, a geologist by academic achievement, a journalist by profession and numismatist by choice has published several articles on epigraphy and numismatics in several research journals. He has also written ten books on the subject and this book under review is his tenth. His main concentration is on coins from Karur.

Karur at the mouth of the River Amaravati tributary of River Kaveri, the life time of Cholamandalam is an ancient city with 'hoary past. It is praised and described in Sangam poems, particulary the Ahananuru. This ancient city is still a virgin; the spade of the archaeologist has not yet defiled it. However, the cultural sequence is not expected to be much different from the other excavated sites like Uraiyur, Alagarai and Tirukkampuliyar in the Lower Kaveri basin where the earliest cultural matrix, the fine Black-and-Red ware of megalithic affinity can be stretched back to the 6th–5th centuries B.C.

Be that as it may. The coins collected from the river bed of Amaravati, had been several kilograms, most of which had been melted for its metal. Whatever Sri Krishnamurti could retrieve from the locals, has been studied and published by him.

The present book *Non-Roman Ancient Foreign Coins from Karur* is in nine chapters, the first one with five subdivisions. Each chapter is prefaced with the history of the region from where the coins originated. All the Coins described in this book are from Karur and that too collected from the Amravarti river bed. The first chapter deals with coins from Thrace, Thesaly, Create (one coin from each) Rhodes (four coins) and Seleucid coins (14 - all bronze coins).

Phoenician coins dealt in chapter 2 are from Aradus (2); Sidon (4) Tyre (8) – all copper; the next chapter deals with 2 Askalon copper coins. In chapter 4 Judean Coins are considered which include those of Hasmonean priest-kings; the next described issues of the Roman governers of Judea. In chapters six, seven and eight are studied coins of the Parthians, Edessan and Aksumite coins from Karur. One would wonder how valuable it would have had these coins were found in a stratified context.

Krishnamurthy is of the opinion that western trade with southern India was not a sudden spurt but the result of a "gradual process" developed from proto-historic times, a postulate yet to be proved by the archaeologist's spade. He traces three routes of contact with south India; one originating from Phoenesian cities, second from Greece and the third from Alexandria in Egypt; all with their ultimate aim to reach Muziris on the Kerala coast. However, direct contact with Muziris could have taken place when the Alexandria route became "familiar" with the sailors. In conclusion he avers that Seleucid and Parthian coins reached west coast through the Phoenecian route; Askalon and Judeon coins via the second and the Edessan and Aksuman coins taking the third route. In all the cases it must be understood the Palghat pass played a vital role through which the ancient coins—Roman, Greek, etc. reached Karur by the overland route.

The present book is a wellcome addition as source book for writing south Indian history, particulary Humismatic history. Krishnamurthy's endeavour and enthusiasm has to be praised.

The printing is good. Paper used is of the heavy variety and is expected to last long. The bibliography is exhaustive. The detailed index is a boon to all researchers. Such indices, we rarely come across these days.

K.S. Ramachandran

D.P. Sharma, *Harappan Seals, Sealings and Copper Tablets*, National Museum, New Delhi.

The book is divided into three chapters with an appendix and a select bibliography. A handlist of Harappan seals, sealings and copper tablets in the National Museum collection numbering 258 found in different excavation of Harappan sites is given at the end. A few of them are also illustrated in Black and White. In the introduction, Sharma has given the salient features of this culture starting from Early Harappans (*c.* 3200–2700 B.C.) through Mature and Decline phase. He has also given some recent views of the scholars defining Harappan civilization as Indus-Sarasvati civilization as both the rivers yielded Harappan sites in the basin. He has also opined that Harappan and Vedic people were one and same on the finding of horse bones, fire altars for rituals and terracotta figure.

One of the most outstanding features of the Harappan civilization is recovery of seals, sealings and copper tablets. The production of these items, required great artistic merit and technological skill. The author has also included the latest findings from Dholavira and Rakhigarhi in the book. As these objects were found in West Asia, and Central Asia, a long distance trade of Harappans was confirmed. However, the script on these objects is still to be deciphred.

The work is an excellent publication on art paper and will be useful to researchers dealing with Harappan studies.

K.N. Dikshit

Report of the XXXIII Annual Conference of Inian Archaeological Society held at Pune from 27th through the 30th December, 1999

The Annual conference of the Soceities namely Indian Archaeological Society, Indian Society for Prehistoric and Quaternary Studies, and Indian History and Culture Society, for the year 1999 was held at Deccan College Post-Graduated and Research Institute, Pune, and was inaugurated by the Hon'ble Professor S.C. Gupte, Presidnet of the Institute on the 27th December, 1999.

After the inaugural function, Prof. T.C. Sharma delivered the Presidential address of the Indian Archaeological Society; Shri K.N. Dikshit, delivered the Presidential Address of the Indian Society for Prehistoric and Quternary Studies, and Dr. Mani P. Kamerkar of the Indian History and Culture Society. The valedictory address was delivered by Dr. Y.D. Sharma on the 30th December, 1999.

Programme

27th Decmeber, 1999: Afternoon session

Professor H.D. Sankalia Memorial Lecture wad delivered by Dr. S.P. Gupta on Harappan Studies in the next Century.

Twesday 28.12.1999: Forenoon session

R.S. Bisht
New Light on the Harappan Civilisation in the Light of Dholavira Evidence.

Vasant Shinde
Harappan Civilisation: new Concept about Terminology and origin.

J.N. Pandey
Pre-Harappan/Early Harappan Culture

Malti Shendge
The Language of the Harappans and the Origin of Sanskrit.

AFTERNOON SESSION OPEN SESSION

Ramesh Jain
Harappans Founded Strong Town Planning Tradition.

P.v. Pathak
Fecundity Seal from Harappa as Pictorial Representation of Rigvedic Deity Asvin Twins

Purushottam Singh and Ashok Kumar Singh
Excavation at Agiabir, District Mirzapur, Uttar Pradesh.

V.D. Misra, J.N. Pal and M.C. Gupta
A Preliminary Report on the Excavations at Jhusi

Lajwanti Sahani
Sailing on a Dhow from Gujarat to the Persian Gulf. An Ethno-archaeological construction of seafaring activities from Harappan period onward.

Wednesday 29.12.999: Forenoon Session

Dilip Rajgor
Evolution of the Brahmi Script : A Linguistic Approach.

Atusha Bharucha Irani and Kurush Dalal
The Material Culture and Settlement Pattern in East Gujarat.

T.C. Sharma and Shri Manish Baruah
Glimpses of Brahmputra Valley Civilisation.

N.C. Ghosh, Shanti Pappu and K.V. Raman
Archaeology and Chidren : The Sharma Children's Museum.

Janardan Singh
Non-Vegetarianism in Ancient India : From Earlier Time to the Gupta Age.

R.K. Pancholi
Bhartiya Purakala Ka Udgam : Bhanpura Kshetra

Amrendra Kumar Singh
Destruction of Archaeological Sites : A case Study of Gurgi

Mala Maiya Malla
Bronzes of Nepal

Tama Panda
From Tribal to Feudal Order: Process of Transformation from Tribal to Hindu Society.

Balram Tripathi
Interpreting Early Historic Trade Mechanism in Central Orissa : A Holistic Approach.

AFTERNOON SESSION

V.N. Misra, Vasant Shinde, R.K. Mohanty, Lalit Pandey and Jeeven Kharakwal
Excavations at Balathal - 1998–99 : Preliminary Results.

P. Ajithprasad, V.H. Sonawane, Abhijit Majumdar and Kiran Dimri
The Harappan Cultural Sequence at Rangpur and New Data from Bagasra, Gujarat.

V.H. Sonawanw, P. Ajithprasad, K.K. Bhan, S. Prathapachandran, K. Krishnan and Abhijit Majumdar:
Excavation at Bagasra - 1998–99 : A Preliminary Report.

Sheila Mishra, Sushama G. Deo, Aarti Deshpande - Mukherjee, P.P. Joglekar, Saonali Naik, Savita Ghate, Anupama Kshirsagar and Utpala Adhav
Investigations around Sakshal Pimpri, District Beed, Maharashtra.

Priyadarsini Sengupta
The Neolithic - Chalcolithic Problem in Eastern India : Its Backdrop and Scope for Further Research.

Anup Mishra
Black - and - Red Ware of Balathal and the Cultural Contacts.

P.S. Joshi
Typology of Indian Megaliths : A Re-assessment

K.P. Rao and V. Ramabrahman.
Megalithic Monuments in Chittoor District, Andhra Pradesh : Recent Discoveries.

P. Binodini Devi
The Living Megalithic Traditions found among the Pumais of Manipur.

D.P. Agrawal and J. Kharakwal
Jodhpura - Ghaneshwar Complex, Meluhha and Sociology of Metallurgy

Vishwas D. Gogte
Early Historic Indian Mould Ware at Petra (Jordan) : An Evidence of India-Arabic Maritime Trade.

K.S. Saraswat
Plant Economy of Early Harappans at Ancient Kunal, District Hissar, Haryana

Chanchala Srivastava
Plant Economy at Ancient Mahorana, Sangrur Disrict, Punjab (C. 2300 B.C. – 200 A.D.)

Anupama Kshirsagar
Dating of Bones from Kalpi in Southern Ganga Plain by Fluorine.

POSTERS
30.12.1999

Abhijit Dandekar
Preliminary Analysis of Pottery found during Exploration at the Early medieval Site of Achhala.

Sonali Nai
Nevasa through the Ages.

Shaunak Kulkarni
Megalithic Culture of the Madias of Maharashtra

Shrikant Pradhan
A study of the Shorapur School of South Indian Painting.

P.V. Pathal
Encycoloadia of the Indus and Vedic Cultures

S.N. Karlekar, Sushama G. Deo and P.P. Joglekar
Identification of Spatio - temporal Changes in Mhasala Creek Using IRS-IB Image.

Sheila Mishra, R.K. Mohantym Sonali Naik, Sushma G. Deo, PP. Joglekar, Utpala Adhav and Gurudas Shete
Preliminary Results from the excavation of Karondiya, District Dhar, M.P.

Richa Jhaldiyal
Lithic Weathering Analysis : Its Usefulness for Archaeological Interpretation.

Girish D. Mandke
Ladideva's Step-well Inscription of 1344 A.D. at Manchar, District Pune

B-17, Qutab Institutional Area
New Dehi - 110016

K.N. Dikshit
General Secretary
Indian Archaeological Society

THE INDIAN ARCHAEOLOGICAL SOCIETY
BALANCE SHEET AS ON 31.03.2000

LIABILITIES		AMOUNT	ASSETS	AMOUNT
CAPITAL FUND			FIXED ASSETS	
Op.Balance	1,648,071.99		(As per Schedule 'A'	
Add:–L.M. Fees	18,500.00		attached	12,688,715.00
Income over				
Expenditure	247444.11	1,914,016.10		
Corpus Fund		1,500,000	Current Assets & Investmens	
			Fixed Deposit	1,575,000.00
Building Fund				
Opening Balance	80,47,263.00			
Add:-Receipts during the year	27,06,000	10,753,263.00	Advances	
			(AS per Annexure 'I' attached)	110,732.00
Dr. A.K. Narain (Award) Fund		50,000.00	Delhi Vidyut Board	86,888.00
Projects Fund		218,290.00	Tax Deducted at Source	19,388.00
			Kampilya proj. Balances	
			Central Bank - Kayamganj	17,427.00
Securities		364,374.00	Amount in Cheque	30,000.00
			Cash at site	6,363.00
Expenses Payable		78,928.00	Cash & Bank Balnace	
			S.B.I. - 45062	21,090.79
			S.B.I.-45082	80,280.77
			Indian Bank - 460017	233,601.65
			Cash in hand	7,386.89
		14,876,871.10		14,876,871.10

Sd/
General Secretary

Sd/
Treasurer

Sd/
For Rajan Sharma & Co.,
Chartered Accountant

Place: New Delhi
Daed: 29.09.2000

(Rajan Kumar Sharma)
Prop.

THE INDIAN ARCHAEOLOGICAL SOCIETY

INCOME EXPENDITURE ACCOUNT FOR THE YEAR ENDED 31.03.2000

PARTICULARS	AMOUNT (RS.)	PARTICULARS	AMMOUNT (RS.)
To Honorarium	82,650.00	By Grant from A.S.I.	25,000.00
To Ground Rent	11,500.00	By Grant from I.C.H.R.	45,000.00
To Municipal Taxes	10,800.00	By Donations	17,250.00
To Publication Exp.	76,460.00	By Sale of Publication	45,616.00
To News Paper & Periodicals	626.00	By Bank Interest	209,869.13
To Medical Exp.	1,065.00	By Rent Received	440,625.00
To Telephone Exp.	13,784.00	By Service Charges	300.00
To Conveyance	44,021.00	By Grant - Majuli Project	100,000.00
To Printing & Stat.	6,905.50	By Grant - Kampilya Project from ASI	60,000.00
To Conference Exp.	59,719.00	By Grant - Kampilya Project from VAIS	96,210.00
To Office Expenses	6,160.00	By Bronze Gallery Project	7,770.00
To Repairs & Maint.	149,256.00		
To Staff Welfare	4,652.00		
To Postage & Stamps	11,160.00		
To Accounting Charges	12,000.00		
To Audit Fees	11,000.00		
To Bank Charges	1,997.00		
To Miscellaneious Exp.	5,730.00		
To Professional Exp.	10,750.00		
To Majuli Project Exp.	107,027.00		
To Kampilya Project Exp.	156,210.00		
To Depreciation	16,723.52		
To Excess of Income over Expenditure	247,444.11		
Total	1,047,640.13	Total Rs.	1,047,640.13

Sd/
General Secretary

S/-
Treasure

Sd/
For Rajan Sharma & Co.,
Chartered Accountant

(Rajan Kumar Sharma)
Prop.

Place: New Delhi
Dated: 29.09.2000

OFFICE BEARERS OF THE INDIAN ARCHAEOLOGICAL SOCIETY

Patrons:
Prof. B.B. Lal
F-7, Hauz Khas Enclave
New Delhi

Prof. B.P. Sinha
68, Pataliputra Colony
Patna

Chiarman:
Dr. S.P. Gupta
B-17, Qutab Institutional Area
New Delhi 110016

Vice Chairman:
Dr. Y.D Sharma
B-16, Kailash Colony
New Delhi - 110048

Shri K.M. Srivastava
142, Venus Apartments
Inder Enclave, Rohtak Road
New Delhi - 110087

General Secretary
Shri K.N. Dikshit
B-322, Sarita Vihar
New Delhi 110044

Hon. Tresurer:
Shri K.S. Ramachandran
C-139, Sarita Vihar
New Delhi 110044

Secretaries:
Prof. V.N. Misra
Former Director
Deccan College, Pune

Shri R.S. Bisht
Director
Archaeological Survey of India
New Delhi

Dr. R.C. Aggrwal
Director
Archaeoloical Survey of India
New Delhi

Dr. R.D. Chaudhary
Director General
National Museum, New Delhi

Members of the Executive Committee:
Prof. Vibha Tripathi
Banaras Hindu University
Varanasi

Prof. V.D. Mishra,
Allahabad University
Allahabad

Prof. V.H. Sonawane
M.S. University Baroda
Vadodra

Prof. K.V. Raman
Madras University
Madras

Dr. V.S. Shinde
Deccan College
Pune

Shri J.P. Joshi
Fomer Director General
Archaeological Survey of India
New Delhi

Asst. Secretary:
Shri R.P. Sharma
New Dehi

Editor Manographs/Newsletter
Sh. K.S. Ramachandran
New Delhi

Headquarters:

INDIAN ARCHAEOLOGICAL SOCIETY
B-17, Qutab Institutional Area, South of IIT, New Delhi - 110016
(O) 652-3728 TELE-Fax:011-696-0654
E-mail: ias_newdelhi@yahoo.co.uk
K.N. Dikshit: 694-8971
K.S. Ramachandran: 695-1389

INDIAN ARCHAEOLOGICAL SOCEITY
BOARD OF MANAGEMENT

Headquarters:

B-17, Qutab Institutional Area, South of IIT, New Delhi - 110016
(O) 6960654, 6523728 Fax:011-6960654
E-mail: ias_newdelhi@yahoo.co.uk

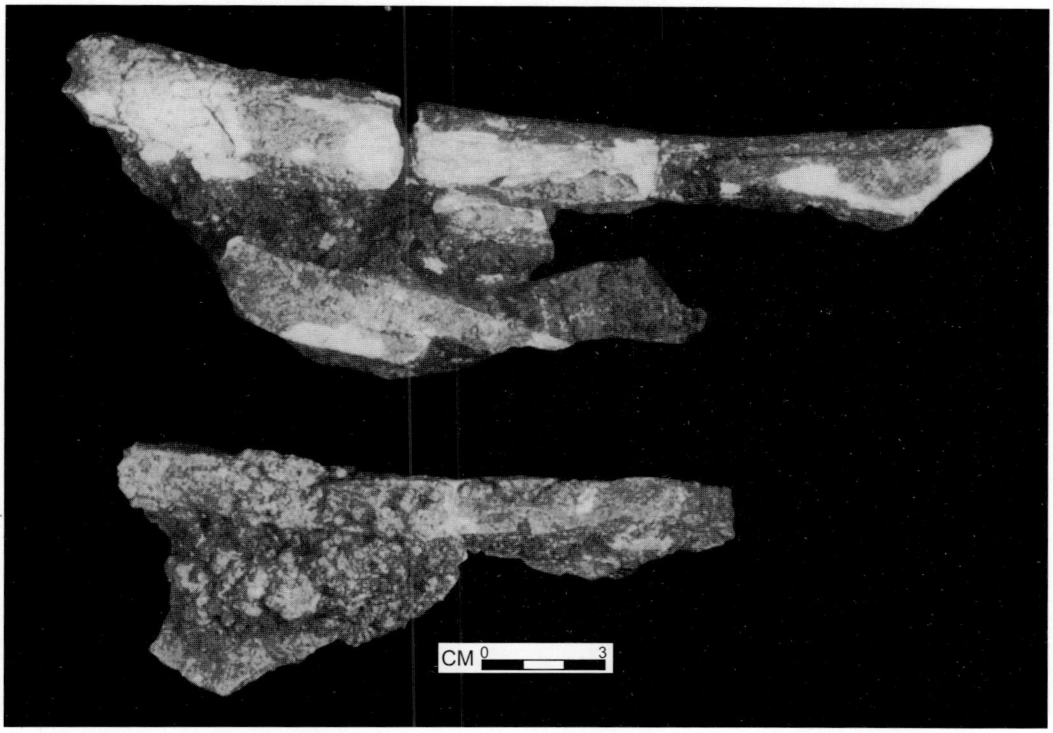

Plate-1. **Isampur,** Long bone fragments of *Bos sp* from Trench 1 Acheulian level **(Paddayya *et al.*).**

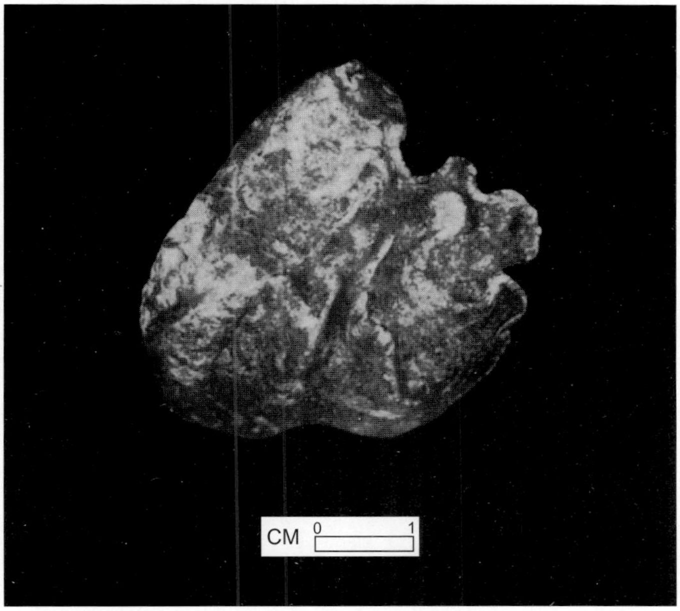

Plate-2. **Isampur,** Left upper molar of a bovid, Trench 5 Acheulian level **(Paddayya *et al.*).**

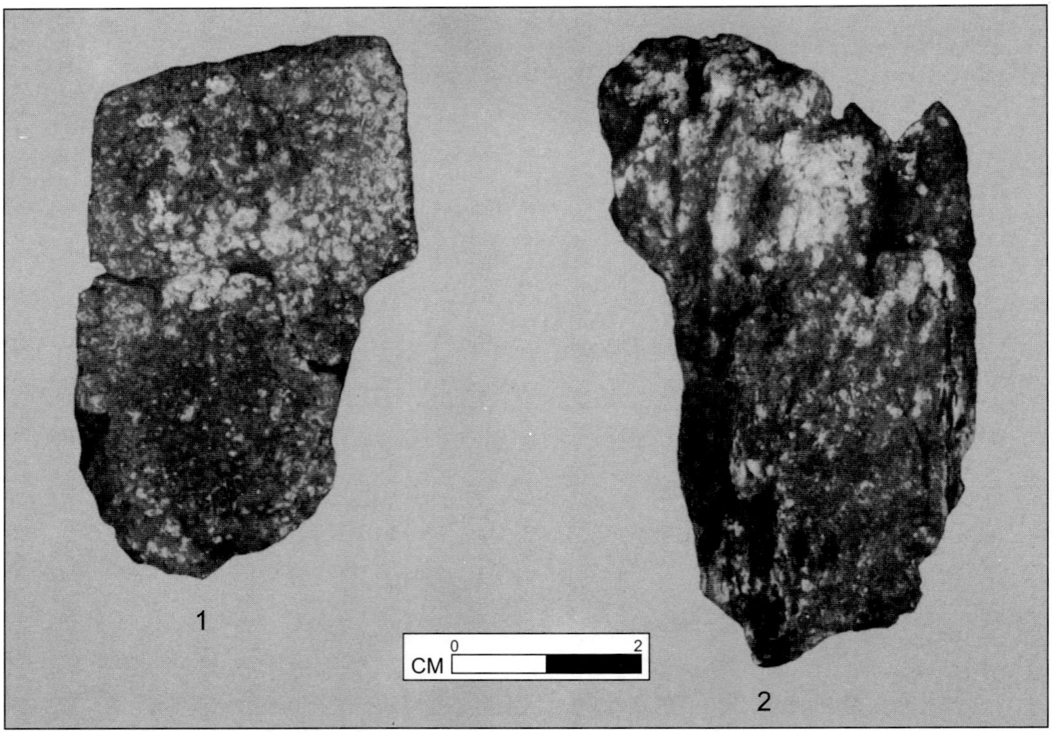

Plate-3. **Isampur,** Fossil fauna - 1) pond turtle 2) horn core of fragment of bovid **(Paddayya *et al.*).**

Plate-4. **Isampur,** Acheulian chipping clusters, from Trench. 1 depth 50 cm. **(Paddayya *et al.*).**

Plate-1. **Ojiyana,** Multichambered house complex **(Meena *et al.*).**

Plate-2. **Ojiyana,** Red ware storage jar with applique designs **(Meena *et al.*).**

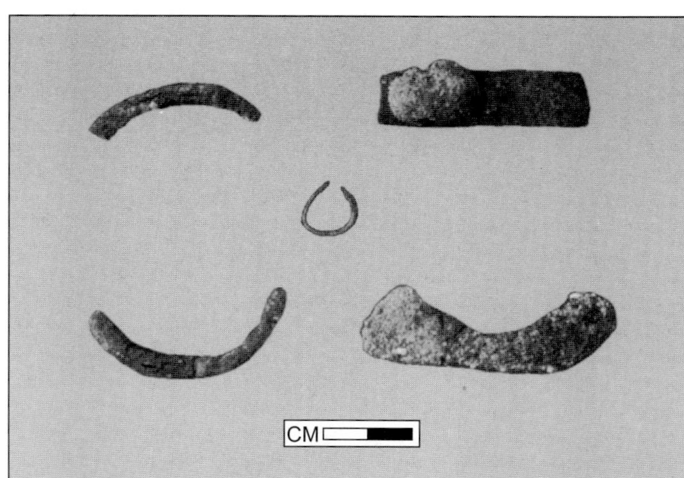

Plate-3. **Ojiyana,** Copper objects **(Meena *et al.*).**

Plate-1. **Dhalewan,** Partially exposed rooms **(Madhu Bala *et al.*).**

Plate-2. **Dhalewan,** Partially exposed room with ovens **(Madhu Bala *et al.*).**

Plate-3. **Dhalewan,** Terracotta cakes and mushtikas **(Madhu Bala *et al.*).**

Plate-4. **Dhalewan,** Semi -precious stone beads, bangles, etc. **(Madhu Bala *et al.*).**

Plate-1. **Chichali,** Plan of rectangular house **(Mitra *et al.*).**

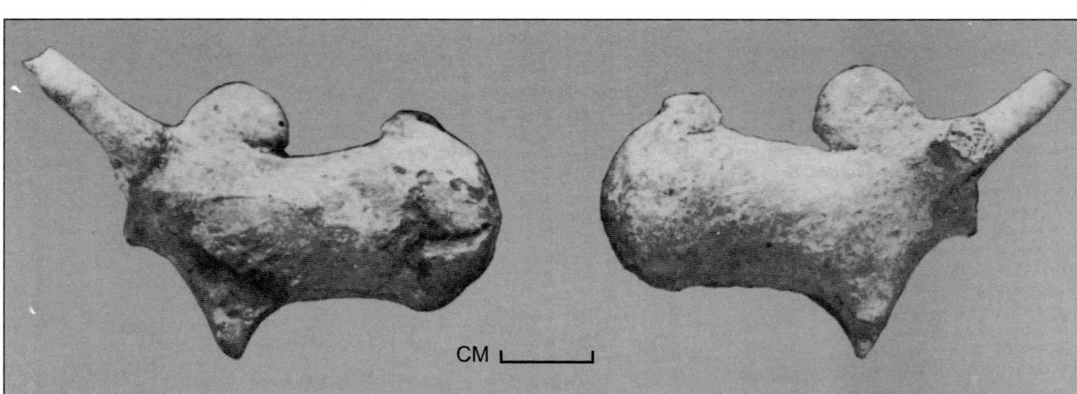

Plate-2. **Chichali,** Terracotta bull—Ahar period. **(Mitra *et al.*).**

Plate-3. **Chichali,** Circular house, Malwa period **(Mitra *et al.*).**

Plate-4. **Chichali,** Pot with whetstones placed in a semi-circular fashion at shoulder level, Malwa period **(Mitra *et al.*).**

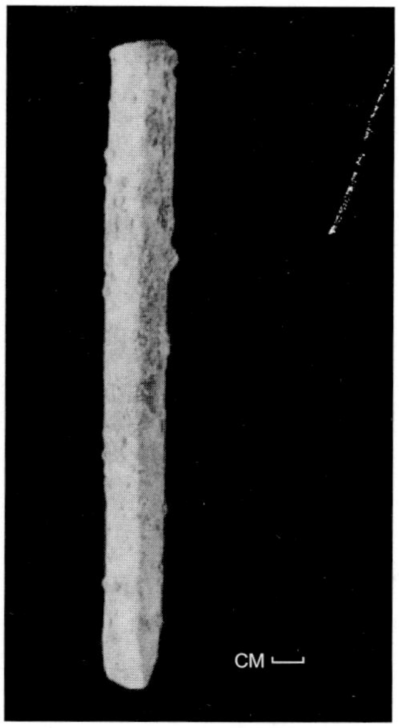

Plate-5. **Chichali,** Copper chisel, Malwa period **(Mitra *et al.*).**

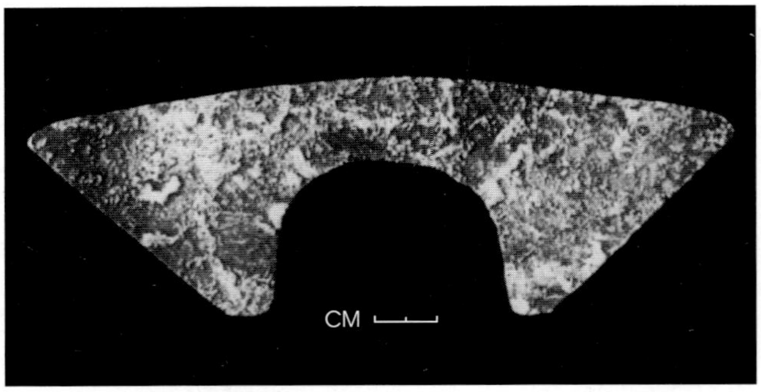

Plate-6. **Chichali,** *Parasu*-shaped copper object, Malwa period **(Mitra** ***et al.*****).**

Plate-7. **Chichali,** Pot with applique design, Jorwe period **(Mitra** ***et al.*****).**

Plate-8. **Chichali,** Three-handled gajamukha jar, Early Historical period **(Mitra** ***et al.*****).**

Plate-1. **Sirpur,** Siva temple **(Joshi *et al.*).**

Plate-2. **Sirpur,** Siva temple, details **(Joshi *et al.*).**

Plate-3. **Sirpur,** Buddha temple **(Joshi *et al.*).**

Plate-4. **Sirpur,** Pillar with *ghata pallava* design from Buddha temple **(Joshi *et al.*).**

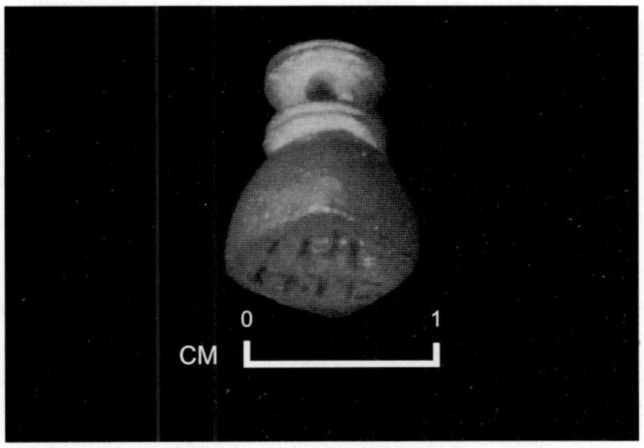

Plate-1. **Budhigarh,** Inscribed pendant seal of red jasper**(Mohanty *et al.*).**

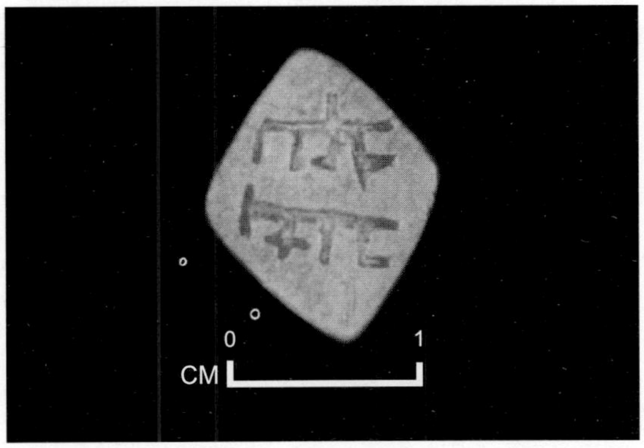

Plate-2. **Budhigarh,** Pendant seal of red jasper showing inscription **(Mohanty *et al.*).**

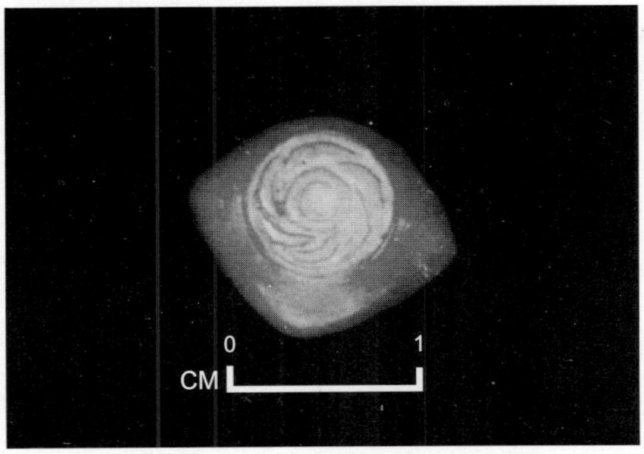

Plate-3. **Budhigarh,** Pendant seal of red jasper showing volute desing **(Mohanty *et al.*).**

Plate-1. **Mansar,**Tools of the Early Stone Age. **(Joshi *et al.*).**

Plate-2. **Mansar,** Stupa-2, *Circa 200B.C.* **(Joshi *et al.*).**

Plate-3. **Mansar,** *Purushamedha* **(Joshi *et al.*).**

Plate-4. **Mansar,** A view of Staircase **(Joshi *et al.*).**

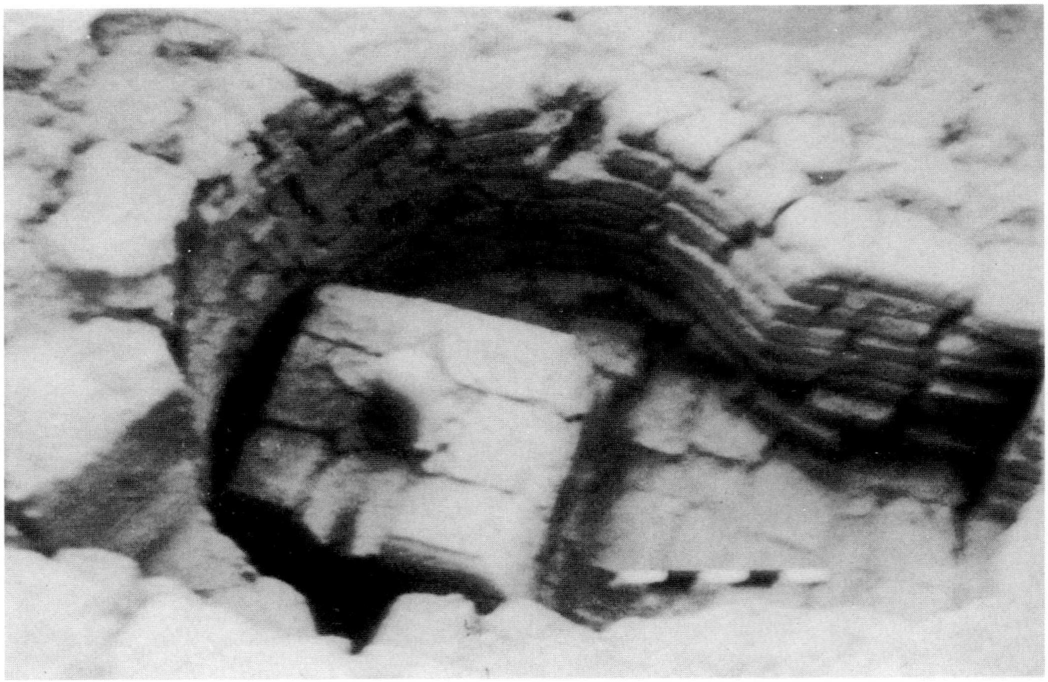

Plate-5. **Mansar,** Sivalinga in a *yoni pitha* shrine **(Joshi *et al.*).**

Plate-6. **Mansar,** Siva shrine. Linga in seen in the background **(Joshi *et al.*).**

Plate-7. **Mansar,** *Kinnara* **(Joshi *et al.*).**

Plate-8. **Mansar,** Sculpture of Lakshmi with attendent **(Joshi *et al.*).**

Plate-9. **Mansar,** Stupa-4. **(Joshi *et al.*).**

Plate-1. **Dihor,** Microstructure of Copper wire showing annealing coins **(Chattopadhyay).**

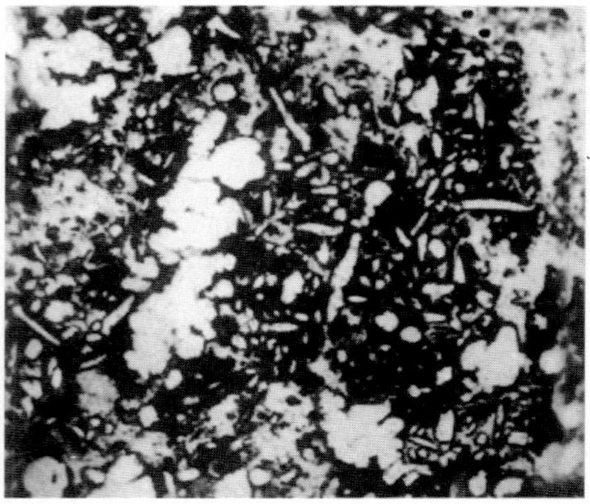

Plate-2. **Dihor,** Microstructure of Copper wire showing dendritic structure 100 X (**Chattopadhyay).**

Plate-1. **Bisokhar,** step well **(Madhu Bala).**

Plate-2. **Bisokhar,** Sculptural representation of Putana vadha and churning of butter **(Madhu Bala).**

Plate-3. **Bisokhar,** Krishna as Govardhanadhari **(Madhu Bala).**

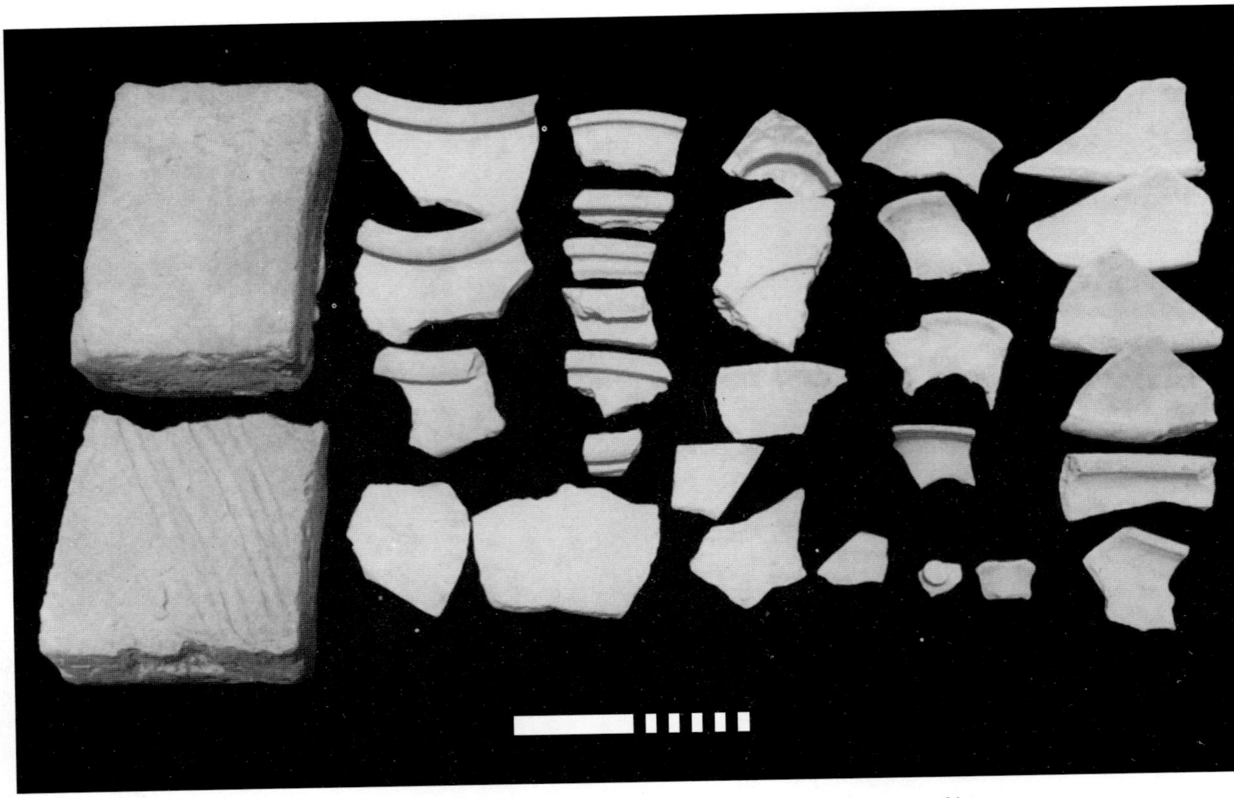

Plate-1. **Mandi,** Burnt-bricks and pottery **(Sharma *et al.*).**

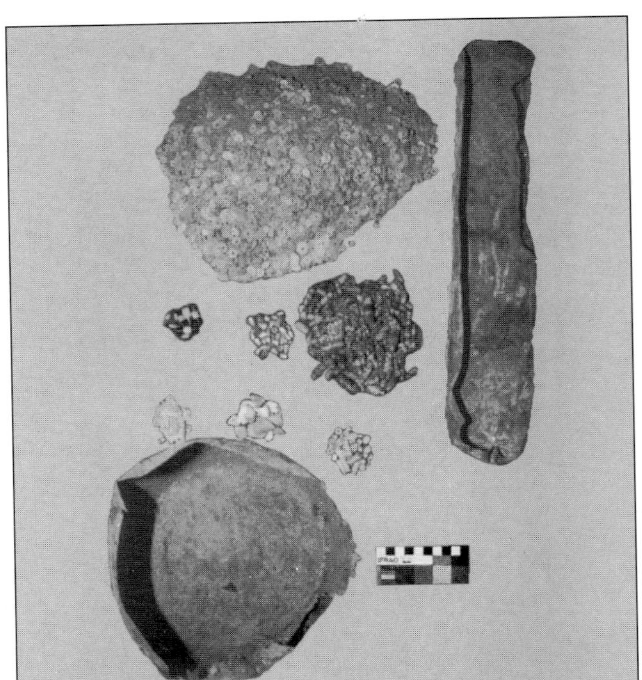

Plate-2. **Muzaffarnagar,** Gold and Copper objects from Mandi kept in the Treasury **(Sharma *et al.*).**

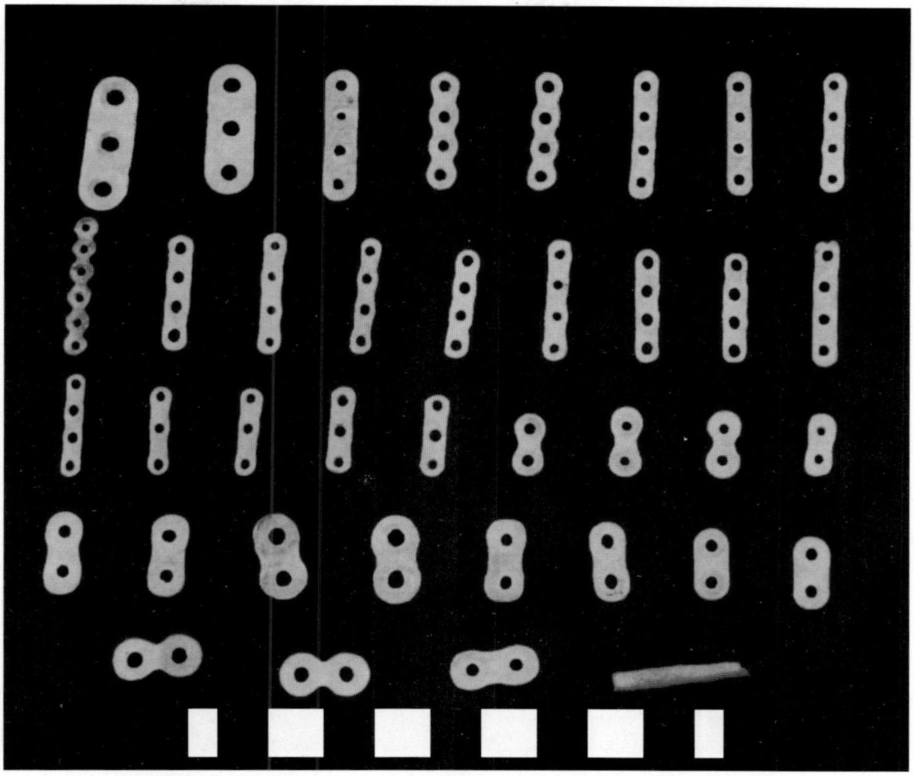

Plate-3. **Mandi,** Gold spacer beads **(Sharma *et al.*).**

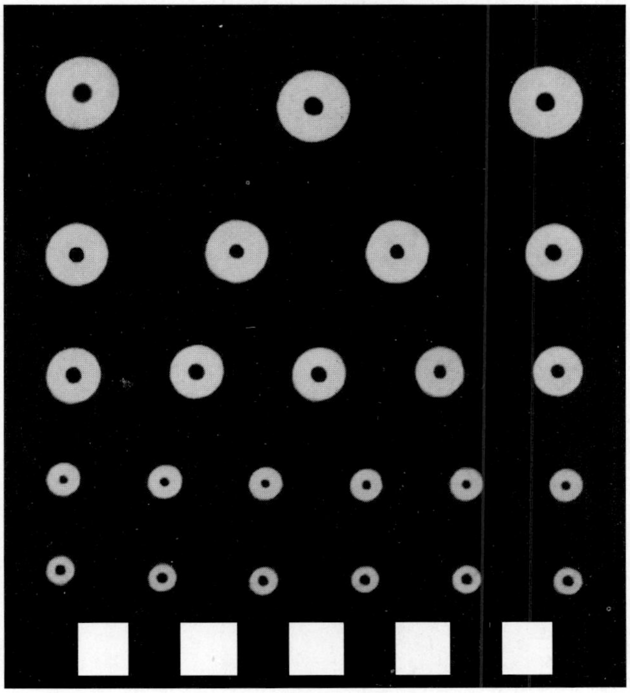

Plate-4. **Mandi,** Gold circular beads **(Sharma *et al.*).**

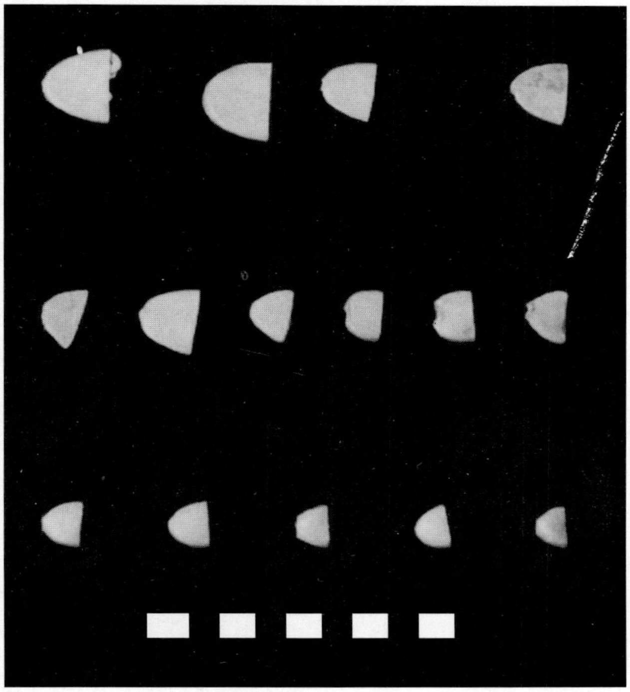

Plate-5. 'D'-shaped gold beads **(Sharma *et al.*, Mandi).**

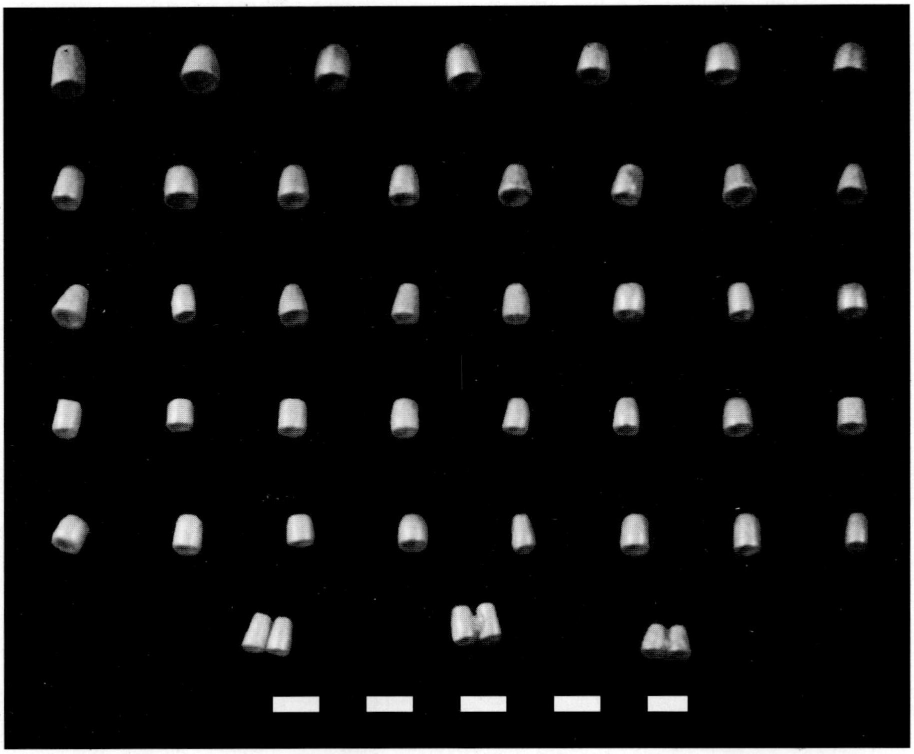

Plate-6. **Mandi,** Bell-shaped gold beads **(Sharma *et al.*).**

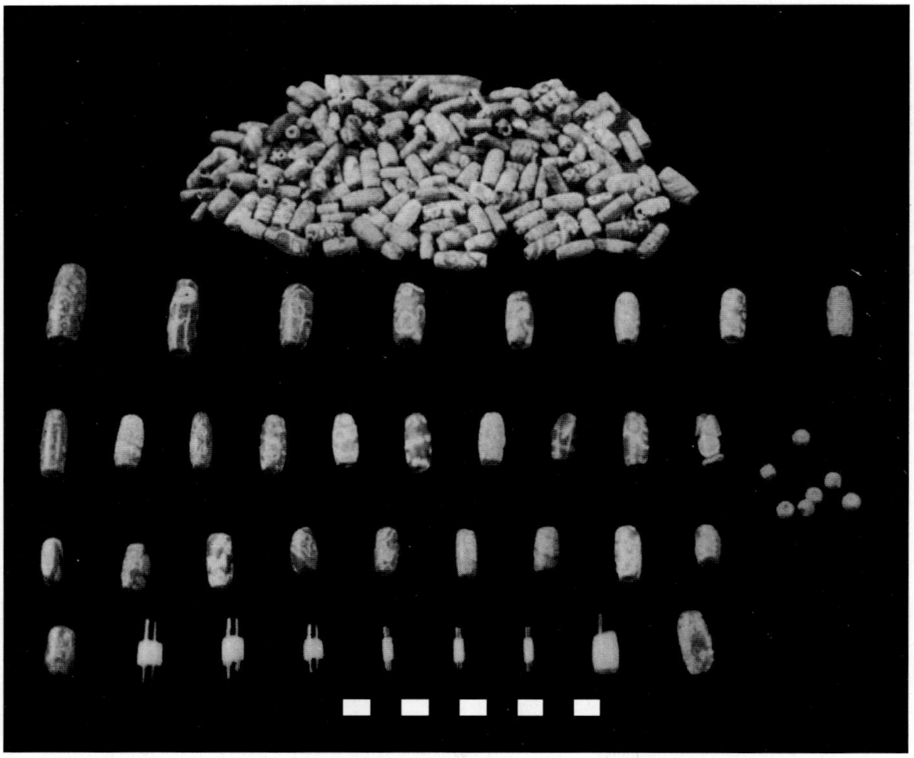

Plate-7. **Mandi,** Beads of semi-precious stones and copper **(Sharma *et al.*).**